# Currents
## in
# Psychoanalysis

# Currents
# in
# Psychoanalysis

*Edited by*

# IRWIN M. MARCUS, M.D.

INTERNATIONAL UNIVERSITIES PRESS, INC.
New York

*Library of Congress Catalog Card Number: 74-139116*

*ISBN:* 0-8236-1105-1

Manufactured in the United States of America

This book is dedicated with gratitude to
Sigmund Freud
and
the generations of humanitarians who have
been our inspiring teachers.

# CONTRIBUTORS

CARL ADATTO, M.D.—Clinical Professor of Psychiatry, Louisiana State University Medical School; Training and Supervising Analyst, New Orleans Psychoanalytic Institute.

JACOB ARLOW, M.D.—Clinical Professor of Psychiatry, State University of New York, College of Medicine; Training and Supervising Analyst, New York Psychoanalytic Institute.

PETER BLOS, Ph.D.—Faculty and Supervising Analyst (Child and Adolescent), New York Psychoanalytic Institute; Consultant, Court Clinic, Jewish Board of Guardians, New York City.

CHARLES BRENNER, M.D.—Lecturer in Psychiatry, Yale University; Training and Supervising Analyst, New York Psychoanalytic Institute.

JOAN FLEMING, M.D.—Professor of Psychiatry, University of Colorado Medical Center; Training and Supervising Analyst, Denver Psychoanalytic Institute.

DAVID A. FREEDMAN, M.D.—Professor of Psychiatry, Baylor College of Medicine, Houston, Texas; Clinical Professor of Psychiatry, Louisiana State University School of Medicine; Training and Supervising Analyst, New Orleans Psychoanalytic Institute.

EDWARD D. JOSEPH, M.D.—Professor of Psychiatry, Mount Sinai School of Medicine, New York; Training and Supervising Analyst, New York Psychoanalytic Institute.

IRWIN M. MARCUS, M.D.—Clinical Professor of Psychiatry, Louisiana State University Medical School; Training and Supervising Analyst in Adult and Child Analysis, New Orleans Psychoanalytic Institute; Professor and Special Lecturer, Tulane University School of Social Work and Teacher Education Center.

HENRY H. W. MILES, M.D.—Professor of Psychiatry, Tulane University School of Medicine, New Orleans, Louisiana; Training and Supervising Analyst, New Orleans Psychoanalytic Institute.

DOUGLAS NOBLE, M.D.—Clinical Professor of Psychiatry, George Washington University Medical School; Training and Supervising Analyst, Washington Psychoanalytic Institute.

EUGENE PUMPIAN-MINDLIN, M.D.—Professor of Psychiatry, Vice-Chairman, Dept. of Psychiatry, The Neuropsychiatric Institute UCLA Center for Health Services; Training and Supervising Analyst, Southern California Psychoanalytic Institute.

VICTOR ROSEN, M.D.—Professor of Psychiatry, Albert Einstein College of Medicine, New York; Formerly Training and Supervising Analyst, New York Psychoanalytic Institute.

HELEN ROSS—Lecturer and Supervising Analyst, Pittsburgh and Washington Psychoanalytic Institute.

HAROLD SAMPSON, Ph.D.—Director of Research, Department of Psychiatry, Mt. Zion Hospital, San Francisco, California.

JAY TALMADGE SHURLEY, M.D.—Career Research Professor of Psychiatry, University of Oklahoma; Senior Medical Investigator (Psychiatry) Veterans Administration.

ALBERT J. SOLNIT, M.D.—Professor of Pediatrics and Psychiatry; Director, Child Study Center, Yale University; Training and Supervising Analyst, Western New England Institute for Psychoanalysis; Faculty, New York Psychoanalytic Institute.

MELITTA SPERLING, M.D.—Clinical Professor of Psychiatry, State University of New York, Downstate Medical Center, Division of Psychoanalytic Education; Training and Supervising Analyst in Adult and Child Analysis at Division of Psychoanalytic Education.

VANN SPRUIELL, M.D.—Clinical Associate Professor of Psychiatry, Louisiana State University Medical School; Training and Supervising Analyst, New Orleans Psychoanalytic Institute.

WILLIAM C. THOMPSON, M.D.— Clinical Associate Professor, Tulane University School of Medicine, New Orleans; Training and Supervising Analyst, New Orleans Psychoanalytic Institute.

HERBERT F. WALDHORN, M.D.—Faculty, New York Psychoanalytic Institute; Consulting Psychiatrist, Hillside Hospital, Queens, New York.

ROBERT S. WALLERSTEIN, M.D.—Chief, Department of Psychiatry, Mount Zion Hospital and Medical Center; Clinical Professor of Psychiatry, University of California School of Medicine and Langley-Porter Neuropsychiatric Institute; Training and Supervising Analyst, San Francisco Psychoanalytic Institute.

# CONTENTS

## PART V—CLINICAL PRACTICE

# ACKNOWLEDGMENTS

A commemorative event cannot in itself give adequate recognition to the many dedicated psychoanalysts who helped us establish and maintain the only Psychoanalytic Institute in this area of the South. That a psychoanalytic institute has existed in New Orleans for 20 years is certainly important. What is really significant, though, and merits commemoration is the vitality and growth of the continuing study and elaboration of the Freudian legacy by the faculty and students who work together at the New Orleans Psychoanalytic Institute.

Two local psychoanalysts, Doctors Samuel Barkoff and Anna Colomb, with the cooperation of Doctors Ernest Hadley of Washington, D. C., and Lewis Hill of Baltimore, established the psychoanalytic study group in New Orleans in 1948. Many prominent members of the American Psychoanalytic Association gave assistance to ensure the development of this small group. These benefactors included Doctors Russell Anderson, Therese Benedek, Edward Bibring, Frieda Fromm-Reichmann, Maxwell Gitelson, Phyllis Greenacre, Bertram Lewin, Helen Ross, Emmy Sylvester, Philip Wagner, and Edith Weigert. With a change from the original sponsoring group—the Washington-Baltimore Psychoanalytic Institute to the Washington Psychoanalytic Institute, other distinguished psychoanalysts contributed to our needs for experienced advisors and teachers. Foremost in this group was Doctor Rex Buxton, assisted by Doctors Alexander Halperin, Leo Bartemeier, Robert Morse, and Lucie Jessner. Development from a study group to a training center and institute presented the usual "special problems." In such instances we normally consulted Doctors Rex Buxton, Bertram Lewin, Helen Ross, and Jacob Arlow. Besides the reliable sources of psychoanalytic knowledge and experience named above, we are grateful to many stimulating visiting lecturers such as Doctors Douglas Noble, Charles Brenner, Martin Stein, Selma Fraiberg, Eli Marcovitz, Eugene Pumpian-Mindlin, Roy Schafer, Otto and Melitta Sperling, Otto Will, and Eugene Brody.

We recently established a Visiting Professorship which included Dr. Jacob A. Arlow 1969–1970 and Dr. Rudolph M. Loewenstein 1970–1971, to be followed by Drs. Albert J. Solnit and Robert S. Wallerstein.

To achieve independence as an Institute at least four training analysts had to be available locally for the essential teaching responsibilities. Doctors Carl Adatto, Henry Miles, Norman Rucker, and I constituted this group which later expanded to include Doctors William Thompson, David Freedman, Robert Gilliland, Edward Knight, Vann Spruiell, Andrew Sanchez, Ernest Svenson and Burton White. Three of our training analysts are now "geographic" (out-of-town) members—Doctors Freedman and Gilliland in Houston, and Robert White in Galveston. In recent years our faculty has expanded to include an energetic group of well-trained, talented, and experienced teaching analysts and instructors. They are Doctors John Albea, Carl Davis, Fred Davis, Merlan DeBolt, Eve Fortson, Robert Long, Monica McGauly, Gunther Perdigao, John Stocks, and William Wiedorn. No list of acknowledgments would be complete without expressing our special indebtedness to our executive secretary, Mrs. Yvonne Christensen, for her invaluable assistance extending over a period of 15 years. It is she who "minds the store." Her indispensable work continues to be conducted with loyalty, cheerfulness, and reliability. Our faculty and candidates regard Mrs. Christensen* with deep affection and regret her retirement this year.

Although 20 years is a relatively short span of time, our Institute now has a faculty of 25 psychoanalysts and the largest candidate group in its history, with a current enrollment of 32 psychiatrists.

---

* The editor notes with sorrow the passing of Mrs. Christensen, prior to publication of this volume.

In view of the modest and tenuous early phase of our development, I shall take the liberty of modifying a well-known quotation affirming how deeply grateful we are to the many who gave so much in the days when we were so few. How fortunate we are to have available the most recent contributions of at least a portion of our benefactors. A special tribute is due to the many additional major contributions offered by our renowned colleagues who join us in this twentieth anniversary volume.

As a parenthetic remark, and with a bit of nostalgia, it should be noted that we could not include in this volume an excellent and provocative paper by the late Dr. Bertram D. Lewin which was presented at our anniversary meeting. Dr. Lewin's paper, "A Meditation of Descartes: A Study of the Pre-Sleep State," was later expanded into a chapter of his last book, *The Image and the Past* and published by International Universities Press. His consistent attendance as a visiting lecturer and advisor over a wide span of years fostered the security that comes from "object constancy" during the developmental years of our Institute's youth. His earlier book, *The Psychoanalysis of Elation,* and his many papers are recognized classics in psychoanalytic literature. We are all deeply saddened by his recent death. It seems so natural that two of the significant figures in our growth were Dr. Lewin and Miss Helen Ross. Their ardent devotion to psychoanalysis produced their collaborational survey, *Psychoanalytic Education in the United States,* a basic reference volume. I wish to thank the Philadelphia Psychoanalytic Institute for granting us permission to publish Miss Helen Ross's paper on "Some Special Aspects of Psychoanalytic Education." It was presented as the First Annual Lectureship on Psychoanalytic Education of their Student Organization in May, 1967.

I am also grateful to the *International Journal of Psycho-Analysis* for allowing us to have the condensed version of Drs. Robert S. Wallerstein and Harold Sampson's paper, "Issues in Research in the Psychoanalytic Process." This paper was presented in May, 1969, as the Frieda Fromm-Reichmann Memorial Lecture at the Department of Psychiatry of the Stanford University School of Medicine.

Dr. Peter Blos' paper on delinquent adolescents was formerly presented as the Nunberg Lecture in March, 1969.

On behalf of the New Orleans Psychoanalytic Institute, I wish to thank my many esteemed collaborators for their contributions to this volume and for their patience in awaiting this publication. Among these colleagues is my close friend, Dr. Carl Adatto, who provided me with his enthusiasm, warmth, and support from the very beginning of this Anniversary Project and at those crucial moments when it was most needed.

With gratitude, I once again acknowledge the untiring help of Mrs. Yvonne Christensen in the many chores related to the preparation of this manuscript and to Mr. H. David Prescott who made certain that I wouldn't stumble over misplaced commas.

I am particularly grateful for the encouragement by the editorial staff of International Universities Press and especially to Mrs. Irene Azarian and Miss Norma Fox.

Finally, I deeply appreciate the cheerful patience and support of my loving wife, Dorothy, who allowed me the many hours alone in my study to accomplish this project. In addition, she and the wives of other faculty members have consistently supported the activities of our Institute. I give special thanks also to my three children, Randall, Sherry, and Melinda, who are now mature enough to make constructive comments on my writing style.

IRWIN M. MARCUS, M.D.

New Orleans, Louisiana
March, 1971

# PREFACE

*Currents in Psychoanalysis* had its origin in papers presented at the Twentieth Anniversary meeting of the New Orleans Psychoanalytic Institute in October, 1968. The faculty proposed that I edit a volume which would provide a representative account of the frontiers in the areas of psychoanalytic education, childhood and adolescence, dreams, theory, and clinical practice. Accordingly, I selected an appropriate sample of the most recent contributions of a number of our creative, highly experienced colleagues, who are active in practicing psychoanalysis, supervising therapy, and other teaching. All are recognized representatives of psychoanalysis. This volume could not possibly attempt a comprehensive survey of psychoanalytic thought and current practice. There are literally hundreds of significant contributions each year; thus, the realities of a single publication dictated the decisions.

The currents in psychoanalysis are more meaningful when there is an appreciation of the past. Man's ability to remember the past, and to phantasize and thus anticipate the future, are perhaps among his most distinguished attributes. Knowing the past allows us to reap the harvest of lessons from errors and to discover new points for departure into the future. The title of this volume suggests an implicit respect for the brilliant contributions of Freud. Without the roots he firmly planted, the fruitful stream of psychoanalytic discoveries could never have been produced. Psychoanalysts have never claimed that psychoanalysis is a complete, comprehensive theory. Freud's career was characterized by his continued revision of theories with the acknowledgment that he was dissatisfied with certain ones and would return to them later. He encouraged his students to modify and extend many of his hypotheses if their contributions evolved from documented clinical observations rather than from philosophizing. Today psychoanalytic theory continues to grow as it has since Freud's earliest concepts were published. Psychoanalysis as a dynamic and growing body of science will continue to expand its horizons into the future. However, the basic discoveries of Freud are still valid: there is mental activity in the unconscious part of the mind influencing behavior, feelings, and attitudes. The vicissitudes of the early developmental stages of childhood are still considered essential elements in personality and character formation. Freud's view of the mental conflicts between impulses and internal controls and of the individual's efforts to work out solutions and adjustments and develop ideals (id, superego, ego, ego ideal) was encompassed in his structural theory. The significant influence of the environment, especially the parents, in the early formation of these mechanisms, and in the conflicts, was another one of his essential contributions.

There are some professionals who have labeled psychoanalysis a rigid belief system. They are usually singularly unfamiliar with psychoanalytic thought; and, when an analyst is known who appears to be flexible in his attitude, they extend him a left-handed compliment by suggesting that he is "different from the others." Freud's excellent scientific training particularly equipped him to carefully distinguish between his discoveries of mental phenomena and his speculations.

Our pioneering colleagues were subject to hostile criticism directed to Freudian theory. The critics seemed most upset about Freud's exposure of the role of sexuality in development and in conflicts. Today sexuality and exposure (literally) are "in," and making adjustments to the environment and having internal controls are "out." Psychoanalysts in our time are criticized for being too careful and controlled in their scientific discipline. These critics champion the idea of immediate gratifications and interaction to make patients feel better "now" and to force or direct behavioral change as a magical way of inducing meaningful personality modifications. It seems to me that the fear of the unconscious part of mental life is still motivating the current critics. The wish to avoid self-understanding and to substitute "acting" and "games" as the short cut to well-being is human but continues to leave man alienated from himself.

Theoretical concepts in psychoanalysis are altered when new observational and other research data indicate that a change is appropriate and useful. The study of the child by developmental psychologists and psychoanalysts has been a most fertile field in this regard.

One of the developments in psychoanalytic theory has been the increased interest in certain ego functions (e.g., perception, language, intelligence, etc.) which may mature relatively free of conflict. The earlier formulations have been modified to include the autonomous functions of the ego without sacrificing that which is still found essential (Gill, 1959; Hartmann, 1964; Rapaport, 1960). Further developments in ego psychology focused on the evolving capacity for relatively stable relationships with "objects." The ability to maintain affectionate ties over a prolonged period (object constancy) is part of our growing knowledge of adaptation. Our theory of the dynamic unconscious including within it a drive-oriented motivational system, conflicts, and the derivatives of these conflicts as expressed in the current life of the individual is of fundamental importance. The five basic metapsychological assumptions which depend upon this essential foundation are the genetic, structural, energic, dynamic, and adaptive theories. The synthetic function of the ego is considered, for the most part, an unconscious process.

Another example of evolution in psychoanalysis is the understanding and utilization of dream material. For many years a careful analysis of each dream was a significant part of treatment. Access to the unconscious derivatives of infantile trauma and wishes was the goal, and dreams were regarded as the expressway toward that end. Theories have become more complex and goals are much more elaborate. With a greater focus on the transference, the intra- and intersystemic conflicts, the function of the superego and the entire development of what is called ego analysis, we have altered our position toward analyzing the patient rather than the dream. We vary in our degree of utilization of the dream during treatment, guided by whether it will or will not advance the analytic work. The dream is still a valuable indicator of conflicts, transference, degree of regression or resistance, and other patterns of functioning. However, because we have learned to observe and study many other sources of information—nonverbal behavior, character patterns, defenses, symptoms, etc.—dream analysis is no longer a dominant activity during treatment.

Transference phenomena and the patient's capacity to develop a transference relationship are considered the *sine qua non* for analysis. Developments in the theory of object relationships have expanded our consideration of transference. We are much more attentive now to the patient's history of object relationships during crucial or critical periods in his development. Child and adolescent data are essential in achieving a more complete understanding of the patient. His environment, family patterns, sibling relations, oedipal and later life experiences—all require a closer examination. Sophistication of the object relations theory also had a modifying effect upon the concept of identification. Thus psychoanalytic theory continues to grow against a background of increasing information and insights provided by many years of intensive study of people.

In the daily work of applying psychoanalysis as a treatment, the analyst is not isolated by theoretical detachment. Rather, he participates in the analytic process and is acutely aware of the patient's uniqueness. With empathy, he feels his way through the labyrinthian complexities of the human psyche, utilizing the illumination available from psychoanalytic theory.

Theory and technique have a reciprocal relationship. The present and the past, the id and the ego, are seen as a continuum interspersed with defenses and exposed to the consciousness by analytic reconstructions through interpretations, with the goal of self-understanding. The science blends with the art of psychoanalysis as individual technical styles appear among psychoanalysts who nevertheless do adhere to the basic psychoanalytic concepts. The personalities of the analyst and the patient present a unique combination in each instance. Recognizing countertransference and its usefulness has been a significant development in psychoanalysis. In a successful analysis, the patient regresses into a transference neurosis and revives not only his own primitive impulses, but manages to elicit the same in the analyst, although—hopefully—only to a minor degree. Thus, the patient becomes aware of the analyst as another human being with human limitations. Neither the patient nor the analyst can, for long, hold on to residual illusions of omnipotence. The patient's ego is strengthened not only by the resolution of conflicts, but also by his learning to deal with the analyst's defects constructively and to understand and eventually forgive him for the occasions of countertransference. The years of intimate work in psychoanalysis become a growth experience for both the patient and the analyst. As the patient's major conflicts are resolved and his fears diminish, he gains confidence which enables him, in Freud's words, "to love and to work."

Psychoanalysis is still dedicated to the goal of knowing one's self as were Socrates, Plato, and their students. Freud and the generations of our colleagues feel that, if man can be liberated from his unconscious conflicts and the spontaneously arrived at poor solutions to these impasses, he can have access to new and healthier patterns in his life. A man with such psychological knowledge of himself would be able to enjoy his relationships to his fellow man—to love, would allow him to be productive in his daily life; to work would constructively engage him with society—all in the service of helping mankind.

In conclusion, during the past half century, we have witnessed the profound impact of psychoanalysis upon medicine, child-rearing, social sciences, literature, and art. Developments in psychoanalysis indicate a healthy trend toward re-examining and modifying many of our premises when based upon carefully documented work, in order to strengthen the theoretical foundations of psychoanalytic practice. Interdisciplinary group research and freer communication among differing groups are increasing. Such trends are characteristic of science.

IRWIN M. MARCUS, M.D.

New Orleans, Louisiana
March, 1971

# Part I
# Psychoanalytic Education

# 1. SOME SPECIAL ASPECTS OF PSYCHOANALYTIC EDUCATION

HELEN ROSS

Psychoanalytic education has passed through historical stages known in all education—from the teacher-disciple duo, as with the mother-child model; to small voluntary groups informally gathered around an inspired leader, as with Zeno in the Stoa and with Christ and his disciples; to a loosely organized school with a more or less fixed meeting place and an informal, nondetailed program, as at first under Freud; and, finally, to a highly regulated, sometimes rigid administration with a consistent curriculum and a panoply of committees to watch over the training from acceptance to graduation, all under the aegis of a national organization.

Eitingon is to be credited for the first organized psychoanalytic school, i.e., the first institute in 1920. It was in Berlin that Freud said of him, "Wherever Eitingon is, there is an institute." We might paraphrase: wherever there is an institute, there is need of a leader. Eitingon was an organizer. He saw that good organization required rules. Indeed, he was the first to propose that everyone seeking to become an analyst should be himself analyzed.

As in industry, a trade was first learned by an apprentice who went from journeyman to master; so, in psychoanalysis, theory and technique were first learned, largely individually, from Freud and then from his followers. A model can be found in the New Testament. With increase in numbers wishing psychoanalytic train-

3

ing and with extension of interest to widespread places, organization and rules have become more complex and may constitute a threat to psychoanalysis itself. The momentum of growth continues and manifests itself in the multiplication of places where psychoanalytic training is offered.

Has it become big business? Freud's own attitude toward his instrument is implicit in a quote from a letter he wrote James Jackson Putnam in 1912: "You make psychoanalysis seem so much nobler and more beautiful: in her Sunday clothes I scarcely recognize the servant who performs my household tasks." Putnam was an early enthusiast and a New England moralist. Freud was a practical man. When someone asked Anna Freud what she regarded as her father's outstanding characteristic, she replied, "His simplicity." Psychoanalysis was his tool, honed to his use.

Freud once said that the three impossible professions (and he disclaimed talent in all three) were "teaching, healing, and governing, and I have been sufficiently busy with the second."

Psychoanalytic education embraces two of these—teaching and healing—and herein lies the syncretism about which the surveyors of psychoanalytic education wrote a few years ago (Lewin & Ross, 1960).

> . . . the psychoanalytic educator has awakened gradually to the fact that education and the psychoanalytic procedure exist in two worlds and that psychoanalytic education, as a concept, is a syncretism . . . the student as a phenomenon fits into two conceptual frameworks: he is the pedagogic unit or object of teaching and the therapeutic unit or object of psychoanalytic procedure. . . . Has the psychoanalyst become something of a teacher and the educator something of a therapist? [p. 47].

We found syncretism in every facet of institute education—in selection, in the training analysis, in supervision, in the prescribed courses and requirements for graduation.

At the time of application for training, the student-to-be is looked at with two main questions in mind: Is he treatable and

---

Presented at the First Annual Lectureship on Psychoanalytic Education of the Student Organization of the Philadelphia Psychoanalytic Institute, May 17, 1967.

is he educable? Will he master the trade? We question his treatability in different ways: Does he have psychological aptitude and perception? Does his neurosis seem too old and deep and unyielding to be alleviated? We do not ask these questions of a new patient, though we may find the answers to them as therapy proceeds. We hold to the fiction that the student, certainly in the beginning, is a patient, but we are influenced by his potentiality as an analyst.

Recently Anna Freud spoke to the Chicago Institute on *Utopia,* the ideal institute, and made some cogent remarks about selection of candidates. She said there is no reason to demand from the candidate ideal qualities and perfections not possessed by the selectors.

"Is he educable?" means in our field more than just "Will he learn his lessons?" It means all those things we expect psychoanalysis to do for him: clear up his neurosis, relieve his blind spots, and disengage the psychic energy he is using neurotically in order to free him for mastering new concepts. It means, too, an acceptance of the unconscious in himself and in his patients. It means, above all, a sincere search for the truth. When a youngster wrote to Anna Freud asking what he should do at an early age to prepare himself for psychoanalytic training, she replied simply, "An analyst first of all must love the truth." In a letter to Putnam, Freud wrote feelingly that his primary concern was for certainty.

It is unlikely today that anyone would apply for psychoanalytic training without some recognition of the existence of the unconscious. The word has virtually become a part of our language. Someone has said it was unfortunate for the development of psychoanalytic theory that in the analytic process, some patients were cured. This observation merits reflection. When a patient loses his symptoms and feels better, he often stops treatment, and the analyst may feel the important work is done. The psychoanalytic student's self-study, however, must go beyond symptom-relief into further reaches of understanding. Interest in analytic education has increased in the last years, sometimes for therapeutic reasons, sometimes for further understanding in a sincere wish to extend the frontiers of his knowledge, and sometimes because psychoanalysis is now better understood and valued as a research tool. The beginning of wisdom is understanding. Healing remains *pure* only so long as seeking for understanding is the aim. Education remains *pure* only so long as seeking for knowledge is the aim.

Anything ulterior in education or in treatment clouds the picture, such as getting a certificate, becoming a member of the local Society and of the American Psychoanalytic Association, seeking office, and getting referrals. All of these pursuits are legitimate as long as they come without too much seeking.

What are we educating our students to be? There are three obvious and primary roles: practitioners of psychoanalysis, teachers of psychoanalysis, and researchers. A fourth role—the propagandist of psychoanalytic insights—should be added. This latter task would be to help not only colleagues in the allied healing professions of psychiatry, psychology, pediatrics, and nursing, but in others such as child-care experts, teachers, social workers, lawyers, parole officers, and so on, whose efforts can benefit from an understanding of the dynamics of psychoanalysis.

What is the content of the training program? First comes the student-analyst—his own id, ego, and superego. He is his own first exercise in psychoanalysis; he learns his own declension, his own conjugation (both regular and irregular verbs), his own figures of speech, his idiom, his symbolism, his design, the economics of his psyche. The analysis itself becomes a reference book, not ended by graduation rites, but constantly extended.

Second comes the training analyst's own patients with supervision, a descendant of the teacher-disciple pattern. The value of supervision depends largely on the willingness to learn from the supervisor and on the satisfaction the teacher has in teaching. The supervisor is behaving not as an analyst, let us say, not as a doctor, but as a professor, alert to the student's deficiencies in understanding. Supervision is not an extension of the analysis, though the student, often in resistance to his analyst, tries to make it so. Since clinical experience is at first limited, the clinical conference makes possible a wide spectrum of cases. Added to this experience are the well-known classical cases, especially Freud's and Abraham's. These are not out of date.

About curriculum, Freud said that it should contain biology, the science of sexual life, the symptomatology of psychiatry, the history of civilization, mythology, the psychology of religion, and the science of literature. He added that, unless the analyst is well at home in these subjects, he can make nothing of a large amount of his material.

Third comes the training analyst's study of the fundamental psychoanalytic writings, especially those of Freud. One finds impatience in the student when he confronts the study of the history of psychoanalytic concepts, as for example, the libido theory. "Why shouldn't we have a text book of currently accepted theory," wailed one student to the surveyors. Need I try to defend the use of history in mastering concepts? Anna Freud's Utopia suggests that there should be a compromise between history and subject matter—perhaps a course called "history of concepts."

Adlai Stevenson used to say to his sons, "Read, read, read!"—a good injunction in our own training course.

The personal analysis, one's own cases and those of one's colleagues, the classical cases, the classical writings on theory: these form the core of the training, and there should be a free-floating relationship among them all. If I may quote the popular McLuhan, the student thus will go "from linear connection to configuration" and, I add, to conceptualization, the earmark of education. I once heard Heinz Hartmann say, "How beautiful an idea becomes when it is clothed in a concept."

All of psychoanalytic training, one might say, is research. The student approaches himself as an object of research; and he assesses his patient in the same way, alert to information from all sources, eager to predict, ready to be surprised, concerned with similarities and differences. A scientist has to be a good observer. The psychoanalyst observes with every sense as well as with the sixth sense, intuition. Students frequently want to know whether intuition can be taught. The analyst can only answer that as the student lifts his own repressions, he sees more and understands more in his patients.

As clinical experience grows, so intuition is fed. Impressions become provable through clinical data. This belief is the watchword of the Hampstead Group under the leadership of Anna Freud.

At Hampstead in the last five or six years, the emphasis has been on diagnosis, an assessment of the patient's intactness of normal development and of his deviation from the normal, measured against his inner potential and environmental opportunities for progression. Those who have read Anna Freud's (1965) book, *Normality and Pathology in Childhood,* appreciate how fruitful her study has been. Experience with the assessment profile proves it to be an unsurpassed tool in diagnosis and hence in choice of treatment. A profile for adult patients is now in use as well.

Teaching is also related to theory as Bertram D. Lewin (1965) indicates in "Teaching and the Beginnings of Theory": "I approach theorizing pragmatically as a branch of pedagogy. Equations, abbreviations, and diagrams that made for good blackboard demonstrations are often good 'theory' . . . The blackboard labored and produced a theory" (p. 138).

This way of thinking leads almost inevitably to research, i.e., to observation, to collection of data, to perception of relationships. Such a process is actually what the analyst does with his patient. The analyst invites him to observe himself, to see into the past, to amass data about himself, and with the help of the analyst's interpretation, to see connections, not in a linear but in a configurative pattern.

As Lewin (1968) indicates in his recent book, *The Image and the Past,* the analyst invites the patient to join him in scopophilia, helping the analyst to construct the patient's past. Lewin prefers construction to reconstruction. "The most general and interesting effect of the communication is that in any case it incites the patient to investigate. It stimulates him to look for something. With sharpened vision, he starts a research" (p. 12).

Though this participation is a special technique in psychoanalysis, we might see, syncretistically, an educational parallel. The teacher, for example, invites the pupil to look at events in the historical past as if in moving pictures, the better to grasp the march of events and the kind of people who took part. In the early grades, there is a similar parallel of using picture books and of role-playing. Though the use of pictures may make a fine argument for TV in the schools, we hope it does not dispose of the person of the teacher, who seduces the student into looking with him to make discoveries and to see significance.

The teacher, like the analyst, shows the student how the long arm of the past reaches into the present—a pedagogical procedure similar to the analytic one and yet not the same. The similarity lies in the dual nature of the looking. The patient presumably wants to get well; the student wants to get educated. The pupil may resist the teacher's explanations just as the patient resists interpretations of the analyst, who may point out connotations uncongenial to the patient.

But we assume the psychoanalytic situation has developed the desirable "therapeutic alliance," such that the patient is willing to look with his analyst into the unconscious. Here the two strive to enlarge the realm of the conscious. The counterpart, in education, we might call "educational alliance." It seems safe to assert that little learning endures which does not have its roots in such an alliance with the teacher. This alliance will reflect the early relationship to the first teacher, the mother, and specifically, to her efforts to train the child to good habits of eating and elimination. During this period he may develop compliance or stubbornness, a desire to please or an urge to revenge, security or insecurity. We are well acquainted with these residues in our adult patients.

Identification is a powerful agent in both kinds of alliance, therapeutic and educational. As the student matures in his wish to master knowledge objectively and the patient begins to pierce the veil of his repressions, identification as the compelling motive drops gradually out of significance. Then and only then, the student or the patient is ready to be on his own.

The psychoanalytic student is often asked to write a paper; the university graduate student labors to present his research in a thesis. Many of us, however, long maintain the infantile wish to please someone from the past with our achievement. Alumni at reunions like to recall what old Professor X used to say; books are dedicated to mothers and former teachers; and Festschriften are produced to honor leaders of thought in academic and professional fields.

This digression shows the similarity between the psychoanalytic school and the everyday school. It may indicate that the psycho-analytic teacher that many will become should be the best educator in the world. He learns to respect the educational alliance as well as the therapeutic alliance. The teacher seldom has an analysand of his own in his class, but such a situation does happen occasionally. His understanding of the influence of the past emotional life makes him a better teacher.

In most of our institutes, the Education Committee, the Curriculum Committee, or some such, are watchful to discern potential teachers among the advanced students, and the students are usually eager to respond. Many earnestly want to teach in identification with their own analyst or some revered teacher from the past, in the knowledge that they will enhance their own perception. Both unconscious and conscious motives are involved.

In a recent little piece, I presented the "teacher game" of childhood as the active side of the passive experience of being taught. In the child's play world, one must take both parts, pupil and teacher, shifting back and forth. In identification with the mother, one must have children, children to be omniscient with, to teach, to encourage, to scold, to punish, and to favor—all variations observable in the teacher game. He will nominate for the game good and bright children as well as dunces and naughty ones. In the child's lexicon, "not smart" nearly always is the equivalent of "being bad." For this game-school, the emotional model is the first teaching situation: mother and child.

A child's wish to have children of his own is well known to child analysts. Little Hans gives us an example in his anal children: "This morning I was in the W. C. with all my children. First I did lumf and widdled, and they looked on. Then I put them on the seat and they widdled and did lumf, and I wiped their behinds with paper. D'you know why? Because I'd so much like to have children; then I'd do everything for them—take them to the W. C., clean their behinds, and do everything one does with children" (Freud, 1909, p. 97). It is to be noted that he had his pupils look at him, just as he looked at them.

Parent, teacher, and child are emotionally interwoven, just as analyst and student-patient. Our patients who are not trainees show us this connection when they decide during the course of analysis that they would like to take up the training. Many settle for kindred work if they do not wish to undergo the rigor of medical education and psychoanalytic training, or if they harbor unconscious reasons, too. The first of the related professions to embrace psychoanalysis fervently was social work, as the psychoanalytic history of this country shows.

Occasionally the analyst is guilty of proselytizing for emotional reasons, unknown to him. Just as there are *ewige Studenten,* so there are chronic teachers—still playing the teacher game—who have need of student-disciples. Sometimes this interest breaks out into a "new school." In other history than our own, examples abound: religious sects, political parties, schools of philosophy, etc., in which professed differences are less powerful than emotional ties which activate adherence to a particular leader.

Some of our thinkers have suggested that the training analyst should be entirely separated from the teaching staff and administration of the training institute, so that the analysis should remain in every sense a joint enterprise between analyst and student and not be corrupted by any spill-over. When the analysis is "finished," the analysand would make application for training.

This method seems drastic indeed in the light of long experience. We complain at every conference about the complications of training as it is now carried on, but we are not universally ashamed of our results. Far from it. We do keep a watchful eye through committees, both local and national. But we have learned how to use our psychoanalytic instrument and to trust its efficacy and continued illumination.

At this point, I might discuss the length of training, the advanced age of the graduate, and the cost of the whole; but these matters are constantly in review and there is little new to be said. Earlier analysis, that is, in medical school, is favored by some. One woman analyst who has two sons said wistfully, "Earlier analyses might make better marriages." Who can say?

Most important to stress is the value of continuing psychoanalytic education beyond the mere receiving of a certificate. Graduate groups in many institutes prove the felt need to pursue their education, not just in keeping up with current papers as in journal clubs, but in constant restudy of the classical writings, especially Freud's theoretical papers. Some study groups have persisted for years and continue with enthusiasm, as, for example, the Kris Study Group of New York, which is notable for its contributions to psychoanalytic theory and practice. Some small groups persist through the years and exhibit great loyalty. "Indeed, neither family connections nor blood relationship bind souls together in a closer or firmer bond of friendship than does a shared enthusiasm for noble studies," Erasmus said in the 15th Century.

Aware that these observations are directed to candidates, mostly still young people, I dare mention a word about wives, who often get restless during a husband's long analysis, an enterprise in which they do not share unless the budget permits. Patience is the watchword. Pleasant social gestures are made within the candidate's organization, but to many a young woman, even not very gregarious, the exclusion from knowing and chatting about the "brass" is unnatural and irritating. She has not even the satisfaction of the old-fashioned doctor's wife who frequently offered a remedy when her husband was unavailable. Eventually, the analytic student does finish his training and becomes a colleague. Fortunate is the wife with a hobby or her own profession. The children may suffer, too, especially if the office is in the home. One analyst's little boy who, when questioned as to what he would like to be when he grew up, answered gravely, "I want to be a patient."

In conclusion, we return to the special aspect of psychoanalytic education, which makes the training so complex: syncretism. The candidate is both patient and student, and he is preparing himself to be both physician and teacher. He enters the training after many years of active study, teaching, and practice, to submit to a passive role. This rigorous discipline exists in no other training I know, except perhaps in the Catholic Church where the student (or novice) must continually make confession and learn how to receive confession. In psychoanalytic training, the student is analyzing while being analyzed, and many think that he should remain in analysis as long as he is in supervision, thus maintaining his dual role throughout.

In *Young Man Luther,* Erikson (1958) reflects: "Young (and not so young) psychoanalysts in training must undergo a training procedure which demands a total and central personal involvement which takes greater chances with the individual's relation to himself and to those who up to then have shared his life, than any other professional training except monkhood" (p. 151).

The verb, *to train,* has two voices, active and passive, and the analyst must master this psychoanalytic grammar—no mean feat in itself, but a rewarding achievement.

May I conclude with a quotation from the late J. Robert Oppenheimer's *Issues in University Education:* "Try to learn something very well indeed. And do not just learn what it is in general terms. Learn it as a practitioner; learn how to do it. And stop while you are doing it long enough to see the beauty of it" (p. 60).

## REFERENCES

Erikson, E. H. (1958), *Young Man Luther.* New York: W. W. Norton.

Freud, A. (1965), *Normality and Pathology of Childhood.* New York: International Universities Press.

Freud, S. (1909), Analysis of a phobia in a five-year-old boy. *Standard Edition,* 10:5–149. London: Hogarth Press, 1955.

Lewin, B. (1965), Teaching and the beginnings of theory. *Int. J. Psycho-Anal.,* 46:137–139.

—— (1968), *The Image and the Past.* New York: International Universities Press.

—— and Ross, H. (1960), *Psychoanalytic Education in the United States.* New York: W. W. Norton.

Oppenheimer, J. R. (1959), Science and the human community. In: *Issues in University Education,* ed. C. Frankel. New York: Harper & Brothers.

# 2. FREUD'S CONCEPT OF SELF-ANALYSIS: ITS RELEVANCE FOR PSYCHOANALYTIC TRAINING

JOAN FLEMING, M.D.

---

Ferenczi (1911) in his paper, "On the Organization of the Psychoanalytic Movement," advocated periodic consideration of the successes and failures of psychoanalysis, saying, "Drawing up such balance sheets from time to time is as necessary in scientific workshops as it is in trade and industry" (p. 299). To follow his advice is especially important for psychoanalytic educators since with expanding knowledge about psychoanalysis, the objectives and methods of educating new generations of analysts need continual review and modification in order to keep pace with the progress of our science. Today more than yesterday, it is the quality of the education we provide for our students which determines the quality of psychoanalytic contributions to knowledge and its practical applications in the years to come. We must continue to examine where we are in the evolution of our educational philosophy, to identify the areas where we feel dissatisfied and in open discussion attempt to find ways to improve our present training programs.

It is in the spirit of Ferenczi that I propose an examination of a persisting question concerning the goal of that cornerstone

14

of psychoanalytic education, the training analysis. A conflict between therapeutic and professional learning goals has been called the "problem of the training analysis" (A. Freud, 1950; Kairys, 1964). Professional goals are seen as reality contaminants of a therapeutic experience and a training analyst is said to be confronted by an irreconcilable dilemma (Lewin and Ross, 1960): should he treat or teach?

I believe it is accurate to say that this question has troubled every analytic educator, including Freud, at one time or another in his career. Treating and teaching are so often held to be mutually exclusive. Insofar as teaching is seen as intellectual and instructional, for an analyst to give instruction is regarded not only as an overemphasis on cognition at the expense of affective experience, but it is also assumed to include recommending a course of action. Such activity by an analyst is considered to be an undesirable manipulation that interferes with the emancipative therapeutic goal of analysis. Therapy, too, has limited definition for many therapists since it is assumed to involve techniques for relieving symptoms, modifying maladaptive behavior of the environment by one manipulative means or another.

Analytic therapy should avoid manipulative maneuvers of all kinds; of that there is no question. Desirable change is produced not by external manipulation but by reliving a neurotically solved childhood conflict under conditions of the analytic situation which facilitate a different, more mature and adaptive solution to a childhood problem. This transference reproduction of the past is, however, only part of the therapeutic goal of analysis. The individuating, integrative experience of exploring oneself in an analytic situation requires a differentiation of past from present, of analyst from transference image—tasks which call on all of the learning capacities and educative skills which analyst and patient possess.

Solving the problem would seem to consist first in finding the factors common to both therapy and learning. If we look at learning and therapy as developmental processes, there is much that they share together. Increased knowledge, freedom to develop to a more mature level, and motivations more realistically determined are shared goals and the person who helps, be he educator or analyst, is one who "leads out from" the bonds of ignorance and irrationality that block freedom to develop. Both are striving for the same results. Even many of the techniques of teacher and therapist are similar, attempting as they do to continue to extend along productive lines the developmental, educative process set in motion at birth and initially guided for better or for worse by the child's first educator and first therapist, his mother.

Without question, our positions on these problems today have their origins in past attitudes and practices. The trouble is that old practices are always subtly modified in one direction or another by various influences coming from both events and people. These changes are often accommodations that become popularized and established as policies without much thought being given to the underlying rationale or the fact that the original accommodation becomes outdated. Earlier policies and procedures may no longer fit the more current situations, yet they continue to be followed or they are changed under influences which often neglect to preserve the best of the old in the service of emphasizing an aspect of the old which seems more imperative at the time. I believe we have become caught by these influences when we forge "to treat or to teach" into such a dichotomy for the training analysis. To follow Ferenczi's stock-taking advice, it becomes necessary to go back into the past, to try to understand what influenced the practices then, what caused the changes that have lead to our present ways of doing things.

With this goal in mind, I reviewed the literature relevant to the evolution of our present-day concept of the training analysis, searching for some clues to "the problem" outlined above. A result of this review was that although I found no satisfactory answers for the causes of change, I was nonetheless impressed with the truth of another statement by Ferenczi (1930) i.e., "We must constantly be prepared to find new veins of gold in temporarily abandoned workings" (p. 120). It is the results of such reworking that I want to present in the current essay with the hope that this effort at stock-taking will help to clarify the issues and lead to more effective educational practices.

Today, everyone agrees that the training analysis is the foundation on which the further development of a young analyst is built. Today, analytic educators consider the training analysis to be the essential educational experience from which learning about theory and acquiring clinical skills proceeds. Yet it has not always been this way. Ernest Jones practiced analysis for eight years before he sought a didactic analysis for himself (Oberndorf, 1953). Bernfeld was told by Freud when he asked about being analyzed, to start with a patient and when he got in trouble they could think about having some analysis for himself (Ekstein, 1953). These two instances bear witness to the fact that in the beginning a training analysis had a purely professional goal, was considered to be a "didactic" (instructional) procedure and was conducted under circumstances which would be labelled "impossible" today. For example, Eitingon went on walks with Freud twice weekly after supper and had his analysis on these walks (Balint, 1954).

When such an analysis was undertaken, it was short and primarily directed toward offering a sample of the activity of the unconscious and a brief opportunity to observe the analytic method. Prior to 1920 there was no formal training program as we know it today. Analysis at that time was more like a game of detection, probing through the wall of infantile amnesia following clues from dreams, symptoms, and slips of the tongue.

It did not take long before the consultations between neophytes and senior colleagues or group discussions about cases revealed how easy it was for a patient to provoke inappropriate responses in the analyst, who seemed unaware of these affective unconsciously motivated reactions. Freud (1912) compared them with transferences and when seen in the analyst called them "countertransferences" which needed "psychoanalytic purification." Since Freud, at that time (1910), considered transference to be an obstacle to analytic work, he felt countertransferences were even more so. A patient's transferences could be resolved with skillful handling, but such was not the case for the analyst himself. Yet Freud realized the importance of bringing such unconscious motivations under conscious control.

Hence, it was in 1910 in a statement that seems to mark the beginning of a shift from a primarily professional objective for the "didactic" analysis to a therapeutic aim that Freud correlated the occurrence of "countertransferences" with the need for "self-analysis." In this paper, Freud felt that self-analysis was a remedy and that "Anyone who fails to produce results in a self-analysis of this kind (should) at once give up any idea of being able to treat patients by analysis." The "countertransferences" were looked upon as symptoms resulting from unconscious conflict and should therefore be treated to "clarify the instrument" to use Isakower's (1957) more current phrase.

Freud's statement in 1910 well describes the informal attitude toward training which prevailed at that time but also the serious-ness with which he made his recommendation. I quote:

> We have become aware of the 'countertransference' which arises in him [the analyst] as a result of the patient's influence on his uncon-scious feelings, and we are *almost* [italics mine] inclined to insist that he shall recognize this countertransference in himself and over-come it. Since analysts have begun to exchange observations with each other we have noticed no psychoanalyst goes further than his own complexes and internal resistances permit; and we consequently require that he shall begin his activity with a self-analysis and con-tinually carry it deeper while he is making his observations on his patients [p. 144].

In this recommendation for a "self-analysis" Freud (1887) is referring to his own experience in analyzing himself which he described in his letters to Fliess. The letters which contain the references to his self-analysis cover a portion of this time, the period from the death of his father in October, 1896 to the fall of 1900, when there was a rupture in his relationship with Fliess which never healed. I intend to review some of the aspects of Freud's self-analysis discernible in his letters and in the commen-taries by Kris (1954), Jones (1953), Buxbaum (1951) and others (Bernfeld, S., 1946; Bernfeld, S. C., 1952; Eissler, K., 1951) as they bear on the acquisition of self-analytic skills and the neces-sity for an interminable application of these skills in the profes-sional work of a psychoanalyst.

However, before presenting that material, I should like to review the changing concepts of the role of the training analysis in the education of an analyst as described by Balint (1954). Balint identified five historical periods, each of which emphasized a different educational philosophy.

The first or instructional period stressed learning the theory and technique by reading books or by a kind of practicing on each other. Knowledge of current theory and the ability to recognize evidence of unconscious activity were the primary learning goals. Didactic analysis apparently was not sought by many until around 1909 and then, according to what Freud said to Ferenczi about Eitingon (Balint, 1954), the model approximated Freud's pattern of self-exploration in which a report of dreams, associations, slips, etc. were discussed.

This kind of limited analytic experience involved more than reading books and became the period of education by demonstration according to Balint's classification. The chief teaching technique was didactic and the expectations were not yet therapeutically direct. In his 1937 paper, Freud described these limited goals in terms of demonstrating intrapsychic processes and techniques of uncovering, stating, however, that "this alone would not suffice for (the student's) instruction" (p. 248).

Even in 1937, however, Freud did not emphasize the "therapeutic need," although he did stress the need for "self-analysis." The 1937 paper assumes a period of analytic work with an experienced analyst, something he recommended as early as 1912. But he also assumes that this period of formal analysis will be "short and incomplete" and that even the "processes of ego transformation" which differentiate the analyzed person are considered to be goals in the service of professional learning. Freud called himself a patient in Letter 67 to Fliess and compared his experiences in his self-analytic work with what he observed in his "other" patients, but, it seems to me, in spite of his depression and confusion, he thought of himself more as a subject of investigation than a patient hoping for relief of suffering. In this sense, he was more like the "normal candidate" of today who resists accepting a need for help even when hurting symptoms are present (Gitelson, 1954).

The normal candidate resists the therapeutic aim of today's training analysis (Greenson, 1967; Bibring, 1954; Kairys, 1964; Fleming, 1969; Greenacre, 1966) and in so doing he recapitulates the "demonstration" phase (Balint, 1954) of early training. In the recommendation to Bernfeld to start with a patient and when he got in trouble to consider analysis for himself, Freud may have been responding to an empathic recognition of the resistance to "being a patient." Consequently, he placed greater emphasis on the professional, rather than the therapeutic value of analysis. For Freud, at that time, analysis was still an intellectual self-discovery, a synthesis of past and present by means of recall of traumatic memories and abreaction of repressed affect. What permitted the recall and freed the repressed in terms of working through the transferences and facilitating the discriminating, integrative functions of the ego had not yet become the focus of investigation.

Balint (1954) comments that no one directed serious thought toward a scientific evaluation of the goals of the training analysis until Ferenczi (1927) began to advocate a "proper analysis"—one as thorough as the therapeutic analysis of a patient. Ferenczi felt that if analysis had beneficial effects on a patient, an analyst deserved the same. He told Clara Thompson (1955) that he sometimes envied his patients who had gained something more from analysis than he did. Balint describes how the opposition to Ferenczi argued that such an analysis, as long and as deep as with the usual patient would involve "tampering" with the character of the analysand. Such tampering was felt to have unforeseen and dangerous consequences. Yet, today, we think of a training analysis as necessarily including the character structure of the candidate. Perhaps Ferenczi's outspokenness offered a displaced target for the resistance latently stirred up by Freud's (1910) statement which advocated self-analysis to overcome the "countertransferences" increasingly visible in consultations about patients and in analytic discussion groups.

Freud wrote little about training as such. Consequently, we are largely in the dark about what he really thought. Yet what appears to be his first published statement (quoted above, 1910) on psychoanalytic training was undoubtedly stimulated by what he felt were manifestations of unconsciously motivated responses from the analyst to his patient—responses which should not be there and

which interfered with the mirrorlike neutrality he considered pro-
fessionally desirable. As far as we know, Freud assumed that all
analysts would be motivated as he was to undergo the trials of
self-discovery in order to increase their professional skill. Apparently in 1910, Freud's feeling of success in his own self-analytic
work made him confident that others could do the same, but it
was only two years later that he (1912) more strongly advised
prospective analysts to undergo "an analysis by someone with more
expert knowledge." In this paper, he compliments the Zurich group
which had begun this practice. Pointing out the rewards accruing
from self-knowledge and self-control, he says: ". . . we must not
underestimate the advantage to be derived from the lasting mental
contact that is as a rule established between the student and his
guide" (p. 117). Here, Freud acknowledges the personal value
of the personal relationship with the analyst, apart from professional advantage. Nevertheless, he again stresses the goal of self-
discovery for its own sake when he takes for granted that,
". . . when it is over (the student) will continue the analytic examination of his personality in the form of a self-analysis, and
be content to realize that, within himself as well as in the external
world, he must always expect to find something new" (p. 117).

With the 1912 recommendation, the institution of training
analyst was thus initiated although the early *Lehranalytiker* and
his student were often neophytes together, since there was not much
difference in knowledge or experience between them (Benedek,
1969). The newly constituted training analysts had probably not
thought of themselves as patients and had not experienced a fully
developed transference neurosis as we expect to have happen today.
In fact, the term "Lehranalytiker" continued to put the emphasis
on the didactic goals of the analytic experience for a student. Nevertheless, as clinical experience with patients (students or otherwise)
continued and deepened under the inevitable dynamic pressure of
transference and the repetition compulsion, beneficial relief of
symptoms, anxieties, and inhibitions were observed.

Balint (1954) attributes to Ferenczi the role of chief advocate
for the shift to stressing a therapeutic aim for the analysis of a
student analyst. Ferenczi (1928) talked of a "fully-completed

analysis" as being something which should be expected of a training analysis. This proposition went beyond his previous position that claimed there should be no difference between a therapeutic and a training analysis (Ferenczi and Rank, 1924). In 1928, Ferenczi stated new goals saying, ". . . that while every case undertaken for therapeutic purposes need not be carried to the depth we mean when we talk of a complete ending of the analysis, the analyst himself must know, and be in control of, even the most recondite weaknesses of his own character, and this is impossible without a fully completed analysis" (p. 89). Here we see a combination of therapeutic and professional aims for the training analysis: therapy for personal advantage as with any other patient, but carried to a high degree of perfection for professional reasons.

Balint (1954) labels what Ferenczi advocated as the fourth historical period where the educational philosophy was one of "supertherapy." Other analysts, notably Nunberg and Eitingon, followed Ferenczi's lead to some extent although their principal objective was to institutionalize the training analysis and make it not an elective procedure but a requirement for becoming an analyst. In 1910 Freud's language was not so strict, but in 1925, Eitingon (1926), half apologetically, said he thought there was "an additional aim, that supersedes or goes hand in hand with the therapeutic aim." Ferenczi in his book with Rank (1924) made this additional aim more specific, i.e., to prepare the student-analyst for the heavy drain on his emotional resources and the strenuous task of strict control of his own responses which treating a patient demanded. In other words, Ferenczi picked up Freud's 1910 statement about self-analysis as a remedy for countertransference and from 1908 until he died in 1933, Ferenczi (1928) stressed the need to recognize what behavior of his own the patient might be responding to.

Because of his interest in the "personal equation" as a factor in analytic work, Ferenczi (1927) attempted to isolate and to define the elements in the analyst's behavior which might influence a patient's reactions, e.g., the cool aloofness, something which analysts consider a proper attitude but which a patient may feel as a rejection. He described in detail and stressed again and again what the analyst is called upon to do at his end of the interpersonal interaction in the analytic situation. He elaborated on how the analyst "has to let the patient's free associations play upon him; simultaneously, he lets his own fantasy get to work with the associated material; from time to time he compares the new connections that arise with earlier results of the analysis; and not for one moment must he relax his vigilance and criticism made necessary by his own subjective trends" (p. 86).

Ferenczi (1928), Robert Fliess (1942), and Hans Sachs (1947) more than others have tried to describe the process in the analyst's mind—the process of stimulus and response sequences, some conscious, many only half-conscious, and many more outside of awareness altogether, that determine the analyst's empathic understanding and his communications to his patient. In Ferenczi's (1927) words, "One might say that the analyst's mind swings continuously between empathy, self-observation, and making judgments. The latter emerge spontaneously from time to time as mental signals, which at first, have to be assessed only as such; only after the accumulation of further evidence is one entitled to make an interpretation" (p. 86). Ferenczi tries to paint in explanatory terms the elements of the self-analytic process which Freud (1887) described experientially in Letters 72, 74, 75, and 130. Freud did not focus on the process of self-analysis after that but paid more attention to motivation, the control of attitudes, and countertransferences.

After the period of "supertherapy," the fifth philosophy of training analysis focused neither on therapy nor instruction, but "research" (Balint, 1954). What happened seems to have been a disillusionment with psychoanalysis as a method of treatment. If the super goals seemed unattainable, it was rationalized that the failure was attributable not to the pathology of the patient or to the inadequacy of the analyst, but rather to the method. Thus the reassuring conclusion could be reached that the method was not designed for such achievements, and, therefore, those ambitions could be given up and attention paid to using "the method" for "research" purposes, i.e., to investigate mental processes. Balint (1954) comments that the advent of the "research" period aimed to avoid the problems inherent in the termination phase of a training analysis with its postanalytic introjection of the idealized analyst. This aspect of continuing transference has been a powerful factor in perpetuating and intensifying the rivalries of the training analysts in the "supertherapy" period. If the "research" emphasis is in the service of carrying on a mutually gratifying self-exploration and discovery that leaves the analyst divested of omniscience and the student-patient free to individuate himself, then "research" in the sense of self-discovery might well become the goals of the training analysis. Freud's self-analytic effort accomplished both. He discovered things in himself which freed him from his dependence on Fliess and he was able to conceptualize his findings with benefit for general psychology. His attitude of self-inquiry and the courage to struggle with inner resistances in unremitting self-analysis is a most valuable legacy for present and future generations of analysts.

Kurt Eissler (1951) compares the creative process and Freud's self-analysis. He stresses that the urge to create, whether in art or science, must always operate against an inner resistance; new forms, ideas, or demands on the self are opposed by strong forces striving to maintain the status quo in comfort. He describes Freud's self-analysis as "so to speak, against human nature; without prospect of reward, without an inner compulsion or impulsion, the ego seems out of its own resourcefulness to have evolved the firm intuition to withstand an inner revulsion and to bear voluntarily and of its own accord that pain which is for several reasons the most difficult to bear" (p. 322).

Eissler thinks that Freud's heroic effort cannot be repeated. This is true if we think of it as a unique, unassisted struggle across uncharted seas. But now the seas are charted to some extent and the initial avoidance resistances are not dealt with entirely without help. A method for self-discovery has been provided. Its application sets going a self-analytic process and skills in this direction can be developed. The training analysis is the start of that voyage. Other learning experiences continue the process and sharpen the skills. The source of the motivation to continue the effort on one's own is the chief unknown. Some of it apparently comes from neurotic suffering and some from an untraceable thirst for knowledge.[1]

When Freud began his self-analysis he was already using the skills of free-association, introspection, and interpretation on his own dreams and with his patients. At that time (prior to 1896) these tasks had a more professional and scientific, rather than a personal goal. He used his skill in introspection to bring into conscious focus peripheral associations and his skill in interpretation to find links between associations, the symbolic meanings and the connections between conflict and repressed affect.

In 1896 and 1897, however, several events seemed to converge and disturb his inner equilibrium. In his own mind, the most impactful event (Freud, 1900) was the death of his father in October, 1896. "Torn up by the roots" (Letter 50), he was grief-stricken and began a mourning process which inevitably stirred up old memories, painful ambivalences, and problems of separation and individuation. A second external influence seems to have been his patients whose preoccupation with their recall of sexual seduction aroused buried affects and impulses in Freud himself which broke through the repression barrier and found an outlet in his dreams and intruding thoughts and feelings (Letters 58–60). A third set of circumstances appears to have been a recurrent sense of failure with patients who interrupted treatment before Freud thought they were through and the recurrent disappointment over not receiving his professorship. These three experiences apparently touched off unconscious conflicts with all of their erotic, aggressive and envious affects which began to be felt in relation to Fliess, as the letters of the spring and early summer of 1897 reveal (Letters 60, 64, 65). His practice was going well and he even had "a real pupil from Berlin" (Letter 62, May 16, 1897) but he felt exhausted by the demands of 10 patients a day (Letter 58). This exhaustion must have decreased his resistance emotionally as well as physically

---

[1] It is not my intention to recapitulate Freud's self-analysis. The Fliess letters (Freud, 1887), however, contain such valuable information and insights into the process of self-analysis that I will present here significant excerpts in order to make the data readily available. What is reported here should not substitute for rereading the letters.

and so played a part in his depression which became evident in Letter 65 of June 12, 1897.

Three authors, Kris (1954), Jones (1953), and Buxbaum (1951) have given us extensive commentaries on Freud's self-analysis based on the data in his letters to Fliess and the analyses of dreams reported in *The Interpretation of Dreams* (1900). Each of these authors stresses a different aspect of the self-analytic work. Kris focuses on Freud's attempt to reconstruct childhood events occurring chiefly before the age of three; Jones emphasizes the work on his own dreams. From a detailed study of dreams reported in the dream book published in 1900 with the account of the same dreams sent to Fliess in letters containing much other personal material (not published until 1950), Buxbaum stresses the evidence for a symptom neurosis which by June, 1897 was disturbing Freud's work. She calls our attention to the transference phenomena in his relationship with Fliess and concludes that we "have to look upon the development of his thoughts and feelings toward Fliess in the light of a transference analysis" (p. 200).

Freud's letters to Fliess began in 1887 and continued until 1902. We are indebted to Wilhelm Fliess for preserving these letters, to a German bookseller for offering them to Marie Bonaparte, and to Mme. Bonaparte herself for recognizing their unique historical value and for resisting Freud's plea that they be destroyed (Jones, 1953). The dramatic story of their rescue from the Nazi persecutions is recounted in Jones' biography of Freud. The letters themselves with the accompanying drafts of Freud's theoretical thinking at the time provide us with an awesome view of the vicissitudes of creative work as it begins, unfolds, and progresses against both inner and outer obstacles. These letters and drafts reveal the origins of a vast body of theory which has relevance to all of the behavioral sciences and the world of the arts. Other scientists and artists have given us the story of their lives and insight into the flowering of their creativity, but in these letters Freud, unknowingly, made a unique contribution to our understanding of the psychoanalytic process when he accomplished the monumental task of bringing together what he was experiencing with what he understood his experiences to mean in cognitive conceptual terms. Nor did he stop with this large achievement. He went on to describe his aware-ness of the process—actually a process of creating which he called his self-analysis. It is the evidence for this aspect of his analysis of himself that I wish to collate here since it has significance for our understanding of self-analysis as a goal for the training analysis and other learning experiences in the education of an analyst.

I have already indicated that Freud was using the analytic skills of introspection, association, and interpretation with his patients and on himself prior to the month of July 1897 when Kris and Buxbaum date the beginning of his self-analysis. I have discussed to some extent the precipitating events and now I would like to discuss further the transference phenomena which seem to have intensified during the spring of 1897 and to have developed into a transference neurosis which caused Freud great anguish during June, July and August of 1897. Freud's struggle with his trans-ferences and with Fliess' countertransference reactions on this as yet uncharted sea offer psychoanalytic educators today much to think about. Freud's beautiful descriptions of his self-analytic efforts, the experiencing of resistances, the importance of surrender to preconscious working through, and the gradual emergence of insight are most relevant to the implementation of an educational program which must integrate experiential and cognitive learning more deliberately than is necessary in most disciplines (Fleming and Benedek, 1966).

Before and during June 1896, Freud's (1887) relationship with Fliess was exaggeratedly positive. In this month his father became ill (Letter 48) and in the next published letter, four months later (Letter 49), he announces his father's death. In Letter 50, November 2, 1896, "torn up by the roots," he grieves but his work and practice move on—especially his work on his own dreams and on the mechanisms of hysteria. During this period from October through April, 1897, he is able to keep his grief over his father's death from interfering with either his work or his positive attachment to Fliess. He sends drafts to Fliess on hysterical mechanisms, on his theory of seduction, on the relation between hysteria and perversion. In January, 1897, he describes himself as in the "full swing of discovery." In February, he learns that he may be considered for a professorship. Exhausted by his 10 patients, and working some 12 hours a day, he finds it necessary to postpone "all attempts to obtain understanding." Here it would seem that the drain of energy coming from his clinical work prevents him from having any left over to devote to the work of conceptualizing. This circumstance must have produced some conflict and frustration since Freud had a tremendous investment in this aspect of his creativity. It may have disturbed his equilibrium with Fliess since he felt their respective scientific discoveries were an important bond between them. Some regression seems to have occurred, undoubtedly reinforced by his mourning for his father.

I base these suppositions on the fact that on April 28, 1897 he introduces a dream of being irritated at Fliess "as if you were always claiming something special for yourself" (p. 194). We do not know whether Fliess may have written something to provoke this thought, although we hear in January that Fliess seems not to be feeling well. In the April 28 letter, there is a hint of disagreement about "father-figures." In May, Fliess is refreshed and Freud feels "impelled to start writing about dreams" (p. 200). "Inside me there is a seething ferment, and I am only waiting for the next surge forward" (p. 200). He is proud of having a real pupil from Berlin and feels Fliess approves of the dream project (Letter 62).

In Letter 64, May 31, 1897, Freud sends Fliess Draft N in which he talks of hostile impulses against parents. "It seems as though in sons this death-wish is directed against their father and in daughters against their mother" (p. 207). An editorial footnote identifies this as the "first hint of the Oedipus complex" (p. 207).

Earlier in this letter Freud calls Draft N "a few fragments thrown up on the beach by the last surge" (p. 206). He half apologizes for them saying, ". . . I know they are only suspicions, but something has come of everything of this kind. . . ." (p. 206). He makes a reference to the concept of the system Pcs which is not elaborated and then adds, "Another presentiment tells me, as if I knew already—though I do not know anything at all—that I am about to discover the source of morality" (p. 206).

He then tells of two dreams. In the first he feels overaffectionately towards Mathilde (his daughter). "The dream, of course, fulfills my wish to pin down a father as the originator of neurosis and to put an end to my persistent doubts" (p. 206). The second is a dream of climbing a staircase not fully clothed; he meets a woman; is paralyzed but erotically excited. (See also, Freud, 1900, pp. 238–240.)

In Letter 65, June 12, 1897, his professorship is voted on favorably by the medical faculty but his appointment is delayed by the administration (footnote to Letter 62). Freud is depressed. He tells Fliess, "I have never yet imagined anything like my present spell of intellectual paralysis. Every line I write is torture" (p. 210). We note that this month is the anniversary of his father's final illness. About a month later (Letter 66) he says,

> I am a useless correspondent just now. . . . I still do not know what has been happening to me. Something from the deepest depths of my own neurosis has ranged itself against my taking a further step in understanding the neuroses, and you have been somehow involved. My inability to write seems to be aimed at hindering our intercourse. I have no proofs of this, but merely feelings of a very obscure nature. Has anything similar been the case with you? For some days past an emergence from this darkness seems to have been in preparation. I notice meanwhile my work has made some progress, and every now and then I have started having ideas again. No doubt heat and over-work have contributed [p. 212].

In spite of intense resistance, there is some relief in this letter and Freud makes some conceptual formulations comparing dreams and neurotic symptoms.

In August (Letter 67) there is no doubt that Freud has accepted himself as a patient he is trying to analyze. But, "This analysis is harder than any other. It is also the thing that paralyses the power of writing down and communicating what so far I have learned. But I believe it has got to be done and is a necessary stage in my work" (p. 214). In this letter, recognizing his "little hysteria" and his resistances, he continues to link his self-analytic motivation to scientific discovery and his professional work.

He writes to Fliess of his fears and anxieties (Letter 68), realizing that his fear of a railway accident is associated with some feeling about Fliess. In the letter, Freud backs away from the hostile component and reports that the fear left him when he thought of the fact that Fliess and his wife would be on the train. It is easy to believe, however, that Freud was aware of the full interpretation but just could not put it down on paper for Fliess to read. The basic trust necessary for the expression of such transference wishes was not strong enough. Neither Freud nor Fliess possessed at that time the insight into transference and counter-transference phenomena which Freud learned later and passed on to us. In the light of subsequent events in his relationship with Fliess, however, it is possible to speculate that the feelings he describes in this letter represent an aspect of his self-analysis which he could not objectify until later.

After a long vacation, toward the end of September (Letter 69) he feels better, knows he has been through a period of great turmoil and disillusionment but is coming out of it. In the letters of October, Freud is turning more to attempts at recall and to following out associations not necessarily connected with dreams. In Letters 70 and 71 he describes the material of his self-analysis as it took shape out of the analysis of his dreams and the childhood memories which his associations recovered. Apparently, he is less involved with any transferences to Fliess except what is appropriate to a working alliance when the process of synthesis and integration of the past in relation to the present is dominant and transference reliving is less active as a form of resistance to remembering. His relationship with Fliess is still manifestly positive.

All of this time he also generalizes from his own and his patients' experiences and is able to apply to some of his patients what he learns from his self-analysis, e.g., an idea about resistance. An editorial footnote comments that, "Many of the phenomena of resistance seem to have become intelligible to Freud through his self-analysis" (p. 226). The experience of resistance is more intense in self-analysis than with an external analyst present. When Freud entered upon an analytic pact with himself, he had no way of knowing what lay in store for him. Today, having experienced resistance in an analytic situation and having struggled with it there, we are better prepared for the phenomenon when it occurs during a self-analytic effort. We know it can be overcome with persistent effort and in time. In the analytic relationship there is always assistance available when indicated. In a self-analysis, the assistance comes from an attitude toward one's self, a desire for self-discovery and a willingness to make a persistent effort. When this attitude is coupled with empathy for oneself in the struggle with resistance, an intrapsychic alliance of sorts can operate. It temporarily relaxes conscious effort and relies on a continuation of the analytic process preconsciously. In other words, the process of realignment and reorganization begun in the training analysis can continue on a self-analytic basis provided motivation, knowledge of the analytic process, and introspective skills are there.

Through October and early November, 1897 (Letters 73, 74), Freud tells Fliess, "My self-analysis is stagnating again, or rather it trickles on without my understanding its progress" (p. 228). Then, in Letter 75 (November 14, 1897), after describing the birth of a new piece of knowledge, he makes a contradictory statement. He says, "Before the holidays I mentioned my most important patient was myself and after my holiday trip my self-analysis, of which there had previously been no trace began" (p. 231).

It would seem that on the one hand he needed to protect himself from the transference neurosis of the summer months and to take comfort in the professional value of his self-analysis (Letter 67). In addition, Freud found gratification in being able to recall and reconstruct the past—analytic objectives originating in the period of hypnosis and basic to his theory of etiology. That he could demonstrate these theories on himself, including the phenomenon of resistance, restored his self-confidence, shaken by the regressive experience of elements of his own Oedipus complex during the summer of 1897. So far as we know, however, although he felt resistance as tangible (Letter 72) and sensed the significance of his ambivalent feelings toward Fliess, Freud did not correlate his own transference phenomena and his experiencing of Fliess' countertransferences with either the process of his self-analysis or the later conceptualization of the same phenomena observed in others.

After his statement in Letter 75 that there was no trace of his self-analysis before his return from his 1897 holiday, Freud tells Fliess about his latest ideas on repression and remembering. He ends with a paragraph about his self-analysis saying, "My self-analysis is still interrupted. I have now seen why. I can only analyze myself with objectively acquired knowledge (as if I were a stranger); self-analysis is really impossible, otherwise there would be no illness. As I have come across some puzzles in my own case, it is bound to hold up the self-analysis" (pp. 234–235).

Here Freud describes the objectivity necessary in an analyst whether it is directed toward his patient or himself. Today we speak of this attitude as belonging to the empathy of the analyst and the development of the self-observing function of the ego. Freud's self-observing function was developed to an extremely high level, something he begins to conceptualize in this letter. Today, the operation of this function of the ego is a part of the self-analytic skills developed in a training analysis without which therapeutic insight and professional objectivity are lacking. Today, we recognize the contribution to the development of this skill made by the objective, uninvolved attitude of the analyst, something Freud defined in Letter 75 as appropriate to a stranger, a bystander in the struggle.

In the fall of 1897, disagreements between Freud and Fliess begin to appear. They have to do with Fliess' theories of left-handedness, bisexuality and questions of priority. In a letter written by Fliess in 1904 (Freud, 1887, footnote, p. 241) Fliess recalls Freud's resistance to the ideas about bisexuality at their meeting in Breslau and accuses Freud of failing to give him credit for priority, a problem which led to their final estrangement. Here we see more overtly expressed some of the countertransference reactions in Fliess. Freud (Letter 80) tries to treat the disagreements as something that can be scientifically and objectively reconciled. Only much later did he realize that Fliess had a more personal investment in proving himself right and claiming priority for a discovery.

Through January and February (three letters) the subject of Freud's self-analysis is only vaguely mentioned. During this period he seems less dependent on Fliess, working more alone with himself. In March, he reaches out to Fliess a little and sends him what is to be the second chapter of the book on dreams. Freud seems to be trying to appease Fliess by belittling his own work. But Fliess evidently approves the second chapter and Freud feels good (Letter 86). April, May, June and July continue the work on dreams with feelings of uncertainty and hesitation about sending the chapters to Fliess, "but our intellectual honesty to each other required it" (Letter 92, July 7, 1898) (p. 258). In September Freud makes reference to the problem of psychology versus biology as if Fliess felt they disagreed which Freud denies (Letter 96). In October, his practice is flourishing and leaves him exhausted. In December, Freud reports he is reading the literature on dreams.

The next reference to his self-analysis is in a letter of January 3, 1899 (Letter 101). ". . . I have accomplished a piece of self-analysis which has confirmed that phantasies are products of later periods which project themselves back from the present into earliest childhood; and I have also found out how it happens, again by verbal association" (pp. 270–271). This work led to the paper on *Screen Memories* (Freud, 1899; Bernfeld, 1946). He feels creative again and attributes it to a meeting with Fliess just before this January letter. But he wonders if this upsurge is due to Fliess' period theory and hopes "the dynamic aspect is not ruled out." In May (Letter 107), he has great confidence in the dream book making a great contribution. "None of my works has been so completely my own as this; it is my own dung-heap, my own seedling, and a nova species mihi (sic!)" (p. 281). He is not bothered by the fact that ". . . the ten analyses have not come off" (p. 282).

In July (Letter 110), Freud is feeling good and recalls an early meeting with Fliess in 1890 or 1891 when "you witnessed one of my very finest attacks of travel-anxiety at the station" (p. 285). Freud seems to feel independent enough of Fliess to report a critical thought at that early meeting about feeling oppressed by his superiority and that Fliess had not yet found his vocation "which later turned out to be shackling life with numbers and formulae" (p. 285). He seems unaware of the not so subtle depreciation of Fliess' life work in this remark.

In August (Letter 113), still riding high, Freud turns again to the problem of bisexuality. But here he only mentions it since the dream book is progressing. His success in nearing its completion intensifies his anticipation of a hostile reception. "When the storm breaks I shall fly to your spare room," (p. 295) he tells Fliess. "You will find something to praise in it anyway, because you are as prejudiced in my favor as the others are against me" (p. 295) (Letter 117).

On September 21, 1899 (Letter 119), Freud mentions that he is astonished at how often Fliess appeared in his dreams. "In the *non vixit* dream I find I am delighted to have survived you; is it not hard to have to hint at such things—to make them obvious, that is, to everyone who understands?" (p. 299).

On October 27, 1899, Freud thanks Fliess for his kind words about the dream book and then goes on to mention five more books he has in mind. The dream book came out in November (Letter 123) and Freud immediately begins on the "choice of neurosis" and its relation to sexual theory (Letter 125).

On March 11, 1900 (Letter 130) Freud remarks about not having heard from Fliess for about a month. He thinks they would both be sorry if their correspondence dried up, yet it seems to be becoming less frequent. The reaction to the dream book was not all Freud expected and he is disappointed. He is more aware of the vicissitudes of the creative process and is better reconciled to its slow pace and to the social isolation which his way of living and his discoveries brought about at this time.

March 23 (Letter 131) introduces a new feeling in Freud's relationship to Fliess. He withdraws from the prospect of meeting him at Easter because of "an accumulation of imponderables" (p. 314) and a fear that with Fliess he might regress into envy and dissatisfaction and again have to go through the depression he feels he has been climbing out of. "No one can help me in what oppresses me," (p. 314) he tells Fliess, but we do not know if this is something uncovered in his self-analysis or if it represents his slowly increasing distance from Fliess.

April 14, 1900 (Letter 133) marks the first report to Fliess concerning transference as it occurs in therapy. Its dynamics and technical handling were not yet understood although Freud (1905) was working with Dora during this period and formulated a theory of transference on the basis of his frustrating experience with that case.

His disappointment in not being acclaimed for his dream book is still bothering him and Fliess' praise does not comfort as it used to (Letter 134, May 5, 1900). Depressive discouragement sets in again.

An arrangement was made in July (Letter 138) to meet around the first of August. Apparently, the two men quarreled at this meeting. Fliess says Freud showed an unintelligible violence toward him which seemed to Fliess to be rooted in envy. After this meeting Fliess "quietly withdrew from Freud and dropped our regular correspondence" (ed. ftn., p. 324). The next letter from Freud in the published series was dated October 14 (Letter 139) and the next was January (Letter 140). Neither refers to the meeting in the summer. The first reference is in Letter 142 dated February 15, 1901. He says, ". . . the congresses themselves have become relics of the past; I am doing nothing new, and, as you say, I have become entirely estranged from what you are doing" (p. 328).

What has happened? It would appear that Freud has become increasingly disenchanted with Fliess, both regarding his theories, his claims to priority, and his praise of Freud's dream book. Apart from the reality assessment of Fliess' scientific theories, it would seem likely that Freud grew increasingly distrustful of the ambivalence underneath the praise as is indicated in Letter 134 written in July before the fateful meeting at Aachensee.

Freud continued to write to Fliess with the usual news and not until Letter 145 in July 1901 does he explicitly comment on the fact that they have drawn apart. Freud feels hurt and depreciated by Fliess' accusation of "merely reading his own thoughts into other people" (p. 334). He defends himself against the accusation of plagiarism. Then he tells Fliess that his next book will be called *"Bisexuality in Man"* and "it will tackle the root of the problem and say the last word which it will be granted to me to say on the subject—the last and the deepest" (p. 334). This sounds provocative which Freud must have realized because he goes on to say, "The idea itself is yours . . . So perhaps I shall have to borrow still more from you . . . or even co-author the book" (p. 335). He hopes this "will satisfactorily unite us again in scientific matters" (p. 335).

Then he fulfills his long cherished desire to go to Rome. After his return from this "overwhelming experience" (Letter 146) he tries to answer complaints from Fliess that Freud is not interested in his work. Freud pleads ignorance of mathematics and tells Fliess of his hurt and his feeling that if an interpretation to a patient makes Fliess feel uncomfortable so that he accuses Freud of projecting, then ". . . you really are no longer my audience, and you must regard the whole technique as just as worthless as the others do" (p. 337).

The complicated transference-countertransference reactions intimated in this letter make the reader sad that this friendship had to end in this way. Neither one fully understood the dynamic forces in operation that generated the transferences from Freud to Fliess in the beginning or the countertransferences from Fliess to Freud in the end. Freud's disillusionment with Fliess and with himself must have been extremely painful and may have left him especially vulnerable to the rivalrous transferences which appeared among his students as time went on. He was able to study the transference phenomena that arose from a patient to his analyst, but he had little to say about countertransferences in an analyst except that they should be overcome by self-analysis.

From this resume of Freud's self-analysis as he reported it in his letters to Fliess, and in the dream book, we can see the dedicated self-discipline with which he devoted himself to the effort to penetrate his resistances. We marvel at the way in which his introspective, associative, and interpretive skills developed and sharpened as his professional and self-analytic work went on. For Freud, the two kinds of analytic situations went hand in hand, each one of benefit to the other. We stand in awe of his ability to grasp the inner processes of this struggle with resistances and to conceptualize the experiences he observed in himself, whether they were available to conscious recall and interpretation or only vague bubblings from within.

Several aspects of Freud's self-analysis have definite bearing on the goal of the training analysis as an educational experience for present-day students of analysis. The record documents the importance of experiencing the phenomena of resistance and of learning through persistent use of the method of free-association that new knowledge and new integrations can occur when resistances are overcome. Experiencing the phenomena of transference as a special form of resistance is of paramount importance for a student-analyst. Today, he can read about these things and understand them intellectually but the vitality of conviction comes only from having lived through the regressed ego state of a transference neurosis and worked through the differentiation of what belongs to the past from what is more appropriate to current reality. There is an emancipating value in this therapeutic experience. Ferenczi's aim of "supertherapy" focuses on this point in terms of the "depth" and "completeness" of the affective experience and the insights into the student-patient's personality structure which a training analysis can achieve. During this therapeutic experience any patient, whether he is a student or not, becomes able to develop his own observing and interpreting functions and apply them to himself. These functions in the beginning of an analysis are carried out mainly by the analyst, but as the process goes on, the patient becomes freer and more skillful in making his own interpretations independent of assistance from his analytic mentor.

But there is another kind of experience which is equally valuable, perhaps even more so, in preparing a student to become an analyst of others as well as of himself. I refer to a different level of learning on which the affective experiences are given cognitive and explanatory meaning (Fleming and Benedek, 1966). When a student is able to objectify his experiences as a patient, and to anchor these fleetingly conscious moments in a cognitive framework, he enlarges the scope of his empathic understanding and knowing, and thereby "adds a dimension to his professional work ego" (p. 27).

Throughout the record of Freud's self-analysis there is evidence of his constant effort to describe, objectify, and explain what was going on within him. At times he was only painfully aware of feeling but not knowing (Letters 130, 72, 74, 75). The necessity to communicate with Fliess by letter facilitated this process of objectification. It forced Freud to put his experiences into words and to write them down for Fliess to read. There must have been at times a cathartic effect from this procedure as well as a penetrating of the barriers to consciousness. It might have stopped there, but Freud went beyond describing in words what he was experiencing and developed explanatory generalizations. This latter activity was also part of what he communicated to Fliess.

The most significant difference between Freud's self-analysis and that possible today is the analytic work on the transference-counter-transference reactions (Benedek, 1969). This latter experience changes the self-analytic situation. Before we are on our own, we have had the assistance of a well-analyzed, well-educated analyst who has himself worked through many of his transference conflicts and has developed his own self-analytic skills. Fliess was not an analyst and therefore could not provide the kind of assistance in preparation for continuing self-analysis that we expect for our students today. He did supply a listening ear and as the relationship between them grew more intimate, Fliess became an object for Freud's transferences. Neither one understood what was happening as it can be understood today. In Freud's intense dependence, admiration, and idealization, there were all the ingredients for the reproduction of childhood envy, jealousy, and competition, something which did happen and which Freud faithfully recorded. As these negative affects became more clear-cut, and as Freud's success in grasping the emotional and dynamic mechanisms determining behavior became more obvious, Fliess seemed to feel threatened and reacted with a counter-hostility which shocked them both. Neither understood this as a reproduction of a childhood rivalry with siblings and a powerful father, although by way of his dreams Freud was able to realize that he was behaving toward Fliess as he had toward objects of rivalry in the past. In being able to do this Freud kept a hold on current reality and experienced a complicated conflict over his current attitudes to Fliess. He expected tolerance, understanding, and scientific objectivity from him. Instead Fliess began to withdraw without explanation after the angry confrontation at Aachensee in 1900. The experience of Freud's own negative transference shook him deeply, but out of it came a formulation of the Oedipus complex. His experiencing of Fliess' negative countertransference, however, was even more profound and disturbing. Perhaps this explains why Freud said so little about his analytic work with Fliess during his lifetime and why he was so cautious about talking of countertransference among the early analysts as revealed in the 1910 paper. He must have felt that the younger colleagues of the early 1900's would resent being told they needed therapy (just as they do today). Perhaps he was reluctant to stir up the negative reactions toward himself that he had experienced toward Fliess and had not thoroughly worked through. Actually, of course, what he feared did come to pass with a number of "deviationists."[2]

Freud's faith in self-analysis as a means of learning how to be an analyst went through several ups and downs. I have already referred to Freud's recommendation in 1910 for a self-analysis because of countertransference. I have indicated the tentativeness of his recommendation at that time and his firmer statement concerning analysis with an experienced analyst, which he made two years later.

Strachey (1957) in an editorial footnote to Freud's (1914) history of the movement does us an important service by pulling together several of Freud's references to self-analysis which indicate this oscillation of attitude toward its value. Discouraged in 1897 (Letter 75), Freud feels that genuine self-analysis is impossible. In 1910, he recommended it; in 1912, he felt a more formal analytic relationship was important; in 1914 ". . . I soon saw the necessity of carrying out a self-analysis, and this I did with the help of a series of my own dreams which led me back through all the events of my childhood; and I am still of the opinion today that this kind of analysis may suffice for anyone who is a good dreamer and not too abnormal" (p. 20). In 1916 in the *Introductory Lectures,* Freud said, "One learns psychoanalysis on

[2] See Jones (1953, pp. 315–317) for an account of what appears to be an intense countertransference conflict in relation to Jung. The issue was over priority credit and occurred in 1912.

oneself by studying one's own personality" (p. 19). This statement could include both kinds of analytic situations. E. Pickworth Farrow (1942) published an account of his self-analysis for which Freud (1926) wrote a preface. He comments on Farrow's "systematic application of the procedure of self-analysis which I myself employed in the past for the analysis of my own dreams."

Near the end of his life, Freud (1935b) wrote a short paper on "The Subtleties of a Faulty Action" in which he struggles to explain a slip of the pen in writing an inscription on a gift to a woman friend. Having written the word *"bis,"* he then crossed it out as inappropriate, attempting to analyze why it should have been written at all. He arrived at an explanation satisfactory to himself which he recounted to his daughter who reminded him that the word "bis" could also refer to the fact that Freud was repeating a present, since he had given this friend a similar gift once before. Freud analyzes the slip further in this short paper, something not as pertinent to our immediate purpose as his reference to self-analysis. In spite of his pleasure in the solution before he spoke to his daughter, he concludes that "in self-analysis the danger of incompleteness is particularly great. One is too easily satisfied with a part explanation, behind which resistance can easily keep back something that is more important perhaps" (p. 314). With this I am sure we would all agree, but today a well-educated analyst has learned to take resistance and the partialness of insight into account. Such an analyst expects incompleteness, has learned to respect resistances whether in himself or someone else, and can wait for signs in dreams and other behavior that the "autoanalytic process" is continuing. Here, I use Maria Kramer's (1959) term accepting her stress on the necessity for preconscious activity to work with resistances before a new integration can add anything to conscious insight.

Strachey's (1957) last comment in his editorial footnote refers to Freud's 1912 paper and the advice in *Analysis Terminable and Interminable* (1937) that training analyses should be undertaken with a training analyst. It is interesting that Strachey neglects to comment on the strong recommendation in this last paper for a continuing self-analysis as well as additional periods of formal analysis every five years. It is here that self-analytic skills are described as a part of an analyst's professional equipment albeit often in need of objective assistance from a colleague when transference phenomena appear as resistances too strong to be worked through alone. It is in this paper, one of his greatest, that Freud discusses the effect of analytic work on the patient's ego. He says, "Is it not precisely the claim of our theory that analysis produces a state which never does arise spontaneously in the ego," a state which "constitutes the essential difference between a person who has been analyzed and a person who has not" (p. 227). This state comes about, he says, when analysis of the infantile defenses against instinctual forces enables the ego to revise and strengthen its defenses and achieve freedom from their dominance. In these remarks Freud is expressing what would be an ideal analytic result and what analytic theory postulates as possible. True to his ever-present scientific skepticism and his reliance on clinical experience for evidence to support his theories, Freud recognizes that the hopes of psychoanalysis are not always fulfilled. He cautions against coming to settled conclusions and against the inadvisability of trying to activate dormant conflicts for the sake of the analyst's therapeutic ambition. In other words, a training analysis should terminate, even if it begins again later.

In 1937, as in 1910 when he spoke of countertransference phenomena, Freud counted the analyst's ego of equal significance in influencing the prospects of analytic treatment. He recognized the special conditions of analytic work which "cause the analyst's own defects to interfere with his making a correct assessment of the state of things in his patient and reacting to them in a useful way" (p. 248). He sets high goals for an analyst whose love of truth is paramount since "it precludes any kind of sham or deceit" (p. 248). Realizing the unachievable ideal which he has just described, with sympathetic humor, he asks, "But where and how is the poor wretch to acquire the ideal qualifications which he will need in his profession?" He answers, ". . . in an analysis of himself, with which his preparation for his future activity begins" (p. 248).

Freud then proceeds to outline what he expected of a training analysis. He says, "Its main object is to enable his [the analyst's] teacher to make a judgement as to whether the candidate can be accepted for further training. It has accomplished its purpose if it gives the learner a firm conviction of the existence of the unconscious, if it enables him, when repressed material emerges, to perceive in himself things which would otherwise be incredible to him, and if it shows him a first sample of the technique which has proved to be the only effective one in his analytic work" (p. 248). This statement may sound superficial to us since it seems to stress more cognitive aspects of the analytic experience. However, Freud, as late as 1937, was still optimistic about self-analysis and by that time had seen the evidence for alterations in the ego brought about by the analytic method. Because he says it so much better than I can, let me present it to you in his words which set a course toward a hoped-for goal while at the same time they chart some of the shoals and narrows.

He feels that the analytic experience described above would by itself not be sufficient for a prospective analyst's education.

> . . . but we reckon the stimuli that he has received in his own analysis not ceasing when it ends and on the processes of remodeling the ego continuing spontaneously in the analyzed subject and making use of all subsequent experiences in this newly acquired sense. This does in fact happen, and in so far as it happens it makes the analyzed subject qualified to be an analyst himself.
>
> Unfortunately something else happens as well. In trying to describe this, one can only rely on impressions. Hostility on the one side and partisanship on the other create an atmosphere which is not favorable to objective investigation. It seems that a number of analysts learn to make use of defensive mechanisms which allow them to divert the implications and demands of analysis from themselves (probably by directing them on to other people) so that they themselves remain as they are and are able to withdraw from the critical and corrective influence of analysis" [p. 249].

Freud recognized the hazards of analytic work for an analyst. He saw a danger in the power with which a patient endows his analyst and warned against the temptation to misuse it. He saw a danger to the analyst's impulse control from "a constant preoccupation with all the repressed material which struggles for freedom in the human mind" (p. 249). He compared the effect of this danger on an analyst with the effect of X-rays on technicians who do not take special precautions, and advised periodic return to analysis, "without feeling ashamed of taking this step" (p. 249).

I hope I have made the point that in this final statement of Freud's ideas about how to become an analyst, he stressed the need for a therapeutic experience plus a never-ending self-scrutiny in order to manage the inevitable countertransferences which confront an analyst. Freud told Jones (1953) that he devoted the last half-hour of every day to his own analysis. In other words, he consciously continued to employ self-analytic skills in an attempt to make contact with preconscious processes, to widen the horizons of knowledge and to integrate experience with cognitive functioning. (For a late example, the reader is directed to Freud [1936a].)

Today we have an opportunity to make explicit this kind of activity as a skill to be taught during the education of a young analyst. The learning experiences of the training analysis and supervision can and do reinforce both the incentive and the know-how. Even the transferences in those situations can contribute to developing this skill if the ongoing nature of the self-analytic effort is focused on as a professional objective by the student's teachers. I stress this because I have seen a tendency among the faculties of Institutes to expect the training analysis to end the need for analytic effort. This tendency is only rarely stated as such, but implicitly carried out in at least two not uncommon instances. The first can be inferred in the practice of prolonging a training analysis. It is as if there is some lack of confidence in the student's being able to work on his own without benefit of his training analyst. Other circumstances and other dynamics in the training analyst may and do influence interminable training analyses but time does not permit discussion of these variables here. The second instance can be inferred from the taboo on discussing countertransferences in a supervisory situation. Supervisors in turn are sometimes reluctant to deliberately structure the supervisory situation (such as, frequency and explicit learning tasks) to encourage a student's assumption of a more independent position (Fleming and Benedek, 1966).

In this essay, one of several devoted to problems of psycho-analytic education (Fleming, 1961, 1969; Blitzsten and Fleming, 1953), I have attempted to review: what are the origins of a training analysis; what did Freud have to say about it; what were the first stated objectives; how were they implemented in the early days; how did experience modify these beginnings; and what were Freud's later compared with his earlier ideas. This stocktaking effort is based on the conviction that the thought we give to the education of new generations of psychoanalysts is an investment in the future of psychoanalysis. If the education is good, it will provide experiences that stimulate a spirit of inquiry and a wish to push back the frontiers of knowledge as well as acquire the skills to use the analytic method for therapeutic purposes. I believe the problem also concerns the thought we give to the education of the teachers of the new generations of analysts, since it becomes more and more clear that the principal difficulty in learning to conduct an analysis *and* in learning to teach it is the "personal equation," for which an ongoing self-analytic effort is an invaluable corrective.

The therapeutic advantages of a training analysis we tend to take for granted, but the additional aim which Eitingon (1926) mentioned we can today spell out more specifically. It is the aim of assisting a student-analyst to develop the self-analytic skills of introspection, empathy, and interpretation not only for acquiring insight into himself but as a built-in part of his "work ego." A basic attitude toward continuing self-exploration and a beginning development of the basic self-analytic skills are expectable results from a training analysis which has both therapeutic and professional aims.

In other words, the "problem" of a training analysis need not remain such an irreconcilable dilemma if we keep in mind the goal of self-analytic skills to be developed in the service of both therapy and professional work. Today, training analysts have techniques for increasing the depth of personal insight and professional attitudes. To enlarge on these techniques is beyond the scope of this essay, but it is an important task to which analytic educators should attend (Fleming, 1969). The position stated in our book on supervision (Fleming and Benedek, 1966) stresses the need to make self-analytic skills the principal educational objective for student analysts, an objective that is contributed to by every phase of analytic training. We need to integrate the aims and techniques of treating and teaching, a philosophy of education for an analyst which includes Freud's original ideas and also makes use of the advances in theory and technique of both therapy and learning.

## REFERENCES

Balint, M. (1954), Analytic training and training analysis. *Int. J. Psycho-Anal.,* 35:157–162.

Benedek, T. F. (1969), Training analysis—past, present and future. In: *Training Analysis: A Report of the First Three-Institute Conference,* ed. C. G. Babcock. Pittsburgh: Pittsburgh Psychoanalytic Institute.

Bernfeld, S. (1946), An unknown biographical fragment by Freud. *Amer. Imago,* 4(1).

Bernfeld, S. C. (1952), Discussion of Buxbaum. Freud's dream interpretation in the light of his letters to Fliess. *Bull. Menninger Clin.,* 16:66–73.

Bibring, G. L. (1954), The training analysis and its place in psychoanalytic training. *Int. J. Psycho-Anal.,* 35:169–173.

Blitzsten, N. L. and Fleming, J. (1953), What is a supervisory analysis? *Bull. Menninger Clin.,* 17:117–129.

Buxbaum, E. (1951), Freud's dream interpretation in the light of his letters to Fliess. *Bull. Menninger Clin.,* 15:197–212.

Eissler, K. R. (1951), An unknown autobiographical letter by Freud and a short comment. *Int. J. Psycho-Anal.,* 32:319–324.

Eitingon, M. (1926), An address to the international training commission. *Int. J. Psycho-Anal.,* 7:130–134.

Ekstein, R. (1953), On current trends in psychoanalytic training. In: *Explorations in Psychoanalysis,* ed. R. Lindner. New York: Julian Press, Inc., pp. 230–265.

Farrow, E. P. (1942), *A Practical Method of Self-Analysis.* London: Allen & Unwin.

Ferenczi, S. (1911), On the organization of the psychoanalytic movement. In: *Final Contributions to the Problems and Methods of Psychoanalysis,* ed. M. Balint. 3:299–307. New York: Basic Books, Inc., 1955.

—— (1927), The problem of termination of an analysis. *ibid.,* pp. 77–86.

—— (1928), The elasticity of psychoanalytic technique. *ibid.,* pp. 87–101.

—— (1930), The principles of relaxation and neo-catharsis. *ibid.,* pp. 108–125.

—— and Rank, O. (1924), *The Development of Psychoanalysis.* New York, Washington: Nervous and Mental Disease Publishing Company, 1925.

Fleming, J. (1961), What analytic work requires of an analyst. *J. Amer. Psychoanal. Assn.,* 9:719–729.

—— (1969), The training analyst as educator. Read at the Second Three-Institute Conference, Topeka, 1969. (To be published)

—— and Benedek, T. (1966), *Psychoanalytic Supervision.* New York: Grune & Stratton.

Fliess, R. (1942), The metapsychology of an analyst. *Psychoanal. Quart.,* 11:211–227.

Fliess, W. (1906), *In Eigener Sache. Gegen Otto Weinninger und Hermann Swoboda,* Berlin. Translated and referred to in footnotes to p. 241, 324 in *The Origins of Psychoanalysis.* New York: Basic Books, 1954.

Freud, A. (1950, 1938), The problem of training analysis. In: *The Writings of Anna Freud,* 4:407–421. New York: International Universities Press, 1968.

Freud, S. (1887), *The Origins of Psychoanalysis: Letters to W. Fliess, Drafts and Notes, 1887–1902,* eds. M. Bonaparte, A. Freud, E. Kris. New York: Basic Books, 1954, pp. 168–345.

—— (1899), Screen memories. *Standard Edition,* 3:303–322. London: Hogarth Press, 1963.

—— (1900), The interpretation of dreams. Preface to the second edition. *Standard Edition,* 4. London: Hogarth Press, 1953.

—— (1905), Fragment of an analysis of a case of hysteria. *Standard Edition,* 7:3–125. London: Hogarth Press, 1953.

—— (1910), The future prospects of psychoanalysis. *Standard Edition,* 11:141–151. London: Hogarth Press, 1957.

—— (1912), Recommendations to physicians practicing psychoanalysis. *Standard Edition,* 12:111–120. London: Hogarth Press, 1958.

—— (1914), On the history of the psychoanalytic movement. *Standard Edition,* 14:7–66. London: Hogarth Press, 1957.

—— (1916–17), Introductory lectures on psychoanalysis. *Standard Edition,* 15 and 16. London: Hogarth Press, 1963.

—— (1926), Foreword to E. Pickworth Farrow's *A Practical Method of Self-Analysis,* London, 1942. *Standard Edition,* 20:200–250. London: Hogarth Press, 1959.

—— (1935), The subtleties of a faulty action. *Standard Edition,* 22:233–235. London: Hogarth Press, 1964.

—— (1936), A disturbance of memory on the Acropolis. *Standard Edition,* 22:239–248, London: Hogarth Press, 1964.

—— (1937), Analysis terminable and interminable. *Standard Edition,* 23:210–253. London: Hogarth Press, 1964.

Gitelson, M. (1948), Problems of psychoanalytic training. *Psychoanal. Quart.,* 17:198–211.

—— (1954), Therapeutic problems in the analysis of the 'normal' candidate. *Int. J. Psycho-Anal.,* 35:174–183.

Greenacre, P. (1966), Problems of training analysis. *Psychoanal. Quart.,* 35:4, 540–567.

Greenson, R. R. (1967), *The Technique and Practice of Psychoanalysis.* New York: International Universities Press.

Isakower, O. (1957), Problems of supervision. Report to the Curriculum Committee of the New York Psychoanalytic Institute. (Unpublished)

Jones, E. (1953), *The Life and Work of Sigmund Freud.* New York: Basic Books, Inc.

—— (1959), *Free Associations.* New York: Basic Books, Inc.

Kairys, D. (1964), The training analysis: a critical review of the literature and a controversial proposal. *Psychoanal. Quart.,* 33:485–512.

Kramer, M. (1959), On the continuation of the analytic process after psychoanalysis (a self-observation). *Int. J. Psycho-Anal.,* 40:17–25.

Kris, E. (1954), Introduction to *The Origins of Psychoanalysis.* New York: Basic Books, Inc.

Lewin, B. D. and Ross, H. (1960), *Psychoanalytic Education in the United States.* New York: W. W. Norton & Co.

Oberndorf, C. P. (1953), *A History of Psychoanalysis in America.* New York: Grune & Stratton.

Sachs, H. (1947), Observations of a training analyst. *Psychoanal. Quart.,* 16:157–168.

Strachey, J. (1957), ed. Footnote to: On the history of the psychoanalytic movement. *Standard Edition,* 14:20. London: Hogarth Press.

Thompson, C. (1955), Introduction to Ferenczi's *Final Contributions to the Problems and Methods of Psychoanalysis,* Vol. III. New York: Basic Books.

# Part II
# Childhood and Adolescence

# 3. OVERVIEW

DAVID A. FREEDMAN, M.D.

---

Given the theme of this volume, it seemed to me appropriate to model my introductory remarks after F. L. Allen's *Only Yesterday* (1931) and *Since Yesterday* (1940). More specifically, I thought it might be of interest to enumerate some of the items in the literature with which candidates at the New Orleans Psychoanalytic Institute are expected to be familiar today and which were either unknown to me, unavailable, or literally nonexistent 19 years ago when I became a student in the then New Orleans Psychoanalytic Study Group.

Lest the reader dismiss what I have to say as reflecting simply the special conditions of a new, small facility, I hasten to remind him that by 1948 the authorities in the American Psychoanalytic Association had, in the fullness of their wisdom, seen to it that such a study group as ours would be sponsored. We were under the aegis first of the Washington-Baltimore Institute, and, when it mitosed, of the Washington Institute for Psychoanalysis. Our curriculum was planned with the approval of their education committees, and much of the teaching was done by members of their faculties. That is, what was taught during our early years in New Orleans, at least insofar as intended content was concerned, was considered in Washington and Baltimore to be what was required for the educating of a psychoanalyst.

It goes without saying that then, as now, the reading of Freud's writings was a major item in the training of an analytic candidate.

51

Indeed, if one wished to be nostalgic for the good old days, his best justification would be that in those times a somewhat greater proportion of his time would have been spent with Freud's writings. However, one's sentimental yearnings might be a bit mitigated if he stopped to consider that the volume entitled *Origins of Psychoanalysis* (1954), that is, the letters to Fliess and the Project, was not available to even the German-speaking student of psychoanalysis until 1950, and to the English-speaking student, not until 1954. How much less difficult it would have been to follow Chapter 7 even in Brill's tortured translation of *The Interpretation of Dreams* (1938) (the only one available to us in 1949) or *Beyond the Pleasure Principle* (to cite another item) had we been aware of Freud's earlier psychological and neuroanatomical speculations.

In addition to Freud's writings, we read some Abraham, some Jones, some Ferenczi, and a great deal of Fenichel's (1945) textbook. Of the postclassical literature, i.e. the literature to which we refer so much today, Anna Freud's *Ego and the Mechanisms of Defense* (1948), had been published only three years prior to my becoming a candidate. I have the year 1950 marked in the flyleaf of my own copy. Although the first of the Hartmann, Kris, and Loewenstein papers appeared in 1945, it was not until 1951 that Rapaport's anthology, *The Organization and Pathology of Thought* made most of us aware of Hartmann's basic work. It was not until 1958 that his *Ego Psychology and the Problem of Adaptation* (1958) was available in complete form. The New Orleans Psychoanalytic Institute was by then a full-grown and fully accredited organization, and I myself had completed my psychoanalytic training and was eligible for membership in the American. If it comes as a surprise to recall that so profoundly important a work has been generally available for only 10 years, consider that such major synthesizing works as *Psychoanalytic Concepts and the Structural Theory* by Arlow and Brenner (1964) and Anna Freud's *Normality and Pathology of Childhood* (1965) are relatively contemporary works.

Turning from metapsychological matters to the more empirical literature, it is of interest to consider the time at which the work of Spitz came to the attention of most of us. The two papers on

Hospitalism appeared in the first and second volumes of *The Psychoanalytic Study of the Child* (i.e., in 1945 and 1946). One might cite, however, as further evidence that our experience in New Orleans was not distorted, the fact that in the 29-item bibliography which Spitz attached to the first paper, there is not a single citation to a psychoanalytic journal. In this vein, it is impressive, too, that his paper on the smiling response, which also appeared in 1946, was published in *Genetic Psychological Monographs* (1946b). It was an unusual psychoanalyst, let alone candidate, who kept up with that publication. It was not until 1950 (the same year, incidentally, that Dr. Lewin's *Psychoanalysis of Elation* appeared) that one finds mention of the smiling response in *The Psychoanalytic Study of the Child*. By then, when the series was in its fifth volume, the response is mentioned only by Spitz himself in an article entitled "The Relevancy of Direct Infant Observation" (1950). The paper seems to have been intended to convince analysts that it might be germane to look directly at child development. Spitz's three major monographs, *A Genetic Field Theory of Ego Formation* (1959), *The First Year of Life* (1965), and *No and Yes* (1957) have all appeared within the last 14 years. I have elected to cite some dates in connection with his work because he is such a towering figure in the field. All of us can certainly supplement this list of major contributions both from Spitz's bibliography and those of Fries, Mahler, Escalona, Erikson, and Bowlby, to name just a few of the workers in the area of infancy and early childhood. Suffice it to say that the impact their work has had on thinking in both metapsychology and psychopathology has occurred since this Institute was organized.

Yet another radical change needs to be noted. We are all aware both of Freud's feeling that he was forced to work in isolation for many years, and of the accusation from many nonanalysts that psychoanalysis is an isolated, esoteric discipline divorced from the mainstream of science and medicine. For me one of the more exciting developments of these past 20 years has been the acceleration of the process of dissolution of the barriers which have kept us isolated. I say this although I am fully aware—from very personal experience—that this has not been an unmixed blessing. No doubt it has to do with my not purely rational commitment to analysis, that I derive so much gratification from the fact that the dissolution of barriers has much more to do with other fields' catching up with us than with changes in analysis. The image of a dedicated behaviorist like Harlow being forced by his own data into an approximation of a psychoanalytic way of thinking is, for me, a source of much satisfaction.

The same catching-up phenomenon can be seen in neurophysiology. Advances in instrumentation and the possibility of studying experimentally a freely moving organism, for example, had to precede Pribram's (1963) discovery of the relevance of Freud's early speculations to current neurophysiology.

The concept of critical periods has relevance to two other major areas of investigation which have become of increasing importance in psychoanalysis during the past several years. I refer to ethology and to Piaget's work. Critical periods, after all, is a term introduced to behavioral science by the ethologists. Twenty years ago, indeed 15 years ago, don't believe I had heard of Lorenz, and the relevance of ethological literature to our work was, if at all recognized, certainly honored in the main by being ignored.

Instinct theory, as we learned it then, did not get much beyond the expositions by Freud and Abraham. Although (unbeknownst to most of us) Freud (1896) was already diagramming critical periods on May 30, 1896, and the libido theory is certainly predicated on the assumed existence of critical periods, it was as we studied it, a first approximation. Even Abraham's (1924) subdivision of the oral and anal periods, and Glover's (1956) further refinements, were only bare beginnings of our recognition of the complexities of the emerging phenomena.

Equally as relevant to their role in drive theory seems to me to be our increasing awareness of the importance of critical periods or at least of timing sequences in problems of cognition. In this regard yet another name unfamiliar to most of us 19 years ago has assumed increasing importance. I refer, of course, to Piaget, who, despite or perhaps because of his disdain for matters relating to affect and motivation, has been able to provide us with so much data concerning what a child is capable of comprehending and, therefore, with what manner of ego equipment he is operating.

Of necessity this has been a very cursory review. Its intention has been to call attention to some of the developments both within psychoanalysis and in other fields which have affected my thinking and the nature of what I find to be of relevance to teach an analytic candidate in 1968.

Twenty years ago, entering the field as an ex-half-trained psychologist and a reasonably competent neurologist, I could see little in my past experience which was applicable to my new interests as an analyst. Today I don't think I could come to the same conclusion. At least in the three fields I have cited, people seem to have caught hold of the possibility that internal sources of motivation, psychic determinism, and changes in cognitive function as well as drive pattern with maturation and development are (as we already knew) extremely relevant matters. As a consequence, they have made observations which both supplement the data on which our theories are based and at times seem to require the rethinking of some of our assumptions.

## REFERENCES

Abraham, K. (1924), A short study of the development of the libido, viewed in the light of mental disorders. *Selected Papers on Psychoanalysis*. London: Hogarth Press, 1948, pp. 418–476.

Allen, F. L. (1931), *Only Yesterday; An Informal History of the Nineteen-Twenties*. New York: Harper and Brothers.

—— (1940), *Since Yesterday; The Nineteen-Thirties in America, September 23, 1929–September 3, 1939*. New York: Harper and Brothers.

Arlow, J. and Brenner, C. (1964), *Psychoanalytic Concepts and the Structural Theory*. New York: International Universities Press.

Fenichel, O. (1945), *The Psychoanalytic Theory of Neurosis*. New York: W. W. Norton & Co.

Freud, Anna (1948), *The Ego and the Mechanisms of Defense*. New York: International Universities Press.

—— (1965), *Normality and Pathology in Childhood*. New York: International Universities Press.

Freud, S. (1896), Letters to Wilhelm Fliess. *Standard Edition,* 1:175–280. London: Hogarth Press, 1966.

—— (1887–1902), *The Origins of Psycho-Analysis*. New York: Basic Books, 1954.

—— (1938), The interpretation of dreams. *Standard Edition,* 4 & 5. London: Hogarth Press, 1953.

Glover, E. (1956), A psychoanalytic approach to the classification of mental disorders. In: *On the Early Development of the Mind.* New York: International Universities Press, pp. 161–186.

Hartmann, H. (1958), *Ego Psychology and the Problem of Adaptation.* New York: International Universities Press.

Lewin, B. D. (1950), *The Psychoanalysis of Elation.* New York: W. W. Norton & Co.

Pribram, K. H. (1963), A neuropsychological model: some observations on the structure of psychological processes. In: *Expression of the Emotions in Man,* ed. P. H. Knapp. New York: International Universities Press, pp. 209–230.

Rapaport, D. (1951). *The Organization and Pathology of Thought.* New York: Columbia University Press, pp. 362–392.

Spitz, R. A. (1945), Hospitalism: an inquiry into the genesis of psychiatric conditions in early childhood. *The Psychoanalytic Study of the Child,* 1:53–74.

—— (1946a), Hospitalism: a follow-up report. *The Psychoanalytic Study of the Child,* 2:113–117.

—— (1946b), The smiling response: a contribution to the ontogenesis of social relations. *Genetic Psychol. Monogr.,* 34:57–125.

—— (1950), The relevancy of direct infant observation. *The Psychoanalytic Study of the Child,* 5:66–73.

—— (1957), *No and Yes.* New York: International Universities Press.

—— (1959), *A Genetic Field Theory of Ego Formation: Implications for Pathology.* New York: International Universities Press.

—— and Cobliner, W. G., (1965), *The first Year of Life: A Psychoanalytic Study of Normal and Deviant Development of Object Relations.* New York: International Universities Press.

# 4. ANNA FREUD'S DIAGNOSTIC PROFILE: A DISCUSSION

## HELEN ROSS

Diagnosis used to be a magic word, even a magic concept, as if the pronouncement would assure the cure. To satisfy the universal need to know, the meaning of the word took on the essence of the absolute. It was felt by the laity that it would answer the question, "What is wrong?" Indeed this is the question I recall in my childhood long before the Greek derivative came into the layman's use.

A story is told in the Freud family circle that when the Professor one evening crossed the hall from his office into the family quarters and found one child feverish, he asked the unruffled Frau Professor, "Have you sent for Dr. Rie?" She replied, "No, I have not decided yet what is wrong." Dr. Rie, the father of Marianne Kris, was the family pediatrician.

A few years ago (1961), the Hampstead Clinic made application to the NIMH for a grant to study diagnosis of children's emotional disorders. The staff had kept regular, meticulous records of child psychoanalytic cases. So also have many other groups. At the Hampstead Clinic, however, no record ever had the requiem mass, so often appended: "Case closed." Here no case is closed so long as the record yields some data useful to later study. Every finding becomes an item of research.

To this end, the Index, now famous, was started: to find a way

57

of making material available to researchers and to provide the therapists themselves with the assurance that the effort involved was not wasted. Taped records have not been used at Hampstead. Each student-analyst is required to write a brief weekly report on each case, at intervals of three to six months, a lengthier report, and at termination a report of the total treatment process to be read to the whole group and discussed. From the weekly reports, the Index is made and then presented to the Index Group for discussion before it finally reaches the file. Some of you are acquainted no doubt with the Index Manuals.

It became clear in the process of indexing that some psychoanalytic concepts require more accurate definition; and, accordingly, a concept study group was formed. This succession of studies is characteristic of the Hampstead group: a new study group is formed when its necessity is evident, a truly dynamic approach.

Recognizing the need for an intensive study of diagnosis of childhood disorders, the NIMH made a second grant to the Hampstead group, to extend and clarify their clinical research. I quote from the application itself. "Emphasis is laid throughout on seeing childhood pathology against the background of a hypothetical developmental norm, and to assess its severity from the aspect of interference with normal development. Assessment becomes the substantive rather than diagnosis."

This emphasis is pursued in Anna Freud's book, *Normality and Pathology in Childhood*. (Please note the order of the two words, normality and pathology.) "Normal" has no static definition. What is often taken for pathology is found, on clinical evidence, to be characteristic of certain conditions and periods of growth, especially to be observed at moments of transition in development.

I emphasize this point of view because it is liberating child study from the formal growth schedules so popular two and three decades ago and because it opposes the more recent tendencies to force growth and intellectual productivity.

Anna Freud once remarked that the precedence given to developmental considerations over considerations of symptomatology and manifest abnormal behavior is the essence of this approach and forms the basis of its conceptual framework.

As an aid to assessment of the normal, Anna Freud presents the "Concept of Developmental Lines" in Chapter III, before she outlines the Profile. She points out that the developmental sequences we know from psychoanalysis are valid only for isolated parts of the child's personality, not for its totality. She writes;

> What we are looking for are the basic interactions between id and ego and their various developmental levels and also age-related sequences of them which, in importance, frequency, and regularity, are comparable to the maturational sequence of libidinal stages or the gradual unfolding of ego functions [p. 63].

Later, she adds,

> . . . There are similar lines of development which can be shown to be valid for almost every other area of the individual's personality. In every instance, they trace the child's gradual outgrowing of dependence, irrational, id- and object-determined attitudes to an increasing ego mastery of his internal and external world [p. 63].

You will recall the prototype given, "From dependency to emotional self-reliance and adult object relationships," the basic developmental line recognized in our psychoanalytic studies.

When this concept of developmental lines was first presented in New York about seven or eight years ago, some analysts steeped in theory regarded these several lectures as too simple; but only within the framework of her total study of normality and pathology does one see the soundness of this approach to the assessment of a disorder.

A study of developmental lines shows how fundamental in the training of child analysts is a thorough knowledge of child development, psychological and physical. Such a course is included in the child analysis curriculum of all the institutes though it is sometimes resisted by students who demur that they have "taken" it in earlier studies.

Anna Freud calls the developmental lines "historical realities" which give a vivid picture of a child's personal achievements and personal failures, his going forward, his stopping at a point he finds more comfortable than going ahead, and his dropping back.

Some developmental lines toward body independence are out-lined: from sucking to rational eating, from wetting and soiling to bladder and bowel control, from irresponsibility to responsibility in body management, from egocentricity to companionship, from the body to the toy, and from play to work. The steps under each heading are carefully outlined as they are affected by object rela-tionship, and it is noted that many children show a disequilibrium between these lines. Here, as in many parts of this book, the author warns against seeing pathology in moderate disharmony, reminding the reader that moderate disharmony does no more than prepare the ground for "the many variations of normality with which we have to count," and warning the trouble seekers that "no child should be expected to maintain his best level of performance for any length of time" (p. 92).

This chapter could be condensed profitably as a brief manual of child development.

There follows logically a long chapter on regression as a principle in normal development, again a little text book in itself. Anna Freud begins with a discussion of three types of regression as set forth originally, in addition to those in *The Interpretation of Dreams* (Freud, 1900)—topographical, temporal and formal; and she translates the earlier topographical concept into later structural terms. She warns against such glib explanations as the patient "has regressed from the phallic-oedipal phase to the oral or anal phase," (p. 96), since this does not give the form, scope and significance of the regressive movement that has taken place. Those of us who supervise students are well acquainted with this recourse to the-oretical terminology, not just because of ignorance (their state-ments are often correct), but because of lack of close observation as to what the patient says and does. Short-hand is too easy. Clinical evidence must be presented before the short-hand. If the child has retreated from masturbation because of some threat, real or imagined, he may find satisfaction in old oral pleasures. A bottle of Coke may be the comforting substitute, more acceptable to his ego than thumbsucking, more permissible than genital play.

Keeping the reader constantly aware of the use of regression in normal development, Anna Freud mentions fatigue, boredom, pain, illness and distress—all the usual occurrences in a child's life; and as a subtle warning to those who wish conformity and precocious achievement, she concludes: "According to experience, the slow method of trial and error, progression and temporary reversal is more appropriate to healthy psychic growth" (p. 99). This sentence as many others in this little volume constitutes a rubric for those concerned with the rearing of children.

It is not easy to determine the depth or permanence of regression at the diagnostic stage; so far no criteria for this exists, though on this evaluation depends decision regarding treatability.

Psychopathology in children does not have its own nosology; the "revolutionary spirit of the child analyst has exhausted itself in the areas of technique and theory" (p. 110), while classification of child disorders has fallen back, unsatisfactorily, to those in the field of adult analysis, psychiatry, and criminology. Descriptive terms are used, such as truancy, temper tantrum, and separation anxiety, though each case may be different in that they may have totally different pathogenesis. For example, a temper tantrum may be a direct motor-affective outlet in a young child who has no other means and is likely to disappear as a symptom, or it may be an aggressive-destructive outburst, or it may be an anxiety attack. The foregoing represents an abbreviation of her statement.

Truancy, vagrancy, or wandering have varied causations as does separation anxiety. These terms, in short, are descriptive; but thinking in descriptive terms does not help in analytic therapy. Lying and stealing may be considered pathological only within certain developmental stages: "Altogether, the symptomatology of immature individuals is much too unstable to be relied on in assessment" (p. 120).

In this book, defense falls into its proper place within the context of child development, normal and pathological. In her earlier work (1946), which has since become a classic in ego psychology, the mechanisms of defense had been brilliantly defined. Students of psychoanalysis and teachers took this book as guide and mentor. Indeed there was a pitfall in our avidity to recognize and name defenses, sometimes too glibly, as if the label itself were our explanation, a satisfaction similar to that of the diagnostician who falls back on his rigid nosological categories. Without supporting clinical evidence, naming the defense has little meaning.

Before the metapsychological profile is presented formally, criteria for assessment of severity of disorder are presented. The analysts base their assessments on the degree of impairment of functioning, notwithstanding the fact that this factor is one of the most revealing criteria for the pathology of adults. Uneven drive and ego progression, disharmony between developmental lines, permanence of regression, and type of anxiety and conflict are discussed simply and pungently. Following this, certain general characteristics are offered as measurements: frustration tolerance and sublimation potential, mastery of anxiety, regressive versus progressive tendencies. These latter categories I have found useful in helping those who are not analytically trained in making judgment regarding large numbers of children whom they must serve.

The *Profile* itself (beginning on p. 140), unfortunately, but not surprisingly, looks forbidding. I believe one cannot usefully begin with the outline and try to fit a given case into its logically designed categories. It is neither a questionnaire nor a case history, but a living instrument. Mastery rests on an understanding of its theoretical foundations set forth in the early chapters; therefore, I recommend to students a careful reading of the book through to the end. Only after the student recognizes the variations in normal development and the strains attendant upon transition stages is he ready to grapple with severe deviations.

We pause here in appreciation of Anna Freud's exposition of the vicissitudes of normal growth. This has led to a greater enlightenment in the handling of the manifold disturbances that appear daily in our child psychiatric clinics and has given encouragement to parents and teachers.

Sidonie Gruenberg, one of the founders of the Child Study Association, once told me she started with a little group of young mothers when she, a young woman, discovered her first born, a little boy, was lying to her and taking things that did not belong to him. Committed to truth, she told her story and so freed the other young mothers to give their own experiences with their innocents. Thus the Child Study Association came into being.

The discovery of infantile ingredients in adult neurosis made many intelligent parents fearful of what their children would become. It has taken a long time to undo these anxieties and to show the progressive and regressive trends in every child.

The *Profile* has undergone some slight modifications since its publication. It continues at Hampstead to be discussed with every new case, at the diagnostic stage, after periods of therapy, and at termination. The general organization has remained almost unaltered, as it was based on psychoanalytic assumptions well tested over many years. As the *Profile* was applied to clinical material of the most diverse order, many questions arose and study groups were set up to grapple with problems posed by, for example, blind children, the borderline patient, and the delinquent personality. A profile for the assessment of adolescent disturbances was developed by M. Laufer and has appeared in *The Psychoanalytic Study of the Child,* vol. XX. In the same volume, there appears "Assessment of the Adult Personality—A Diagnostic Profile" by Anna Freud, H. Nagera, and W. E. Freud. It is of some interest that currently a baby Profile is being developed. A geriatric Profile might be anticipated. The additional adaptations in no way detract from the original invention; the essence remains. They are all instruments of psychoanalytic study, guide posts only; and as in all psychoanalysis, they are not to be regarded as finished products.

The *Profile* is now well known and is being used in many clinics in this country. I shall not attempt to outline it here but wish to note that I have found it invaluable in my work with students.

There follows in the book a discussion of some infantile prestages in adult psychopathology as well as certain categories of severe disturbance, in which the age factor, psychological and legal, determines whether the disorder can be called antisocial, dissocial, delinquent, or criminal. The newborn is a law unto himself, and the mother is the first law-giver. This exposition is influencing the writing of family law and giving new meaning to the age-old legal wording: "in the best interests of the child." Homosexuality—a normal expression at certain developmental levels—and perversions such as transvestism, fetishism, and addictions are given developmental explanations as deviations from the norm chronologically and quantitatively. These are concise, useful expositions, of value to the clinician.

The concluding chapter reviews therapeutic possibilities applicable to the whole range of childhood disturbances. I advise students to read this last chapter (6) before the preceding one lest they become fascinated with the symptomatology of the more deviant forms of behavior. The end chapter keeps the focus on general principles of child pathology and on the goal of psychoanalytic treatment, while pointing out that the young patient makes use of the analyst's technique as his pathology requires. The child patient tells the story which we hear only if we listen.

Diagnosis has become an ever-expanding concept. The word is not self-limiting. In a famous decision Justice Holmes (1918) said, "A word is not a crystal, transparent and unchanging. It is a skin enclosing a living thought, influenced by changing circumstances and conditions."

In a recent issue of the *Massachusetts Review,* Robert Coles (1966) has a sensitive piece, "The Achievement of Anna Freud," written upon the occasion of Anna Freud's 70th birthday. Though he had never studied with her nor indeed at that time even met her, he caught the essence of her books and many papers, all of which he read in sequence of their appearance. In conclusion he states,

> Anna Freud has remained fittingly loyal to her father by refusing to stand in useless awe of his many accomplishments. She has gone forward where he left off, giving her life to children from unhappy homes, to children in the midst of the terrors of war, to normal children in their puzzling inspiring variety. All the while she has written the clear, civilized prose of the confident scientist, the warm good-humored prose of the kind and sensible human being. One can fairly glide along the pages of her latest book. . . . The most complicated idea emerges so effortlessly that it seems to be pure "common sense" [p. 220].

## REFERENCES

Coles, R. (1966), The achievement of Anna Freud. *The Massachusetts Review,* Spring.

Freud, A. (1946), *The Ego and the Mechanisms of Defense*. New York: International Universities Press.
—— (1965), *Normality and Pathology in Childhood*. New York: International Universities Press.
Freud, S. (1900), The interpretation of dreams. *Standard Edition,* 4 & 5. London: Hogarth Press, 1953.
Justice Holmes (1918), Towne vs. Eisner 245, *U. S. 418,* 425.

# 5. ADOLESCENT CONCRETIZATION: A CONTRIBUTION TO THE THEORY OF DELINQUENCY

". . . Nier ce qui est, et
expliquer ce qui n'est
pas . . ."
J. J. Rousseau
(*Nouvelle Héloise*)

PETER BLOS, PH.D.

I have chosen a topic for investigation that is remote from psychoanalysis as a therapeutic technique and yet, at the same time, it is close to the heart and mind of everyone who practices it. If we look at people of all ages whose emotional maldevelopment has brought them into disharmony with themselves or with their environment—a disharmony causing a kind of misery that inexorably works its way down the generational lineage—and if we then look at our psychoanalytic expertise, we cannot escape the conclusion that the vast majority of those afflicted by emotional maldevelopment is immune to the benefits derived from the standard psychoanalytic technique, even if such a utopian availability of analysis

Herman Nunberg Lecture, March 3, 1969.

were within everybody's reach. There is no need to let matters rest at this point, because psychoanalysis as a general psychology has flung open many new gates inviting us to walk on untrodden ground.

Psychoanalysis has always recognized the limitations of mutability within the instinctual and adaptive life of man while, at the same time, it has demonstrated the extent of personality transformation that lies within the resourcefulness of man. As analysts we work and exist within the awareness of the unalterable boundaries of human nature; in fact, the exploration of their extent and flexibility is the aim of our science. It is dedicated to the affairs of man and to the facilitation of individual self-realization. Psychoanalysis has always held firmly and passionately to the humanist tradition. Nothing remains more valued and worthy of our endeavor than the harmonizing influence we can exert on the life of man through our science. Contemporary history urges upon us a quest for rational means of intervention that will moderate man's destructiveness and brutality in relation to himself and his fellow man. Any contribution—no matter how slight, if it enlarges our knowledge of these blind forces, of their ontogenetic sources, and of their ways of transformation—answers a communal quest.

I have singled out for this psychoanalytic exploration a group of white adolescent delinquent boys who were adjudicated by the juvenile court. The puzzlements which these cases present in terms of their assessment and rehabilitation have kept my curiosity at a high pitch for a long time. After decades of concentrating on child and adolescent analysis, I have, as it were, returned to my analytic beginnings. August Aichhorn's example, his work with delinquents, and his personal tutorship have strongly influenced my choice of profession. I fulfill a legacy of these early years of apprenticeship when I now explore some clinical problems of delinquency. With the widening of explanatory concepts, extending deeply into the preoedipal stage of development, there has evolved a more complex model of delinquency. This is to say that we speak of a multitude of delinquencies; they are united by only one characteristic, namely, the engagement of the action system in problem solving and the use of the environment as tension regulator. Both these factors work against internalization and against changes within the self.

I have come to the conclusion that acting out, the hallmark of this group of asocial adolescents, is a species of behavior with many distinct subspecies. It has been my endeavor to study such identifiable varieties and to distinguish one from the other. My considerations are limited to a subspecies of behavior which we call, generically, acting out. Within this narrow context, I shall focus on the processes of internalization and ego differentiation, with special reference to the function of memory and symbolic speech.

The subspecies of acting out behavior, which is the subject of this paper, possesses certain characteristics I shall now describe. In the first place, the action system has assumed to a significant but restricted extent an ego function that belongs, normally, to symbolic speech. The maladaptive behavior impresses the observer as a gestural communication, the content of which is seemingly unknown to the gesturer. Bypassing the language channel of expression, it appears that only concrete modalities are found adequate for the expression of thought, memory, affect, or conflict. The main vehicle of communication is action. It is not simply random action, but neither is it action with volition and intentionality. In analogy to the attention cathexis, as characteristic of thought, one might say that action, as considered here, is selectively cathected in relation to certain affects and ego interests. The absence of symbolic speech, but only and exclusively in reference to these selective and delineated areas of mental life, precludes their integration into higher and more complex mental functioning. Consequently prelogical mentation survives side by side with age-adequate language usage and learning capacity. We correctly suspect the continuation of magical thought from early childhood into adolescence.

It follows that action, being a gestural communication, does not necessarily express an unequivocal statement, consisting of discrete elements such as we can discern in verbalized, logical thought, but such action is a syncretic formation with an implicit irrationality, alien to the communicative use of language. Such syncretism is known to us from dreams in which a person can be several persons at once, without arousing a sense of unreality in the dreamer. Long ago, Greenacre (1950) has called our attention to a predisposing factor to acting out that lies in "a distortion in the relation of action to speech and verbalized thought" (p. 227).

We can distinguish two extreme forms resulting from this distortion, either concretism through action or concretism through eidetic imagery; the adolescent can describe both while they both remain inaccessible to verbalized interpretation. I have found that imagery, as known from daydreams, is more prevalent among girls, in contradistinction to the boy who, normally, resorts more quickly to action. Both modalities can constitute an equivalent of verbalized thought, in the same manner as we consider thought an action equivalent. An adolescent girl I had in analysis told me that she has a picture in her mind for every thought and feeling. She, for example, might avoid writing a difficult school assignment by imagining that she rides a horse and gallops over the prairie. This imaginary action *is* the school assignment; one can say that it is written through the action fantasy that allows a syncretic imaginary resolution with no action taking place in reality. Interpretations of concretism in either action or eidetic imagery remain ineffectual because the implicit primitive, prelogical thought countermands the comprehension of the discrete elements of language that are governed by the secondary process. Only when the concreteness of eidetic imagery fades into pictorial language and metaphorical speech or, conversely, only if the gesture is replaced by words, do we know that the reality principle has intervened. The irrationality of thought with which certain delinquents justify, explain, and defend their asocial behavior possesses a fixity and immutability that is reminiscent of a delusional system. Yet, no thought disorder and no distortion of reality, due to psychosis or organicity, are in evidence. On the basis of the characteristic features of this particular subspecies of acting-out behavior, I have called it "concretization." This term has its established place in the theory of psychosis, but, in contrast, I propose to use the term with a developmental reference. Within this context, concrete and abstract thought describe stages in the ontogenesis of the comprehension of and interaction with the outer world (Piaget). The concreteness of action and of thing representation, its transition to symbolic speech and concept formation, represents a pivotal developmental point, on which hinges not only the individual mode of communication, but its progressive usefulness for adaptive mastery of the internal and of the external world.

I am often reminded of the analysis of dreams or parapraxes, when I attempt to reconstruct the coherent, latent content of action from the manifest action which appears, usually, disjointed, seemingly irrelevant, extraneous and incidental, with meaningless details that look like fortuitous expressions or accidental occurrences. Seasoned analytic experience is the *sine qua non* for this kind of work. An action specimen of concretization will help us along at this point. An adolescent car thief brushed aside all accusations regarding his offense by reiterating, ad nauseam, the fact that the owner of the automobile was, after all, insured and could not possibly care if his car was stolen as long as he got the money. The boy felt that police and court conspired to exonerate the car owner of his money-grabbing greed by branding him, the boy, a thief and a criminal. In defiance he told police and court to "go to hell" because they did not know what they were talking about. At the assessment interview, the boy presented the typical indifference to and disinterest in discussing his actions. I realized that his obstinacy was not due to his unwillingness to say anything but to the fact that he had nothing to say. He had said it all in his action and in his commentary that followed. The *idée fixe* with reference to the car owner convinced me of the concretizing nature of the theft. Indeed, the theft proved to be a condensation of perceptual, cognitive, and affective determinants. The transposition of the manifest into the latent action theme reads as follows: "When I was a little boy of six, my father died; all my mother cared about was the insurance money. She did not mind that he was dead, as long as she got paid for the loss. My mother never loved my father. I hate her for that. She wants to control and baby me now. I do not trust her. She is selfish. She should go to jail. She is a criminal." It is not necessary to dwell in this connection on the meaning of a stolen car and the symbolic father representation, because these are matters with which we are thoroughly familiar; they are, however, only tangentially useful for the comprehension of the theft and for the choice of the rehabilitative intervention. All I can say at this point is that life history and adolescent conflict coalesced here in a particular form of antisocial behavior. It is obviously not a metaphorical statement, when I call concretization a private language, because action has usurped a language function which has, however, no communal reference and remains idiosyncratic in character. It should follow from this point of view that the theft, as described, is not simply a displacement, but rather a communicative interaction with the environment, a statement of a memory and a thought in juxtaposition with developmental recapitulations and, in this case, abortive resolutions.

Such cases have always impressed me by the absence of conflict and of guilt. Yet, we do not deal with a psychopath and, furthermore, the superego defect is highly selective and, by no means, pervasive. Here, we might ask ourselves the simple question: How could it be otherwise? The boy, after all, exonerates his dead father and wrests his exalted image of him from the malevolent archaic mother. A hero fighting for a great cause feels not guilty about any of his actions but, quite to the contrary, his actions relieve him from the guilt of passive acquiescence to a crime to which he was and remains a living witness. Should we emphasize in the clinical picture the absence of conflict as well as the absence of guilt, and make these findings the basis of our assessment, then we have mistaken the appearance for the substance or the manifest for the latent content.

I have recognized in concretization a nonconflictual ego function. The apparent absence of conflict is due to the fact that concretization can accommodate antithetical strivings and thoughts within its organization. This can be expressed in terms of object relations by saying that the perseverance on the level of ambivalence has prevented the fusion of the need-gratifying and the frustrating, namely, tension-inducing object. This perseverance on the archaic object experience never fails to leave its imprint on cognition and on the function of language, both being rendered unable to rise above the prelogical stage of communication and tending, therefore, to rely heavily on pictorial mentation—"a special emphasis on visual sensitization" (Greenacre, 1950)—and on gestural communication of various kinds—"a largely unconscious belief in the magic of action" (Greenacre, 1950).

The concretizing delinquent attests to a reality of his past and to isolated and forgotten (preconscious) memories. These remain excluded from cognitive integration whenever they are openly contradicted or pointedly ignored by the environment. Ego discontinuity is thus inflicted on the child by the ego pathology of his significant caretakers, usually the parents, whose enclaves of denial contradict the child's perception by withholding consensual validation. There we find an additional cause for the survival of the concrete, due to the fact that sanity hinges on the identity of perception and reality, memory and fact.

The concretizing adolescent uses the environment not only for the gratification of infantile wishes but, simultaneously, he tries to extricate himself, through his actions, from infantile object dependencies; in short, he aims at activating the second individuation process of adolescence. He obviates or corrects through action a piece of reality. The denial of reality is of a peculiar kind in the cases I shall present, insofar as what is denied is a piece of unreality which was thrust upon the child by authority figures, through commission or omission, as positive or negative reality.

Concretization implies, by its very nature, a continued and tenacious dependency on the environment. The silent mastery of tension through thought, fantasy, recollection, anticipation—briefly, through processes that are the result of internalization—appears inadequately developed in these cases. Constantly, environmental participation is elicited by provocation. The environmental retaliation and apprehension is not something to be avoided but rather something that is sought. The three institutions—family, school, and court—are aroused to counteractions which render realness to what the concretizing adolescent gestures in helpless but determined pertinacity.

Before I present further clinical illustrations, there remains a matter that has to be clarified. We are accustomed to speak of thought as trial action. The economy of thought lies in the reduced expenditure of energy. Thought anticipates the outcome of action, weighs the pleasure-unpleasure balance, and settles on a course of action that is a compromise formation. The conscious, often preconscious, process uses awareness and memory via word representations to synthesize a conclusion or a decision. Tensions which arise in this dialectic process are resolved through the mediation of alternatives that lie within the scope of ego and environment. The point I endeavor to make concerns the fact that thought implies potential consciousness and awareness of tensions that are attached to disequilibrizing strivings or affects vis-à-vis a given situation. The outcome of thought is a deliberate act, positive or negative. In contrast, the concretizing adolescent acts without thinking and without internal resolution of, or accommodation to, tension. He is, thus, predestined to get into conflict with the environment, to be a delinquent, even if not necessarily a delinquent who is ever confronted by the law. The economy of action blurs the awareness of contradictions in relation to affects, thoughts, and memories.

The reliance on action as tension-regulator indicates a state of ego undifferentiation that is noticeable in the vague and fluid boundaries between perception, feeling, and thought. The confusion between the internal and the external, namely, the subjective and the objective (the "adualism" of Piaget) should have been dispelled by the end of the latency period. Not so in the concretizing adolescent. He seems to be up against a barrier in the path of development which he cannot surmount. He hopes that the environment will surmount it for him. Consequently, the more he struggles against the barrier, the more he falls back into helplessness and rage. This could not be different because—Odier (1956) quoting Piaget—"objectification and consciousness are mutually exclusive" (p. 113). It follows that the ego of the concretizing delinquent is inimical to insight which is rooted in introspection and contingent on internalization and verbalized thought.

Here, the influence of an impersonal authoritative institution, namely the court, acts as a coercive force, thus lending an effective leverage in an otherwise hopeless situation, provided this power is used judiciously. Toward this end, psychoanalytic psychology illuminates the intricacies of concretization and points the way to a helpful intervention in the vagaries of these recalcitrant and antagonistic subjects.

## THE CASE OF RUBIN

After having described the developmental characteristics of the concretizing adolescent, I shall now speak of a 13-year-old delinquent boy. In his case, it was indeed possible to "unhitch a developmental catch," to use Winnicott's expression.

Rubin was raised in an orthodox Jewish home. On Yom Kippur he had broken into the Yeshiva of his temple where he stole a box of nails and some pencils. This burglary, in conjunction with his chronic truancy, brought Rubin to court. The judge requested an assessment of Rubin for the adjudication of his case. For the reader to appreciate the assessment process to its conclusion, certain facts about Rubin's life have to be told.

The boy and his mother had always lived in the Williamsburg section of Brooklyn. His father was a junk dealer, who had died when Rubin was six-years-old. The child, then, attended a Yeshiva. At the age of 12, he refused to continue his religious education and transferred to a public school, where his truancy began. The mother complained bitterly about Rubin's antagonism to religious observances and his preference for non-Jewish friends. Through their company he was introduced to petty stealing which resulted in an accumulation of bicycle parts that filled the back yard of his house. Rubin's disobedience only intensified the mother's fervor to make her son conform to an orthodox life. These data, which were part of the case history as collected by court, school, and social agencies, hardly sufficed for adequate comprehension of Rubin's behavior.

We are accustomed from our analytic work to gain unexpected insight into a case through minor details, through isolated oddities of thought or behavior, through circumstantial coincidences, if viewed against the major events of a life history and against the developmental state of the moment. I was curious to know where the boy had spent the endless hours of his truancy. He told us that he used to cross the Williamsburg Bridge to Manhattan and would wander aimlessly through the Bowery. His father's junk shop was once located here, where the little boy had done his first carpentry work under his father's tutelage. He still wanted to become a carpenter. The theft of nails was related to Rubin's early adolescent struggle to come to terms with his father whom he had lost at the height of the oedipal period. Mourning had to be completed in adolescence. But why did he steal the box of nails on Yom Kippur and why from a holy place? Rubin concretized in this action the parental fights over religious observances by allying himself with the agnostic father who had never had any use for Orthodox Judaism. The mother's religious coercion of the son brought the preoedipal fears of the archaic, castrating mother into prominence around this issue. The mother was, indeed, unrelenting in her determination to make out of Rubin a better Jew than his father had been. Yet, young Rubin defended his identity through the collection of junk that he carried home from his exploits in the streets. The mother tried in vain to rescue her son from the father's influence by eradicating the dead man from his memory or, at least, by rendering him an unspeakable and unthinkable object. We cannot fail to detect in the boy's action an effort to protect his sense of reality that is contingent on ego continuity and memory cathexis. The deciphered language of Rubin's delinquency spoke eloquently of his adolescent struggle to rescue the positive father image and of the anxiety engendered by the archaic mother. Rubin had no capacity for verbalization nor any interest in insight. There was ample reason to expect that he could make good use of an environment that would offer the appropriate growth-promoting experiences for a boy of his age and kind. While he would not speak of his father, he was eager to identify with him vocationally; this, in turn, might reduce his fear of the archaic mother and his need for delinquent concretization. The thought occurred to me that the desecration of the holy place unified antinomical thoughts, namely, on the one hand he defended the agnostic father and, on the other hand, he accused him of a crime. Rubin knew right from wrong. The intervention that promised to intercept a delinquent career was the removal of the boy from his mother's fanatical interference with her son's adolescent psychic restructuring. What was at stake was the completion of mourning, the positive identification with the father and, generally, the process of adolescent socialization.

The mother rejected the court's remand, refusing to release her son to an unorthodox residential treatment center, even though Rubin wanted to go. Time being of the essence, we resorted to a shortcut in order to implement the rehabilitative strategy of choice. We turned to the rabbi, whose authority the mother respected, and asked him for a dispensation which he granted. Soon thereafter Rubin left home in haste and hope. In the stern voice of authority that ordered him away from home, Rubin heard, I suppose, a whispered message that told him that it was the mother who had to be taken away from him because the judge condemned her destruction of the oedipal father.

Once established in the residential institution, Rubin never missed a day of school; he selected carpentry as his vocational training. He fitted smoothly into the new environment, displayed no deviant behavior, and related well to peers and adults alike. Understandably, he was not eager to make home visits. An autonomous integration of the parental religious antagonism became finally evident when Rubin, voluntarily, began to attend religious services. Two years have passed since his appearance in court; all that can be said today is that Rubin could extricate himself from a catastrophic developmental impediment, once the environmental conditions facilitated psychic differentiation, internalization, and vocational identity. Rubin is an exceptional case, a simple case I might say, which should not necessarily allow undue optimism toward the treatment of the concretizing adolescent.

Before I proceed to a more complex case, I shall deal with some objections and queries that have no doubt been raised by the foregoing material. After all, acting out has been dealt with exhaustively by many analytic writers and it seems uncalled for to split off a unique category from the established concept of acting out. Why do I not simply speak of the externalization of unconscious conflicts, of acting out as an adolescent-specific modality of behavior, as a defense against a depressive core and object loss, as a form of remembering, as a symbolic replication of the past—and let it go at that? I have always adhered to the opinion that acting out within the analytic situation reserves a theoretical position of its own in contradistinction to extra-analytic acting out as observed, for example, in delinquency. Anna Freud (1968) remarked at the 1967 Symposium on "Acting Out" that ". . . re-living in the transference was increasingly taken for granted; and the longer this happened, the more often was the term 'acting out' not applied to the repetition in the transference at all, but reserved for the re-enactment of the past outside the analysis." She continues: "Personally, I regret that change of usage since on the one hand it obscures the initially sharp differentiation between remembering and repeating and on the other hand it glosses over the differences between the various forms of 'acting out.' " One of these various forms—what I have called a subspecies of acting out—I venture to comprehend in the concept of concretization. Perhaps the one factor that sets this form of acting out apart from the others—in spite of their sharing many similarities—is the effort to uphold a sense of reality and autonomy both of which are kept in constant jeopardy by the environment. They are, reactively, stabilized in concretization which is experienced, subjectively, as a lowering of tension and a restoration of self-esteem.

In Rubin's case, the sense of reality and autonomy remained in jeopardy from two sides; namely, from the reality distortions or the denial which the mother impressed on the ego of the grieving child, and furthermore, from the inability of the child's ego to cope, integratively, under these conditions, with selective memories and affects. We have always recognized certain preconditions that are characteristic for all forms of acting out. Could it be that the preponderance of one of the preconditional factors is responsible for the various forms of acting out? I expect that the case I am about to report will sharpen the line of demarcation that sets off concretization from other forms of maladaptive behavior generally, and from other forms of acting out, in particular.

## THE CASE OF EDDY

Eddy was a 15-year-old car thief, a chronic truant, and a wild boy who was beyond the control of his parents. In desperation, they took him to court after he had smashed up a stolen car and nearly killed himself. He had talked about suicide before. In speaking about his accident he presented an amused and detached attitude: he was just playing a game of brinkmanship with death. Some time before, Eddy had, with burglary on his mind, acquired a master key to his apartment house.

Each family member—mother, step-father and older sister—contributed a casual strand of information out of which the total fabric of Eddy's history was painstakingly woven. In piecing these random strands together, there finally emerged a picture that illuminated the boy's behavior in an unexpected perspective of historical continuity.

Eddy's father had died when the child was two-and-a-half years old. Over the years many versions of his death were given to him, all of which the boy had brushed aside as unacceptable. Eddy had only one certainty about his father, namely, that he was dead. He did not know his vocation nor his family background, nor his paternal relatives, nor the location of his grave.

The relevant facts of the father's life can be told briefly. He was a professional crook, who specialized in thievery. Working in a hotel he procured a master key and burglarized the rooms. One day when he had stolen goods in his automobile he was, accidentally, followed by a police car. He panicked, tried to escape by speeding, lost control, and smashed into a stone wall where he met his death.

In comparing the father's criminal career and the son's delinquency, we are struck by the replication of crucial details of which the child, supposedly, had no knowledge. While he was never told of the facts he sensed, no doubt, that the facts were of an unspeakable and unthinkable nature. Here, we must remind ourselves that such denials or repressions are nothing unusual in the lives of children. Why, then, did it invade Eddy's adolescent action system with a force so compelling that it remained totally unaffected by any outside interference?

It has been my impression that there are two qualitatively different kinds of secrets which parents keep from their children. The essential difference lies in the degree of reality with which the parent himself endows the facts he keeps from the child. It is simpler for the child to deal with prohibitions and taboos, than with contradictions, confusion, and inconsistency. Eddy's case demonstrates how the mother's enclaves of denial infiltrated her reality testing and prevented the child from ever dealing integratively with his father's life and death. The mother could offer the child neither a consensual validation of his perceptions nor a consistent refutation of them. Therefore, no intrapsychic settlement of the catastrophe was feasible; action language remained the only communicative modality by which contact with perceptual memory could be maintained. I conceive of this ego effort as the driving force in Eddy's maladaptive behavior and, consequently, I attribute a subordinate role to identificatory processes in this case.

This leads us to a consideration of Eddy's object relations. It became immediately apparent upon meeting this boy that he was passionately involved with the members of his family. He dated the onset of his delinquency as coinciding with his step-father's leaving the family on one of his mysterious absences, lasting several months. Only the mother knew that he was on a gambling spree. The boy resented the paternal absenteeism and blamed the mother for condoning it. This hardboiled delinquent said with tender feelings: "I thought my [step] father left us because he didn't love us. I wanted so much to have him as my real father." The child had wooed his new father ever since his mother's remarriage when he was four years old; he used the step-father's last name even though he was not legally adopted. Eddy was a fatherless son in search of a father. It is one of the requirements of adolescence to come to terms with the oedipal father. Preconditional for this task is the establishment of historical ego continuity as independent from parental sanctions and complementations. Here, then, was the point where an early catastrophic developmental impediment became manifest. Through his actions the boy made it known that he possessed a preconscious, if hazy, knowledge of all the relevant facts surrounding his father's life and death. This was confirmed when the father's history was imparted to the boy. How this shared knowledge and the implicit validation of his shadowy perceptual memories affected his behavior is of particular interest. Concretization, suicidal brinkmanship, and provocative behavior declined markedly. In addition, changes in the boy's affective life were noticeable. As one of them I shall mention the emergence of the boy's tender feelings to his natural father, his grief and compassion for a man who, so he thought, was not loved enough to value life more than death. He rediscovered his father's family on his own initiative, learned about his father's grave, took a job at a paternal uncle's store, moved to a paternal aunt's family, and fell in love with a neighborhood girl. Through action, rather than through insight, he tried to assimilate his unconsummated past. With adolescent exuberance he turned to the environment for the support of his adaptive efforts.

Concretization, by its very nature, implies an infantile dependency on the environment. Paraphrasing Spitz's remark, we might call Eddy's actions a permanent dialogue between the self and the environment. Concretization always represents a primitive form of adaptation. Consequently, it depends on the responsive cooperation of the environment at the point of crisis whether this developmental impasse can be overcome and the arrested internalization process carried forward. Parents whose need for denial is not fixed and compelling will often be able to contribute their share to the adolescent's progressive development. But in cases similar to that of Eddy, their participation in a renewed growth process will never occur spontaneously. The mother who had twice chosen a husband with asocial inclinations was unable to participate in her son's socialization. The step-father's sadomasochistic relationship to his step-son had entered a crisis when puberty added a homosexual threat to a latent perverse attachment of long standing.

The adaptive changes in Eddy's life came to an abrupt halt when his girl friend left him. He felt he was wronged and sought restitution. For this he returned to his family where his birthright to unconditional love and acceptance became his battlecry. The inevitable happened: he reverted to asocial behavior, arrogantly calling his parents the true villains and considering himself their victim. Luckily, the law again intervened when the mother had found some "pills" (Methedrine) in his coat pocket. She called the police and Eddy, being just 17, was sent to the City penitentiary on Riker's Island. I visited him there after two months of incarceration in order to determine whether it should be recommended to the court that he be remanded to an open residential treatment center in Manhattan.

What struck me in my talk with the boy was the fact that his preoccupation with and idealization of his dead father was now replaced by that of his present parents. He held no grudges against his mother who was directly responsible for his being in jail; at least she cared, so he felt. He remembered perfectly well his parents' double-talk and selfishness but he assured me that all this was a matter of the past. He insisted that they both had changed in heart and mind. This firm belief highlighted the boy's need for all-good parents who would protect him against the revival of his infantile greed and rage that had landed him behind bars. Here his reality testing proved defective due both to his primitive ambivalence and his belief in magic. It is a characteristic of the concretizing adolescent that his need tension creates that imaginary environmental correspondence which will keep such tension in tolerable bounds. A rehabilitative strategy was designed which took its cue from the compelling, maladaptive predilection that he conveyed so convincingly to me in the interview.

I concluded from my work with concretizing delinquents and family myth cases that, where verbal communication fails to affect behavior and cognition, a carefully chosen concretization, introduced by the therapist, would substitute for symbolic speech. The therapist thus communicates by inducing a specific action. It must be kept in mind that the function of language has miscarried only selectively, as with attention decathexis, and by no means constitutes a comprehensive language abnormality or thought disorder. At any rate, it occurred to me that through induced concretization a bridge might be built to perceptions and affects that had not advanced to word representations or were excluded from them by either ego arrest or dissociation. I shall now discuss a case in which I applied the principle of induced concretization or—if you permit the expression—of "guided acting out."

## THE CASE OF MARIO

Some years ago I was consulted about an 18-year-old boy, Mario, who had been in psychotherapy for several years. School failure, uncontrollable behavior, and aimless indifference, coupled with extreme intolerance of frustration, had worn down the endurance of home and school alike. Mario had no capacity for insight nor could he view his actions or experiences within a time continuum. His only time reference remained the present. Consequently, treatment had deteriorated to a drawn-out stalemate.

Mario had been adopted in Italy by an American woman. He was almost five years old when he left the orphanage where he had lived since birth. Three findings became apparent in the consultation as significant: first, Mario's driven and insatiable pleasure-seeking behavior, in conjunction with a resigned acceptance of his weaknesses and failures; second, his incapacity to project himself into the future or into his manhood, except via regressive need-gratifying expectations; and third, his complete amnesia for his life before the adoption. His earliest memory was his Atlantic crossing, reflecting a catastrophic anxiety of annihilation which he described in these words: "Big waves were splashing against the porthole; I was afraid they'd get me and I'll drown." From this time on, Mario's memory proved to be excellent. I attributed particular importance to the fact that nearly five years of his early life were totally unavailable to him for adolescent psychic restructuring and, furthermore, that he was unable to use language for the purpose of reaching, cognitively and affectively, the formative stages of his development. The ego functions which normally facilitate reconstruction were, for all practical purposes, nonexistent. His maladaptive behavior was a groping effort to touch rock bottom of his life. He could neither move forward nor go backward: he held frantically to his shaky sense of pretrauma object hunger by meaningless and endless sexual attachments. His was a problem of identity or, saying it differently, of an impasse in ego differentiation.

The thought occurred to me then that, through sensory contact with his early childhood environment, a continuity in the ego might be affected which would lift the primitive, preverbal use of action to a higher level of integration. What I had in mind was the revisitation of the pretrauma locale, the visual reminder of a once familiar scenery, the inner echo of his childhood language and the music of churchbells, the intrusion of smells and of lights. This romantic composite of sensations attests to my ignorance of what, in particular, might touch him. As you will see, I could not have foretold what actually happened.

I recommended that the boy visit his native hill-top village in Umbria. Mario received this suggestion with eager delight and confessed that this had been his secret wish for a long time. He set out to travel to the place of his birth in the company of a college student who spoke the boy's native tongue. When Mario descended from the bus that delivered him to the village piazza, he was recognized by an elderly woman who shouted his name and threw her arms around him. She was the matron who had taken care of him during his orphanage years. In a flash he knew who she was. His first step in his native village carried him right into the depth of his childhood. Next, he investigated his origin. He discovered the circumstances of his illegitimate birth which followed the seduction of a young farm girl by an older man. What was more natural now than to search for his mother? This, I knew, he intended to do, but I also knew that any verbal advice on this score could only remain meaningless to him. He found out who his mother was and where she lived. But at the point when the search of a lifetime seemed to have come to an end, Mario abruptly turned his back on his past.

What made him shrink back from meeting his mother in person when she was, finally, in physical reach? In his own words, it was the realization that his appearance would destroy her marriage and her happiness. This decision reflected empathy and altruistic protectiveness; yet, the decisive factor, in terms of progressive development, lies, in my opinion, in his volitional move not to seek her, thus turning passive abandonment into active separation and leave-taking. I must confess my amazement upon hearing that this boy who never before considered the feelings of others in the pursuit of his desires, had practiced forethought and empathy on the threshold of an emotional fulfillment.

The effects of the induced concretization became slowly apparent after Mario's return to his adoptive country. Most noticeable was a growing capacity for introspection and compromise. He came to recognize limitations within himself, instead of feeling limited by the malevolence of the environment that had, and would again, abandon him. Not that he remembered actual childhood events after his Umbrian voyage, but the view of his future became more organized and real. What accrued from the experience was a greater fluidity of thought and emotion, as if the seal that had enshrined his past was broken, bringing his total life experience into the mainstream of the adolescent process. With the spontaneous decline of the hypomanic behavior, Mario experienced and tolerated—under the influence of the therapeutic situation—the depressed affect of his early childhood that had been abruptly lost when his traumatic dislocation came to pass. Concurrently with these affective changes he developed a relatively stable and positive relationship with his male therapist. He had now found a model for identification after having used his therapist for years as the target for his helpless demandingness or cynical vindictiveness. When circumstances, finally, imposed a geographical separation and, hence, a termination of therapy, Mario turned to writing letters. This time, he did not allow circumstances to annihilate his relationship. Consequently, he did not fall back into the monotony of his former pleasure-driven behavior, but developed a more modulated way of life with an active search for an appropriate, if commonplace, work situation that afforded him a sense of satisfaction and accomplishment. This does not, however, mean to imply that Mario had repaired the total damage that had been inflicted on his personality; far from it. But, within the irreversible limitations of object relations and ego differentiation, he had found an adaptive compromise which was, peculiarly, his own.

A significant characteristic which the concretizing adolescent demonstrates lies in the participation of ego interests in his maladaptive behavior, in contrast to the purely instinctual gratification in other forms of acting out. It always remains a question of balance or preponderance. Even where a breakthrough of id impulses is unquestionably in evidence, the decisive promoter of the acting out can, nonetheless, be found in an ego interest. Again, a case will speak for itself.

## THE CASE OF STEVE

A 14-year-old boy was brought to court for assaulting a woman with a dangerous weapon. The boy, Steve, had rung the doorbell of a lady that lived next to his apartment. For the occasion he had pulled a pillowcase over his head and held an open scout knife visible in his hand. The neighbor, terrified by the sight, grabbed the boy's hand and cut herself in the process. Steve, so he said, only intended to frighten her. This act proved to be a concretization of an unthinkable fact, of the unknown, which I shall briefly sketch out. Steve's maternal grandfather, bedridden for some time, lived three flights above the victimized lady's apartment. The sick man was attended by a nurse with whom Steve's father entertained an affair. Steve and his father had always been pals; they both belonged to a boy scout troop of which the father was the leader. The knife in question was the father's scout knife. The father's vaguely perceived infidelity and disloyalty hurt Steve beyond endurance. His degradation had lowered the boy's self-esteem to a point where he struck out in desperation. His aim was the rescue of his ego ideal, the father, who was in danger of being destroyed by the predatory woman, the castrating, archaic mother. Here, an adolescent ego interest asserted itself, to which I assign a top order in the hierarchy of determinants. At any rate, this boy was not a homicidal maniac who had to be isolated from society. He was a little boy who claimed the father whom he loved. After Steve was helped to know the unthinkable, he bridged, rather rapidly, the gap between concretization and verbalized thought. Due to this fact we recommended that his case be dismissed by the court. Psychotherapy seemed to be the intervention of choice in order to neutralize antisocial concretization. Two years of treatment have borne out this expectation.

Sartre (1952) has given a vivid description of the making of a criminal in his biography of Jean Genet, the illegitimate child, ward of the state. Little Jean was declared by his foster parents to be a thief when he was 10 years old because he had stolen some sweets. Sartre writes:

> He [Genet, the child] regards the existence of adults as more certain than his own and their testimonies as truer than that of his consciousness. . . . Therefore, without being clearly aware of it, he judges that the appearance (which he is to others) is the reality and that the reality (which he is to himself) is only appearance. . . . He refuses to hear the voice of the *cogito* . . . In short, he learns to think the unthinkable, to maintain the unmaintainable, to pose as true what he very well knows to be false [pp. 46–47].

It is perhaps the most provocative finding about the category of cases of which I have given you some representative specimens, that they had all suffered a disastrous loss which they were never able to put to rest nor replace. Yet none of them showed the clinical signs of depression or withdrawal. Quite to the contrary, they seemed to cling to the living and to social participation with an astounding pertinacity. They seem to want something from the environment on which their survival depends. Generally, one internalizes—for better or for worse—the lost object. Whenever vague and contradictory awareness of the lost object interferes with this process, the original ambivalence, attached to it, remains unchanged. The incapacity to synthesize the good and the bad part of the lost object relegates the loss complex to primitive and prelogical integration. This type of mastery is characterized in my cases by the magic of action or, in other words, by the concretization of dissociated memory-traces. The projective mechanism is invariably at work and blurs the boundary between the self and the object world. It does not by any means operate in the service of defense, but represents the primitive form of dealing with the outside world on the level of animism. This primitivization, however, remains attached to a restricted psychic content, namely, to unassimilated experiences. Concretization acquires the function of preventing a merger of self and object, of keeping the noxious influence of the environment from spreading through the total personality and, last but not least, of assimilating a loss by rendering it real, validated by snatches of memory, inferences, and suppositions. We can observe how concretizing behavior tries to avert regressive engulfment while, simultaneously, giving in to it. This process has reached a disastrous impasse when the concretizing adolescent is brought to court. Psychoanalytic understanding of this impasse and of its historical determinants is called for at this point in order to avert, if at all possible, the extreme calamity of developmental stagnation or regression.

It was the purpose of my chapter to lay before you the theoretical and practical conclusions I have derived from my study of a special form of acting out which I have called concretization. The analyst, standing today vis-à-vis the vast spectrum of adolescent maladaptive behavior, is expected to offer modalities of intervention that are not part of his customary armamentarium. These modalities have to be invented. It will be no surprise to me if such inventions might seem to many a reader, nothing more than the result of intuitive, empathic, or identificatory, in essence highly personal predilections, which are interesting but, strictly speaking, lie outside the psychoanalytic science. It has been my special effort to show that we possess no better guide in the field of adolescent maladaptive behavior than the rigorous application of psychoanalytic psychology. Of course, everyone who has worked with adolescents has taken, at times, recourse to all kinds of so-called unorthodox measures in the face of emergencies. Some of them have proven exceedingly effective and even lasting. What I propose is simply to study such seeming effectiveness, because restorative processes always lay bare, for our investigation, the nature of developmental and maturational anomalies.

I hope I succeeded not only in contributing to our insight into adolescent maladaptive behavior, but also in generating a kind of concern and interest that will entice others to further the study of those forms of social maladaptation which still elude our full comprehension. A sentence from a Freud letter (1932) befits this mood and I shall close my lecture with the words he wrote in his 76th year to his friend Arnold Zweig. There he said: "Oh, das Leben könnte sehr interessant sein, wenn man nur mehr davon wüsste und verstünde!" In English: "Oh, life could be very interesting, if only there was more about it that one knew and understood!"

## REFERENCES

Freud, A. (1968), Acting out. *Int. J. Psycho-Anal.*, 49:170.
Freud, S. (1932), *Sigmund Freud-Arnold Zweig, Briefwechsel.* Frankfurt am Main: S. Fischer Verlag, 1968, p. 52.
Greenacre, P. (1950), General problems of acting out. In: *Trauma, Growth, and Personality.* New York: International Universities Press, 1969, p. 227.
Odier, C. (1956), *Anxiety and Magic Thinking.* New York: International Universities Press, p. 113.
Sartre, J. (1952), *Saint Genet.* New York: George Braziller, Inc., 1963, pp. 46–47.
Spitz, R. A. (1965), *The First Year of Life.* New York: International Universities Press, p. 42.

# 6. THE INTERDIGITATION OF PSYCHOANALYSIS AND PIAGET'S DEVELOPMENTAL PSYCHOLOGY

DAVID A. FREEDMAN, M.D.

At least two monographs published in the last few years (Gouin-Décarie, 1965; Wolff, 1950) as well as a chapter by Cobliner in Spitz' *First Year of Life* (1965), and papers by Anthony (1956, 1957), bear testimony to the unique impact of Piaget's work on psychoanalysis. I don't think it is an exaggeration to say that at this time the relation which obtains between these two approaches to human psychology is analogous to that which held for so long in physics between the wave and corpuscular theories of light. Each is of great value in studying and explaining some phenomena, but neither is adequate to help one deal with all the problems he encounters in the study of behavior. While it is to be hoped that a synthesis will ultimately be achieved, as yet this has not been accomplished. In what follows, therefore, I will limit myself to a review of what I consider to be some of Piaget's more important contributions, and indicate where, in my opinion, an understanding of them may be relevant to the practice of psychoanalysis.

In the first place, one must understand that Piaget's whole approach to the study of behavior is radically different from that of Freud as well as of psychoanalysts since Freud. Originally a zoologist, Piaget became interested in the theory of knowledge (Flavell, 1963). From the beginning, his concern has been almost exclusively with how one develops the capacity to think and understand. Just as psychoanalysts have tended to take cognitive development for granted, so has Piaget disregarded the vicissitudes of emotional development. Problems directly relating to the genesis of affect, intrapsychic conflict, and human interrelations have played an exceedingly minor role in his work. Secondly, since he is not a physician, both the clinical problems which bring people to our attention and the limitations imposed on us in research by our therapeutic goals have been irrelevant to his work. He has never, for example, had occasion to rely on the use of retrospection as a primary investigative technique. Rather, he has engaged in a series of methodical observations and experiments designed to answer specific questions which derived from what he observed. These have enabled him to follow the evolution of cognitive and other intellectual functions from birth through adolescence in great detail and with much precision. While his field of interest has been from our point of view restricted to aspects of ego and superego function, what he has studied, he has studied meticulously. The observations, made on his own three children, which established the six stages of sensorimotor evolution, have now been confirmed many times and in many hundreds of youngsters.

Perhaps as good a way as any to illustrate the differences between what Piaget studies and what is significant to us is to compare his outline of developmental periods with Anna Freud's (1965, Chapter 3) developmental lines. Miss Freud lists six parallel lines of development along which she feels children progress. Each line consists of a sequence of steps which follow one another in a predictable order (see this volume, pp. 59–60). Piaget also considers six lines of sequential cognitive development. Their designations, however, are (1) imitation, (2) play, (3) the object concept, (4) space, (5) causality, and (6) time. Just as we can in the course of psychoanalytic work demonstrate empirically that continua such as Anna Freud describes do exist, so does Piaget demonstrate that there is for each of his categories an identifiable sequence of developmental phases which follow one another in a predictable way.

The period of sensory motor evolution, which in itself is subdivisible into six clear-cut stages, is followed by the period of preoperational thought. This, in turn, is followed by the period of concrete operations which then gives way to the period of formal operations. As is true of our developmental lines, the emergence of a new phase in Piaget's system does not mean the abolition of the preceding one. Rather, the new is superimposed on the pre-existing organization even as we would conceive it to be the case in psychoanalysis. Finally, he recognizes a process of assimilating and accommodating to new experiences followed by a state of equilibrium which, like the Nirvana-principle, seems to refer to homeostasis; i.e., a dynamic equilibrium state which must be achieved before the child can go on to the next phase of development.

Before I proceed to elaborate further the various periods and stages of cognitive development, I would like to point out that there is implicit in all psychoanalytic theory, the assumption that one's cognitive capacities change in the course of development. A way of characterizing the anal phase, for instance, would be to say that the perception and understanding of the child between the ages of roughly two and four is filtered through his preoccupation with the function of that zone. Again, by way of illustration, it is self-evident that the effect on a child of witnessing the primal scene is, among other things, a function of the construction he places on it because of his limited ability to understand what he is witnessing. If one considers the problems of cognitive functioning from this standpoint, it is possible to say that Piaget's contribution has been to add immeasurably to our understanding of what a child at a given age is capable of comprehending and therefore to help us understand in what context he will both assimilate and accommodate to (Piaget's terms) any new piece of experience.

Piaget has been able to identify the four periods of cognitive development which I have already enumerated. He has also determined, at least approximately, the ages at which one may anticipate that a child's perception and interpretation of the world will be patterned by the characteristics which define any one of these phases. Thus, he designates the first 18 to 24 months of life as the period of sensory-motor operations. The period is further subdivided into six stages which can be identified through successive changes in the child's behavior. Because it is the developmental sequence with which I am most familiar, I will illustrate this period by following the development of the concept of an object. In the first two stages; i.e., roughly the first four months of life, the child shows practically no awareness of the existence of objects. Beyond some following with his eyes, he gives little, if any evidence of awareness of or even of being influenced by them. Some time after the fourth month, he shows a new response which marks the beginning of stage three. At this time the infant can be shown to continue to follow with his eyes in the direction in which a dropped object disappears. By the time he is nine months of age (upper limit), if you only partially hide something from him, he will grasp the exposed portion and recover the object. At this time a completely hidden object—even if the hiding is done before the child's eyes—will be treated as though once it is covered, it is gone forever. The child makes no effort to seek out the "lost object." Even though he may have been actively playing with it before it was hidden and seizes it with great enthusiasm once it is again shown to him, he acts as though it no longer exists. (One can wonder, what connection this cognitive state might have with the contemporaneous phenomena of stranger and separation anxiety.) During the next three stages, which cover the period whose outer limits are from eight through 20 months, the child successively is able to recover an object hidden from him in full view; is able to recover it if, in his presence, it is removed from one hiding place to another (at first he will invariably return to the first hiding place even though he watches the displacement); is able to recover it after successive displacements outside his field of vision, and finally will actively seek out an object he desires not only without any regard for the place at which he last saw it, but also hours or even days later.

Having, unlike Bishop Berkely, become convinced that objects continue to exist outside his perception of them, he has now entered the period of preoperational thought. Over the next five years he progresses from an organism whose most intelligent functions are sensorimotor acts to one whose upper limits are inner-symbolic manipulations. In its earlier period, this phase of cognitive evolution is coincidental with the anal phase or what Glover (1935) refers to as the phase of obsessional primacy, and Mahler (1958) calls the period of separation-individuation. Later it coincides with what we all refer to as the oedipal period. It is striking that the earlier portion of this period (up to five years) is the least well-studied by Piaget, whereas the later portion (five-seven years) is probably the best studied. During this period the child develops the capacity for "action-contemplative" behavior as opposed to simple acting. Because thought is separated from direct motor expression, it is possible for him to synthesize a whole series of experiences rather than be tied to the sequential steps implied in any direct motor expression of thought. It is Piaget's conviction that this is also the first period of his life in which the child must assimilate new experiences and accommodate to them on the basis of an equilibrium state which has existed before.

Object constancy does not do too well as a model for illustrating the relevance of this phase to psychoanalysis. However, according to Piaget, the belief that objects maintain an existence outside of one's perception of them, is only one of a series of "eternal verities" (my term) in the mind of the two-year-old. From the cognitive standpoint of the toddler there is no more reason to doubt the appropriateness of his spontaneous behavior and techniques for need gratification than there is to doubt object constancy. The introduction at this time both of prohibitions and demands for performance will therefore inevitably lead to conflict between what the child conceives of as inevitable and what the new circumstances demand. Not only is the child expected to modify an ongoing way of behaving for reasons which his cognitive position cannot assimilate but also with the expectation comes—implied or explicit—a threat to the stability of important affective relationships.

M. Wulff (1951) describes a poignant example of this dilemma—a two-and-a-half-year-old girl was brought to him because she was obsessed with the need to be clean and keep everything in her environment clean. Wulff found that in the course of attempting to toilet train her, the child's father had urged her to "be clean." From her cognitive standpoint "clean" meant to pick up and be neat and tidy. The more her father urged her, the harder she tried, all the while being unable to make the shift from her fixed conception of the connotation of the word to her father's particular metaphorical use of it.

Examples of similar misunderstandings on the part of the preoperational child are, of course, innumerable. Whether the outcome will be cute and amusing in the eyes of the beholder or the source of distress between parent and child would be a function of those affective aspects of the relation which Piaget tends to ignore and with which we tend to concern ourselves.

An observation from the preoperational period which will serve to illustrate the kind of problem Piaget studies is the development of the concept of volume constancy. Until the very end of this period, the notion is beyond the cognitive capacities of the child. Thus, presented with two cylinders filled with fluid, he will continue to insist that the taller and narrower contains more fluid than the shorter wider one, even though it is shown to him repeatedly that the fluid when passed back and forth exactly fills each vessel.

I will touch only very briefly on the next two stages of cognitive development—those of concrete operations and formal operations. Chronologically, they cover the period between seven years and the end of adolescence. In these periods, the child begins to look for and utilize the various kinds of logical interrelationships which obtain between objects and events. General principles are deduced and alternative logical possibilities are utilized; i.e., in situations such as the problem of volume constancy the child is able to withdraw his attention (decenter in Piaget's terms) from the height of the cylinder and focus on the amount of the water.

During the period of concrete operations this is possible only in relation to specific systems where the possibility exists that specific motor acts can be carried out. The stage of formal operations (the ultimate stage of cognitive development), which in its onset is coincidental with puberty, is marked by the capacity to think in terms of the formal properties of interrelationships; i.e., to manipulate symbols and ideas rather than specific concrete objects and situations. It is at this stage that the individual can question, wonder, and anticipate the future without regard for the particular circumstances which surround him. That this sort of shift in cognitive style does characterize adolescence we all recognize. It was, after all, described by Anna Freud (1946) many years ago. I would only reiterate that Piaget has investigated the details of the change and demonstrated the implications of this new cognitive position both for adolescent and for subsequent adult intellectual operations. Again, here as elsewhere, he has not concerned himself particularly with problems of drive and affect; i.e., of motivation.

The indicator of the beginning of each successive stage of cognitive evolution is a phenomenon reminiscent of both regression and the repetition compulsion. The child approaches the newly perceived problems in a highly personal, egocentric fashion. In effect, he sees the world from his own point of view, without knowledge of the existences of other viewpoints and perspectives. He is, to quote Piaget, "a prisoner of his own perceptions." Paradoxically this implies that he is at this stage least aware of himself as well as least capable of perceiving and discrimination. In our terminology he fails to differentiate self from object. It is, I guess, not by accident that I should reserve mention of this point for after a consideration of adolescence. It is important, however, not to lose sight of the fact that the description is equally as relevant to the posture with which the child approaches each of the stages of cognitive development.

In addition to his studies of cognitive development, Piaget has also devoted some attention to moral development. Nass (1966) recently reviewed this work and attempted to relate his observations to the development of the regulatory agencies (superego and ego ideal) of psychoanalytic theory. Briefly, Piaget recognizes up to the age of seven or eight; i.e., the beginning of the period of concrete operations—a morality of restraint. This is characterized by such features as (1) objective responsibility, (2) unchangeability of rules, (3) absolutism of value, (4) transgression defined by punishment, (5) duty as defined by obedience to authority, (6) ignoration of reciprocity, (7) expiative justice, (8) immanent justice, (9) collective responsibility. The older child, as egocentricity diminishes, gradually develops the "morality of cooperation." This is relatively autonomous and is characterized by (1) responsibility for intent, (2) flexibility of rules, (3) relativism of value, (4) moral judgments made independently of sanctions, (5) duty defined in terms of peer expectations, (6) reciprocity, (7) restitutive justice, (8) naturalistic causality, (9) individual responsibility. Again, as was noted in the case of cognitive development, it is possible to demonstrate empirically such a shift in point of view, as well as predict by extrapolation how it will influence behavior. Furthermore, if one allows for a difference in terminology, the characteristics of the morality of restraint seem to be indistinguishable from those of the primordial punishing superego, while those of the morality of cooperation are certainly congruous with the characteristics of the adult superego.

However, as it appears to be the case throughout his work, in this area too Piaget seems to take drive and conflict for granted. While he describes the so-to-speak formal characteristics of conscience, he seems to contribute little or nothing to those questions of their derivation from instinctual drive and motivation which are our primary clinical concern.

The importance of Piaget's work not only in dealing with children but also in our efforts to reconstruct the etiology of adult adaptive problems is, I think, clear. He has established beyond any serious possibility of doubt that both moral and cognitive development do follow clearly defineable sequences and that the steps involved are invariant in their relation to one another. However, he contributes nothing to our understanding of the reasons for arrests in development, i.e., for the persistence of earlier modes of functioning and the adaptive problems they imply. Nor does he help us understand how the disturbances in adaptation which we observe in the clinic reflect the operation of cognitive functions.

### Summary and Conclusions

Piaget's systematically executed investigations of cognitive development provide the practicing psychoanalyst with a wealth of normative data. On the basis of his findings, it is possible to have a much clearer picture of the world as it is perceived by the young child. The relevance to psychoanalysis of such data seems to me to be self-evident. Assumptions about the cognitive state of the maturing individual can be made with a precision unavailable to us in the past. On the other hand, Piaget contributes nothing to those problems of motivation, drive, and energy distribution which play so prominent a role in the clinical practice of psychoanalysis.

## REFERENCES

Anthony, E. J. (1956), The significance of Jean Piaget for child psychiatry. *Brit. J. Med. Psychol.,* 24:20–34.

—— (1957), The system makers: Piaget and Freud. Symposium on the contribution of current theories to an understanding of child psychiatry. *Brit. J. Med. Psychol.,* 30:155–269.

Flavell, J. H. (1963), *The Developmental Psychology of Jean Piaget,* Princeton, N. J.: D. von Nostrand Co.

Freud, A. (1946), *The Ego and the Mechanisms of Defense.* New York: International Universities Press.

—— (1965), *Normality and Pathology in Childhood,* New York: International Universities Press.

Glover, E. (1935), Developmental study of the obsessional neuroses. *Int. J. Psycho-Anal.,* 16:131–144.

Gouin-Décarie, T. (1965), *Intelligence and Affectivity in Childhood.* New York: International Universities Press.

Mahler, M. (1958), Autism and symbiosis, two extremes of identity. *Int. J. Psycho-Anal.,* 39:77–83.

Nass, M. L. (1966), The superego and moral development in the theories of Freud and Piaget. *The Psychoanalytic Study of the Child,* 21:51–68. New York: International Universities Press.

Spitz, R. (1965), *The First Year of Life.* New York: International Universities Press, pp. 301–356.

Wolff, P. H. (1950), *The Developmental Psychologies of Jean Piaget and Psychoanalysis.* [*Psychological Issues,* Monogr. 5.] New York: International Universities Press.

Wulff, M. K. (1951), The problem of neurotic manifestations in children of pre-oedipal age. *The Psychoanalytic Study of the Child,* 6:169–179. New York: International Universities Press.

# 7. ADOLESCENCE AND THE CHANGING REALITY

ALBERT J. SOLNIT, M.D.

In this report I shall examine adolescence as a critical phase of development and assess the advantages and disadvantages that accrue to this critical phase in the light of certain environmental and biological trends. These trends can be viewed as potentialities made possible by man's increasing mastery of his environment through technological knowledge about nutrition, chemistry, transportation, communication, nuclear energy, and the capacity to prevent or effectively treat previously fatal or crippling diseases. As we examine the development of adolescents in a world whose technology has influenced their biological timetable, as well as their expectable environment, we are confronted with a magnification of contrasting extremes. The extremes of hippy passivity and nonviolence are accompanied by the revolution of adolescent aspirations. The insistence on a significant and responsible voice in the affairs of the University—the declarations of Peace Yes—Viet Nam No—are contrasted by the ruthlessness of youth delinquency and violence, and by an interest in experiences with mood-altering drugs. How can psychoanalytic perspectives clarify this current canvas of extremes?

This work has been supported in part by the Children's Bureau and The National Institute of Mental Health, U.S. Department of Health, Education and Welfare; the Connecticut State Department of Health; the Connecticut State Department of Mental Health and the Grant Foundation.

98

## BIOLOGICAL AND SOCIAL PERSPECTIVES

Adolescence as a normative developmental crisis appears to have been altered by biological and technological conditions in a changing world. Although there are, of course, significant differences between the adolescent development of boys and girls, this report will not focus on these differences. Also, the observations will concentrate on children who are members of our affluent society, though much of what emerges will be applicable to those who are otherwise disadvantaged or from a variety of social, ethnic, economic, and educational backgrounds.

Predetermined patterns of adolescent development can be influenced by experiential factors, but by and large these innate or maturational changes and patterns are relatively resistant; there is evidence that they have been accelerated by improved nutritional and health care. These accelerations are most dramatically demonstrated by the fact that our children grow taller at an earlier time in their lives and that there has been an earlier onset of menstrual periods (J. M. Tanner, 1960, 1962; R. Dubos, 1965, 1967). Since 1880 when records in Scandinavia were first kept, girls in the United States and Western Europe experience menarche on the average about six months earlier each decade. Had it been feasible to keep such records, it is reasonable to infer that the index of sexual maturation in boys, such as the age of the production of semen or of the first ejaculation, would also have shown evidence of a steady acceleration. The height of young men and women, their shoe sizes, and their physical feats—such as breaking the four-minute mile and swim speed records—continue to extend the limitations of the past and present. These changes in the biological timetables are associated with a persistent increase in the average height of boys and girls. The acceleration and elaboration of these biological processes has been related by many authorities to the improvement in nutritional experiences and to the increased effectiveness of preventive and therapeutic medicine (*Lancet,* 1960 and *British Med. Journal,* 1961).

All cultures have to cope with the natural turbulence of adolescence, though the degree to which it is given institutional

expression varies from culture to culture. How adolescent changes
are expressed and how adolescent behavior is evoked in a particular
environment is a crucial consideration in our attempts to understand what Helene Deutsch (1967) terms "the battlefield of the
adolescent's struggle." She views the struggle as taking place on
two fronts:

1.   "The inner world of conflicts which are to be resolved;

2.   The relationship to the external world (this refers to their
nearest and to their more remote environment) which needs to
be stabilized" (Deutsch, 1967, p. 20). Although this dilemma is
not new, in their interactions the balance of biological, social, or
environmental and technological characteristics and influences has
changed. I believe it is essential that we review the balance at
this time when so much of our history is being made or influenced
and when this history for which we are responsible is being challenged by the older adolescents and by those to whom Helene
Deutsch refers as postadolescents. A historical review of this perspective may be helpful.

> But when, by what test, by what indication does manhood [or
> womanhood] commence? Physically, by one criterion [and a changing
> one at that], legally by another, morally by a third, intellectually by
> a fourth—and all indefinite. Equator, absolute equator, there is none
> [Kiell, 1964, pp. 855–856].

This formulation provided by Thomas De Quincy in the late 18th
century (*Autobiography,* 1785 to 1803) is still timely in demonstrating that certain dilemmas are the same although they deal
with change and an altered balance of forces.

### EXPERIENCE AND TECHNOLOGY

In reviewing the relationship between the adolescent's maturation
and the conditions of his environment, there are many factors that
impinge on the more exuberant biological growth of this period.
One major factor which directly conflicts with changes in the biological timetables, is our society's demand for an extension of the
adolescent social and economic moratorium. The need for a longer

period of education as preparation for adult opportunities and responsibilities becomes society's demand for this extended moratorium. In this way the adolescent can gain access to institutionalized channels for a relatively safe and guaranteed passage to adulthood. In many cultures in the 1960's and 1970's, the pursuit of knowledge is the most assured way to be able to leave one's childhood home effectively and yet to postpone the establishment of one's own family and home. The adjective "safe" as a modifier of the word "passage," is ironic in view of the situation in recent years in Berkeley, Paris, Cambridge, Chicago, San Marcos, Peru, Mexico City, and at many United States high schools and universities in the past months.

Contemporary student uprisings and assertions reflecting the age-old and the new.dilemmas of youth, are illuminated and elucidated by certain psychoanalytic perspectives about individual development. Such perspectives are gained from the analytic treatment of adolescents, from the reconstruction of adolescence in adult analysis, from the analysis of parents of adolescents, and by other clinical and direct observations of these youthful representatives of our society. We can approach this question by further inquiry into the environmental stimuli and demands as well as the technological influences that impinge on our adolescents whose sensitivities can be viewed as the magnifying lens and reflecting mirror of their society.

The changing experience of adolescence can be viewed in terms of man's use of his newer knowledge and inventions or technologies. The following outline suggests these relationships and the directions of the changing adolescent experience.

## Communication and Transportation

The discovery and elaboration of electronic methods of communication have established the daily experience and expectation of instant auditory and visual communication. Such instant communication has many advantages, but it also changes the experience of distance and time, shrinking the world geographically and conveying a sense of an increasing velocity of historical change.

These changes in human experience are heightened and further elaborated by our modern capacities for rapid transportation, especially that which has become a daily experience in the use of automobiles, jet airplanes, and the dawning of rocket-power propulsion. Now an individual can span a continent, conduct his work for several hours in one day, and return home the next day. Truly the velocity of history as perceived and lived has increased and continues to accelerate.

For the adolescent these external changes in life's experiences are presumed to influence his internal psychological and emotional changes. These internal changes are also undergoing and reflecting the increased velocity of biological and psychological developments that characterize puberty and adolescence. For example, the adolescent is confronted with much more awareness and information about his world and with modes of life that invite him to carry out many more acts in a much wider geographic range. His developmental need for privacy and for opportunities to experience changing body boundaries and sensations are under a more intense demand for responses to the contemporary environment. For the current adolescent, the sense of reality and reality itself seem to have lost the delay and distance factors that formerly encouraged the individual to have inner privacy while exploring the social and physical environment. Technology offers instant gratification and challenges the orderly development of a sense of reality through reducing the apparent opportunities for feeling the insulating qualities of distance and waiting that facilitate the individual's capacity to deal simultaneously with what may be termed inner and outer reality in an imaginative and organizing manner. Visual, auditory and kinaesthetic appetitive longings can be more easily and repeatedly saturated by television, amplification of sound and vision, rapid air speeds, and by the increasing ease with which such opportunities are available. Instant communication and transportation, at the least, have an unsettling impact on one's sense of boundaries and on time-space relationships. Adolescents experience our new world of high speed and acceleration as disorganizing as well as stimulating and gratifying. Sensory tolerances and appetites at a time of rapid change (puberty and adolescence) can be stretched and depleted, possibly contributing to the alteration of the biological timetables. The television intrusiveness of instant auditory and visual news from local, national and worldwide sources is perhaps the most important technological inference to study for its advantages and disadvantages to children, but especially to younger adolescents.

Although we have no adequate specific studies by which to examine these clinical impressions, it would be conservative to assume that these changes in modern life are likely to sharpen the dilemma of the increased rate and extent of biological change and the expected delay in assuming adult opportunities and responsibilities. Such trends do not basically alter the adolescent experience but they do point to the advantages of more knowledge and to the disadvantages of prolonging the social, economic, and emotional dependency while the biological timetables have been accelerated. The evidence of pathological passivity in many of the younger generation may be one of the outcomes of this dilemma. Other outcomes include the critical demand increasingly dramatized by our youth for a correction of the inequities and corruption in our society.

## INSTANT DESTRUCTION AND POLLUTION

The harnessing of nuclear energy has created the feasibility of instant and total destruction. The adolescent's sense of inner volcanic forces and his phantasies of destruction are matched by the threat that adult men and women are in poor control of their lives, the space they inhabit, and the resources upon which they depend for sustaining life. The youth peace movement and the hippy retreat from conventional life styles represent opposite reactions to this intolerable awareness of man's capacity for and tendency toward annihilation.

The daily evidence of air and water pollution and man's inability to regulate his environment to insure human survival is perceived by adolescents as further evidence that those who govern, those who lead, those who represent us are unable to harness or limit man's destructiveness. Until very recently (the 1940's) the adolescent could use comfortably and reassuringly the belief that the heavens and earth were infinite in their resources and boundaries. Pollution confronts all of us, but most forcefully the teenagers, with the depressing and frightening awareness that our environment is finite and that we are incapable at present of regulating and limiting our technology in order to avoid the dire consequences of being destroyed by our consumption and exploitation of the environment. The withdrawal of many small groups of adolescents may be their reaction to feeling that we are being lived by our technology and that we are helpless to turn off this juggernaut.

## MODERN MEDICINE

The prevention of illness and the cure of infectious and congenital or degenerative diseases by antibiotics and transplant surgery represent great hopes and promises in valuing each individual, at the same time that they promote magical thinking to a dramatic degree. However, man's capacity for microbiological warfare again reveals the alternate destructive bent.

## DRUGS

We have been properly termed a chemical society. One aspect of our universal use of chemicals has been youth's attraction to drugs. There has been a popularization of drugs that alter mood and perceptual capacities. The use of these drugs may subtly persuade the user that the self-destructive effects of certain drugs are warranted because of the associated relief experienced from tense social self-consciousness or from the painfulness of depressed feelings in adolescence. There is also the lure of selective expansion of certain perceptions at the expense of other capacities of the mind. This further invitation to passivity and regression is clothed in reassurances that now one is close to one's peers and can avoid painful or intolerable self-consciousness, loneliness, and the anxiety of giving up infantile ties. Many of our lotus eaters have painful difficulties in coming to grips with their poorly synchronized capacities to individuate and to sublimate. On the other hand there are drugs that serve the health aims of relieving pain, replacing deficient bodily supplies, and combating infection.

## ENDOCRINE AND GENETIC CONTROLS

The advent of chemical control or regulation of endocrine and genetic systems, especially as related to pregnancy and birth, and to the prolongation of life have also created invitations and confrontations for all of us. These are particularly stimulating to and demanding of the adolescent. Whether it's the sense that the cycles of life and death can be influenced, the technical capacity to select male or female external equipment, the control of which baby will be admitted and which will be discarded before embarking upon the passage to life, or the maintenance of vegetating man, the adolescent's inner tasks are complicated and challenged by these elaborating technological influences. Some of these inner tasks are: an acceptance of the inevitability that biological and psychological reality converge in the constancy of sexual identity as a man or woman; the inevitability of giving up childhood dependencies and ties; the recognition that death is unavoidable; and developing one's capacities to plan and work, practicing these capacities as a preparation for work stabilization and career choice. Such adolescent individuation also is accompanied by selectively forming new and intense love object relationships as the exploration of life and responsible behavior are balanced in young adulthood. These tasks are immensely complicated by the increasing realization of how short the distance is between man's constructive and destructive behavior, e.g., we can afford to go to the moon but we can't afford a first-class educational system. We can afford to build nuclear missiles and ABM's but not to increase our support of the U. N. Regressive forces appear to promote destruction more quickly than the ego's regulative and reality-testing capacities can harness the primordial instinctual drive forces for construction, cure, and prevention. This awareness or sense of a negative balance has a sharp and sustained impact on the adolescent experience.

In outlining the relationship of the adolescent's inner tasks to his social and technological reality, Helene Deutsch (1967) has raised "the question of whether the adolescent of our times has psychological problems that are different from those faced by his counterpart two and three generations earlier as well as to what extent his expression of these problems has changed with the social structure of his society."

Our psychoanalytic perspectives can only be outlined because our knowledge in this area is incomplete and not systematic. A contributing factor to our inability to consider this area systematically is the increasing velocity of technological change and history. Fortunately, psychoanalytic knowledge does not become obsolete at the same rate as does our knowledge about the physical sciences and technologies. The selective consideration of a psychoanalytic view of youth, 1970, indicates that the changes in our environment and technologies clearly influence but do not explain adolescence and youth. A psychoanalytic view about youth and their world can be inferred from the outline of the six technological influences that are assumed to have changed our outer world sufficiently to challenge the inner world and development of the adolescent. In summary, the technological changes are: 1. Instant communication; 2. Instant transportation; 3. Progressive destructiveness and pollution; 4. Cure or death by medical means; 5. Popularization of new and old drugs; and 6. Biological control techniques that appear to be far advanced over our ethical wisdom.

To what extent do these technological influences have an impact on adolescent development? They offer a wider, more intense and more rapidly changing reality. For example, the current generation of adolescents have lived their whole lives in the shadow of nuclear destruction. This reality is one in which the total world destruction by man is technically possible, which can be grasped intellectually by studying physics and mathematics. However, to grasp this emotionally is particularly painful and threatens to be overwhelming for adolescents since their own explosive instinctual energies have just become more rapidly available for limited avenues of expression. This takes place at a time when the concept that inevitably everyone dies has become fully formed and has at times been directed at one or both parents. Thus, the technical acquisition of the ability to make the H-Bomb challenges the ego's capacity to grasp the implications of this acquisition, at the same time as the reality of nuclear destruction appears to heighten the claim of the id and its destructive instinctual drives. The outer world and the inner world, tending to be less clearly differentiated, appear too similar for safety and comfort. This blurring of realities and the attending discomfort and anxiety leads to an exaggeration of the obligatory regression (Blos, 1968) including passive withdrawal, or to the adolescent's intense effort to ward off the threatening regression through protest and hyperawareness of the social and technological environment.

These inferential views lead to the need for more detailed psychoanalytic studies of regression in adolescence, and of challenges to the capacity for reality testing and to the viscissitudes of the synthetic function of the ego in adolescence. These central functions of the ego in adolescence have been well summarized as the four preconditions for progressive development in adolescence. According to Blos (1967, 1968), these are:

1.   The advent and resolution of the second individuation, i.e., the loosening of the infantile object ties and the new individuation that proceeds to the crystallization of identity and the adult character structure.

2.   The reworking and re-integration of residual trauma.

3.   The establishment and clarification of ego continuity—there is no future without a past—the partial acceptance of the inevitability of life, death and limitations of function.

4.   The resolution of the sexual identity.

Another central task of adolescence is the elaboration and refinement of the differentiation between external, objective reality and inner subjective reality. While the adolescent maturational process comprises both adaptation and an increased capacity for reality testing, nevertheless there are also the accompanying normative regressive forces that are characteristic of adolescence. These regressive reactions are observed in the unevenness and eruptibility of the instinctual energies and in the disynchronization of the erratic, instinctual drive energies and configurations with the advancing and regressing ego capacities. Thus, at the same time as there is an increased capacity for reality testing, there is also an intensification of narcissism that interferes with the struggle to discern and respond effectively and adaptively at the same time to the external objective reality and the inner subjective reality.

It is an essential characteristic of human development, especially vivid in the adolescent period, that regressive experiences are prerequisites for mobilizing the resources of ego and id in preparation for forward steps in development. When the balance is delicate and unstable, as is normative in adolescence, the influence of the environment, the invitations that promote the dynamic balance of progressive and regressive developmental forces, can be a significant one.

In observing and studying contemporary adolescents there appears to be a less stable and more sensitive balance to the regressive and progressive forces influencing their behavior. This could have been brought about by the convergence of the changing biological timetables, the technological influences on the conditions of human experience, and society's demands for a prolongation of education and preparation for social and economic adulthood. This convergence suggests that we study psychoanalytically and in other ways how these three vectors, biological, technological, and societal expectations tend to promote or interfere with sublimation, developing a sense of reality, and the capacity for tenderness in object relationships. For example, biological precocity in the context of our modern technology may offer satiation of the senses and a widening contact with reality while it concomitantly promotes regressive tendencies which are further encouraged by the expectations of the family and community that the individual should extend the adolescent moratorium in order to complete his education. Biological precocity often appears in this way to be associated with a relative failure of sublimation and of the capacity for tenderness.

On the other hand, biological precocity or exuberance combined with opportunities for developing and expressing a social conscience may exploit the technological aspects of our environment and maintain a developing capacity for tenderness in the context of completing one's education or training. This implies that the community must offer viable alternatives in socialized and institutional forms in order to offer a balance to the regressive forces that tend to be promoted by many of the technological influences on our contemporary scene. Many of our youth struggle to resolve their dilemma through seeking attachments and activities that will enable them to develop and act upon a firmly held social conscience.

## SUMMARY AND CONCLUSIONS

The experiences of adolescents in our world of unrest are complexly and significantly influenced by the rapid convergence of: the improved health and nutritional care that is available; the demands for more education as the institutionalized means of achieving freedom and independence; the impact of instant audiovisual communication and rapid transportation; and the increasing velocity of history with its constructive and destructive technological capacities. Our observations and theory strongly suggest that the changes in the biological timetable in the direction of a more rapid and elaborate maturation, and the necessity for a longer and more complicated moratorium to achieve the desirable education and training, intensify the conflicts and dilemmas of the adolescent in our society. These intensifications are increased and further influenced by our technological capacities for perceiving and mastering our physical environment in a variety of ways. The intensification of the adolescent dilemma offers the advantages of more alloplastic resolutions and viable alternatives. At the same time, there are the compelling disadvantages of a more rapidly changing environment whose technological characteristics and capacities can encourage the adolescent's regressive forces, strengthen his infantile fixations and fail to provide institutionalized channels for the expression of a rapidly developing social conscience.

In order to acquire the knowledge necessary for the full liberation of the adult from adolescent and infantile ties and dependency, and to achieve a balance between conformity and alloplastic influences upon one's environment, a prolonged education—an extension of the adolescent moratorium—is necessary. This extension is in conflict with the increased rate of maturation made possible by the technological advances in the health field including nutrition. The earlier and more exuberant advent of adolescent appetites, sensitivities, and creative leaps are confronted by the demands for more education, more specialization, and by an increased velocity of history. Change takes place more rapidly and the sense of time, the rate at which we move toward desperate choices and unavoidable inevitabilities, is a repetitive and at times an unrelenting pressure upon adolescents who need time to dream, to explore, to be wrong and to be right without submitting to the desperation of our times.

## REFERENCES

Blos, P. (1967), The second individuation process of adolescence. *The Psychoanalytic Study of the Child,* 22:162–186. New York: International Universities Press.

—— (1968), Character formation in adolescence. *The Psychoanalytic Study of the Child,* 23:245–263. New York: International Universities Press.

*British Medical Journal* (1961), Early maturing and larger children. 2:502–503.

Deutsch, H. (1967), *Selected Problems of Adolescence.* New York: International Universities Press.

Dubos, R. J. (1965), *Man Adapting.* New Haven and London: Yale University Press, pp. 77–85.

—— (1967), Biological remembrance of things past. *Bull. Philadelphia Assn. for Psychoanal.,* 17:133–148.

Kiell, N. (1964), *The Universal Experience of Adolescence.* New York: International Universities Press, pp. 854–856.

*Lancet* (1960), Continuing secular trend in growth. 1:1336.

Tanner, J. M. (1960), *Human Growth.* New York: Pergamon Press.

—— (1962), *Growth at Adolescence.* Oxford: Blackwell Scientific Publications.

# 8. THE TRANSITION OF THE BODY IMAGE BETWEEN MIDDLE AND LATE ADOLESCENCE

VANN SPRUIELL, M.D.

I

Adolescence is the period between childhood and adulthood. It is also, as Spiegel (1959) has emphasized, a process which consists of at least two phases. It is a fairly common misconception that adolescence represents one distinct phase of life. On the contrary, early and middle adolescence together are almost as different from late adolescence as the latency period is from the phallic. It is important to spell out the phase differences and to understand the transitional period between them.

This paper will examine the transition from middle to late adolescence, particularly from the viewpoint of alterations in the body image in response to psychological, environmental, and biological changes. Theoretical and clinical material will be presented to demonstrate that in most people there rapidly develops a new organization of ego processes, a sort of jelling of the personality, at this time. On the other hand, failure to negotiate the transition results in a chaotic condition within the ego associated with the use of extreme mechanisms of defense.

111

## II

Even the definition of adolescence varies, depending on the stance from which it is viewed. Biological, social, and psychological disciplines describe the period in overlapping, but not identical terms. Biological adolescence is usually understood as beginning when the first external bodily changes appear, although we know that these external changes are preceded by gathering shifts in endocrine balance. As a matter of fact, there is no precise way to date all these internal phenomena; some even begin about the age of nine. They approach a kind of crescendo during the six months preceding the first signs of the growth spurt and the external changes in the primary and secondary sexual characteristics, and, of course, continue for a long time after pubescence.

Biological adolescence is at an end when stature and the capacities for procreative sexuality have reached an adult level. This occurs at about the age of 16 for most young people. Some changes of course, continue, just as they do throughout life. But for all practical purposes, biological adolescence is at an end at about 16 years of age.

Social adolescence depends upon the society. It encompasses the period between childhood, with its relatively quiescent and nonprocreative sexuality, its lack of decision-making and other responsibilities, to the time the culture accepts the young person as adult in terms of marriageability, responsibilities, and prerogatives.

In most cultures social adolescence ends with the achievement of physical and sexual maturity, just as biological adolescence does. In complex cultures, where there is considerable division of labor, some individuals are selected in various ways for more training, and are not accorded full adult status for several years—in some cases for many years. Our own culture is an example; some individuals destined for unskilled work are considered adult by about the age of 16. For other groups, destined for professional lives, adult status may not be reached until the thirties, or even later.

It is much more difficult to define the limits of psychological adolescence. Again, it begins about the age of 12 when many psychological shifts take place in response to the biological and social changes. It is at an end when the individual has succeeded in elaborating an idiosyncratic, more or less stable conflict and drive constellation, when he has realized a capacity to work and to love as an adult. This implies the emancipation from dependence upon the parents and the ability to love and commit himself to another in both a nonnarcissistic and nonincestuous fashion, in the relative sense of these terms.

It is obvious that this is not a completely adequate way to spell out the end of psychological adolescence since by implication every neurotic would be a continuing adolescent. In a sense, every neurotic does continue adolescent conflicts. But if his emotional processes have become fixed, stereotyped, and show no promise of change, he cannot be considered to be functioning as an adolescent. The very essence of adolescence is flux and change. In *this* sense, some individuals have never had a psychological adolescence at all.

## III

Bernfeld (1923) wrote, "Adolescence manifests itself in various areas: physiological, psychological and sociological. Confronted by the enormous variety of individual, social, cultural, historical and physical differences in the group, one is tempted to question the validity of classifying all these manifestations under the one heading of adolescence" (Quoted by Spiegel, 1951, p. 377). But breaking the one heading is not easy. Common sense tells us that the 13-year-old in the midst of an adolescent storm is dealing with one set of conditions while the "hippie" in his late teens or early twenties is fighting other wars. The majority of psychoanalytic writers divide this period into phases—for instance, early, middle, and late (Panel Report, 1959). Spiegel (1958) speaks of a beginning point, middle point and end point, with the mid-point occurring at about 16. Continuing, he says, "It would be illuminating if the course of adolescence could be described in chronological terms; if we could describe the changes in psychic structure over the entire period. However, it is not possible to ascertain way stations over the course of adolescent development" (p. 301).

Blos (1962) is similarly pessimistic about achieving precision about the phases.

> Naturally, any division of phases remains an abstraction; there is no such neat compartmentalization in actual development. The value of this kind of formulation about phases lies in the fact that it focuses our attention on orderly development sequences. . . . Transitions are vague and slow and beset with oscillating movements; larger and smaller remnants of a seemingly completed phase of adolescent development nevertheless persist for a longer or shorter time during subsequent phases. These irregularities are apt to blur the developmental schedule if it is applied too narrowly and too literally [pp. 72–73].

He goes on to divide the period into four phases: preadolescence, early adolescence, adolescence proper, and late adolescence. The latter three, based primarily on narcissistic, bisexual, and heterosexual object findings respectively, are apparently comparable to the early, middle, and late periods mentioned above.

On one point most psychoanalytic authors agree: the therapeutic work in late adolescence—usually explicitly or implicitly assumed to be from about the age of sixteen—is different from the earlier stages. Most workers believe that a true, analyzable transference neurosis becomes possible in late adolescence, and that analysis becomes essentially like that done with adults (Spiegel, 1951; Geleerd, 1958). On the other hand, psychoanalytic work in the earlier phase or phases must be so modified that debate arises whether it is actually psychotherapeutic rather than analytic (Josselyn, 1954).

Sullivan (1953) spoke of early and late adolescence, the latter extending "from the patterning of preferred genital activity . . . to the establishment of the full human or mature repertory of interpersonal relations" (p. 297). Most clinical papers also make do with concepts of early and late. This paper will deal with the "midpoint" of Spiegel, or the progression from "adolescence proper" to the late adolescence of Blos, or the transition from the middle to late adolescence of other authors.

Is this transition imperceptible and slow, or is it rapid and obvious? Is it true that there are no way-stations with which to identify it? My own interest began with the observation of periods of rapid consolidation and change in some adolescents which at first were ascribed only to the effects of therapy. Later I came to see them as results also of maturation, a maturation which is practically universal, although the psychological consequences to it are not.

## IV

It is not only psychoanalysts who find that their dealings with adolescents change in the mid-teens. Our culture itself acknowledges certain profound changes in a variety of formal and informal ways. All cultures develop standard attitudes, values, ways of coping—in short, institutions—for dealing with their young at various stages, and adolescence is no exception. These institutions are developed from two sources. One has to do with the biological facts of life, which are very similar in all humans. The other has to do with particular needs of a given culture.

It would be tempting to discuss the importance of sociological and anthropological material, but this paper will confine itself to intrapsychic considerations and will use clinical material for theoretical rather than technical implications. While there is no reliable investigative tool other than the psychoanalytic method to use in reconstructing the history of adolescent development in its intrapsychic sense, it is understood that there are certain pitfalls in its use. Sufficient material is often missing, or it may be selectively distorted.

The reasons for this are complex and have been discussed by Lampl-de Groot (1960) and others. The problem has to do with such factors as the primary analytic interest in historical material from early childhood, communication difficulties peculiar to adolescence, and defensive processes relating to the recall of adolescence in either the transference or countertransference, or the use of adolescent material to screen earlier memories.

My own research data came from three sources: adult analysands, adolescent patients, and a large group of nonpatient medical students who were studied for several years. I found that the adults fell into three groups: the aforementioned patients who supplied little valid information about their adolescent years, some who provided ample material indicating the rapid development in the mid-teens of a clearcut phase of late adolescence, and some who seemed not to have moved through the usual phases. Of necessity, the first group will be left aside and most attention will be paid to the second.

As for the minority of analysands who provided sufficient material, but who seemed *not* to have gone through the usual phases of adolescence, most of them apparently had by-passed the usual phases. An obsessive-compulsive physician, for instance, had apparently undergone an extraordinarily smooth life as a youth. He was a good compliant boy, who never rebelled and was a delight to parents and teachers alike. However, he never formed adequate relationships with peers. After a long period in analysis dealing with his latencylike personality, adolescent conflicts began to emerge—apparently for the first time in his life.

There are other individuals in which this integration does not take place, either because of inabilities of the individual, special defenses of denial, unusual demands of the environment, or all three. The individual remains either an infantile or a chaotic personality, attempting to function as a young adolescent, or, more likely, regressing to earlier levels. Frequently the underlying lack of organization may be hidden behind a fase, schizoid, or "as if" personality facade.

My material does not allow me to comment on unusually early or unusually late maturation except to say that in one psychoanalytic case I was able to see the "primitivization" described by Blos (1962). The patient had had a precocious adolescence and had to meet unusual demands for early maturation. By the age of 14 he was functioning sexually and at work as a man in a man's world. His perceptions of most of the normal conflicts of adolescence were either lacking or blunted by denial. These conflicts eventually emerged in the transference neurosis.

Most of the people we are able to study, and presumably most people in general, have much more ordinary experiences in adolescence. They cope with them in ordinary ways by developing healthy or unhealthy adult character traits under the pressures from id, superego, the ego itself, and the environment.

The environment, although listed last, is not necessarily meant to be least. For instance, one youngster, a boy named Freddy, was seen in psychotherapy from the time he was 15 through the age of 17. During this time he moved into full physical maturity. He had been referred initially because his immature behavior was disruptive at school and at home. Indeed, he behaved more like a disturbed latency child than a teenager.

The boy's parents had been divorced when he was 11, after an "emotional divorce" of several years. The mother's remarriage when he was a pubescent 13-year-old did not dislodge him from an intense incestuous and pregenital bond. Freddy had never worked through the normal problems of latency, and accordingly his early adolescence indicated an infantile character which was felt to be a function of lack of progression, rather than regression. Some of the early therapeutic work had to do with helping the mother achieve a measure of separation from Freddy thereby allowing the boy to repress some of the more infantile contents. This, however, resulted in changes which disturbed the neurotically complementary relationship of mother and step-father.

All through early adolescence there had been outbursts of violence between Freddy and his step-father which served to discharge hostile feelings, provide control for Freddy, and unconsciously gratify homosexual feelings in both. There came a day, however, when the step-father was unable to overpower the boy and found himself thrown out of the latter's bedroom.

At this, both went into a panic, precipitating the man's referral for psychoanalysis. Unlike other adults in Freddy's environment, the step-father's neurosis had led to denial of awareness of the boy's physical maturity (which the latter had denied for other reasons) until the defense was shattered in the physical confrontation. In this case, there was a radical change in the way the therapy proceeded thereafter, particularly in dealing with depression. Outside behavior also changed rather suddenly.

Most adults perceive the growth of their relevant young people with intensity and the affects aroused may be complicated. They are always mentally measuring and comparing, assessing and evaluating. Adolescents are aware of this interest, pleased by it, and annoyed by it. Or, like some of the adults, they must deny, displace, repress, or otherwise handle the associated affects neurotically.

A "My, how you've grown," from an adult can both gratify and irritate at the same time. The irritation is particularly apt if the young person has not indeed grown since the last time the adult saw him. The young person may be aware that his image has somehow shrunk in the adult's mind and may even be half-aware that the adult does not *want* him to grow up.

The parental love and pride and identification with the young, even when genuine and not the result of reaction formations, only partially compensate for unacceptable feelings: envy, genital erotic stimulation, competitiveness, and mourning for the lost dependent child. And the young sense this and respond to it; they have their own equivalent basic feelings and equivalent defenses. All of these interactions, reactions, and counter-reactions are inextricably bound up in the mind of the young person with his own body and the bodies of others.

Adolescents in the early and middle phases have internal reasons for the intensified conscious and unconscious preoccupations with their bodies. These have to do with several factors: There is a quantitative increase in instinctual pressure; there is an increase in narcissistic concerns which results both from beginning decathexes of the objects of childhood and the related diminution of external sources of self-esteem; besides the rapidity of growth and maturation disturbs the reliability of the body image.

The adolescent is seeking to integrate his conception of himself in the face of these rapid external changes and rapid internal cathectic shifts. He must somehow deal with unfamiliarity with his body and unfamiliarity with feelings stirred up by a variety of shifting personal relationships. His uncertainty about his body and its feelings is welded to an uncertainty about the bodies and feelings of others. His unconscious struggle dealing with the wish and fear to maintain incestuous and pregenital attachments is complicated by whatever confusions exist as a result of the negative oedipal situation. A related complication is the experience of tender feelings in middle adolescence for others of the same sex.

An example of these uncertainties and confusions about the body was provided by a patient in his fifth year of analysis. He suddenly became aware of heightened perceptions of the analyst which were confusing in their variability. "I got anxious when I realized I couldn't keep you in my mind. One time you look taller than me, then shorter. You look old. Then you look young. You look calm and friendly. Then you look mean and hateful." His associations moved to memories of exactly similar perceptions of himself during his fourteenth and fifteenth years.

During a period of very rapid growth, caught up in the midst of a threatened divorce of his parents, he had gone through a period of extreme instability, recalling it vaguely as "nightmarish." He had shown the familiar paradoxes of adolescent turmoil in that he had been alternately rebellious and meek, inhibited and licentious, reserved and loudly overbearing. Above all, he experienced utter uncertainty about himself and about his objects.

A period of calm had developed later in his junior year in high school, a calm that hid an inner despair. He developed a fixed conception of himself in terms of his body and his meaning to others. Outwardly he was attractive, an intellectual, a student leader, a dater of pretty girls; inwardly he knew he had no conscious feelings for the girls, that he entertained perverse sadomasochistic masturbation fantasies, saw himself as a secret physical coward, weak and incapable. As "hypocritical" and as tragically split as he felt, he was at least *stable* in comparison to the earlier period. And others came into stable, albeit psychoneurotic relationships with him.

His confused perceptions of the analyst came at a transition point in the transference neurosis. The patient's material was moving from regressive equivalents of oedipal conflicts consisting of sadomasochistic material relating to mother, to much more explicit positive and negative oedipal strivings and fears. However, the preoedipal determinants continued to be associated with this material, e.g. the perceptions of the analyst betrayed their origins in primal scene traumata, along with the effects of the mother's intense interest in a minor defect in his penis throughout childhood. These perceptions were further analyzed as related to warded-off interests in the father's erections. All this material surfaced and was buried again in adolescence. The analyst later bec me the recipient of transferences and projections which, when understood and worked through, allowed the development of a new body image to replace the stable, but crippled, distorted and bisexual body image integrated in mid-adolescence. After this work the patient developed his first mature love affair.

A similarly intense concern about the body was shown by another adult whom we shall call Russell, who remembered with great clarity an experience during the spring of his sixteenth year, when he was looking in the mirror. For some months he had been minutely inspecting himself. He looked at every pimple, every blemish, every good quality and every bad. He studied himself with a variety of costumes and expressions. He scrutinized every orifice concerned with every function. He was particularly interested in seeing himself masturbate in different positions. Yet for all this he could not seem to come to any conclusions.

But this particular occasion was the first time that he had ever *seen* himself in profile, although of course, this could not have been literally true. He was utterly shocked and dismayed upon noting that he had a thin face and an aquiline nose, claiming to have never before known this. He had always simply looked at his face head-on, or at the most from a slight angle. He looked, or so he thought, exactly like the most disgusting, effeminate boy in his school, a boy he regarded as vaguely "sinister."

"People have been seeing me this way all along," he said to himself with horror, "and I never knew it."

This boy seemed to be constructing, or reconstructing, his body image in a new way. Although the new dimension brought up a distorted perception—that is, other people did not really see him as "disgusting, effeminate"—the new way of seeing himself represented an advance beyond the inflated and narcissistic image of younger years. It represented a new "framework," as Spiegel (1951) has termed the achievement of self and object representations, a framework still betraying the homosexual object choice of middle adolescence (which had specifically neurotic features). At the same time, the unacceptability of part of the perception presaged a rapid synthetic development of the ego.

To examine the context of this clinical vignette in more detail, Russell began his analysis when he was in his late twenties. At that time he was a young lawyer who really wanted to be a novelist; his inability to finish writing what was apparently a "black humor" type novel was one of the factors leading him to seek treatment. He had complained also of doubts regarding his capacity to love, uncertainty of his goals, and feelings of depression. As a lawyer he had been acknowledged to have a brilliant future, particularly in politics. A behind-the-scenes representative of older politicians, he had planned a large-scale political coup which nearly succeeded; its failure was another reason for his having sought analysis. He found himself feeling that everything he did was "phoney"—he did not believe in his public career, nor did he believe in himself as an author. Although he had left Roman Catholicism, he felt troubled by fragments of his previous beliefs, particularly in regard to sexual matters. He fought off masturbatory fantasies of a homosexual nature, and while promiscuous heterosexually, he doubted that he would ever be able to love anyone.

Russell was a personable, athletic man whose charm and wit had a youthful quality. He adapted himself to the analytic process readily. For some reason—perhaps because he was still so obviously struggling with unresolved adolescent conflicts—he brought up an unusual number of memories from that period. The focus here will be that development, and will largely ignore the vicissitudes of the analysis itself.

Prior to the experience with the mirror, Russell had been preoccupied with his fear of going out for spring football practice. He had told everyone that he had to work in his maternal grandfather's sporting goods store. That was not true; he had simply been afraid. It was not so much that he was afraid of other boys on other teams, or that he was afraid of the physical pains of football. Russell was, however, afraid of his own team-mates. He was afraid of locker room nakedness, practice performance, or not being respected for his guts, or his penis, or his endurance. He did not know what lay behind these and similar fears. Later he understood that he loved, feared, and hated the big boys. He still saw himself as a little boy.

For several years he had been involved in every kind of imagining, in essential loneliness and isolation, in a chaos of day-dreams of power and sex that frightened him and made him feel "different." These were mostly military fantasies, having to do with the states of the country having been broken up into separate nations. The state to the east would invade his own state. On the verge of defeat, he would lead a band of his peers into his grandfather's store and they would take the necessary guns, ammunition, and other supplies. Fighting as a guerilla band in the neighboring county, they would, after all sorts of hardships, eventually drive the invaders out and force the evil dictator of the neighboring state to abdicate. While the variations and elaborations of this story mostly had to do with combat, with heroics and physical injury and hardship, there were also sexual escapades of every sort worked into it.

The authoritarianism—to which he reacted in later life by being very insistent about his civil libertarian beliefs—expressed and fought off powerful anally sadistic expressions of murderous oedipal impulses, and also served to defend against passive longings and fears of disorganization.

In relations with older people he was, of course, far from the heroic young leader. On the contrary, he acted in a generally clumsy and abashed manner. Later, as an adult, he saw this as an unconscious attempt to disguise his motives by representing himself as a harmless fool. Though he admired his grandfather, he felt unable to talk to him. He was totally isolated consciously from his father whose inferior job and submissive status at home fed Russell's feeling of contempt.

For a time Russell showed an exaggerated devotion to his religion and a priest accused him of the sin of "scrupulosity." On the other hand, his teachers became concerned because his school work had fallen apart. They told his mother he seemed distant and unreachable.

In summary, by that spring, he was a polymorphously perverse, bright, withdrawn, lost, goal-less, disorganized boy in middle adolescence, trying to abandon mothers and avoid fathers. He sought regression in secret ways, since there seemed no public future. Communication with adults was practically out of the question.

For all this, during the succeeding summer, he began fumbling experiments with the future. Clandestine smoking began. He made friends with some seriously delinquent boys, but did not become really involved in their delinquencies. Dancing with girls came to be more fun. On dates he began to experiment in a certain amount of petting. But though he felt sexually excited, he would also experience feelings of distance from the girls and explained this to himself in terms of his pimples and the imagined ugliness he had seen in the mirror. He felt a blind envy for boys who were more successful and hid the envy behind sarcasm and contempt.

Finally, he mastered his fear sufficiently to go out that fall for the football team. To his surprise, he found that he was a good player, and he met test after test. Although his achievement of a new sense of himself was a gradual process, he remembered one particular incident with clarity: the time he proved to be the fastest man on the team. More and more, he came to love, in his own words, "the part-scared, part-vicious feelings of the game," the solid violence of physical contact. He loved to hit.

It was only during this period that it dawned on him that he was in fact a *big* boy, not the biggest, but bigger than most. He saw his body in an entirely different light, which later he described as "all together," as a unity in itself. He was very proud of himself—but he still felt secretly that some un-namable thing was wrong.

During that same first year of football, there was a coming together of intellectual processes as well. He read a book by Philip Wylie, *A Generation of Vipers,* a slashing attack on the contemporary values of the time. It both shocked and thrilled him. For the first time he acknowledged himself to be an agnostic, and refused to deal any more with his "mother's church." He decided that much of what he had been taught was propaganda. He began to generalize from these thoughts, and an excited period of intellectual discovery began. He did not settle on a particular profession, but for the first time "really" knew that he would achieve one. The future became real and with the excitement of ambitiousness came new fears of future dangers. Death also became "real" to him. He had periods of poignant, but undefined sadness. At the same time, he developed an absorption in himself which was expressed in a host of new ways. He became conscious of an intense hatred for his mother, which later was seen to be partly defensive in nature. All feelings were seen in a new light. He tried to analyze himself and to realize his feelings and paradoxes by writing short stories. A romantic set of values and morals emerged, and his fantasies dealt more with what he could be, might be, wanted to be.

Although there were many vicissitudes in this later adolescence—indeed, some aspects of it continued into the period of analysis—the outlines of the psychoneurosis became crystallized in a few short months of his sixteenth year. The transition was brief. The psychoneurosis itself, was, of course, determined in early childhood. Adolescence brought a reissue of the problems and with the reissue a second chance at their solution. The patient did partly solve them. But the "closing of the epiphyses" psychically brought both gains and losses. The patient developed a split of sorts in his self-image (along with specific chronic pathology relating to his ego-ideal). In part he saw himself as the effeminate, weak, but somewhat sinister figure in the mirror who represented his still active pregenital wishes. In part, his body image was that of a powerful hero, aggressively capable of mastery of a hostile world. The gains had to do with achieving some measure of stability. The losses had to do with the fact that the structuring of the conflicts and drive systems made further change difficult except through the use of psychoanalytic process.

I have had a number of adolescent patients in whom it has been possible to observe similar rapid transitions. One gifted 16-year-old boy, considered a child prodigy as a sculptor, was seen because of extreme disorganization, uncontrolled impulses, and failure at school. He used psychotherapy as a supportive, organizing sort of experience. He seemingly had unusual access to unconscious processes, but nevertheless, his often brilliant—and accurate—"psychoanalytic" interpretations of himself were treated as essentially intellectualizations and attempts to both please and subvert the therapist. He grew to a larger than average size and began to test his body in a number of ways: diets to lose weight and provide supplements for muscular development, weight-lifting campaigns, basketball, etc. The work began to shift. He went through a provocative period in which he threatened to be literally destructive to the therapist or to his office. Finally he announced, "I could do it, you see. I'm big enough to hurt you. But I won't because *I* won't. Oh, I know that it wouldn't be a good policy—you probably wouldn't see me any more if I broke things or something like that. But *that* isn't the only reason. It's just that I won't."

In the next session he brought in the first piece of sculpture he had made since childhood. Afterwards, he began seriously to plan to finish high school so that he could go to art school. He suddenly saw himself as The Artist, or at least a future artist. A short time later he fell in love with a girl for the first time, although he dared not approach her. The patient continued to show signs of serious character disturbance, but the material became quite different in that it dealt with a new kind of felt anxiety relating to oedipal themes. Pregenital material continued to abound, but was not believed to be usable therapeutically.

Achieving adult stature seemed to initiate the processes of synthesis which have been the theme of this paper. With the synthesis a psychoneurotic kind of anxiety became realizable. Gitelson (1948) wrote, "The 'pure fantasy' of childhood becomes realizable during adolescence. A 16-year-old, speaking of his father, told the author: 'It frightens me that I could now really kill him—a weak little man' " (p. 422).

This realization at a certain age that all impulses, thoughts, affects, and fantasies exist in a different context—the context of a mature body—and are thereby different themselves, was illustrated by another imaginative and intelligent adolescent.

Laura was first seen as a 14-year-old. Two years before, her parents had divorced after a stormy marriage. Laura had sided with her father and chosen to live with him. Six months before, the father had remarried. Laura had approved, admired her new stepmother, and for a time compared her mother very unfavorably. She was in real life a "Member of the Wedding," except that instead of having to bear the frustration of realizing her loss and her smallness she became a sort of Member of the Marriage.

Disillusionment came soon, of course, signalled by outbursts of rage toward the stepmother, defiance toward the father.

Laura was a gifted, introspective girl who followed a variety of intellectual and artistic interests in succession, abandoning each whenever adults demonstrated much interest. She had been exposed to rich, cultural stimulation, and to it added very wide reading. She considered herself a Communist and had very sophisticated opinions about art, music, history, and her father's profession. But in spite of her erudition, close scrutiny revealed these interests to have little real depth. They were largely second-hand and internally inconsistent. They were both defensive intellectualization and expressions of phallic wishes. She was a sort of Diana, the Huntress of the Mind.

Laura was not really close to girl friends and was not interested in boys. She was pretty, but was not like her peers in dress or interests. She knew a lot about sex and thought it was "funny."

The work with Laura made it clear that there was massive repression of pregenital impulses and fantasies, along with an obvious continuation of oedipal wishes relating to her father. But as she had to recognize that the step-mother could neither be destroyed nor ignored, anxiety and rage mounted. After a particularly painful rejection by her father when she was 15, she impulsively placed herself in a physically and sexually dangerous situation—the effects seemed to be traumatic. A six-month period of chaos followed, gradually resolving as she brought up intense hostility toward her father, a rediscovery of her by now much happier mother, awareness of deepening attachments to girl friends, and a variety of positive interests in her body.

One day she came into the office presenting what appeared to be a totally different manner. There was nothing obviously different about her clothes or grooming. It was a demureness which had not been present before. She had suddenly become a very pretty young woman. At the same time communication had become blocked. Finally she was able to say that she was in love with a boy a year older. "For the first time I know what it must feel like to be a woman. It isn't just a sexy feeling—I've felt that way before. It's a different feeling all over."

It became clear that psychotherapy could not compete, and it was interrupted for some months at Laura's insistence. When she came back, she was still involved with her boy friend, was intermittently doing better at school, but was having more storms at home. She had gone on binges of reading—novels now rather than the nonfiction of old—and had dropped most of her previous intellectual values. She was experimenting with keeping herself awake for long periods and also with complicated diets.

But most obvious was her disillusionment with her father. The earlier resentment was replaced by both sadness and contempt as she recognized many features of his own problems. She had become particularly aware of how he was recreating in his second marriage the same conditions that had destroyed the first. Laura now allied herself more and more with both her mother and step-mother. However, the alliance was not like her earlier childish alliances, but rather a product of more mature identifications. At the same time a new and more appropriate ego-ideal developed which allowed Laura to become realistically involved in the future. Her later adolescence continued to be stormy, but she handled it well, finally emerging into young adulthood apparently successfully.

This patient's transition into late adolescence was preceded by a disorganized period in which she was beginning to separate from parental objects. In the meantime narcissistic self-interest was vastly increased. Late adolescence began quite abruptly with the elaboration of a new body image and the investment of a new, and more nonincestuous relationship. Ultimately, she felt like a new person, and appeared this way to others. Mourning for her lost father became possible. There had been a diversion of some of the narcissistic cathexis to more realistic ego interests in the future. Along with this, the earlier involvement with girl friends and older women came to be replaced by an effective ego-ideal.

Laura's case illustrates some of the intellectual, physical, and emotional extremes many young people undergo in order to define themselves and their limits. These extremes may go beyond excessive reading and athletic activities to include alcohol, drugs, sexual escapades, or serious delinquencies of a "testing" variety. Her case also illustrates the rapid synthesis of identifications which takes place in the transitional period.

This synthesis may be more or less successful. At times, it may be syncretic in an extreme way. A patient in analysis, a young woman diagnosed as an anxiety hysteric, had developed markedly conflicting identifications as a result of repeated traumatic separations. It was possible in the analysis to demonstrate a partially successful attempt to synthesize these identifications in a setting of heightened interest in the maturity of her body. Yet the syncretism was evident in the fact that she became a sort of subclinical multiple personality; that is, she maintained several contradictory self-images, although only one external personality was apparent to others. She emerged with it at 16, like a butterfly from a cocoon. At the same time she fell in love for the first time. From a morose, shy, unattractive girl, she made herself into an externally aggressive, seemingly erotic, castrating type of woman. Insofar as she failed in the synthesis, the other identifications appeared as dissociated versions of herself. This organization was maintained until the analysis was practically completed.

## V

Two lines of research further support the notion that integration of ego operations occurs at about the age of 16. Wolfenstein (1966) studied the mourning process in children and adolescents and concluded that a true process of mourning does not become possible until at least mid-adolescence. Implied is a new development of an adult capacity to both relate to and separate from objects.

Similarly, Piaget and Inhelder (1958) were able to show in their experiments that fully operational thinking—the ability in an adult manner to utilize abstract thinking, formal logic, verbal abstractions, conceptions of the future, conceptions of possibilities, conceptions of what is not—only develops at an age of 16 or 17. According to these authors, complete maturation of the neural apparatus occurs at that time.

While it is questionable that the capacity for operational thinking depends entirely upon maturation of the neural system, since not only primarily autonomous functions of the ego are involved at this level of its operations, but presumably some which have become secondarily autonomous but arose out of conflict, the evidence is consistent with the essentially biological nature of psychoanalytic theory. In adolescence, as in earlier childhood, psychological maturation cannot occur unless the physical apparatus is ready for it.

The changes in the body image during the integrative period are part of a complex series of structural and intrasystemic alterations. Blos (1962) has beautifully described the instinctual vicissitudes, the processes of identification, new defensive maneuvers, superego and ego-ideal alterations, and cathectic shifts. Blos, of course, discussed the body image. Before him, Freud (1923) regarded the body image or body ego as the very foundation of the ego. A long list of contributors, including Schilder (1950), Fenichel (1945), Hartmann, Kris and Loewenstein (1946), Hoffer (1950), Greenacre (1958), Kaufman (1958), and Jacobson (1964) have traced its development and progressive modifications, along with its importance to other operations of the ego.

Without the body image as its base, conceptions of self and object representations have an ethereal or disembodied quality. If we think about the endless testing of physical limits and prowess and endurance, of the limits of pain, of the experimental alterations of costumes, of the fascination with the extensions of the body image by way of automobiles and tools, we can see that the middle adolescent is seeking to reconstruct his body image and the images of others, to either rid himself of the representations of the other sex or to settle for them, to free himself from old images out of his childhood, and above all, to incorporate his newly functioning genitalia as a narcissistic center of his body image. It can then become the focus of his tender contacts with the functioning genital of another, with foreplay subsuming the residual pregenitality.

This progression from the shifting bisexual concerns of middle adolescence is in most young people powerfully facilitated by a new inner awareness of biological parity, physically and even intellectually, with adults. The awareness, related as it is to the body image, is facilitated further by perceptions of acceptance of the new status by the environment and inhibited by rejections.

Normally, the process is relatively smooth. Its success is most often indicated by the achievement of the first love relationship, whether neurotic or relatively nonneurotic, relatively incestuous or not, relatively pregenital or genital. Often these relationships are kept as deep secrets. When they are heterosexual in nature, and manifest, they are often called "puppy" loves, pejorative terms invented by defensive adults.

The impact of the possibility of mature functioning makes the decathexis of the infantile objects a crucial task. The unbound energy, for economic reasons, tends to be reinvested in the new, tender, erotic, relatively nonincestuous, heterosexual relationships, while identification with the bisexual objects tends to consummate the development of the ego-ideal. Under the new organization, some of the narcissistic investment becomes available for intellectual and other ego interests in the individual's future, and this used in consonance with external reality.

To return to our original questions: are there way-stations to distinguish middle from late adolescence, and is the transition rapid or slow? Material has been presented to indicate that there is a way-station in the form of physical maturity, and that way-stations can be determined clinically by the use of indicators of inter- and intra-systemic structure, particularly by the status of the body image.

The middle adolescent must play out his sexual and aggressive fantasies with the body of a child in relation to the bodies of other children and the larger, complete bodies of adults. In late adolescence, the individual is biologically, and in some cases, socially, on a par with adults—if not in fact in a superior position. If he is able to incorporate perceptions of this in his body image, there results intrapsychically something like the "closing of the epiphyses." There results, colloquially speaking, "a whole new ball game."

The great creative act of the child emerging into latency is the recognition that he is indeed small and must renounce, or at least hide, his grandiose ambitions. The great creative act of the young person emerging into late adolescence is that he is indeed big and capable of nonincestuous sexual and aggressive transactions with others—or that he must use psychoneurotic "solutions."

Thus the achievement of a stable body image is both a consequence of the complex changes going on and an *organizer*. Hopefully, psychoanalytic research in the future will be able to clarify in detail these changes and their sequences.

## VI

The thesis has been proposed that the achievement of physical maturity is the biological demarcator of the beginning of late adolescence. In most people the corresponding psychological events involve a rapid restructuring within the ego of a new and more unified body image, of more mature self and object representations, along with the structuring of a more or less stable drive and defensive hierarchy. These things tend to occur whether the individual is essentially normal or neurotic. The Oedipus complex is revived, but in a new context of body image parity with adults. Later adolescence is taken up by the reworking, consolidation, and eventual solution of the problems of being able to work and to love. Failure of the process results in a continuing chaos within the personality, although the chaos may be hidden behind defensive maneuvers which further impoverish and constrict the ego.

## REFERENCES

Bernfeld, S. (1923), Über eine typische form der männlichen pubertät. *Imago*, IX. (Translated and quoted by Spiegel, 1951, reference below).

Blos, P. (1962), *On Adolescence*. New York: International Universities Press.

Fenichel, O. (1945), *The Psychoanalytic Theory of Neurosis*. New York: W. W. Norton and Co., p. 36.

Freud, S. (1923), The ego and the id. *Standard Edition*, 19:125–126. London: Hogarth Press, 1961.

Geleerd, E. R. (1958), Borderline states in childhood and adolescence. *The Psychoanalytic Study of the Child*, 13:279–295. New York: International Universities Press.

Gitelson, M. (1948), Character Synthesis. *Amer. J. Orthopsychiat.*, 18:422–431.

Greenacre, P. (1958), Early physical determinants in the development of the sense of identity. *Int. J. Psycho-Anal.*, 6:612.

Hartmann, H., Kris, E., and Loewenstein, R. (1946), Comments on the formation of psychic structure. *The Psychoanalytic Study of the Child*, 2:11–38. New York: International Universities Press.

Hoffer, W. (1950), Development of the body ego. *The Psychoanalytic Study of the Child*, 5:18–23. New York: International Universities Press.

Inhelder, B. & Piaget, J. (1958), *The Growth of Logical Thinking from Childhood to Adolescence*. New York: Basic Books.

Jacobson, E. (1964), *The Self and the Object World*. New York: International Universities Press.

Josselyn, I. (1954), Ego in adolescence. *Amer. J. Orthopsychiat.*, 24:223–237.

Kaufman, I. and Heims, L. (1958), The body image of the juvenile delinquent. *Amer. J. Orthopsychiat.*, 28:146–159.

Lampl-de Groot, J. (1960), On adolescence. *The Psychoanalytic Study of the Child*, 15:95–103. New York: International Universities Press.

Schilder, P. (1950), *The Image and Appearance of the Human Body*. New York: International Universities Press.

Solnit, A. J. (1958) (Reporter), The vicissitudes of ego development in adolescents. *J. Amer. Psychoanal. Assn.*, 7:523–536.

Spiegel, L. (1951), A review of contributions to a psychoanalytic theory of adolescence: individual aspects. *The Psychoanalytic Study of the Child*, 6:373–394. New York: International Universities Press.

—— (1958), Comments on the psychoanalytic psychology of adolescence. *The Psychoanalytic Study of the Child*, 13:296–308. New York: International Universities Press.

—— (1959), The self, the sense of self, and perception. *The Psychoanalytic Study of the Child*, 14:81–109. New York: International Universities Press.

Sullivan, H. S. (1953), *The Interpersonal Theory of Psychiatry*. New York: W. W. Norton & Co.

Wolfenstein, M. (1966), How is mourning possible? *The Psychoanalytic Study of the Child*, 21:93–123. New York: International Universities Press.

# Part III
# Dreams

# 9. OVERVIEW

WILLIAM C. THOMPSON, M.D.

The enthusiastic interest of psychoanalysts in the very live area of dream research during the last decade or so has acquired a more temperate and reflective quality as data accumulate, and as we have time enough to reflect on the inconsistencies, deficiencies, and most important—the implications of what we are learning.

Michel Jouvet (1967), who has done much of the definitive physiological and biochemical research on the states of sleep, has recently said, "Dreaming itself, particularly the question of its evolutionary origin and what function it serves, is still one of the great mysteries of biology" (p. 72). Though he does not refer it to psychology, Jouvet's work, with that of the many other researchers of sleep and dreaming, has strengthened the biological base of psychoanalytic concepts, and no less for stimulating consideration for refinements and changes in psychoanalytic theory itself.

The Kris Study Group Monograph (1967) on the place of the dream in clinical psychoanalysis lists several of the wide range effects of these nonpsychoanalytic experimental findings which have relevance to problems of clinical psychoanalysis. They are:

1. Every person dreams a good portion of every night, and people vary only in their ability to recall and report their dreams.

2. The greatest proportion of dream reports are obtained from the last two REM periods of sleep. The likelihood of recall is

135

greatest when the awakening takes place at the end or soon after the end of a REM period. Vividness and completeness of recall of dream narrative is also greater the shorter the interval between dreaming and awakening. A subjective awareness of such vivid recall may contribute to the frequently encountered report of the "instantaneous" dream.

3.   The proposition that the dream is the guardian of sleep would require some revision to accord with the experimental findings. All that can be stated with precision is that the REM state is obligatory, and that REM deprivation leads to an inexorable effort in subsequent periods of sleep to make up lost REM time. The role that dreaming plays in preventing awakening and consequent disruption of the REM period is not clear. Some discussants felt the entire proposition might better be covered by the statement that, psychologically speaking, we sleep in order to dream, while others still subscribe to Freud's belief that we dream in order to preserve sleep.

4.   None of the reported psychophysiological research has been able to throw significant light on the psychological function of dreaming, or on the details of the dream work, either from the point of view of the connection of day residues with infantile wishes, or as regards the techniques of regressive distortion of the latent content.

5.   The demonstration of the cycle of penile erection coincident with dreaming throws into higher relief the question of the role of instinctual tensions contributing to or being dealt with by dreaming. Fisher (1965) raises the question that whenever drive pressures are increased and there is an accompanying weakening of defenses, there will be an increase in REM time and dreaming.

6.   The occurrence of bed-wetting apart from dreaming in very deep sleep has sharply challenged the view that enuresis is always a psychogenic symptom. The possibility that the bed-wetting episode may be triggered off by some preceding non-REM mentation, not identical with dreaming but with psychic content of a significant character, remains to be studied.

Surprisingly, at least in proportion to the amount of research done over the last 12 years, these analytically relevant data are not yet extensive, and lend very little to the psychology of dreams. As Dr. Lewin remarked in this context during a visit to the New Orleans Psychoanalytic Institute: "They [the physiologists] haven't told us a thing we didn't already know." Yet, there seems little doubt that the new biology of dreaming, of the third organismic state, as Snyder (1963) has called it, will profoundly influence future development of both theoretical and clinical aspects of psychoanalysis.

## REFERENCES

Fisher, C. (1965), Psychoanalytic implications of recent research on sleep and dreaming. *J. Amer. Psychoanal. Assn.,* 13:271–303.
Jouvet, M. (1967), The states of sleep. *Scient. Amer.,* February, p. 72.
Snyder, F. (1963), The new biology of dreaming. *Arch. Gen. Psychiat.,* 8:381–391.
Waldhorn, H. F. (1967), *The Place of the Dream in Psychoanalysis* [Kris Study Group Monogr. II]. New York: International Universities Press.

# 10. CHANGING CONCEPTS OF DREAMING

Jay T. Shurley, M.D.

The study of dreams has ceased to be the exclusive domain of the clinical practitioner. Freud's preoccupation with the meaning of dreams had a tremendous heuristic value for the sciences of psychoanalysis, psychology, and psychiatry. Today's preoccupation by a number of workers with the concomitant relationship between dreaming and the Rapid Eye Movement State (REMS) has had and is having a similar heuristic value for the new scientific discipline of psychophysiology.

That aspect of universal human experience which is commonly referred to as the dream has, from antiquity, been associated with that state of the human organism simply denoted as "sleep." Not until the end of the last century was it convincingly argued by Freud (1900) that the content of the dream was meaningfully and significantly associated, however, with the dreamer's past waking life experiences, as well. It remained for the mid-twentieth century scientists, Aserinsky and Kleitman (1953, 1955), Dement (1960, 1965), and Snyder (1963) to demonstrate that, while sleep was a necessary condition for dreaming, it was not a sufficient condition. For what we knew as "sleep" has now been shown to be not one solid, unitary state, but a repetitive cycling of at least two distinctive organismic states, together with greater or lesser amounts of seeming transitional states between them and waking.

These two are now referred to primarily as Rapid Eye Movement (REM) and as Slow Wave, or NREM, sleep, although both now have a number of meaningful synonyms. REM sleep is referred to as low voltage fast sleep, active or activated sleep, rhombencephalic sleep, paradoxical sleep, and finally, simply as dreaming sleep. Non-REM sleep is also called Slow Wave sleep, synchronized sleep, slow sleep, cortical sleep, and nondreaming sleep.

While the Slow Wave sleep state is apparently not wholly devoid of mental activity, Rapid Eye Movement sleep is often richly dramatic and presented in visual and auditory images. This is in fact what we generally mean when we speak of a "dream." Because of its exclusively subjective nature, the dream has always been a difficult phenomenon for most scientists to deal with scientifically. For them, it was a "hypothetical construct," open only to introspective observation, and thus highly suspect.

Stoyva and Kamiya (1968) have rightly pointed out that dream research suddenly became much more respectable and interesting for experimental psychologists and others when Aserinsky and Kleitman (1953) discovered the Rapid Eye Movement indicator of dreaming, insofar as this development offered a new "construct validity" for that which had been previously considered hypothetical. In fact, the electrophysiological study of dreaming has become the prototype of a whole new and exciting strategy in the study of consciousness, which complements and extends the introspective and psychoanalytic methods. It even becomes possible once more to consider unravelling further the phylogenetic history of the evolution of consciousness. The new strategy involves the logic of what are called *converging operations,* which make it possible to eliminate whole series of alternative hypotheses which might explain a given result. Although not referred to by this name in the literature, this strategy is hardly new to the psychoanalyst, for it has constituted one of the means by which the existence of the unconscious itself has gained credence. It is worth noting that Kamiya (1968) by using the strategy of jointly incorporating physiological measures, verbal reports, and operant conditioning (with its built-in information feedback procedures), has given his subjects the power of conscious control over the "on" and "off" of their own electroencephalographic alpha rhythms. There are certainly other applications in the study of waking or sleeping mental activity formerly open only to introspection yet to be exploited by this strategy.

Having commented on some of the strategy evolved, and one of the more startling results of its application—the discovery of the two distinctive types of sleep—I now wish to turn back to a consideration of some possible and probable impacts of the new information on the theory and practice of dream interpretation.

First, however, let me recapitulate briefly some of the essential aspects of what Snyder (1963) called the "new biology of dreaming." It is central to this view that dreaming is the experiential aspect of a third physiological state which is distinct from sleeping, in the usual sense, and from waking. The course of nocturnal sleep is periodically interrupted by four or five periods of low voltage, fast, desynchronized electroencephalographic rhythms coincident with bursts of fast conjugate movements of the eyes, and markedly decreased tonus of the submental musculature. In the young adult, this "activated sleep" occurs at roughly 60 to 90 minute intervals, with progressively longer episodes, so that approximately 22–26 per cent of total sleeping time is passed in this state. Arousal during or immediately after this Rapid Eye Movement period reveals that the subject can relate details of a vivid visual dream in all but five to 20 per cent of arousals. Triggered by tonic and phasic discharges from a discrete midbrain-pontine nuclear structure known as the locus coeruleus, activation of the limbic circuits and cortex equals or surpasses that seen in the waking state, but both incoming sensory messages, and outgoing motor activity is sharply curtailed, in what has been called a functional deafferentation, and de-efferentation. From a steady, quiescent state, all variables monitored by the autonomic nervous system appear to become highly variable, concomitantly with bursts of rapid conjugate eye movements, and contractions of the small muscles of the middle ear. In the male, there is an accompanying partial to full penile erection co-terminous with the duration of the REM period. It has not been technically possible to obtain satisfactory genitograms from the female, so that a similar genital response pattern in the female must remain for now a moot question. Both Huttenlocher (1961) and Evarts (1962) have shown, in single neuron studies in the mesencephalon and primary visual cortex in animals, that there is a dramatic increase of 10 to 40 times, and 70 per cent, respectively, in spontaneous firing, indicating intensive neuronal activity throughout the nervous system. Kanzow (1962) found an increase of 30 to 50 per cent in cortical blood flow over that of the rest of sleep. In brief, the evidence is overwhelming in favor of a qualitatively different mode of neural functioning, distinctive from both waking and the rest of sleep, which, by conservative estimate, has exclusively occupied approximately six years of the life of a 70-year-old person. The experience of visual dreaming apparently extends throughout most of this time, and very little into the rest of sleep, by empirical test.

Freud's (1900) well-known hypothesis, that the specific function of the dream is to guard sleep against disruption by anxiety-provoking unconscious impulses, is now under sharp attack and defense as a result of the host of new findings regarding the physiology of sleeping and dreaming. I will refer you to papers by Fisher (1966), Whitman (1963), and Altshuler (1966) for some of the detailed arguments. It is quite remarkable to this reviewer to realize the degree to which so many of Freud's observations and theories foreshadowed, or at least remain compatible with recent findings. He advanced the notion that active psychic processes go on throughout sleep, that dreaming occurs in a state of arousal, and that motor mechanisms were paralyzed, while incoming sensory stimuli were occluded during dreaming, as examples. Nevertheless, new and alternative hypotheses are now making their appearance. One of the more interesting of these is the so-called "P" or "Programming" hypothesis of Newman and Evans (1965) and of Dewan (1968). It is a working hypothesis, and should not be considered at this stage as either true or untrue. It proceeds from the consideration that all higher organisms must continue to adapt to continuously changing circumstances throughout their lives, with many alterations in their goals. These changes would seem to require some kind of functional reorganization of their brains. As humans, we face entirely different sorts of problems at different life periods, and we change our goals, interests, etc. as this happens. We forget information that is no longer useful—languages we no longer use, for example—and lose unused abilities. We appear to use all our brain for present purposes. It is as if healthy brains were constantly being reorganized functionally. Here, Dewan draws an analogy with the computer—one of many that can be usefully drawn—and states that it is as if the brain *spontaneously reprograms itself* continuously. This is the essence of the Newman-Evans-Dewan "P" hypothesis.

When we re-examine the meaning of this hypothesis a little more closely, we see many interesting parallels with living; i.e., brain, processes. In the computer, a program can be regarded as its "potential behavior," or its functional structure. The computing elements are organized, by the input of mathematical formulas, to solve certain mathematical problems. In some computers, these are *wired in,* and fixed (as in lower life forms). In other computers, the programming is in terms of long lists of instructions stored in memory devices. There are many categories of these—input programs, for example, which tell the computer what to do with new input information; others process this information, and still others determine what is to be done with the output. Sometimes, this output is converted into signals which activate other devices in a system of which the computer is but one component, as, for example, in a space vehicle. Many more obvious analogies with brain function suggest themselves; but we haven't, in the case of the brain, the foggiest notion of how such programming is accomplished physically or chemically. Thus the term, "functional pathways."

We see, further, that the spontaneous process of self-programming (P) of the brain must involve some kind of "principle of optimality." It selects certain information and programs, making "decisions" which can only be made by help of certain criteria. The way it makes these decisions, we assume, is in the way which is more or less optimum for its needs—that is, the selection is optimized with respect to the needs and drives of the organism. The only way this can be accomplished is by means of a system which uses feedback. The ability of the simple technical feedback control system (e.g., the thermostat) to "home in" on their "goals" is so well known it needs no elaboration here. In the case of the brain, the goal of the system which programs is to create a functional organization of its constituent elements which, on the average, is adequate, or even optimum, for its needs. (Even the process of evolution would have the tendency to organize systems somewhere near an optimum of some sort.) One consequence of the requirement that our hypothetical P-system is, in point of fact, a feedback system, is that it would then display various behaviors related to overshooting and undershooting its goals, and various other "stability" phenomena, as temporary or permanent transitions to abnormal modes of function. In other words, it can be expected to "break down" occasionally. Indeed, this is what we do see, in the case of the human brain.

Two considerations in particular motivate the hypothesis that REM (i.e., REM sleep), is necessary and sufficient for "P":

(1)    Phylogenetically, most mammals exhibit a per cent REM that does not differ significantly from that of man. Lower forms of life, however, which are "fixed programmed" have much less REM, or none at all. (Hartmann, 1966; Jouvet, 1965).

(2)    Ontogenetically, we see that per cent REM is higher in immature animals than in adults. Human infants spend 50 per cent of their sleep in REM, compared with 20 per cent in adults (Roffwarg, et al., 1966). It is estimated that, at about 24 to 30 weeks of gestational age, the human fetus spends nearly 100 per cent time in REM (Parmalee, 1964). In other words, a large amount of programming takes place at the start of an animal's life. The plasticity of behavior seen in children and immature animals would seem to reflect the action of "P" hypothesis. Even "imprinting," the so-called "permanent learning" which takes place particularly in birds at crucial life periods, is well explained by "P."

In addition to reprogramming, two other functions appear to be associated with REM: the "consolidation" from recent memory into more permanent storage of the input from the period since the last sleep, and the clearing out of older, no longer useful, programs. "P," or self-initiated programming, would seem to be, as well, a way of "preadapting" in line with expectations of the future. Thus, there may be a bit of literal truth, yet, in the folk-belief that dreams, in some way, help foretell the future.

A partial confirmation of Freud's assumption that all the dreams in the course of a night are related to a single theme, with the impulse becoming bolder and less disguised, and, in paired dreams, a condition-consequent relationship between them, was made by Kramer, Whitman, et al. (1964) in an ingenious application of the REM indicator to capture the entire dream series, and then subject these to psychoanalytic analysis of the content. These same authors had previously pointed out that discrepancy (1963) between the fact that Freud and other analysts have seldom noted or commented on dream series beyond pairs, while it has been convincingly demonstrated (Dement and Kleitman, 1957) that three to five periods of dreaming, and discrete dream reports, can be ascertained in almost any adult. They suggested that the particular dream or pair selected for recounting by the patient was determined by the transference relationship to the listener. Now they report the results of collecting every dream, every night, from two volunteer experimental subjects over a long series of consecutive nights, and subjecting these to analysis. While 50 per cent of the dreams so collected from single nights did confirm the previously described sequential pattern in which each dream solution acts as a "night residue" for the next dream, they also found a second pattern in over 30 per cent of dreams in which the same problem was repetitiously restated over and over in each dream. This, of course, immediately suggested a parallel with the behavior of dreams in cases of traumatic neurosis, where the dream material repetitiously repeats the same conflictual situation, without progression or regression to various solutions. They also described and gave a clinical example of an intermediate pattern, suggesting that the two major patterns described form two ends of a dynamic continuum.

Whitman (1963) has also made use of the Dement-Kleitman technique of dream recovery to re-examine the metapsychology of the forgetting and remembering of dreams. He attributes failure to recall dreams on the basis of primal repression to several factors, including (1) the difficulty of conceptualizing primary process thinking in secondary process terms, (2) excessive energy demands on the ego, and (3) the difficulty in recalling a completed (oral) experience, in comparison with an uncompleted one (the Zeigarnik effect). Forgetting of dreams, on the other hand, is attributed to the action of repression proper, in which the latent content is endopsychically perceived by the dreamer, judged to be ego-alien to his waking self, or unacceptable to the listener. Based on Gifford's (1960) observation from some of Kleitman's original work that, at about three months of age, the number of night feedings drops exactly at the time the mean hours of sleep per night goes up, Whitman speculates that dreaming, at this point, takes over the function of an unconscious wish-fulfilling hallucinatory experience which enables the infant to continue asleep. He notes that the number of dreams on a given night is roughly equivalent to the number of night feedings of a neonate. But the interesting part of his speculation is that the dream not only discharges some drive cathexis, but is also, in and of itself, a gratifying oral (visual) experience which substitutes for a primary nursing experience. This gains interest in the light of Forrer's (1960a,b) demonstration that many hallucinatory episodes in young schizophrenic patients could be quickly terminated by a milk feeding! The main point I wished to make, however, is that such a view is not incompatible with Freud's basic postulate of the sleep (REM sleep?) protecting function of the dream.

When researchers turned their attention to children's sleep, it was totally unexpected to find that the neonate, where it is difficult to conceive of dramatic visual dreams, had not less, but more REM sleep. Roffwarg, Muzio, and Dement (1966) showed that the one-month-old neonate spends one-third of his day, and one-half of his sleep in REM. Parmalee and co-workers (1964) showed that an even higher percentage of REM was found in prematures, and in the fetus at 39 weeks gestational age. This led Roffwarg, et al., to formulate the hypothesis that the REM mechanism serves as an endogenous source of stimulation, furnishing to higher centers great quantities of excitation which assist in structural maturation and differentiation of key motor and sensory areas within the CNS. The elaborate controlling mechanisms for integrating eye movement with vision, in particular, would benefit from such "warm-up" stimulation. Shapiro (1967) went even further by speculating that the phenomena of REMS provides a patterned input into central nervous system structures, in order to offset the deteriorating effects of disuse and of sensory isolation periodically produced by the sleep cycle itself in adults.

At this point I wish to turn away from the ontogeny of REMS to some facts about its phylogeny. Snyder (1964) studied the Virginia opossum, a "living fossil" marsupial mammal, surviving at least 130 million years since the separation of the placental and marsupial branches of the mammalian tree, and found unmistakable evidence that the opossum spends a longer period of its day in REMS than in waking, at least under laboratory conditions. REM sleep has been demonstrated in the mouse, rat, rabbit, cat, dog, sheep, monkey, and chimpanzee, in addition to man. This past summer, I (1969) had the good fortune to be able to demonstrate both REMS and SWS in the first marine mammal so studied, the pilot whale, *Globicephalus scammoni*. It is reasonable to assume, therefore, that REMS is found in all mammalian species. It is not, however, found in the amphibians and reptiles, and it is questionable whether it is found in birds. The amount is quite variable—from two per cent in the adult sheep—perhaps much less in the whale—up to 60 per cent in the cat. The cycle length seems to vary with size of the animal and metabolic rate, from three to four minutes in the mouse to 90 minutes in man. Since the physiological mechanism is clearly extremely old phylogenetically, and exists under conditions where it is inconceivable that visual dreaming in the sense that we know it in ourselves occurs, we are left with the strong supposition that the psychological function ascribed to dreams simply makes use of, or becomes secondarily associated with a pre-existing biological cycle which it does not govern or control in any sense. Some experiments have shown that, while many strong external and internal stimuli become incorporated into the dream text of a person in REMS, no one has been able to demonstrate that a REM cycle can be stimulated by such stimuli; it occurs with almost clocklike regularity, and is followed by a refractory period of at least 15 minutes before another can be stimulated by direct pontine stimulation in the laboratory cat (Jouvet, 1963).

This quality of REMS, and the increasing "pressure" for REMS demonstrated when a subject or cat is deprived of his REMS for successive nightly periods, resulting in a final build-up to a point where it can no longer be delayed, and shows a strong "rebound" tendency, point strongly in favor of some biochemical substance which is elaborated in the brain and periodically reaches an excess, whereupon it is destroyed by the REMS experience. Dement (1965) and Jouvet (1964), in particular, have been extremely diligent in the effort to unravel the chemistry and pharmacology of REMS, but have found it extremely difficult to do. It appears, nevertheless, that we may one day have a chemistry of dreaming (as Freud predicted), but it is unlikely we shall have a chemistry of the dream (to paraphrase Kety's famous statement on memory).

I would be even more remiss than I have been in omitting so many important findings in recent sleep research from this review, if I did not comment upon some aspects of the "other" part of sleep, the non-Rapid Eye Movement Sleep (NREMS) and mention some of the pathological conditions affecting sleep and dreaming.

Narcolepsy, which is an uncommon but not rare disorder of sleep, often associated with attacks of cataplexy, sleep paralysis, and hypnagogic hallucinations, has been shown by Rechtshaffen and Dement (1967) and others, to be characterized by a disorder of the REMS mechanism itself, in that both their nocturnal and diurnal naps are initiated with a period of REMS, followed by SWS, instead of the reverse. Instead of hallucinatory arousal and motor inhibition, as in normal REMS and narcolepsy, another set of pathological conditions of sleep is characterized by the reverse: motor arousal and hallucinatory inhibition.

It is now quite clear, through the work of Broughton (1968), Gastaut (1963), Jacobsen, et al. (1965), and others, that the tetrad of sleep disorders known as enuresis, somnambulism, the incubus or nightmare, and the night terrors, occurs preferentially during arousal from Slow Wave sleep, and virtually never are they associated with REMS. The symptoms appear to be based on physiological changes which are present to some degree throughout the night, and are simply reinforced or markedly accentuated during arousal from Slow Wave sleep, reaching a clinically overt level on occasion (Broughton, 1968). Slow Wave sleep arousals are normal cyclic events, being apparently the most intense recurrent arousal regularly experienced by any individual. Broughton stresses that these conditions are better considered disorders of the arousal mechanism than of the sleep mechanism. While conceding that diurnal psychic conflicts may be the determining factor causing the accentuation of the symptoms of normal arousal, he has been unable to demonstrate either any potential psychological causative factors, as, for example, in dreams, or even "psychological void" just prior to the attacks. Obviously, further studies need to be done to elucidate the process of cyclic arousal from NREM sleep.

In conclusion, what I have to report is that the young science of psychophysiology, as applied to sleep and dreaming, is in a healthy and rapidly expanding state of confusion, somewhat akin to the state of psychoanalysis itself in its younger years. Altshuler (1966) commented in a recent paper, "It is more parsimonious and in keeping with the data [of sleep and dream research and of psychoanalysis] to assume that conflictual and analyzable mental activity is not confined to REM periods, but occurs throughout the night—as indeed it does throughout the day. What is different is the mode of representation and the clinical availability" (p. 236). We have just seen that there are clinical disorders of the mechanism associated with REM sleep. Perhaps the latest theoretical model of the neural states which underlie the three organismic states is that put forth by Globus and Gardner (1968), of the NIMH, who take the view that these states are not always in a one-to-one relationship with mutually exclusive underlying neural systems, as assumed, but actually are the complex resultants of coterminously active underlying neural systems, and thus they propose a "trireme," or three-tiered Grecian galley, model to account for some of the confusion!

## REFERENCES

Altshuler, K. Z. (1966), Comments on recent sleep research related to psychoanalytic theory. *Arch. Gen. Psychiat.,* 15:235–239.
Aserinsky, E. and Kleitman, N. (1953), Regularly occurring periods of

eye motility and concomitant phenomena during sleep. *Science,* 118:273–274.

—— (1955), Two types of ocular motility occurring in sleep. *J. Appl. Physiol.,* 8:1–10.

Broughton, R. J. (1968), Sleep disorders: disorders of arousal? *Science,* 159:1070–1078.

Dement, W. C. (1960), The effect of dream deprivation. *Science,* 131:1705–1707.

—— (1965), Recent studies on the biological rate of rapid eye movement sleep. *Amer. J. Psychiat.,* 122:404–408.

—— and Kleitman, N. (1957), Cyclic variations in EEG during sleep and their relations to eye movements, body motility, and dreaming. *EEG Clin. Neurophysiol.,* 1:673–690.

Dewan, E. M. (1968), Tests of the programming (P) hypothesis for REM. *Psychophysiol.,* 4:365. (Abstract)

Evarts, E. V. (1962), Activity of neurons in the visual cortex of cat during sleep with low voltage fast EEG activity. *J. Neurophysiol.,* 25:812–816.

Fisher, C. (1966), Recent trends in dream-sleep research in the United States. *Proc. IV World Congress Psychiat.,* Madrid, 3:168–177.

Forrer, G. H. (1960a), Effect of oral activity on hallucinations, *Arch. Gen. Psychiat.,* 2:100–103.

—— (1960b), Benign auditory and visual hallucinations, *Arch. Gen. Psychiat.,* 3:95–98.

Freud, S. (1900), Interpretation of dreams. *Standard Edition,* 4 & 5. London: Hogarth Press, 1953.

Gastaut, H. and Broughton, R. (1963), Paroxysmal psychological events and certain phases of sleep. *Percept. Mot. Skills,* 17:362.

Gifford, S. (1960), Sleep, time, and the early age. Comments on the development of the 24-hour sleep-wakefulness pattern as a precursor of ego functioning. *J. Amer. Psychoanal. Assn.,* 8:5–42.

Globus, G. and Gardner. R. (1968), CNS function underlying states of waking, sleeping and REM-sleep: A trireme model. Abstract read at the Annual Meeting of the Association for the Psychophysiological Study of Sleep, Denver.

Hartmann, E. (1966), The D-state: a review and discussion of studies on the physiologic state concomitant with dreaming. *Int. J. Psychiat.,* 2:11–47.

Huttenlocher, P. (1961), Evoked and spontaneous activity in single units of medial brain stem during natural sleep and waking. *J. Neurophysiol.,* 24:451–468.

Jacobsen, A., Kales, A., Lehmann, D., and Zweizig, J. R. (1965), Somnambulism: all-night electroencephalographic studies. *Science,* 148: 975–977.

Jouvet, M. (1963), The rhombencephalic phase of sleep. *Progr. Brain Res.,* 1:406–424.

—— (1965), Paradoxical sleep: a study of its nature and mechanisms. In: *Progress in Brain Research: Sleep Mechanisms,* eds. K. Akert, C. Bally, and P. Schade. Amsterdam: Elsevier, 18:20–62.

Kanzow, E., Krause, D., and Kuhnel, H. (1962), Die vasomotorik der hirnrinde in den phasen desynchronisierter EEG-aktivität in natürlichem schlaf der katze. *Pflugers Arch. Ges. Physiol.,* 274:593–607.

Kramer, M., Whitman, R., Baldridge, B. J., and Lansky, L. M. (1964), Patterns of dreaming: the interrelationship of the dreams of a night. *J. Nerv. Ment. Dis.,* 139:426–439.

Newman, E. A. and Evans, C. R. (1965), Human dream processes as analogous to computer programme clearance. *Nature* (London), 206:534.

Parmalee, A. H., Akiyama, Y., Wenner, W., and Flescher, J. (1964), Activated sleep in premature infants. Paper read at the Annual Meeting of the Association for the Psychophysiological Study of Sleep, Palo Alto.

Rechtshaffen, A. and Dement, W. C. (1967), Studies on the relations of narcolepsy, cataplexy, and sleep with low voltage random EEG activity. In: *Sleep and Altered States of Consciousness,* eds. S. S. Kety, E. V. Evarts, and H. L. Williams. ARNMD, Vol. 45. Baltimore: Williams & Wilkins.

Roffwarg, H. P., Muzio, J. N., and Dement, W. C. (1966), Ontogenetic development of the human sleep-dream cycle. *Science,* 152:604–619.

Shapiro, A. (1967), Dreaming and the physiology of sleep. A critical review of some empirical data and a proposal for a theoretical model of sleep and dreaming. *Exp. Neurol. Suppl.,* 4:56–81.

Shurley, J. T., Serafetinides, E. A., Brooks, R. E., Elsner, R., and Kenney, D. W. (1969), Sleep in cetaceans: I. The pilot whale, *Globicephala scammoni. Psychophysiology,* 6:230. (Abstract)

Snyder, F. (1963), The new biology of dreaming. *Arch. Gen. Psychiat.,* 8:381–391.

Stoyva, J. and Kamiya, J. (1968), Electrophysiological studies of dreaming as the prototype of a new strategy in the study of consciousness. *Psychol. Rev.,* 75:192–205.

Whitman, R. (1963), Remembering and forgetting dreams in psychoanalysis. *J. Amer. Psychoanal. Assn.,* 11:752–774.

—— Kramer, M., and Baldridge, B. J. (1963), Which dream does the patient tell? *Arch. Gen. Psychiat.,* 8:277–282.

# 11. EXPERIMENTAL AND NEUROPHYSIOLOGICAL INVESTIGATION IN RELATION TO DREAM THEORY

Douglas Noble, M.D.

For nearly half of a century after the publication of *The Interpretation of Dreams* (1900) few additions were made to Freud's theory of dream interpretation. Significant exceptions to this period of latency were, however, provided by the work of Ella Sharpe (1949), French (1941), Isakower (1939), and others. A resurgence of interest in the dream then came about in the late forties with a series of papers by Bertram Lewin (1950) in which he developed his concepts of the Dream Screen, the Oral Triad, the processes involved in the forgetting of dreams, and the resemblance of the manic state to an unfinished dream in which denying secondary elaborations were preponderant.

Concurrent with Lewin's contributions was the sudden expansion of interest in the dream as a result of the discoveries of Kleitman (1955), Aserinsky (1955), Dement (1957), Fisher (1954, 1957), Jouvet (1961), and others, which have since stimulated investigative work in many laboratories. These researches into the REM states have revealed the existence of what Snyder (1965) has called the third organismic state, the paradoxical phase of sleep in which physiological alterations have been found in every organ system that has been studied in man and in many mammals. From these studies much has been learned of the mutual relationship of neurophysiological, biochemical, and endocrinological components of dream function; on the psychological side they have led to confirmation of some aspects of dream theory and modification of others.

I would like to expand the area of discussion in this paper beyond the consideration of neurophysiological research indicated in the title and to include a review of a number of diverse laboratory studies which serve to illustrate the application and some future possibilities of laboratory studies in the psychobiology of dreaming.

In the early fifties, Charles Fisher (1954, 1957) was pursuing important studies in the role of subliminal perception in dream formation. He repeated and confirmed Poetzl's (1960) findings that parts of tachistoscopically produced images which were not perceived at the time of exposure often appeared in dreams. From his demonstration of the immense participation of preconsciously perceived perceptions in dreams, Fisher concluded that preconscious percepts were connected with deeply repressed material; they represented an earlier mode of psychic function that with maturation of the perceptual apparatus became inhibited and replaced by the adult form of reality-oriented perception. These conclusions recall Freud's description of the dream as having preserved a sample of the psychical apparatus's primary method of working which was later abandoned as inefficient and replaced by the secondary system.

The regressive mode of perception which Fisher found to be operative in dream formation had been compared by Schilder (1953) with the perceptual processes seen in some organic brain disturbances. Price, Gilder and I (1954), studying a group of patients with neurological diseases, found evidence which supported this view. In one instance the appearance of the primary mode of perception was related to a denial of personal and bodily loss. The patient in question had a left hemiplegia and manifested the phenomenon of anosognosia, stating that his paralyzed left arm belonged to the patient in the next bed. He himself had a phantom right arm in addition to his healthy arm. He had named the phantom arm, which was stretched across his chest in something like an embrace, "Oscar," claiming that Oscar was the name of a druggist who had befriended him in boyhood and had recently died. It seemed that the loss of the friend, and the limb, the one introjected, the other denied by the phantom, had combined with the confusion accompanying the loss of the brain function to bring about a regression of the perceptual process with an inability to distinguish between self and nonself.

From his experiments on subliminal perception Fisher (1957) drew certain conclusions regarding the dream process. He had found that perceptions were subject to distortion, condensation, and symbolic representation in close temporal relationship to the perception and saw this as initiating the first stage of the dream process. This modified Freud's view that distortion took place only after the state of sleep had been established. Fisher found that the transference onto the experimenter was of great importance in activating unconscious wishes and in selecting, at the time of tachistoscopic exposure the percepts to be included later in the dream. In the second stage of the dream process after sleep, the stage of regression to perception, the unconscious wish is again activated and memory pictures from the past are covered by the percepts connected with the day residues. Fisher stated that memory pictures from the past did not appear in dreams unless screened by a recent visual percept. In this sense visual images in dreams required a cover from something seen during the dream day comparable to Freud's description of speeches in dreams as made up of speeches heard or read on the day before. A dream, wrote Fisher, cannot create a new visual structure. Fisher saw no necessity for postulating the existence of a regressive pathway when the unconscious wish was activated during sleep and described the dream work both in the first and second stages as following progressive pathways. He thus moves towards the structural theory which Arlow and Brenner have outlined. Fisher further suggested that subliminally incorporated auditory perceptions might enter into dreams but he did not pursue investigation of this.

Some years ago, when teaching at the New Orleans Psychoanalytic Institute, Dr. William Thompson and I undertook as a teaching device some crude experiments in auditory perception. We moved into a room adjacent to the classroom and carried on a muffled conversation almost inaudible to the candidates in the classroom. In the prearranged conversation, Dr. Thompson criticized the dream course saying he found it very boring. Candidates were asked to write down what they heard at the time and to report their dreams in the seminar the next day. Dreams that were reported frequently included references to the experimental situation; connections between the dream material and the muffled conversations was, however, not clearly established. Rosenberg and I (1967) later elaborated the experiment when we placed auditory stimuli consisting of two scrambled conversations on a tape recording; usually, the one conversation in the foreground dealt with trivialities, the other in the background concerned tragedy and violence. A second type of stimulus was devised by playing a taped narrative at twice the ordinary speed so that the words were practically unintelligible and sounded like the quack-quack of a Donald Duck cartoon. These experiments have been reported in detail elsewhere. Although it was not possible to exclude the element of chance and the influence of incidentally perceived stimuli unrelated to the experiment, some of the elements in manifest dreams and associated thoughts resembled so closely the content of the hidden material that we believed that these background messages had been preconsciously perceived and incorporated into dreams. In one instance where the Donald Duck type of recording was used, a subject who heard only one word of the stimulus during the waking state had a dream in which elements of the taped narrative appeared in some detail. He was so impressed with one part of his dream which resembled closely an element in the hidden stimulus that he made a drawing of the dream without having been asked to do so and brought it to the seminar. This strong impulse to make a drawing of the dream had been observed by Fisher who compared it to automatic writing.

We found that perception of the stimuli was influenced by personal problems and transference to the experimenters. Material from the auditory stimuli usually appeared in dreams in visual form and in only rare cases were actual speeches part of the manifest dream. The appearance of speeches seemed to be related to the emergence of powerful ambivalent feelings which had been transferred onto the experimenters. This finding supported Fliess's theory that speeches in the manifest dream are a regressive superego manifestation which occur in the presence of a threatened crisis when the dreamer seeks parental protection and direction. A military officer listened to the stimulus which contained in the background the critical statement, "This is a very boring course." He heard nothing of this element. He dreamed, however, that a superior officer met him and his wife and addressed his wife sharply saying, "Do you have intercourse with your husband?" On the next day, when the background stimulus was played clearly to him he immediately connected the phrase, "This is a boring course" with the speech in the dream. Further associations showed obvious transference feelings related to the experimenter.

These experiments should be repeated in the sleep laboratory if more accurate data are to be obtained. In an assessment of more than 600 REM reports, Snyder (1967) found a constant accompaniment of conversational and other auditory material, and in a later study reported verbal interaction in 76 per cent of subjects studied with alleged quotations in 26 per cent. He stated that verbal and auditory experiences occurred in dreams much more often than is usually believed. Snyder noted also that color appeared in the majority of dreams but was only brought out when subjects were questioned about it. He considered memory for auditory aspects of dreams and for color to be evanescent.

During the day we continually shut out the background of sound surrounding us though we attend to sounds that hold significance for us and are aware of the change when accustomed sounds cease. In a somewhat similar way we are often unaware of color in the environment. Walking on a busy street on a week-day we may be aware only of a general grayness whereas on a Sunday morning, when the streets are empty, we are likely to perceive a rich variety of color. My own observations support the idea that color appears very frequently in dreams but is usually not reported. Some experience with artists has led me to believe that they report dreams more often. Snyder's work suggests that external sounds are incorporated into dreams more often than has been believed. When incorporation of external sounds occurs the sounds are usually transformed into visual images. This regressive manifestation may well be facilitated by the absence of feedback from accustomed sounds which takes place in the waking states.

Berger (1963) found in the sleep laboratory that spoken names which were meaningful to his subjects and presented to them at random during REM states were incorporated into dream material. Subjects correctly matched stimuli and dreams in 32 out of 78 instances. Berger confirmed what has always been known regarding the ability of a sleeper to remain aware of meaningful sounds as in the case of a sleeping mother hearing the baby's cry but demonstrated also that this discrimination enters into the dream work. Rechtschaffen and Foulkes (1965) exposed stimulus cards to sleeping subjects whose eyes were taped open; there was no evidence that these visual stimuli were incorporated into dreams. It would appear that the discriminatory function is utilized by the dream work to deal with external sounds which we cannot shut out as we can by closing our eyes during sleep.

The researches in the rapid eye movement states that have been made in the laboratory, the phenomenon of dream deprivation described by Dement (1957), of penile erection in dreams demonstrated by Fisher (1963) and many other evidences of physiological alterations accompanying the REM states are well known and will not be reviewed here. I would like, however, in the remainder of this paper to direct attention to particular studies in the sleep laboratory which have illustrated correlations between dream physiology and psychoanalytic theory, and between laboratory and clinical investigation.

Jouvet (1961) found that tonic muscle activity in the neck of the cat disappeared during REM sleep; Hodes and Dement (1964) showed that the onset of the REM state is accompanied by a dramatic reduction in certain spinal reflexes. Berger (1963) found in humans that tonic muscle activity beneath the chin disappeared during REM periods. These tonic and reflex changes apparently help to maintain the organism in a resting state supporting the idea expressed by Freud in his "Project for a Scientific Psychology" (1950 [1895]) that a loss of prespinal cathexis occurred during dreaming which, because of the motor paralysis it imposed safeguarded us against acting out our dreams. Jouvet (1961) demonstrated that the tonic muscle changes were controlled through a center in the nucleus locus coeruleus and that cats in which this nucleus is bilaterally destroyed show periods of REM sleep accompanied by aggressive, sexual and other behavior which may represent the acting-out of dreams.

Despite the arrangements to bring about motor paralysis, Baldridge, Whitman, and Kramer (1965) have shown that motor impulses are generated during REM states and break through in a muted, abortive fashion. Phasic twitching about the face and hands is prominent during REM sleep in infancy with manifestations of sucking, chewing, and smiling. In adult mammals abortive manifestations which take the form of walking or running movements have been observed. Fisher (1965) has demonstrated that penile erections occur in most REM states. All of these findings tend to confirm the idea that an instinctual discharge function exists in the dream.

Jouvet (1961) and his co-workers indicate that the REM state depends upon a primitive brain-stem mechanism which involves the limbic system. Subsequent studies have implicated the hippocampus in the expression of basic biological drives and memory and probably in the regulation of the REM state. Jouvet considers telencephalic or NREM sleep as a condition of cortical inhibition and rhombencephalic REM sleep as performing an arousal and discharge function. Rhombencephalic sleep is controlled from the nucleus within the pons which at the onset of the REM states inaugurates a diverse group of manifestations. Tonic muscle activity is suppressed, thresholds for external stimulation are raised; at the same time, excitations from the pons activate structures within the limbic system which provide an expression for basic drives in the hallucination of the dream. The involvement of visual mechanisms in the dream formation has been demonstrated by Bizzi (1965) and others who demonstrated the activation of lateral geniculate nuclei during REM states. The changes attendant upon REM sleep are dramatically visible in the subject in the sleep laboratory when almost suddenly, restlessness ceases, rapid eye movements commence, and the dreamer becomes engrossed with endogenously produced perceptions, the dream content. Fisher has compared this phenomenon with the manner in which the audience in a theatre settles down when the curtain goes up on the play.

Meissner (1968) finds an analogy between the two states of sleep and the primary and secondary processes. He pointed out that individuals who do not remember dreams well have, in addition to a repressive posture in regard to inner experience, a diminished REM time. Meissner suggests that telencephalic mechanisms are hyperactive in these people. With children in whom telencephalic mechanisms are less highly developed, REM time is greater and undisguised wish-fulfillment is therefore more likely to occur. Freud stated that two fundamentally different kinds of psychical processes are concerned with the formation of dreams, that the activity of the first system is directed towards securing the free discharge of the quantities of excitation and that the second system succeeds in inhibiting this system. Meissner's comments that the rhombencephalic pattern is, like the primary process, also primary, and Freud's statement that it is only in the course of life that secondary processes unfold, can be considered as descriptive of the telencephalic pattern emerging with cortical maturation.

Fisher and Dement (1963) reported that in dream deprivation the discharge of instinctual energies was disrupted with accompanying disturbances in ego-functioning, difficulty in concentration, tension, and anxiety. It became clear from these observations that the REM state plays a significant role in adaptation of the organism. Meissner (1968) believes that the disturbance in functioning in dream deprivation is due to interference with the function of the limbic system which he has shown to be involved in the organization of emotional and cognitive experience. A disorganization within the limbic system is brought about also, according to Meissner, as the result of deprivation of sensory input during normal sleep but, in contrast to what occurs in sensory deprivation with waking subjects, ego disruption does not occur because a regulatory mechanism is put into play. A regression to more primitive levels of organization and functioning occurs with a regulated discharge and binding of unconscious energy.

Hawkins (1966) expressed the idea that in addition to discharging instinctual tension the dream aids in the resolution of conflict situations. In the dream process, it is necessary to dispose of the excess sensory input of the day before, to wipe the slate clean; in this effort the dream work functions in a manner similar to that of a computer operation in storing material away. Hawkins (1966) states that the rhombencephalic mechanisms function in the re-establishment of the pattern of sensory input, in the manipulation of symbolic material and in the sorting out of drives and affects. These processes free the mental apparatus for dealing with the perceptions and problems of the following day and facilitate the solution of current problems. At the same time, the loss of sensory input during sleep is compensated for by the endogenous sensory input emanating from the dream perceptions which produce an arousal effect and keep the perceptual apparatus ready to re-establish a normal pattern of operation. Hawkins adds that it is as though the motor were being "revved up" regularly to keep it ready for operation at brief notice. What is now known of the functioning of the limbic system in the assimilation of emotional and cognitive material would support the view.

Freud (1900) stated that the solution of a problem when it appeared in a dream represented the emergence in the latent dream thoughts of a solution which had been arrived at preconsciously in the waking state. There is some question in the light of laboratory researches, however, whether such a sharp distinction can be made between a problem which has been solved prior to sleep and one in which the dream work participates. Fisher (1963) has expressed the view that from his studies in perception the first stage of the dream process begins almost immediately following the perception; he has also traced preconscious perceptions through the NREM periods to the point of contact with the REM state when activation of the unconscious would seem to occur. In their passage through the NREM to the REM state the perceptions undergo increasing distortion. (In recent studies by Baekeland et al. [1968], a high percentage of references in dream content to associations prior to sleep support Fisher's findings.) Again, Offenkrantz and Rechtschaffen (1963) studying sequential dreams in the laboratory reported that solutions of current problems became apparent in later dreams of a series during the same night. It must also be remembered that many dreams are not reported to us in clinical and laboratory studies. Present findings suggest that problem-solving plays a greater part in dreaming than has previously been believed.

Whitman (1963) studied in the sleep laboratory the problem of forgetting of dreams in two patients who were undergoing intensive psychotherapy. He noted that there was a difference in the content of dreams that were told to the laboratory aide and those told to the therapist. Dreams which contained transference material related to the therapist, especially when this was of a sexual or hostile nature, would be reported to the laboratory aide but not to the therapist and vice versa. Thus, both in dreams that were reported on awakening in the sleep laboratory and those reported the following day, the relationship with the listener became crucial to the process of recall. From 10 to 30 per cent of dreams are not reported when subjects are awakened in the sleep laboratory. Whitman compares this type of forgetting with Freud's primal repression. Dreams which would have been remembered if the subjects had been awakened in the laboratory have been subject to what Freud described as repression proper. It is a constant finding, in this connection, that even with the best motivated subjects only one or two dreams are reported in the morning out of a large number that have occurred during the night.

Whitman suggested that the hallucinatory experience of the dream provides a partial oral satisfaction and that the dream is introduced in the third month of life to replace the night feeding which is usually omitted at that time. Thus the dream serves multiple functions in replacing the missing feeding, providing oral satisfaction, and preserving sleep. This is consistent with Fisher's observation that with the development of dreaming as a psychological event with the capacity for instinctual drive discharge, earlier modes of discharge used by the infant by motor pathways during REM states can be replaced by the dream so that REM sleep diminishes in quantity.

Another area in which sleep laboratory and clinical studies have been usefully combined is that of an investigation of psychosomatic states by Nowlin, Silverman et al. (1965). They found, in four patients with angina pectoris, that out of a total of 39 episodes of nocturnal angina which occurred in the sleep laboratory, 32 were associated with REM periods. Dreams which preceded awakening with pain were concerned with strenuous physical activity or emotions of fear, anger, and frustration. Armstrong et al. (1965) reported elevations of HCl in peptic ulcer patients during REM states, elevations which do not occur normally.

In a recent paper in which he formulated a theory of psychosomatic disorders, Reiser (1966) pointed to the analogy between the disturbances in the REM states and those observed in the neonate and in certain psychosomatic illnesses. These similarities involve alterations in range and lability of autonomic functions as well as biochemical and endocrine changes. It has also been shown that deep visceral functions involved in psychosomatic disorders may be altered by manipulation of subcortical structures involving the limbic system. Mason (1960) et al. have delineated circuits from the hippocampus to the hypothalamus which are involved in release of adrenal hormones; Friedman (1963) and Wolff (1964) demonstrated correlations between the effectiveness of ego defenses under stress and hormone levels. (Schur had previously described an altered state of consciousness and a regressed ego state as the psychological substrate for the precipitation of disease.) In the light of these findings and concepts Reiser (1966) suggests that central connections for the psychosomatic diseases are part of the normal structure of the brain and that under certain conditions specific neural circuits may be discharged into the body, thereby activating endocrine and visceral structures. One physiological state that may provide the appropriate condition for facilitating this process is REM sleep. Accordingly, in conditions of ego defensive breakdown, and perhaps, altered states of consciousness, the REM state will function to precipitate the kind of pathological disturbance such as occurred in those patients with nocturnal angina and alterations in gastric HCl. Reiser points out that this theory is subject to further experimental testing in the sleep laboratory.

Finally, I would like to refer to certain combined clinical and laboratory studies of the manic-depressive psychosis. Bunney and Hartmann (1965) in a longitudinal study of a patient who alternated every 48 hours between mania and depression found that in manic states the corticosteroid levels were low and in depressed states high. They believed that it was the presence, however, of the defense of denial rather than the state of mania itself that was accompanied by the low steroid levels. Hartmann (1968) later reported that he had observed that changes from depression to mania tended to occur during sleep. Mendels and Hawkins (1968) found diminished REM time and diminished sleep in both depression and mania.

Snyder (1968), confirming their findings, reported also that in a study of depressive psychoses clinical improvement was accompanied and sometimes anticipated by a compensatory increase in REM time. In one involutional patient in whom considerable REM compensation occurred there was no clinical improvement. Snyder ascribes this to the fact that sleep was not replaced. He believes that the loss of sleep is cardinal in severe depressions and that a vicious cycle is created with the accompanying loss of REM. Some psychotic and nonpsychotic depressive patients have unusually intense rapid eye movements within their REM periods. This may be a further attempt at compensation. The question arises as to whether the REM deficit and the need for compensation may not be compounded by a disruption in the ability of the manic-depressive patient to utilize the dream in achieving discharge in the manner that seems to occur in infancy when, with diminution in REM time, the dream function is able through the hallucinatory process to take over a discharge function.

In the manic patient, as Lewin has suggested, the unfinished, undischarged dream is continued into the waking state in which a continuation of denying secondary elaborations and motor discharge is manifest. This solution, because of his different defensive structure, is not available to the depressed patient.

As yet, only a beginning has been made in these investigations of the manic-depressive states, but they have opened up an area of collaborative research by psychiatrists, psychoanalysts, physiologists, and psychologists which has already been extended to the study of schizophrenia and other psychotic states.

## SUMMARY

In summary, we have reviewed some experimental observations, psychological and physiological, which have broadened our understanding of dream functioning in its relationship to clinical psychiatry and to psychoanalytic theory. Investigations of REM sleep have in some respects confirmed Freud's original ideas and in others have led to some modification of them.

Freud's conception of a loss of pre-spinal cathexis during dreaming, of the wish-fulfilling discharge function of the dream and the participation in dream functioning of internal endogenous stimulation to replace a loss of sensory input have been confirmed by laboratory investigations. They have indeed been related to certain specific brain areas involved with the limbic system. Freud's idea that the majority of dreams has a sexual aspect is supported by the observations of sexual activation in REM states shown in sustained penile erections and in the motor, especially oral activity of the neonatal period.

The role of problem-solving in dreams would appear to be a greater one than Freud had believed. As to the function of the dream "as guardian of sleep" some modification is necessary since we know that dreaming goes on during specified and physiologically determined periods during the night while sleep continues when we are not dreaming. During the REM states, however, the dream would appear to coordinate its psychological with an existing organismic function to provide an opportunity for instinctual discharge and perhaps, during these periods, to preserve sleep.

On the clinical side, the opportunities for research in the rela-

164     CURRENTS IN PSYCHOANALYSIS

tionship of the dream and REM states to the psychosomatic disorders and to the psychoses has been discussed.

REFERENCES

Armstrong, R. H. et al. (1965), Dreams and gastric secretions in duodenal ulcer patients. *New Physn.*, 14:241.
Aserinsky, E. and Kleitman, N. (1955), Two types of ocular motility occurring in sleep. *J. Appl. Physiol.*, 8:1–10.
Baekeland, F. et al. (1968), Presleep mentation and dream reports. *Arch. Gen. Psychiat.*, 19:300–312.
Baldridge, B. J., Whitman, R. M., and Kramer, M. (1965), The concurrence of fine muscle activity and rapid eye movements during sleep. *Psychosomat. Med.*, 27:19–26.
Berger, R. J. (1963), Experimental modification of dream content by meaningful verbal stimuli. *Brit. J. Psychiat.*, 109:722–740.
Bizzi, E. (1965), Discharge patterns of lateral geniculate neuroses during paradoxical sleep. Association for Psychophysiological Study of Sleep, Washington, D. C.
Bunney, W. and Hartmann, E. (1965), Study of a patient with forty-eight hour manic-depressive cycles. *Arch. Gen. Psychiat.*, 12:611–618.
Dement, W. and Kleitman, N. (1957), The relation of eye movements sleep to dream activity. *J. Exp. Psychol.*, 53:339–346.
Fisher, C. (1954), Dreams and perception. *J. Amer. Psychoanal. Assn.*, 2:389–445.
—— (1957), A study of the preliminary stages of the construction of dream images. *J. Amer. Psychoanal. Assn.*, 5:5–60.
—— and Dement, W. C. (1963), Studies on the psychopathology of sleep and dreams. *Amer. J. Psychiat.*, 119.
—— (1963), Dream development in relation to NREM and REM stages of sleep. Association for Psychophysiological Study of Sleep, Washington, D. C.
——, Gross, J. S. and Zuch, J. (1965), A cycle of penile erections synchronous with dreaming (REM sleep). *Arch. Gen. Psychiat.*, 12:29–45.
French, T. M. (1941), Goal mechanism and integrative field. *Psychosomat. Med.*, 3:226–252.
Freud, S. (1900), The interpretation of dreams. *Standard Edition*, 4 & 5. London: Hogarth Press, 1953.
—— (1950 [1895]), Project for a scientific psychology. *Standard Edition*, 1. London: Hogarth Press, 1966.
Friedmann, S. B. et al. (1963), Urine 17-hydroxycorticosteroid levels in parents of children with neoplastic disease. *Psychosomat. Med.*, 25:364–376.
Hartmann, E. (1968), Longitudinal studies of sleep and dream patterns in manic-depressive patients. *Arch. Gen. Psychiat.* 19:312–330.
Hawkins, D. R. (1966), A review of psychoanalytic dream theory in the

light of recent psychophysiological studies of sleep and dreaming. *Brit. J. Med. Psychol.*, 39:85–104.

Hodes, R. and Dement, W. C. (1964), Depression of electrically induced reflexes in maintaining low voltage EEG "sleep." *Electroenceph. Clin. Neurophysiol.*, 17:617–629.

Isakower, O. (1939), On the exceptional position of the auditory sphere. *Int. J. Psycho-Anal.*, 20:340–348.

Jouvet, M. (1961), Telencephalic and rhombencephalic sleep in the cat. In: *Ciba Found. Symposium on the Nature of Sleep*, eds. G. Wolstenholme and M. O'Connor. Boston: Little, Brown and Co., pp. 188–208.

—— (1967), Neurophysiology of the states of sleep. *Physiol. Rev.*, 47:117–177.

Lewin, B. D. (1950), *The Psychoanalysis of Elation*. New York: W. W. Norton & Co.

—— (1952), Phobic symptoms and dream interpretation. *Psychoanal. Quart.*, 21:295–322.

—— (1953), The forgetting of dreams. In: *Drives, Affects, Behavior*, ed. R. M. Lowenstein. New York: International Universities Press, pp. 191–202.

—— (1955), Clinical hints from dream studies. *Bull. Menninger Clin.*, 19:73–85.

Mason, J. W. et al. (1960), Limbic system influences on the pituitary-adrenal cortical system. *Psychosomat. Med.*, 22:322.

Meissner, W. W. (1968), Dreaming as process. *Int. J. Psycho-Anal.*, 49:63–79.

Mendels, J. and Hawkins, D. R. (1968), Sleep and depression. *Arch. Gen. Psychiat.*, 19:445–453.

Noble, D., Price, D. B. and Gilder, R. (1954), Psychiatric disturbances following amputation. *Amer. J. Psychiat.*, 110:609–613.

—— and Rosenberg, S. (1967), Auditory residues in dream formation. In: *Crosscurrents in Psychiatry and Psychoanalysis*, ed. R. W. Gibson. Philadelphia: J. B. Lippincott Co.

Nowlin, J. B. et al. (1965), The association of nocturnal angina pectoris with dreaming. *Ann. Int. Med.*, 63:1040–1046.

Offenkrantz, W. and Rechtschaffen, A. (1963), Clinical studies of sequential dreams. *Arch. Gen. Psychiat.*, 8:497–508.

Poetzl, O. (1960), The relationship between experimentally induced dream images and induced vision. [*Psychological Issues*, Monogr. 7]. New York: International Universities Press, pp. 41–120.

Rechtschaffen, A. and Foulkes, D. (1965), Effect of visual stimuli on dream content. *Percept. Mot. Skills*, 20:1149–1160.

Reiser, M. F. (1966), Toward an integrated psychoanalytic-physiological theory of psychosomatic disorders. In: *Psychoanalysis; A General Psychology*, eds. R. M. Loewenstein et al. New York: International Universities Press, pp. 570–582.

Schilder, P. (1953), *Medical Psychology*. New York: International Universities Press.

Sharpe, E. F. (1949), *Dream Analysis*, London: Hogarth Press.

Snyder, F. (1965), The new biology of dreaming. *Arch. Gen. Psychiat.,* 8:381–391.

—— et al. (1967), Phenomenology of dreaming. Paper presented at a meeting of The Association for the Psychophysiological Study of Sleep, Washington, D. C.

—— (1968), Sleep disturbance in relation to acute psychosis. From draft of paper presented at Symposium on Physiology and Pathology of Sleep. U.C.L.A., May 22–23.

Whitman, R. M. (1963), Remembering and forgetting dreams in psycho-analysis. *J. Amer. Psychoanal. Assn.,* 11:752–774.

Wolff, C. T. et al. (1964), Relationship between psychological defenses and mean urinary 17-hydroxycorticosteroid rates, I & II. *Psychosomat. Med.,* 26:575–609.

# 12. DREAMS, TECHNIQUE, AND INSIGHT

HERBERT F. WALDHORN, M.D.

It will be the aim of this presentation to discuss some theoretical and technical problems relating to the goals of dream interpretation in psychoanalysis. A sizeable number of historical factors can be seen to play a role in determining a special emphasis on dreams in the writings and clinical work of many analysts. Essentially, this reflects a tendency to consider the dream as a unique element of mental life, governed by psychological rules and requiring technical approaches different from those applicable in the analysis of the remainder of a patient's psychic productions. Experience has shown that this tendency can lead to distortions and error in therapeutic work. This is suggested by the appearance in the literature, at periodic intervals, of injunctions warning against special interest in or inappropriate technical interventions relating to dreams. It may be that the opportunity to place the development of some of these ways of looking at dreams in psychoanalysis in historical perspective can be of help in diminishing the misconceptions and technical difficulties which often accompany them. At the same time, certain principles of psychoanalytic theory and technique may be reexamined with relevance to the goals of dream interpretation. One way of focusing such a survey would be to consider the far-reaching significance of the therapeutic goal of insight and the technical implications involved in the achieving and integrating of insight in analysis. This represents one of the points at which the theory of therapy intersects with the theory of the psychic apparatus and psychic functioning. This provides us with a valuable opportunity to access both the suitability and theoretical consistency of our technical procedures, since we are able to examine clinical phenomena from more than from one critical vantage point.

In a contribution to the Symposium on "The Theory of Technique" at the Centenary Scientific meetings of the British Psycho-Analytical Society in 1956, Ernst Kris noted that the history of psychoanalysis could be described in terms of the continuing interaction between theory and technique. He spoke of the impact on technique of the access to new clinical pictures in the course of the expansion of psychoanalytic experience. As an example, he cited the important influence of fully analyzed, obsessional neuroses on Freud's thinking at the beginning of the century, and he went on to point to other clinical phenomena of special significance since that time. Among these were the scanty first contacts with psychoses, the work with character neuroses after the First World War, the stimulating expansion of child analysis in the twenties, and the treatment of borderline cases as well as the regular contact with psychotic patients in the forties and fifties. Kris did not overlook the fact that technical advance was often instigated from the side of theoretical innovation, but he was especially interested in the study of clinical experience as the matrix within which to place and to examine incompletely understood aspects of our science. He expressed the hope that changes in technique would be studied by ". . . a percipient, historically minded, but clinically versed and interested group of colleagues . . ." using the clinical literature and the writings on technique as their sources.

The past decade or two has seen a number of such efforts undertaken, and several authors (Arlow and Brenner, 1964; Brenner, 1955; Fenichel, 1938–39; Hartmann, 1964; Hartmann, Kris, and Loewenstein, 1964; E. Kris, 1951, 1956) have shared the impression that this has been a period in which many aspects of psychoanalytic conceptualization and technical development should be reappraised in the light of the theoretical advances made by Freud and others. However, both in regard to teaching and clinical work concerning dreams, the lag in the full and consistent application of the dual instinct theory and the structural hypothesis has perhaps been most evident. No doubt, this relates to a number of historical factors, including the extraordinary impact of the publication of Freud's *The Interpretation of Dreams* (1900). The topographic hypothesis detailed in the seventh chapter had particularly been spared any extensive change through the various editions, despite Freud's many alterations in and additions to the earlier sections of this monumental work.

There are two well-known quotations from Freud's (1900) preface to the book on dreams which bear on his special attachment to this work: "During the long years, in which I have been working on the problems of neuroses I have often been in doubt and some-times been shaken in my convictions. At such times it has always been *The Interpretation of Dreams* that has given me back my certainty" (p. xxvi, Preface). "Insight such as this falls to one's lot but once in a lifetime" (p. xxxii, Preface). Now, the fact is that Freud said many different things about dreams, at different times. For example, in 1923:

> What conclusions can one draw from a correctly translated dream? I have the impression that analytic practice has not always avoided errors on this point, partly owing to an exaggerated respect for the 'mysterious unconscious.' It is only too easy to forget that a dream is as a rule merely a thought like any other, made possible by a re-laxation of the censorship and by unconscious reinforcement, and dis-torted by the operation of the censorship and unconscious revision [p. 112].

Nevertheless, the first pair of quotations have been cited on numer-ous occasions as an implied justification for the retention of the topographic hypothesis as a basis for clinical understanding and theoretical orientation, with certain technical consequences. Kris (1954), in a critical essay written on the occasion of the appear-ance of volumes IV and V of the *Standard Edition,* places Freud's remarks in an illuminating historical perspective, but the weight of imposing tradition still seems to be demonstrated in current literature and training curricula as a special emphasis on the study of dreams. Greenson (1967) for example, gives well over a hundred clinical vignettes in which he describes the technical procedures (and problems) involved in analyzing resistance and transference phenomena. Only about a quarter of these have to do with dreams, and in most instances the therapeutic work cited is not dream analysis. It is accomplished by skillful and persistent elucidation of the unconscious meaning and interrelationship of slips, symptoms, affective responses, nuances of wording and allusion, nonverbal behavior, and features of the course of events within and outside of the analytic sessions. Nevertheless, he states: "Dreams are the single most important means of access to the unconscious, to the repressed, and to the instinctual life of the patient" (p. 67).

The theoretical conception of the neurosogenic role of "repressed" unconscious material was the cornerstone of early analytic understanding. This led to the stress in analytic work on the uncovering of unconscious infantile sexual wishes and to the conviction that the affect-laden airing of these hidden residues was the therapeutic event *par excellence*. Such an attitude, echoes of which can be heard in the sentence quoted above, was consistent with, and, in a certain sense, demanded by the topographic theory of mental functioning. As our theories have become more internally consistent and sophisticated, and our understanding of neurosogenesis centered more verifiably on the phenomena of anxiety and conflict, a greater diversity of approaches to the problems of analytic technique has evolved. We now believe that the mental life of patients, as conveyed by their communications and behavior in the analysis, reflects more than the influence of their repressed instinctual wishes and the breakdown of repression leading to symptomatic discharge. Defensive, adaptive, moralistic, and conflict-free responses also find expression in the behavior and character of every patient, and contribute to the complex compromises which determine every moment of mental life, including dreaming. Accordingly, the theory of therapy must conform to the technical demands (and opportunities) occasioned by this increasing understanding of the complexity of mental life, in regard to which the structural hypothesis appears to offer the most valuable and instructive guide.

In the early period of analysis, the newly explored science was defined as a depth psychology, and dream analysis was considered the paradigmatic essence of therapeutic psychoanalysis. One of the invaluable legacies of this period has been the genetic approach to the understanding of mental phenomena. The modern reliance on the structural theory seems, to some analysts, an insufficient or misleading approach to some aspects of clinical work, as if this approach caused a disregard of the memories to be mined in the realm of the unconscious, especially by means of work with dreams. Far from contradicting the genetic emphasis in analytic investigation, it may well be that our comprehension of the inter-systemic and intrasystemic conflicts often provides the most effective, workable data for therapeutic developments. Such a viewpoint enriches our ability both to connect the present with the past and to convey the subtlety often involved in transference reliving. Many aspects of unconscious fantasy life become understandable only when the role of aggression, guilt, the vicissitudes of conflict-determined self-representation, and the operation of the many defensive operations encountered in anxiety-induced regression are taken into account.

Moreover, the analytic process has a temporal aspect, and its unfolding confronts us with the possibility of reexperiencing in our clinical work the relevant features of the genesis of the content under study. Precisely because we observe a great array of data progressively appearing in a certain sequence, with a certain degree of repetitiveness, with a certain tempo of development and elaboration, and with varying degrees of transience, we must bear in mind the necessity of considering knowledge as provisional and incomplete, often for a long period of time. This is what lies behind the technical rules about working through and the need for patient observation of confirmatory information and developments before we can feel convinced about our therapeutic achievements. Despite the general readiness to accept the inevitable gradualness of our understanding and the slow, irregular growth of the patient's ability to comprehend and use what we interpret to him, dreams are often treated as affording opportunities to make giant leaps (even back to intrauterine existence, according to Kleinian authors), and to lead to ready-made insights into pathogenic wishes and conflicts.

The historical features alluded to above account for some of the preoccupation with the dream as a separate and unique mental phenomenon which is epitomized by the reference to "the royal road to the unconscious." In part, this is an example of the well-known phenomenon, encountered in many sciences, of a lag in the acceptance and application of theoretical advances. In each case, the determinants of this lag are always multiple and varied. To begin with, the delay in the integration of newer psychoanalytic theory into clinical writing and technique is a consequence of the existence of long-established patterns of analytic thought and teaching which are not easily dislodged. In addition, we find that there is a widespread and quietly persistent psychological resistance to the unpalatably fundamental role of sexuality and aggression in Freudian theory. This is a resistance which is encountered anew in each generation of students, indeed, in each individual. Added to this, there is a special resistance occasioned by the complexity of a great deal of post-Freudian analytic thought. The combined impact of these and many other factors has frequently led to over-simplifications and vulgarizations in the literature, often despite manifestly good intentions.

Kris' (1956) paper, mentioned at the beginning of this contribution, stands at the other extreme, and demonstrates the inestimable value of a consistent, systematic application of the dual instinct theory (extended by the inclusion of the concepts of neutralization and deneutralization) and the structural hypothesis as a model for psychoanalytic investigation. His discussion was made even more felicitous by his abstraction of the "good analytic hour" with its culmination in a piece of insight. At a later point, we will be referring to the phenomenon of insight, its development, extensiveness, miscarriage or persistence as we examine questions about dreams and technique, but for the moment we may approach this matter along a different course.

Interpretation is the prime tool of psychoanalysis, and the interpretation of the transference is considered one of the hallmarks of analysis as a distinct psychotherapeutic technique. What we ultimately find to interpret, in the course of considering all the material brought to us by our patients—speech, behavior, characteristic rhythms and patterns of functioning, life styles—are the derivatives of unconscious conflicts. The genetic, dynamic, and economic aspects of psychic functioning, as reflected in the associations and other data from the couch, determine, by their simultaneous and constantly changing interplay, the nature of the challenge to understanding faced by the analyst at each moment in his work. Waelder's (1930) formulation of the principle of multiple function and the consideration of the structural significance and interrelationships (conflicts) of mental processes, make it possible at each point to assemble some picture of the nature of the clinical problem before us. While Freud (1912) warned against attempting to ". . . formulate a case scientifically while treatment is proceeding . . ." and urged a readiness to be led by the patient to something different from what was expected, we inevitably construct some sort of temporary framework for understanding (Fenichel, 1941), allowing for modification of our assessments as experience unfolds. For this purpose, we make use of the symptomatology, impressions of the personality, behavior of the individual, and aspects of his history and memories.

At this point, it might be well to recall Glover's (1931) differentiation between incomplete interpretations and inexact interpretations. The perils connected with the inexact interpretation have been described and documented in many contributions. They result from the avoidance of the pertinent unconscious or infantile details which are sidestepped in the interpretation. This enables the patient to repress, or otherwise defend against the deeper and more threatening meaning of his conflicts. Despite the consequent improvement or stabilization of functioning that can sometimes result from the displacement of the patient's real problems onto the formula offered in the inexact interpretation, genuine knowledge is forfeited by the procedure. In addition, the new defensive structures which are elaborated receive so strong a reinforcement that they tend to become extremely persistent or even unmodifiable.

The incomplete interpretation is, of course, the commonest form in analytic work, for it is the means by which we gradually approach the unconscious significance of the psychic material under observation. Our ability to reach an understanding of the unconscious conflicts of our patients proceeds in small analytic steps (including detours and setbacks). Moreover, our ability to deal with the additional impediments to the readiness of the patient to accept, comprehend, and integrate the interpretation we offer, also depends upon a gradual and multi-pronged attack. Definitive progress in analytic work depends most often on the confluence of resistance interpretation, instinctual pressure in the patient (especially as manifested in the transference), superego enhancement of honesty and diligence in the patient's participation in the work, and the meaningfulness of successful genetic connections, among other factors.

In the paper referred to initially, Kris emphasized the ego side of this array of developments, when he spoke of the crumbling of a resistant structure as a prelude to the appearance of insight. The contributions which are derived from tensions and economic shifts involving the other realms of the psychic apparatus, and even those which reflect influential impacts from external reality, must not be disregarded in the effort to understand therapeutic change, even if it is true that the ego's functioning is the final common path for the expression of the relevant psychic phenomena. It is as incorrect to consider psychoanalysis equivalent to ego analysis as it is to conceive of it as primarily the search for the derivatives of the repressed id. This is not contradicted by the fact of the enrichment of our technical armamentarium ever since the implications of the structural hypothesis, especially ego functioning, have been explored and tested in clinical work. The key to an optimal technical approach is strongly indicated by our concept of psychoanalysis as the science of human mental conflict, and by our appreciation of the principles of psychic causality and overdetermination. In this connection, Hartmann's (1951) consideration of the multiple appeal of interpretations has an important place alongside of Waelder's aforementioned reminders about the principle of multiple functioning.

Certain problems of interpretation can be examined in the light of these observations. It can be seen that premature constructions of the details of infantile events from initial screen memories can tend to be hindering and misleading. Nevertheless, the temptation to make such formulations is often very great, especially if the analyst experiences anxiety and a sense of impotence when the clinical picture is confusing, and his understanding of it is incomplete. Such partial understanding must be accepted and patiently dealt with at every stage of the analysis.

The traditional view of psychoanalysis as a psychology of the depths, and the accompanying view of dreams as offering more direct access to unconscious contents than other psychic productions, can make it more enticing to attempt such premature leaps. We know that problems of defense and resistance, as well as those derived from superego pressures and the desires for transference gratification, require the gradual use of preparatory interventions, in addition to care in the timing, dosage, and sequence of our interpretations. Despite this, the appearance of a dream report seems, to some analysts, to be a license for the abandonment of analytic precision and tact. Fenichel (1941) stated the problem succinctly:

> What has been said about the dynamics and economics of interpretation in general, applies, of course, to the dream. Dream interpretations that are incorrect from the economic standpoint [i.e., which are offered without suitable regard for the therapeutic needs and psychological realities of the moment] are not only not accepted, but make the analysis difficult or spoil it for later on, because through such interpretations the patient gets a premature, intellectual familiarity with the ideational content of his unconscious, and the analyst is then in the position of one who has shot off his ammunition before it was possible to hit the mark [p. 50].

When Kris (1956) abstracted "the good analytic hour" as the culmination of certain advances in the analytic work with the patient, he anchored his approach in the discussion of the integrative and synthetic functions of the ego, with its resultant achievement of a new configuration of ideas, a new insight. He noted that not infrequently, a dream and accompanying associations may combine with some affect-laden memory as a precursor to the sudden beginning of an all-inclusive comprehension. New elements may appear ". . . as if they had always been familiar, so well do they seem to fit into things. And when the analyst interprets, sometimes all he needs to say can be put into a question. The patient may well do the summing up by himself, and himself arrive at a conclusion" (p. 446). Kris explicitly considered as inadequate the explanation that such a confluence of events merely represented the tendency of the repressed to reach consciousness (even in the allegedly less distorted channel of a dream). He took pains to point out that such results are the reaction to preceding analytic work, including ". . . the crumbling of a resistant structure (not the random interpretation of an isolated evidence of resistance) . . ." (p. 447). The entire presentation emphasized that the development of insight, just as any other manifestation of a patient's psychic functioning, must be examined in the context of the entire analytic situation and the patient's response to the analytic process itself.

It is in regard to the discussion of miscarriages of insight that we find clinical observations of considerable technical significance. In what might be called deceptively good hours, insight appears under the influence, for example, of a wish to merge with the analyst, or to win his praise or love. At other times or in other patients, such aims may be defended against with the appearance of a competitive display of independence. Such pseudo insights always tend to reinforce resistance, leading in the most obvious instances to the growth of intellectualization, but in the common, insidious example, to the emptiness of insight and the lack of any therapeutic advance. ". . . partial or pseudo insight tends to become a façade behind which illness and character deformation can proliferate . . ." (p. 499). Kris urged that the function of the insight and the use to which it is put always be scrutinized for the degree of instinctual gratification or defense involved.

Such scrupulous and thoroughgoing analysis, applied to the long-awaited and struggled-for insights, seems in notable contrast to the technical approach which some analysts appear to believe is warranted for dreams. We have noted that there are many occasions where such special attention to dream interpretation seems equated with a relaxation of analytic rigor. The extreme example of this attitude is represented by the assumption that the manifest content of a dream can regularly be interpreted without the patient's immediate associations. While familiarity with a patient's style, defensive patterns, preoccupations, and preferred symbolic usages may on some occasions make educated guesses possible, so many meanings may simultaneously be expressed by even a single dream element that reliance on the associations of the hour is clearly indicated. The ability to translate symbols and to understand the possible allusions in a portion of the *latent* content of a dream develops piecemeal, and, as was said before, leads to tentative assumptions before validated interpretations are reached. In any event, and certainly insofar as *manifest* content is concerned, we should always make a distinction between what the analyst understands about the dream (or other item of material), and what is presented to the patient in connection with it. Accordingly, we speak of the need for correlating the dream work with every other pertinent aspect of the clinical picture at the moment, rather than adhering to a view which singles out dreams as an atypical communication with rules of interpretation unique for it. Another of Freud's (1911) basic injunctions covers this ground very well, yet it often seems not to have had the impact one would expect:

> I submit, therefore, that dream interpretation should not be pursued in analytic treatment as an art for its own sake, but that its handling should be subject to those technical rules that govern the conduct of the treatment as a whole . . . [The] analyst should always be aware of the surface of the patient's mind at any given moment . . . he should know what complexes and resistances are active in [the patient] at the time and what conscious reaction to them will govern his behavior. It is scarcely ever right to sacrifice this therapeutic aim to an interest in dream interpretation . . . [p. 94].

On many occasions, one hears of dreams being accorded a prime role in the confirmation of interpretations and reconstructions. This view was especially prominent in the early days of analysis, and it has largely given way to an understanding that a wide array of subsequent phenomena may bear on the accuracy of an interpretation. Among others, these include the appearance of further associations, affects, memories, a new understanding or acceptance of the relevance of previously unconnected experiences, a change in the patient's unconscious fantasy as reflected in diminution of anxiety or symptoms, including nonverbal bodily responses, and changes in the transference tension. They may all make their appearance, severally or individually, with or without a dream which elaborates what has been presented and worked on. Any of the above, as well as other responses, can offer productive leads for the pursuit of the deeper meaning and essential connections of the data at hand. This is a fact which one would less likely overlook or neglect if the value of working with (and the waiting for) dream confirmation were kept in proper perspective.

The same sort of broadening of viewpoint can be observed in the crucial work of reconstruction, for the shifts in and extensions of Freud's theoretical approach can be clearly seen in the difference between his elaboration of the Wolf Man's history and his (1937) paper on "Constructions in Analysis." In the latter work, he identifies the sources of the material to be used in recovering lost memories as dream contents, the patient's free associations (ideas) and his accompanying or suppressed affects, especially as seen in repetitions and transference. Even in his laborious work with the Rat Man, as depicted in the daily notes of the therapy (translated, 1955) Freud makes reference to dreams only about a dozen times, and the notes seem to show that he predominantly focussed his efforts on the wishes and conflicts exposed and elaborated in the patient's symptoms, obsessive formulae, slips, and other associations and behavior in the hour. Freud's technical injunctions in his 1911 paper on "Dream Interpretation" seem to have been firmly based on his own clinical experience, and the main theme of working within each hour has had its value amply proven, before and since.

Let us return to the topic of analytic insight. We think of insight appearing as the end result of a long process which, on the part of the analyst, involves a considerable amount of preparatory work before the crucial interpretations are arrived at. Loewenstein (1957) offers an extremely penetrating discussion of the variety

and function of the limited interpretations, clarifications, and confrontations involved in the therapeutic process, and speaks of the
way in which they coalesce therapeutically in the preparation of
the patient for this crucial next step. To begin with, we see a facilitation of recall, and what Loewenstein refers to as a significant
regrouping of material that, together, enable the patient to make
connections between present and past, and other dissociated content. In addition, there is a reciprocal extension of comprehension
and growing insight in the analyst that increase the likelihood of
an appropriate genetic interpretation and reconstruction. From the
technical side, the information the analyst gleans by closely observing the detailed features of this reciprocal process in himself
and the patient is of the greatest value in helping to choose the
wording, sequence, dosage, and timing of his interpretations, to
be able to proceed with analytic tact. Since, in the last decades,
we have been seeing more patients who are familiar with psychoanalytic formulations as well as a reportedly more widespread use
of jargon and other intellectualized resistances, Loewenstein's
(1951) observations about "reconstruction upward" also have a
considerable pertinence, as they do in many other situations, not
necessarily based on the particular resistances just noted.

It follows that our familiarity with our patient, his level of regression and anxiety, the nature of his current fantasies and transference involvements, the defensive pressures implicit in his associations and behavior, and our understanding of the significance
of the moment in the analytic process, determine our choice of
intervention from hour to hour. The analysis of dream material,
as is the case with all the other data the patient may produce,
will vary in degree of utility, insofar as advancing the analytic work,
from time to time, from situation to situation. Latent dream content
can be used in many ways, if it can be arrived at from the reported
dream and the work with the patient's associations, or from the
hints as to the nature of the distortions involved in the dream
work. It may, for example, yield some insight into the state of
resistance and the defensive patterns related to it. In another instance, light may be thrown on features of the patient's regression,
its depth, or the rate and sequence of the regressive movement

in relationship to conflict and stress. Transference interpretation may be facilitated by discerning allusions to recurring patterns of object relations or libidinal or aggressive discharge tendencies. On some occasions, the fruitful material of the dream interpretation may point to developmental traumata and the resultant ego and superego defects. Sometimes we can learn more about crucial identifications and other psychic residues so that a picture of the character structure can be gradually assembled.

The symbolic language of the dream may be intelligible to the analyst in a technically useful way, provided that he does not fall into the trap of promptly offering translations of symbolic equivalents, and reserves his knowledge for the construction of an interpretation the patient can accept, or at least deal with, without new defensive elaboration. All of these considerations make it likely that some aspects of the dream will have a higher priority for technical attention than others, and that the original goal of the "beautiful dream interpretation" will yield to therapeutic objectives consistent with both the needs of the patient and the demands of theory. This is the rule we apply to all other aspects of our interpretive and reconstructive work carried on through the study of symptoms, defenses, parapraxes, character, behavior and everything else our patient brings to us. Such considerations

> . . . raise a question as to the wisdom, or even the possibility of dealing with dreams by attempting an exhaustive tracing out of *all* the latent thoughts and the delineation of *every* detail of the dream work. Instead, therapeutic requirements would inevitably demand a concentration on limited goals, according to the interplay of [several critical] factors . . . [Waldhorn, 1967, p. 102].

As regards the question of limited goals, just as is the case with all other analytic interpretations, we may say that dreams can be dealt with in two major ways. We can primarily interpret the meaning of a dream or dream element, that is, either the wish or some related aspect of the conflict or compromise involved. Secondly, we can interpret so as to lead to the development of information by the elucidation of latent thoughts, or by an understanding of the intermediate links in a thought chain. The choice is made with reference to the critical factors alluded to above. We can summarize this in another way. The critical factors are those which determine our ability to work with any of our patients' associations: the prior understanding of the relevant material in both patient and analyst, the resistance to such material, based on its anxiety-producing potential, the resistance related to the current transference situation, and the relative importance for the patient of the material involved compared to other simultaneous concerns and productions. A psychoanalytic dream interpretation makes sense and is therapeutically useful only in the context of the total mental functioning of the person.

The dynamic processes involved in the achieving of insight include recognition and recall and, ultimately, cognition and the integration of newly acquired understandings. It is in connection with the recovery of infantile memories, of acknowledged importance in the dynamic processes just mentioned, that the dream is considered by some to have an extraordinary position in technical work. Some of the reasoning involved starts with the fact that the regressive changes attendant upon sleep involve the diminution of certain ego and superego functions. One consequence of this can be an increased ease of expression of drive representations, particularly as the result of the partial suppression of the capacity to test reality. Such shifts in intersystemic relationships occur, of course, in other temporary regressions (daydreams, reveries, fatigue, inattention, excitement, etc.) and they share with the dream varying degrees of reversion to more infantile modes of mental functioning, including a reliance on visual imagery. Nevertheless, some authors still maintain that it is the prominence of visual imagery as an important feature of regressed psychic functioning which endows the dream with a special utility in analysis. They also believe that important memories from early infantile life could only be recovered in the form of visual representations because the incidents referred to come from a preverbal period. With similar logic, it has been claimed that dreams might be especially applicable to the study of psychosomatic illnesses and physiological dysfunction, an idea which is connected with the putative phenomenon of (nonverbal) organ memory.

It is not possible here to treat the entire question of the origins and nature of infantile thought and memory and its relationship to the acquisition of language and the function of speech. We can only make the minimal comment that this is something about which, we must confess, our knowledge is extremely limited. In any event, we are incontrovertibly faced with the fact that verbal formulations and communications provide the content of our analytic sessions in the main, and are the form in which our patients produce dream reports. In addition, many aspects of dreaming are not visual representations and may still be eminently analyzable. These include affective states in the dream situation as well as in the moments of awakening, thoughts and spoken phrases, experienced and reported muscular and other sensations, temporal elements and many others (Arlow and Brenner, 1964). The significance of "seeing" something, which is claimed as a special modality by which a dream conveys a sense of conviction to the patient concerning unconscious phenomena and analytic interpretations, can be overstressed. The application of the idea of "seeing" may be an inordinate extension of a metaphor rather than the meaningful invocation of verified assumptions about psychic functioning and analytic work. In any event, we communicate our interpretations in words, discuss ideas, evoke verbal responses from our patients, while relying upon language as the framework within which recall, understanding, and finally, insight become formulated and integrated. For every patient for whom mental life is a panoply of images, there must be a far greater number for whom language is the foundation of thought. One gets the feeling of the persistence, in the implications of this emphasis on visual imagery, of the oracular prehistory of the interpretation of dreams, of divinations at Delos, and vulgarized, modern-day psychedelia, rather than a sense of the patient humility of psychoanalytic work.

The aforementioned reference to the patient's feeling of conviction can also be used as a point of departure for some additional comments about insight. The appearance of a sense of conviction about interpretations and new understandings will vary extensively in different analyses and at different stages of the analytic work, chiefly in relation to the transference resistances and the patient's needs for his pathological structures. It can be absent, minimal, part of, or colored by an intellectual understanding or even be experienced as a vivid reliving of the genetic sequences and relationships reconstructed in the analytic work. However, as is well known, important insights may not persist in a patient's awareness for more than a short time, and then only in fragmentary form. Just as is the case with the persistence of awareness of insight, a sense of conviction about an insight cannot be considered a fundamental analytic aim in itself, however welcome and gratifying it may be to patient and analyst. The experience of insight involves a change in the relationship of drive derivatives, defense mechanisms, superego functions, and the demands of reality, combined with the subjective awareness of some aspect of this change. But the goal is only to make possible the increased participation of the operative psychic forces (chiefly less conflict-burdened ego functions) in the more economical and adaptive regulation of these conflicting demands. Freud's phrase for this process was the provision of the optimal conditions for the functioning of the ego. As analytic theory and technique developed, many more avenues of access to this goal were discovered and identified beyond those which tended to make the interpretation of dreams, often so impressive to patients, seem so uniquely important.

Dynamic changes of therapeutic value can, of course, occur without insight. In practice, our interpretations are directed, through most of the analysis, at furthering the analytic process and nurturing the patient's capacity to bring therapeutically oriented and operative patterns of functioning to the fore. Improved self-observation, self-evaluation, testing of reality, tempering of affect and activity in favor of thought and free association, increase of candor, diminution of reliance on and need for magical thinking and other infantile, chiefly defensive mechanisms—these are among the familiar areas of patient response which define the subgoals of our work. Such goals are, therefore, the goals of our work with dreams. The progress of the analysis and the slow crystallization of our efforts toward the achievement of insight and therapeutic success may entail a more tedious and less exciting-looking process than that sometimes implied in the literature emphasizing dream interpretation. For example, Altman's (1969) admirable book on *The Dream in Psychoanalysis,* takes pains to indicate that the work with patients involves a great deal more than the interventions clustered around the reported dreams, and that material additional to the reported interpretations contributed to the understanding in both patient and analyst. Nevertheless, the cataloging and titling of the many dozens of dreams, as well as the (necessarily) condensed scope of the clinical presentations, tend to make possible a misemphasis on the discoveries associated with dreams, and on their special leverage in the analytic work. It would be unfortunate if the reader believed that the memories and dynamic connections which are so attractively and wittily presented could not be arrived at in other cases, in other ways as well.

Psychoanalytic technique is a constantly evolving set of procedures, rooted in theory and influenced by a growing body of clinical experience. Each analyst develops greater precision, discipline, and finesse in his work, as his personal experience expands. The limitless diversity of our patients' productions, the absolute uniqueness of each individual's life and of each moment in time, make standardization of technique an impossibility and rigidity of style a handicap. Our literature contains many outstanding contributions from penetrating theoreticians and gifted practitioners, and is thereby an invaluable resource for study and stimulation. The avoidance of mistaken emphases and of undue preoccupation with any one aspect of analytic material over all others is a vital part of the self-critical, self-observant, and self-enriching responsibility of the analyst. Hopefully, this brief discussion of some therapeutic and technical considerations concerning dreams and insight may be of use in such a process of self-scrutiny and analytic development.

## REFERENCES

Altman, L. (1969), *The Dream in Psychoanalysis.* New York: International Universities Press.

Arlow, J. A. and Brenner, C. (1964), Psychoanalytic Concepts and the Structural Theory [*J. Amer. Psychoanal. Assn.,* Monogr. 2]. New York: International Universities Press.

Brenner, C. (1955), *An Elementary Textbook of Psychoanalysis.* New York: International Universities Press.

Fenichel, O. (1938–39), Problems of psychoanalytic technique. *Psychoanal. Quart.*, 7:421–442, 8:57–87, 164–185, 303–324, 438–470.

Fliess, R. (1953), *The Revival of Interest in the Dream*. New York: International Universities Press.

Freud, S. (1900), The interpretation of dreams. *Standard Edition*, 4 & 5. London: Hogarth Press, 1953.

—— (1909), Notes upon a case of obsessional neurosis. *Standard Edition*, 10:151–318. London: Hogarth Press, 1955.

—— (1911), The handling of dream-interpretation in psychoanalysis. *Standard Edition*, 12:91–96. London: Hogarth Press, 1958.

—— (1912), Recommendations to physicians practicing psychoanalysis. *Standard Edition*, 12:111–120. London: Hogarth Press, 1958.

—— (1917), A metapsychological supplement to the theory of dreams. *Standard Edition*, 14:222–235. London: Hogarth Press, 1957.

—— (1923a), Remarks on the theory and practice of dream interpretation. *Standard Edition*, 19:109–121. London: Hogarth Press, 1961.

—— (1923b), Two encyclopedia articles. *Standard Edition*, 18:235–259. London: Hogarth Press, 1955.

—— (1925), Some additional notes on dream-interpretation as a whole. *Standard Edition*, 19:127–138. London: Hogarth Press, 1961.

—— (1937), Constructions in psychoanalysis. *Standard Edition*, 23:255–269, London: Hogarth Press, 1964.

Glover, E. (1931), The therapeutic effect of inexact interpretation. *Int. J. Psycho-Anal.*, 12:397–411.

Greenson, R. (1967), *The Technique and Practice of Psychoanalysis*, Vol. I. New York: International Universities Press.

Hartmann, H. (1951), Technical implications of ego psychology. In: *Essays on Ego Psychology*. New York: International Universities Press, 1964, pp. 142–154.

—— (1956), The development of the ego concept in Freud's work. In: *Essays on Ego Psychology*. New York: International Universities Press, 1964, pp. 268–296.

—— and Kris, E. (1945), The genetic approach in psychoanalysis. *The Psychoanalytic Study of the Child*, 1:11–30.

——, Kris, E., and Loewenstein, R. M. (1964), Papers on psychoanalytic psychology. [*Psychol. Issues*, Monogr. 14]. New York: International Universities Press.

Kris, E. (1951), Ego psychology and interpretation in psychoanalytic therapy. *Psychoanal. Quart.*, 20:15–30.

—— (1952), *Psychoanalytic Explorations in Art*. New York: International Universities Press.

—— (1954), New contributions to the study of Freud's "The Interpretation of Dreams": a critical essay. *J. Amer. Psychoanal. Assn.*, 2:180–191.

—— (1956), On some vicissitudes of insight in psychoanalysis. *Int. J. Psycho-Anal.*, 37:445–455.

Loewenstein, R. M. (1951), The problem of interpretation. *Psychoanal. Quart.*, 20:1–14.

—— (1954), Some remarks on defenses, autonomous ego and psychoanalytic technique. *Int. J. Psycho-Anal.*, 35:188–193.

—— (1957), Some thoughts on interpretation in the theory and practice of psychoanalysis. *The Psychoanalytic Study of the Child*, 12:127–150.

Rangell, L. (1956), Panel Report: The dream in the practice of psychoanalysis. *J. Amer. Psychoanal. Assn.*, 4:122–137.

Waelder, R. (1930), The principle of multiple function: observations on over-determination. *Psychoanal. Quart.*, 5:45–62, 1936.

Waldhorn, H. F. (1967), The place of the dream in clinical psychoanalysis. [Monogr. II: *Monograph Series of the Kris Study Group of the New York Psychoanalytic Institute.*]

# 13. THE DIAGNOSTIC AND PROGNOSTIC SIGNIFICANCE OF CHILDREN'S DREAMS AND SLEEP

MELITTA SPERLING, M.D.

My interest in sleep and dream phenomena of children is of long standing (M. Sperling, 1949, 1952, 1955a, 1958, 1965). I was fortunate in having had the opportunity to follow up some of the cases which I had treated or evaluated at a very early age and to test the reliability of my predictions made then. This paper incorporates some of these experiences and observations from the treatment of severely disturbed children and adolescents in whom specific sleep disturbances had been prominent features of childhood. The treatment of children suffering from enuresis, petit mal, epilepsy, and various psychosomatic disorders such as bronchial asthma, ulcerative colitis, mucous colitis, etc., provided insight into the interrelated dynamics of dreams, sleep, and nocturnal somatic symptoms.

Before presenting some clinical data from which my conclusions and suggestions are drawn, I would like to discuss briefly the psychoanalytic concepts of sleep and dreaming and to correlate them with the findings from recent psychophysiological sleep and dream research. It is hoped that this will provide a basis for a more meaningful discussion of the phenomena with which this paper is concerned.

Freud (1899) introduced into the phenomenon of sleep an active principle—namely, the *wish* to sleep, that is, voluntary withdrawal from reality into sleep. If for neurotic reasons the wish to sleep is either absent or turned into its opposite, we meet with a neurotic sleep disturbance. Freud (1936) has shown that the most common cause of interference with the wish to sleep is anxiety. This anxiety stems from repressed impulses and wishes which threaten to break through during the state of sleep. Freud attributed to dreaming an essential sleep-protecting function. By disguised expression of repressed wishes and impulses in a compromise between wish and defense against it, the dream serves the purpose of drive discharge during sleep and protects sleep against disruption by anxiety-evoking unconscious impulses.

It is of particular interest that psychophysiological research into the phenomena of sleep and dreaming has fully confirmed Freud's early assumptions (Dement, 1964; Fisher and Dement, 1963). The findings of sleep deprivation experiments are particularly interesting in this connection. Serious personality changes and even psychotic episodes have been shown to occur in subjects who had been deprived of dreaming either by forced awakening, total sleep deprivation, or suppression of dreaming by certain drugs. This would indicate that dreaming is not only an essential nocturnal psychological activity as Freud had assumed (Freud, 1899), but perhaps even a physiological necessity.

Nightmares and the phenomena of pavor nocturnus do not seem to fit into the wish-fulfillment theory of dreams. Freud's (1936) explanation of nightmares was that they represent belated attempts at mastery of traumatic experiences which are repeated in a dream during sleep. Mastery over the traumatic stimulus is gained retrospectively through anxiety, the omission of which was the cause of the traumatic neurosis. The question may be raised why mastery of traumatic experiences which had not been possible in the waking state, should be expected to be achieved during sleep.

Jekels (1945) pointed out that sleep on its deepest level represents a danger to the existence of the conscious ego. He ascribed to the dream the function of serving as the waker of the sleeping ego. Freud (1920) had also proposed that above and beyond the function of providing hallucinatory wish fulfilment and of guarding sleep, dreams may have a more basic function, namely to awaken the sleeper and to provide a transition from the sleeping to the waking state. This assumption would seem to be fully confirmed by findings from experimental research which indicate that dreaming with its hallucinatory and especially visual imageries, takes place during REM (Rapid Eye Movement) sleep and that during these phases "A quasi-waking level of physiological activity is attained, which does not occur in any of the other sleep stages" (Fisher and Dement, 1963, p. 116).

In this connection, the findings from the psychoanalytic investigation of sleep disturbances in children and especially of the phenomena of pavor nocturnus, are of particular interest (Sperling, 1958). I described Type II of pavor nocturnus in children, which is characterized by recurrent nightmares leading to abrupt waking up, as "the traumatic neurosis" of childhood, and expressed the belief that the nightmare contrary to being a guardian of sleep and serving belated mastery of traumatic experiences, has the function of waking the sleeping child abruptly and fully because the progressive increase of anxiety during sleep represents an acute danger to the sleeping ego.

The situation is different in Type I pavor nocturnus. Here the child does not fully awaken and the confused delusional dream state continues even though the child may be out of bed, walking or talking, that is, motorically awake. I have described this type of pavor nocturnus as an episodic, psychoticlike attack limited to the night-time and the special conditions of the dream state.

The findings from the most recent dream and sleep research by Dr. Charles Fisher at Mt. Sinai Hospital (1969) in New York are of particular interest for the understanding of pavor nocturnus and nightmares. He found that the most severe nightmares with behavior resembling pavor nocturnus Type I in children (his studies are with adults) do not occur during the REM periods, that is during the superficial stages of sleep associated with dreaming, but during Stage 4, which is the period of deepest sleep. Awakening from these severe nightmares is sudden the subject appearing to be dissociated, confused, hallucinating, and unresponsive to the environment. Brain waves show a waking alpha pattern but the subject is nevertheless not fully awake. Dr. Fisher found that there is a relationship between the depth of sleep and the severity of the nightmare: the deeper the sleep, the more severe the nightmare. According to Dr. Fisher, the REM dream seems to have a mechanism that modulates anxiety, while the Stage 4 nightmare seems to indicate a massive failure of ego functioning and is more like a brief, reversible, psychotic attack which seems to resemble the pavor nocturnus Type I sleep disturbances in early childhood.

Neurotic sleep disturbances in infancy, that is, sleep disturbances for which no external or internal physical explanation can be found, are by no means a rarity. Because infants normally require a great deal of sleep, and in view of the findings from psycho-physiological sleep and dream research concerning the effects of prolonged sleep and dream deprivation, a persistent sleep disturbance in a very young child should be considered to be of serious import, even in the absence of other signs of distress. Because it is not possible to explore the dream life or the sources of the infant's sleep disturbance directly, it is advisable to investigate the mother's feelings about her child in search for the sources which provoke and maintain such a state of tension in the infant. Rarely is a psychiatrist or psychoanalyst consulted for a sleep disturbance in an infant. This is the domain of the pediatrician and here is an added indication for the desirability of educating pediatricians to the awareness of the role of the mother-child relationship in the etiology of neurotic sleep disturbances in young children. I have had an opportunity to learn about and to intervene in several such cases of infantile sleep disturbance in the treatment of the mother, and in one case, in the treatment of the grandmother of the child (Sperling, 1949).

I have treated a considerable number of children, for severely disturbed behavior, in whom sleep disturbance in infancy had been the only manifest neurotic feature of the early life. The atypical behavior and other manifestations appeared later (Sperling, 1954). The youngest child whom I could study and treat for severe sleep disturbances in play analysis was two years old (Sperling, 1952). Linda, from the time of infancy, had suffered from sleep disturbance and attacks of paroxysmal tachycardia which occurred during the night. The sleep disturbance became more intense after a tonsillectomy at age one-and-a-half and the birth of a brother when she was two years old. During this time she began to have recurrent nightmares. She would wake up screaming, confused, and hallucinating, sometimes looking for fish on her pillow who wanted to bite her, or screaming that a kitty or dog was biting her. In play analysis, intense oral-sadistic impulses directed against her mother's breast and her brother's penis were brought to the fore. She had been weaned abruptly at nine months and toilet trained before her brother's birth. She had had a tonsillectomy at one-and-a-half which she had experienced as an oral castration inflicted upon her by her mother. Linda developed fears of dogs and cats, of noises, the dark, and of being alone. The nightmares during sleep and the daytime phobias were an indication that this child felt in danger of being overcome by her threatening impulses. Her nightmares, her paroxysmal tachycardia, and her phobias were an indication that she was defending herself against ego disintegration (Sperling, 1952). The concomitant psychoanalytic treatment of her mother was an important factor in the successful outcome and in preventing a psychotic development.

A persistent sleep disturbance in a young child with recurrent nightmares is an indication that the child's ego is struggling against overwhelming anxiety. If no relief is forthcoming, there will be ego impairment resulting from crippling defenses, leading to phobias, psychosomatic illness, or even psychosis.

I should like to illustrate such a situation with one example. Four-year-old Ruth suffered from a persistent sleep disturbance with recurrent nightmares, especially about a spider in her bed who threatened to take her to the hospital. This was the earliest indication of a schizophrenia with marked paranoid trends which she developed at age eight-and-a-half. As with Linda, in this case as well, the mother had rejected her child from birth because of her sex. Ruth too had been weaned and toilet trained early and had had a tonsillectomy before the age of two which she had experienced as an oral castration inflicted upon her by her mother. She had experienced the birth of a brother at age two and of another brother at age eight, when she had a recurrence of the sleep disturbance with nightmares followed by the onset of the manifest psychosis as a loss of mother-breast-penis. Ruth too was struggling against overwhelmingly strong oral and anal-sadistic impulses, while suffering from intense breast and penis envy. However, her mother was not available for treatment and the brief play analysis at age four brought about a subsidence of the sleep disturbance, but not a change in the child's personality structure nor in a modification of the mother-child relationship (Sperling, 1949). Although it had been insufficient in preventing the psychotic development during puberty, this early intervention was an important factor in rendering Ruth amenable to treatment. She was treated successfully for her psychosis from age nine through adolescence (Sperling, 1955b). This case is cited in order to emphasize the necessity for adequate assessment of such a sleep disturbance in a young child.

During the anal phases, repression of anal-erotic and anal-sadistic impulses takes place. Whenever such repressions are excessive, abrupt, or aggravated by additional traumatic experiences, the first indication will be a disturbance of sleep. According to O. Fenichel (1942), impairment of the function of sleep is the first indication of repressive conflicts, before the individual has learned to avoid struggles by means of rigid ego attitudes, that is, before definite mechanisms of defense and specific symptoms are formed. The prognosis of such sleep disturbances is good and they can usually be handled indirectly by advising mothers to relax their demands for too early and too rigid cleanliness and conformity. In this area, however, one has to be careful of the pitfalls of mothers going to the opposite extreme whereby they set virtually no standards of performance. Substitute gratification and outlets for anal-erotic and anal-sadistic drives through physical activity and appropriate play should be provided. Bornstein (1935), Fraiberg (1950) and Wulff (1927) have described such cases.

However, my experiences from analytic work with children suffering from pavor nocturnus and sleep walking (1952, 1958,

1967, 1969), from deviate sexual behavior (1959), from enuresis (1965), and from various psychosomatic diseases such as bronchial asthma (1963b), mucous colitis (1950), ulcerative colitis (1968), petit mal, and epilepsy (1953) etc., as well as the work done with severely disturbed or psychotic children (1954), have taught me that the role of the anal phases in character and symptom formation is not yet sufficiently considered. During the anal phase, separation conflicts are activated and anal drive and ego development as well as locomotion make their expression possible. Unresolved separation conflicts of the anal phase provide the pathological basis for particularly intense oedipal conflicts. The development during this phase has a decisive influence upon the vicissitudes of the aggressive drives, of narcissism, ambivalence, and bisexuality. The ambivalence, omnipotence, and narcissism which become associated with anal processes and sphincter control may thus become the most important vehicle for control of impulses in general. Conflicts about sphincter control may become equated with control of impulses, that is, of internal reality as well as control of mother and external objects, that is, of external reality, and may also be used for the symbolic expression of separation conflicts. Children of this age will evidence their separation problems in sleep difficulties, fear of the dark, and fear of being alone. This was expressed by a little girl who when put to bed, said "talk to me, Mommy, then it won't be so dark." Some children need substitutes in the form of special toys to take to bed with them. An exaggerated need and attachment to such articles may be an early indication of childhood fetishism (Sperling, 1963a). Other children may show their separation conflicts more manifestly by clinging and holding on to their mothers physically, at bedtime.

If, however, expression of anal impulses and of aggressive drives is severely restricted and at the same time the child is excessively stimulated by anal manipulations and by visual exposure and close body contact, a climate is created which is conducive to the development of pavor nocturnus Type I. This type of pavor nocturnus has in most cases an insidious onset during the anal phases reaching a climax during the oedipal phases when character maldevelopment and symptom formation are beginning to appear as indications of the child's struggle with overwhelmingly strong sexual and aggressive impulses. Because we rarely see the initial stages of this type of sleep disturbance, and because of the prognostic significance it holds for future character and personality development, I should like to discuss and to illustrate such a situation with two cases, one of a young child and one of an adolescent in whose analysis the early sleep disturbance could be reconstructed.

The case of three-year-old Freddie, who at the age of one-and-a-half had begun to have nightmares and occasional night terrors, came to my attention during the treatment of his mother, and could be managed indirectly by modifying his mother's handling of him. Freddie appeared to be too much concerned with cleanliness and showed the beginnings of food and sleep rituals. His mother was preoccupied with anal functions and frequently used suppositories and enemas for herself as well as for Freddie. At age two he had shown a tendency to have temper tantrums which his mother had quickly suppressed. She did not allow him any overt expression of aggression. Freddie also had indulged in a form of anal masturbation by sticking his finger into his anus. This behavior subsided when his mother was able to curtail her preoccupation with the anal functions of her son. She had been in the habit of taking him into bed with her as the "only way" to get him to sleep after he awakened from a nightmare. The practice of taking the child into the parental bed as a means of restoring sleep disturbed by nightmares, serves only to provide an additional source of overstimulation for the child whose disturbance of sleep is an indication of his inability to cope with his (aggressive and sexual) impulses. The fact that Freddie's mother remained in therapy during his oedipal phase development was most beneficial for him. In this case the early intervention through the mother had proved of therapeutic and preventive value.

Twelve-year-old Lenny was referred for severely disturbed behavior and an incapacitating mucous colitis. From the age of three, he had suffered from a sleep disturbance with nightmares. He would awaken in the middle of the night and look for his mother. This became more intense during the oedipal phase when his mother would have to lie down with him and hold his hand and promise that if he should die, she would die with him. With the onset of an overt school phobia and episodic nocturnal diarrhea, his sleep disturbance improved. He developed the full-blown mucous colitis during puberty following a recurrence of the sleep disturbance which reflected the resurgence of the unresolved oedipal conflicts and his masturbatory struggle (1950). During the phase of his treatment when he had given up the mucous colitis symptoms (severe cramps and non-bloody diarrhea), he had a transitory return of the sleep disturbance with nightmares. One recurrent nightmare of an Egyptian "mummy" was particularly frightening and informative. The specific fears caused by this nightmare related to the fears of the anal phase, specifically the fear of separation and death which now served to express his castration fears and feminine wishes. Touching the mummy was fatal because there was a curse that anyone who touched the mummy had to die, it also made the mummy disappear, which was particularly frightening. He had many hypochondriacal fears of a paranoid nature, being especially afraid of poisoning, injections, illness, surgery, etc. He had stopped masturbating and regressed to the anal level of sexuality. The colitis symptoms served both the gratification of and punishment for his aggressive and pregenital sexual wishes.

The occurrence or reoccurrence of a sleep disturbance with nightmares is a typical phenomenon observed during the treatment of children with psychosomatic disorders, such as asthma, colitis, epilepsy, etc. It occurs during the phase of treatment when the child is giving up the psychosomatic symptoms which had provided the needed instant release of the threatening impulses via somatic channels. The character and content of the nightmares and dreams during this period express the child's specific fears and fantasies and are a key for the understanding of the dynamics of the specific somatic symptoms in each case. This aspect of the dream and fantasy life of children with psychosomatic disorders has been dealt with in detail in the published accounts of these respective syndromes (Sperling, 1950, 1953, 1963b, 1968, and many others not listed here). Enuretic children with persistent enuresis usually develop a sleep disturbance with nightmares, for the first time in their lives, during the phase of treatment when they are giving up the enuresis. In these cases the enuresis had served the immediate discharge of their impulses, thus protecting them from a sleep disturbance. During a transitory phase in their treatment, enuretic children may keep themselves up deliberately for many hours during the night in order to prevent themselves from having nightmares or bed-wetting. This is true also for children with psychosomatic disorders and is an indication of their intolerance toward anxiety and impulses which had been released previously in somatic symptoms or enuresis. This intolerance to anxiety and tension is an important differential diagnostic criterion between these children and those who suffer from a neurotic sleep disturbance. I shall return and elaborate on this subject after a brief discussion of neurotic sleep disturbances during the oedipal phase.

The repression of the oedipal wishes and the conflicts about infantile masturbation, with the resulting fears of castration, are reflected in the sleep disturbances of this phase. In most cases these are mild and transitory with occasional anxiety dreams and difficulty in falling asleep. There are typical fears associated with these sleep disturbances. Dreams deal frequently with attack, injury, or death. These are expressions of the child's fear of punishment for masturbation and his castration anxiety. Typical also are fears of monsters, ghosts, burglers, robbers, kidnappers, etc. These fears on closer investigation reveal themselves as projections of the child's own sexual and aggressive impulses directed towards the parent or sibling rivals. While the occurrence of mild and transient sleep disturbances during the oedipal phase can be considered almost a typical feature in our culture, the more severe sleep disturbances of this phase, especially acute exacerbations leading to acute sleeplessness, and anxiety dreams, are pathological phenomena. A persistent sleep disturbance during this phase, in the absence of other symptoms, can be considered a manifestation of the infantile neurosis of the child. From the dream and sleep behavior, it is possible to make a differential diagnosis between neurotic or other more serious psychopathological development of the child. This differential diagnosis is important for the therapeutic approach and for prognosis and prevention. I should like to present a clinical vignette of a neurotic sleep disturbance and then compare it with that of a more serious sleep disturbance in a child of the same age, using this as a basis for the discussion of the similarities and differences in the genesis and dynamics between these sleep disturbances and between the prognostic significance and therapeutic approach.

Six-and-a-half year old Bobby had had a mild transient sleep disturbance between age four and five. For the past year and a half his sleep disturbance had become more intensified; he had difficulty in going to sleep and when he fell asleep he would frequently wake up in anxiety. His mother described him as a model child who was very attached to her and very considerate of his baby brother, one-and-a-half years old. Bobby had frequent dreams about cemeteries and dead people getting out of their graves and coming to fetch him. He was preoccupied with fears of death although he had had no experience of death in his family. He would sometimes cry before going to bed because he was afraid he might die in his sleep. Therapy revealed that his oedipal conflicts had been complicated and intensified by repressed hostility and death wishes towards his brother who had become his immediate rival for his mother's affection at a time when he was at the height of his positive oedipal conflict. Once, when he was five-years-old and driving past a cemetery with his parents, it was explained to him that this was a place where dead people were buried. Also, about that time he had been warned about playing with his penis.

Bobby is a good illustration for the neurotic type of oedipal sleep disturbance. He had a relatively well functioning ego and superego and was able to handle the intensification of his oedipal conflicts, his aggression, and his sibling rivalry by repression. He was able to maintain repression of these impulses during the day without manifest disturbance of his behavior, and was thus able to tolerate a certain amount of anxiety without symptom formation and impairment of ego functioning. However, because he was in a state of acute repression, sleep represented the danger of a breakthrough of these impulses (Fenichel, 1942). He defended himself against this danger by neurotic insomnia, that is, by trying to stay awake or by awakening *fully* with the help of anxiety dreams when these repressed impulses threatened to overcome the sleeping ego.

He had full recall of the events during the time of the night when he was up and was fully aware of his environment and actions. In fact, he rarely got out of bed or disturbed his parents. He was more or less a "silent" sufferer.

The essential difference in the sleep behavior between the child with neurotic insomnia and the child with pavor nocturnus Type I (and sleep walking) is that the child with neurotic insomnia awakens fully from sleep and has complete recall for the events of the night, while the child with pavor nocturnus and sleep walking it not fully awake and has a retrograde amnesia for his nocturnal activities. The child with neurotic insomnia, by awakening fully from the dream, does not permit himself acting out of forbidden or dangerous impulses in reality, while the child with pavor nocturnus Type I, by not awakening fully and by continuing the dream in a partially awake state permits himself to act out in disguise some of his impulses in reality. I would put the differential emphasis between these two groups on *action*. The child with pavor nocturnus Type I and sleep walking needs to act out in reality without being fully aware of his impulses and actions, and with amnesia for them. The dynamic situation, and this is an important factor in the treatment of children with pavor nocturnus and sleep walking, is similar to the situation in patients with character disorders and acting out behavior. There is also a striking similarity in parental attitudes and early childhood experiences found in the histories of patients with character disorders and acting out behavior. These children are exposed to overstimulation and inconsistency on the part of the parents. The oral phases of development are usually more satisfactory, but beginning with the anal phase, there is a progressive pathological development with intensification during puberty and adolescence. These children in contrast to those who suffer from neurotic insomnia, do not have a satisfactory latency period. An important difference is the different character structure and the different mechanisms of defense against instinctual drives used by these children. The urge to act out impulses is particularly strong and the ability to tolerate anxiety, that is, some awareness of these impulses, is very low. This explains the frequent association of pavor nocturnus Type I with psychosomatic symptoms, which serve as emergency outlets, or the replacement of this type of sleep disturbance by psychosomatic symptoms.

I would like to illustrate such a situation with the brief vignette of six-and-a-half year old Charlie. Charlie was referred for treatment because of a school phobia, which manifested itself mainly in somatic symptoms. He was always sick and tired in the morning and his mother would dress and feed him breakfast in bed. Charlie would vomit every morning either before leaving the house, or on the way to school or in school. He finally refused to go to school at all. Although he was a very bright child, his performance had been poor. From about age three he suffered from pavor nocturnus Type I. He would wake up during the night appearing fearful, confused, and unresponsive to his environment, seemingly in a dream state. He would walk into his parents' bedroom and get into bed with his mother. Occasionally he would talk during this state, sometimes saying "I hate you all; I hate this house. I want to leave," and actually attempt to walk out of the house. In the mornings he was tired and sleepy and had complete amnesia for the happenings of the night. During the past year, the pavor nocturnus attacks were less frequent, although Charlie had now developed a severe cough which kept him and his parents up for most of the night. The cough had been diagnosed as allergic but did not respond to medication. He would never go to bed when his mother was not at home and would often sleep with his clothes on. His daytime behavior had become increasingly disruptive and demanding and because of his phobias and abusive behavior towards other children, he was a rather isolated child.

Both parents showed marked anal fixations. His mother overcompensated for her rejection of him by overindulgence but did not allow him appropriate expressions of aggression. She was very controlling and restrictive. Her treatment revealed that she had unconsciously encouraged his phobia by her overprotection and overanxiousness and that he had been used by her for the acting out and gratification of some of her own unconscious needs. Charlie had accommodated his mother in these areas and retaliated by his disturbing and demanding behavior. Unlike Bobby, he was not a silent, but in fact a very noisy sufferer. Preparatory treatment of his mother was necessary in order to modify her relationship with Charlie and to make him amenable to therapy. As is typical for such cases, Charlie was not brought for treatment for his pavor nocturnus and sleepwalking, but under the pressure of the school, for his school phobia and behavior.

Children with pavor nocturnus and sleep walking are rarely brought for treatment because of these symptoms unless their behavior is endangering their own or their family's safety and even then, rarely before school age. Treatment is usually sought because of other symptoms, especially behavior difficulties, school problems, or phobias. Responsible in part for this is the belief of parents, shared by pediatricians, that children outgrow pavor nocturnus and sleep-walking and therefore do not require treatment for these symptoms. This belief is supported by the fact that pavor nocturnus Type I is usually given up during puberty or adolescence. However, parents and pediatricians do not know what my extensive and long experience with children suffering from this type of pavor nocturnus has taught me—namely, that it is given up in exchange for severe character and personality disorders and other behavior and symptoms which neither the patient nor his environment relate to the preceding sleep disturbance. Frequently, these children suffer from so-called allergic conditions such as persistent coughing, hay fever, bronchial asthma, headaches, petit mal, etc., sometimes coexisting and sometimes replacing the pavor nocturnus. These symptoms and the pavor nocturnus Type I are indications of the severity of the pregenital fixations and conflicts. The character structure of these children is predominantly anal with marked ambivalence, bisexuality, tendencies to homosexuality, sadomasochism, and other deviations.

Although Charlie came for treatment at age six-and-a-half, his character psychopathology was already so severe that it required long therapy (under my supervision) and preparatory as well as concomitant treatment of his mother (with myself). His father had also been in analysis with another analyst.

I have now a 19 year follow-up on patient Bill, reported in 1958 (Sperling, 1958). He was treated for pavor nocturnus and sleep-walking from age 9 to 11; he was seen again at age 15 when he was close to a psychotic break. His psychological records, including Rorschach, at that time indicated that he was suffering from a paranoid schizophrenia. That he was amenable to analysis, I attribute as in the case of Ruth, to his previous therapy. From age 20 to 24 he had more analysis to work out his latent homosexuality and other related problems. He is married, has children, and is pursuing a professional career. I am citing this case here to emphasize again the prognostic significance of this type of sleep disturbance.

I have stressed in particular three features as differential diagnostic criteria for pavor nocturnus Type I. One, the fact that the child is only partially awake and behaves as if in a dream state; two, hypermotility, whether the child is in or out of bed; and three, retrograde amnesia. These features are manifestations of strong regressive tendencies and indications of impairment of the ability to wake up fully, as well as a tendency to *act out* impulses in reality. This behavior points to a possible connection with psychotic states. Simmel's (1942) ideas concerning the connection of sleep and psychosis are of interest here. Simmel makes the point that in psychotic states there seems to be a disturbance of the ability to awaken fully during the day. Apparently there is a similarity between the dream state, with partial awakening during the night in pavor nocturnus Type I, and some psychotic states. Observations from recent experimental sleep research would seem to validate my conclusions concerning the difference between pavor nocturnus Type I and other sleep and dream states which have been drawn from clinical psychoanalytic work with children during the past 25 years.

Broughton (1968), a neurologist, reported that in most of the subjects studied, bed wetting, sleep walking, and nightmares of the type described by me as pavor nocturnus Type I, occurred during sudden arousal from slow wave Stage 4 sleep. He observed an increase in physiological activity, mental confusion, and retrograde amnesia in these subjects. He was particularly impressed with their decreased response to light and concluded that these sleep disturbances are essentially "disorders of arousal." Unfortunately however, the drawback with physiological research is the unfamiliarity and often the resistance to psychoanalytic thinking and methods of the researcher. Broughton's explanation for these phenomena is a purely physiological one; he attributes it to predisposing physiological changes in the body. Because he observed little or no mental content on the subjects, he jumped to the conclusion of a "psychological void." He attributed the terror and confusion in this type of nightmare victim to the increase in his heartbeat, rather than to the anxiety which in my opinion causes both the acceleration in physiological activity and the nightmare, with the confusional state following it. Here the superiority of the psychoanalytic method of investigation is unquestionable.

In the psychoanalytic treatment of children suffering from pavor nocturnus, sleep walking, bed-wetting, and other related symptoms, I have succeeded in lifting the retrograde amnesia while restoring the memory and the psychic content of the nocturnal attacks (Sperling, 1958, 1965, 1969c). In this connection, the psychoanalytic work with patients suffering from psychosomatic diseases, in particular, migraine headaches, altered states of consciousness, petit mal, and grand mal epilepsy are of interest (Sperling, 1953, 1969b). With these patients too, analysis succeeded in lifting the amnesia for their petit mal and even grand mal attacks. That it is possible in psychoanalytic treatment of psychosomatic patients to uncover the fantasies converted into and released in the somatic symptoms has been amply demonstrated (Sperling, 1950, 1963b, 1968, 1969b). In fact, the combined physiological and psychoanalytic study of the various sleep states and the phenomena associated with them, may well prove a source not only for a better understanding of dream and sleep mechanisms, but perhaps also for the still "mysterious leap from the mind to the body," and the transformation of psychic content into physiological activity and vice versa.

I have described Type II pavor nocturnus as the traumatic type. Here the onset is sudden, often dramatically following an acute trauma. Such a trauma may be surgery, accident, illness, death in the family, birth of a sibling, etc. This type can occur in children of all ages and is characterized by fitful sleep, crying out during sleep, and waking up in anxiety from a nightmare which may represent a repetition of the traumatic situation which preceded the onset of this sleep disturbance. This type of pavor nocturnus is analogous to the traumatic neurosis of adults and can be considered as the traumatic neurosis of childhood. The revival of the traumatic situation during sleep leads to anxiety, and the continuation of sleep under these circumstances would be dangerous. The nightmare in this situation functions as the abrupt waker and the mastery lies in waking up and escaping the traumatic situation in the dream which the child had been unable to escape and to master in reality. In most cases, waking up from this type of pavor nocturnus is accompanied by relief in contrast to the behavior in pavor nocturnus Type I. This, as well as the acute onset and transitory character, are important differential diagnostic criteria. It is of therapeutic and especially of preventive significance that in traumatic neurosis there is a characteristic incubation period during which sleep is disturbed in this specific way, before the onset of manifestly disturbed daytime behavior. I should like to illustrate this briefly with the case of four-year-old Olga who developed an acute severe sleep disturbance and anorexia following a tonsillectomy. The child had been having repeated nightmares in which she would cry out, "No, no, don't!" Olga had been adequately prepared for the surgery except for the anesthesia, and in her nightmares she relived the struggle against being overcome by the anesthesia against her will, an event which she had been unable to prevent in reality and from which she could escape by waking up when she relived it in her nightmares. It was possible in a few play sessions to reconstruct the meaning which the traumatic events that had caused this behavior had for her and to free her from her symptoms. She has remained well and symptom-free in a long follow up (Sperling, 1958).

However, in an already traumatized child, an additional trauma may have the effect of profoundly disturbing the object relationship and the balance between the libidinal and aggressive drives. These will be experienced as particularly dangerous during deep sleep when the regressive tendencies threaten to overcome the weakened ego of the child. These tendencies have to be counteracted with emergency speed and measures and the sudden and excessive increase in the cardiorespiratory rate and other physiological hyperactivity are indications of the mounting anxiety. Dr. Charles Fisher

(1969) in his research has described how the subject of such a nocturnal attack awakens from deep sleep (Stage 4) when his pulse rate was 60, suddenly with a pulse rate of 150, sweating, agitated as if in great danger. This is exactly how some children with the traumatic type of pavor nocturnus feel and behave. They call in panic for their mother and want to be held and comforted. They may be confused for a while, still under the spell of the nightmare, but they awaken fully and have recall of the nightmare and the events of the night, as was the case with Olga.

In the cases of two-year-old Linda and four-year-old Ruth, the traumatic effects of the tonsillectomy for which both children had not been prepared, was added to an already severe sleep disturbance, thereby contributing to its intensification, but they too were able to remember the nightmare and the events of the night.

Following a traumatic experience, children should be encouraged to verbalize and to abreact their feelings in order to protect them from permanent consequences. After the incubation period, that is, with the subsidence of the acute sleep disturbance, some changes in the child's daytime behavior may appear. These changes, depending on the premorbid personality of the child, may vary from mild phobic to more severe neurotic or somatic reactions.

An adolescent boy whom I treated for severe school phobia and paranoid distrust comes to mind. In this case, the crucial traumatic experience occurred at age four when he had to undergo surgery for which he had not been prepared at all. In fact, his mother, afraid that he would not go to the hospital, had misinformed him. The sleep disturbance following this experience went unnoticed and the subsequent changes in his personality and behavior, in addition to a tendency to develop severe headaches, had not been related to this traumatic experience by him or by his environment. In his analysis it was found that he still suffered from disturbed sleep with episodic nightmares and intense destructive impulses of both a homicidal and suicidal nature.

Sleep disturbances of childhood, like other early established behavior patterns, are frequently carried over into adulthood contributing to the high incidence of neurotic insomnia among the population.

Type III of pavor nocturnus, the neurotic type, has its origin in the conflicts of the oedipal phase and is phenomenologically and dynamically similar to the nightmare syndrome of the adult. The concepts on the nightmare of the adult developed by Jones (1931) apply in some measure to this type of pavor nocturnus in children. Here the superego permits the dangerous and forbidden impulses that were warded off during the day to come out during sleep in the disguise of the dream, but insists upon immediate waking up when there is a danger that the ego might be overcome by these impulses. This type of nightmare occurs episodically, and the child awakens fully in anxiety and with a vivid recall of the contents of the nightmare which may become a lasting memory. It can be revived later in life either in its original or in somewhat changed form.

Here again, Dr. Fisher's research and thinking are most interesting in validating and explaining clinical observations. He states that despite the fact that the REM period is generally characterized by considerable cardiorespiratory activity, anxious REM dreams seem to be accompanied by a motor paralysis that limits physiological reactions to anxiety, and further, that this process keeps a person asleep or prevents too great a disruption should he awaken. He also states that it appears that the REM dream has a mechanism which modulates anxiety by abolishing or diminishing physiological responses. He found that spontaneous awakenings with reports of anxious mental content can occur at any time of night in any of the four stages of sleep, but that the most severe nightmares take place during the period of deepest Stage 4 sleep. On the basis of these findings, one would be inclined to think that the neurotic type of pavor nocturnus is associated with the REM period of sleep, while the traumatic and psychotic type is associated with the periods of deep sleep.

## Summary and Conclusions

In this paper I have been concerned mainly with three aspects of children's dreams and sleep:

One, to establish and to investigate further the relationship of these phenomena with developmental phases and conflicts. My investigations have revealed the importance of the pregenital phases and preoedipal relationships in the genesis of sleep disturbances in children, and in particular the role of anal phase development and conflicts in the genesis of pavor nocturnus Type I. I have expressed my belief that this type of sleep disturbance may be the first indication of serious pathological character and personality development. I have also re-emphasized the prognostic significance of a persistent severe infantile sleep disturbance.

Two, as indicated by the title, I have been particularly concerned with the practical, clinical aspects of these phenomena and their application in assessing existing pathology and predicting, or if possible preventing, future psychopathology in children. For this reason, I have tried to define especially some of the differences between neurotic sleep disturbances and those of the type of pavor nocturnus I and II in children.

Three, I have attempted to correlate psychoanalytic sleep and dream research with findings from recent experimental research of these phenomena (Broughton, 1968; Fisher and Dement, 1963; Fisher, 1969; Dement, 1964).

While experimental research is important in enhancing our knowledge of the physiology of the processes of sleep and dreaming, the psychoanalytic investigation is essential for the understanding of the mental processes involved.

## REFERENCES

Bornstein, B. (1935), Phobia in a two and a half year old child. *Psychoanal. Quart.*, 4:93–119.

Broughton, R. J. (1968), Sleep disorders: disorders of arousal? *Science,* 159:1070–1078.

Dement, W. (1964), Experimental dream studies. *Science and Psychoanalysis,* 7:129–184. New York: Grune & Stratton, Inc.

Fenichel, O. (1942), Introduction to symposium on neurotic disturbances of sleep. *Int. J. Psycho-Anal.*, 23:49.

Fisher, C. and Dement, W. C. (1963), Studies on the psychopathology of sleep and dreams. *Amer. J. Psychiat.*, 119:1160–1168.

—— (1969), The psychophysiological study of nightmares, Freud 19th Anniversary Lecture. N. Y. Academy of Medicine, April, 1969.

Fraiberg, S. (1950). On the sleep disturbances of early childhood. *The Psychoanalytic Study of the Child,* 5:285–309. New York: International Universities Press.

Freud, S. (1900), The interpretation of dreams. Standard Edition, 3 & 4. London: Hogarth Press, 1953.

—— (1920), Beyond the pleasure principle. *Standard Edition*, 18:1–64. London: Hogarth Press, 1955.

—— (1936), The problem of anxiety. *Standard Edition*, 20:77–175. London: Hogarth Press, 1959.

Jekels, L. (1945), A bioanalytical contribution to the problem of sleep and wakefulness. *Psychoanal. Quart.*, 14:169–189.

Jones, E. (1931), *On the Nightmare*. New York: W. W. Norton.

Simmel, E. (1942), Symposium on neurotic disturbances of sleep. *Int. J. Psycho-Anal.*, 23:65–68.

Sperling, M. (1949), Neurotic sleep disturbances in children. *The Nervous Child*, 8:28–46.

—— (1950), Mucous colitis associated with phobias. *Psychoanal. Quart.*, 19:318–326.

—— (1952), Animal phobias in a two-year-old child. *The Psychoanalytic Study of the Child*, 7:115–125. New York: International Universities Press.

—— (1953), Psychodynamics and treatment of petit mal in children. *Int. J. Psycho-Anal.*, 34:1–5.

—— (1954), Reactive schizophrenia in children. *Amer. J. Orthopsychiat.*, 24:506–512.

—— (1955a), Etiology and treatment of sleep disturbances in children. *Psychoanal. Quart.*, 24:358–368.

—— (1955b), Roundtable on childhood schizophrenia. *Amer. Psychiatric Assn.*, Atlantic City, May 12, 1955.

—— (1958), Pavor nocturnus. *J. Amer. Psychoanal. Assn.*, 6:79–94.

—— (1963a), Fetishism in children. *Psychoanal. Quart.*, 32:374–392.

—— (1963b), A psychoanalytic study of bronchial asthma in children. In: *The Asthmatic Child*, ed. H. I. Schneer. New York: Harper & Row, pp. 138–165.

—— (1965). Dynamic considerations and treatment of enuresis. *J. Amer. Acad. Child Psychiat.*, 4:19–31.

—— (1967), School phobias: classification, dynamics, and treatment. *The Psychoanalytic Study of the Child*, 22:375–401. New York: International Universities Press.

—— (1969a), Ulcerative colitis in children. *J. Amer. Acad. Child Psychiat.*, 8:336–352.

—— (1969b), Sleep disturbances in children. *Modern Perspectives in International Child Psychiatry*, ed. J. G. Howells. Edinburgh: Oliver & Boyd, Ltd.

—— (1969c), Migraine headaches, altered states of consciousness and accident proneness: a clinical contribution to the death instinct theory. *The Psychoanal. Forum*, ed. J. A. Lindon. New York: Science House, 3:69–83.

Wulff, M. (1927), A phobia in a child of eighteen months. *Int. J. Psycho-Anal.*, 9:354–359.

# Part IV
# Theory

# 14. OVERVIEW

HENRY H. W. MILES, M.D.

---

There has been no dearth of criticism with regard to psychoanalysis from the practitioners of the "hard sciences," such as physics and chemistry, and from behavioral scientists of various persuasions. They tend to regard our views as imprecise and fuzzy if not actually unscientific. Waelder (1962) answered these criticisms lucidly in his classification of psychoanalytic propositions, which he arranged hierarchically according to increasing remoteness from concrete, clinical observations. Because his paper is well known, I will not give a detailed recapitulation of his thesis except to reiterate that what most analysts find of greatest usefulness in their daily work is clinical theory which constitutes Waelder's fourth level of hierarchical classification. This is made up of concepts which should be verifiable by clinical or experimental observations or both. Waelder's fifth-level propositions, the concepts of metapsychology, are pure constructs and, the pertinent question about them is not so much whether they are "true" but rather how useful they may be.

Warren Weaver (1967) has some very illuminating comments on the terms, "theory" and "explanation." In the physical sciences, a satisfactory theory is defined as one which enables us to control phenomena and to make predictions. It is likely to consist of a body of mathematical equations which state the interdependence of a few or several quantities represented by letters in the equations. "If you point to one of the letters and ask, 'What is this? What

211

physical thing does this represent?'—the answer may well be that you asked an irrelevant and improper question" (p. 40). This formal, abstract type of scientific theory contains nothing which may be said to constitute, in any ordinary sense, explanation. I think it is obvious that the subject matter dealt with in psychoanalysis cannot be expressed by such a theory.

Weaver then goes on to describe what happens to a person confronted by a puzzling phenomenon. "He goes through some process of talking or listening, or reading, or thinking, or experimentation or perhaps all of these. It may take ten minutes, or it may take years" (p. 55). Then he may feel intellectually comfortable and say, "Now I understand better than I did" (p. 55). In other words he can now explain the phenomenon. Most explanations cannot be expressed in an elegant, abstract set of mathematical equations—that is to say, in a formal theory as it was previously defined. What is much more familiar to all of us and much more widely used both by scientists and nonscientists is the type of explanation which consists of describing or restating the unfamiliar in terms of the familiar. This is exemplified in the use of analogies or models or, in a more literary or poetic sense, similes and metaphors. For instance, one could describe electromagnetic waves spreading out from a radio transmitter in terms of the circular ripples expanding on a pond after a stone is dropped. Apart from the obvious incompleteness of such an explanation, Weaver reminds us that, "examples not very much more sophisticated than this have played exceedingly important roles in the development of scientific theories, particularly in physics" (p. 57).

My reason for this nonpsychoanalytic preamble is to emphasize again that our theories and explanations of man's psychological development and functioning must still be expressed by analogies and models. We simply do not know enough to emulate the physicist who can write an equation which predicts accurately that, "under such-and-such conditions, such-and-such will happen and if you change the conditions in such-and-such a way, the results will be altered in such-and-such a way" (p. 56).

One impediment to the ongoing search for better models to explain human behavior, as I see it, is a tendency, especially among those not trained in psychoanalysis, to discard certain fundamental, well substantiated, clinically derived concepts in favor of newer and presumably more "objective" explanatory models. I will mention two examples, encountered recently in browsing through non-psychoanalytic publications.

Geertz (1966), an anthropologist, believes that we can obtain a more precise image of man if we reformulate the determinants of behavior and culture in terms of, "sets of control mechanisms—plans, recipes, rules, instructions, what computer engineers call 'programs' for the governing of behavior" (p. 2).

Reiner (1968), an enzyme chemist, has attempted to integrate modern feedback concepts with various aspects of human functioning from enzyme systems to behavior. To illustrate what he calls an adaptive control device for the regulation of behavior, Reiner takes the example of a man waiting to catch a ball. If the ball in midair were perceived to be something else, such as a live rattlesnake, the man's "standard of operation" would be switched from wanting-to-catch to not-wanting-to-catch. What this type of formulation seems not to explain are the irrational responses in man's adaptive control devices. Figuratively speaking, we may see a patient who correctly perceives the object to be a rattlesnake and fails to change the standard of operation. The switch does not occur and he proceeds to catch the rattlesnake. To put the question in more familiar terms, rather than cybernetic language, why should a man with adequate ability to test reality do such an irrational thing? What are the unconscious determinants of his self-harmful or masochistic behavior? I do not question the ultimate value of the contributions of other disciplines to our understanding of human motivation and behavior. At present, however, we should remember that the data are so complex that it is possible to construct a number of quite plausible theories all of which can "explain" the observations. In the search for better conceptual models, we must be careful not to discard concepts of proven value.

Wittgenstein (1953) has described the progress of human knowledge as a series of ascending plateaus with each new vantage point offering a new perspective. The difficulty, he says, is that one tends to climb on others' conceptions until one understands them—then one tends to "throw away the ladder" and to see the contemporary stage not as one of a series but as "the truth."

Two comments, at this point, are relevant to psychoanalysis. Scientists, such as Geertz and Reiner, however skilled in their own fields, have not mastered the data and the concepts of psychoanalysis. They propose to throw away the ladder without actually having climbed it. Secondly, to explain the phenomena we see every day in ourselves and in our patients, we must make use of such well documented concepts as those of the instinctual drives, of psychic energy, of intrapsychic conflict, etc. These propositions, as is generally known, are not static but are constantly being re-examined, tested, defined more precisely, and modified.

However, in our field there are difficulties unlike those faced by the physicist or chemist. Rapaport (1960) comments that the process of development which brings about the interplay between observables and theories is always slow. In a footnote he says:

> We have some idea why this process is so slow. If logic, methodology, and mathematics were the pacemakers of development in sciences, this development could be fast enough in psychology. But the pacemaker is not methodology—it is human invention. ("Developmental projects," "crash programs," and "interdisciplinary teams" are effective only in highly developed sciences or else in situations where the makeshifts of pooled ignorance are the most that can be had.) . . . human invention consists of discontinuous events, each of which requires long preparation, since in it an individual's thought patterns must come to grips with patterns of nature, and only those rare encounters in which a unique human thought pattern actually matches a unique pattern of nature will matter. If the match is not specific and precise, or if the individual is not prepared to recognize it, or if he does recognize it but is not ready to use it, the moment is lost [p. 37].

I cannot agree with those who imply that the fundamental concepts of psychoanalytic theory have been rendered obsolete and untenable by newer developments in ethology, cybernetics, neurophysiology, molecular genetics, information theory, etc. Psychoanalysis is still, to a large degree, dependent upon the collection of clinical impressions. Introspective reporting occupies an important place in our scheme, and in the long run many issues will have to be decided on the quality of the empirical data presented. Freud (1932–1933) said this long ago, much more succinctly, ". . . we are studying the psychical accompaniments of biological processes" (pp. 95–96).

## REFERENCES

Freud, S. (1932–1933), New introductory lectures on psycho-analysis. *Standard Edition*, 22:7–158. London: Hogarth Press, 1964.

Geertz, C. (1966), The impact of the concept of culture on the concept of man. *Bull. Atom. Sci.*, 22:2 (April).

Rapaport, D. (1960), *The Structure of Psychoanalytic Theory* [*Psychological Issues* Monogr. 6]. New York: International Universities Press.

Reiner, J. M. (1968), *The Organism as an Adaptive Control System*. New Jersey: Prentice-Hall, Inc.

Waelder, R. (1962), Psychoanalysis, scientific method, and philosophy. *J. Amer. Psychoanal. Assn.*, 10:617–637.

Weaver, W. (1967), *Science and Imagination*. New York: Basic Books, Inc.

Wittgenstein, L. (1953), *Philosophical Investigations*. New York: The MacMillan Company.

# 15. SOME PROBLEMS IN THE PSYCHOANALYTIC THEORY OF THE INSTINCTUAL DRIVES

CHARLES BRENNER, M.D.

---

Problems abound in every area of psychoanalysis, as they do, indeed, in every branch of science. Nowhere are they more abundant than in the theory of the instinctual drives. Freud himself seems to have felt this way if one can judge from his joking about the drives as "our mythology." What Freud called "the drives" have to do with basic, human motivation, and it is by no means easy to be clear and certain about the deepest wellsprings of the motives of the human mind. Obscurity and uncertainty are only too likely to intrude.

It was during my experience over a period of several years, in teaching a course at the New York Psychoanalytic Institute, that my attention was drawn repeatedly and insistently to the many problem areas in psychoanalytic drive theory. The following list of such problem areas makes no claim to completeness. It is offered only as an indication of their nature and extent. (1) Vitalism and drive theory. (2) Evidence for a dual drive theory as opposed to a unitary one. (3) Fusion and defusion of drives. (4) The concept of mental energy; its relation to physical energy; its heuristic value. (5) Modes and transformations of mental energy; neutralization and instinctualization. (6) Cathexis and countercathexis; cathexis of mental functions as distinct from cathexis of a mental representation. (7) Economic aspects of mental life; in particular, the relative usefulness and possible disadvantages of explanations based solely on economic or quantitative considerations.

It is clear from the mere listing of these topics that far more than a single paper would be necessary even to begin to do them justice. In fact, the discussion to follow will be limited to a relatively narrow range. As its title indicates, it will deal with some of the problems which are connected with our current theoretical views concerning aggression.

The interval of 20 years is a significant one with respect to any discussion of the psychoanalytic theory of aggression, since it was just 20 years ago that Hartmann, Kris, and Loewenstein (1949) wrote a lengthy paper on the subject. I consider this paper to be of particular importance for two reasons. In the first place, it was the first major statement of the psychoanalytic theory of aggression since those of Freud himself in 1920 and 1933. In the second place, the conclusions and point of view which the three authors put forward have been accepted by most analysts, certainly by most analysts in this country, in all essential respects. The paper thus represents what might be regarded as an authoritative or accepted statement on the subject of the theory of aggression.

Tempting as it is to undertake a detailed review of the paper just referred to, I shall forego the opportunity of doing so at this time, although I will be referring to some of its more pertinent conclusions in the course of the following discussion. Instead, it is my intention to begin by listing for you the particular problems I shall raise concerning the psychoanalytic theory of aggression as an instinctual drive. The first of the problems I wish to discuss are those which have to do with the origin and source of aggression; the second is the problem of the aim of aggression; the third, the problem of the relation between aggression and the pleasure-unpleasure principle, and the fourth, the relation between aggression and conflict.

Let us begin with our ideas concerning the origin or sources of aggression. When Freud (1920) first introduced the idea that an aggressive or destructive drive is of fundamental importance in the mental life of man, what he attempted to do was to derive aggression, as a basic drive in mental life, from a universally active death drive; that is, from a force which he assumed to be present in all living matter and which impels or drives living matter in the direction of death, that is, in the direction of a return to the inorganic state. Freud's argument in favor of the existence of a death drive was a relatively simple one. He noted that all animals sooner or later die. At least, this is true in the case of multicellular animals. Unicellular animals never die; as long as the species survives, the original cell is immortal. Freud explained this difference between unicellular and multicellular animals in the following way. In the case of the former, germ plasm and somatoplasm are identical. In the case of the latter, it is, in fact, only the somatoplasm that always dies; the germ plasm is immortal in the same sense as a unicellular animal is. Perhaps, therefore, Freud reasoned, in the case of germ plasm the death drive is effectively neutralized by the presence of a substantial amount of the life drive. A fusion of the two, he assumed, is what accounts for the immortality of unicellular animals and of the sexual cells of multicellular animals. The death drive, he concluded, is indeed present in all living matter, though its influence can be checked more or less effectively if the life drive is fused with it.

Thus, according to Freud, the source of aggression in mental life is to be found in the death drive, which he assumed to be present in all living matter. Freud believed that aggression in mental life is a reflection or consequence of a universal death drive. Since the relation between aggression and death drive was of prime importance to Freud, it is interesting that Hartmann, Kris, and Loewenstein (1949), though they mentioned it briefly, preferred not to discuss it. It seems likely that their decision to avoid discussion of this point was much influenced by the lengthy and inconclusive statements on the matter that had appeared in the psychoanalytic literature in the decades following the publication of "Beyond the Pleasure Principle" (Freud, 1920). The correctness or incorrectness of assuming a death drive in all of living matter was considered by Hartmann, Kris, and Loewenstein to be a matter for biologists to decide. It is not, they felt, of decisive importance with respect to the correctness or incorrectness of the psychoanalytic theory of the drive of aggression.

Judging from the literature since 1949, most psychoanalysts would concur with the idea that the psychoanalytic theory of aggression as an innate drive in man can properly be divorced from the broad question of whether there is or is not a death drive. It seems to be generally agreed that as psychoanalysts we are under no particular obligation to support the validity of Freud's speculation in this direction. What I wish to emphasize in this connection is the following.

As early as 1915, in "Instincts and Their Vicissitudes," Freud emphasized the impropriety, indeed, the impossibility, of basing a satisfactory theory of instinctual drives on psychology alone, that is, simply on the data of psychoanalysis. Drives, he emphasized, are a borderland concept. They are, as it were, intermediate between mental and physiological phenomena, representing the demands of the body on the functioning of the mind. For all these reasons, Freud maintained that a satisfactory theory of drives must rest, in part at least, and probably in major part, on biological data other than those accessible through the use of the psychoanalytic method. The clinical practice of psychoanalysis cannot, he felt, be used by itself as a reliable basis for drive theory, that is for the acquisition of data on which to base a theory of drives.

It seems safe to assume that these considerations played a decisive role with Freud in his statements and hypotheses concerning aggression as a drive in the mental life of man.

Neither in 1920 nor later was Freud prepared to alter his conviction that any theory of drives must be based on more than psychoanalytic data. This conviction was one to which he adhered throughout his life. Consequently, when he was ready to introduce the concept that aggression is no less a driving force in human mental life than is the urge for sexual gratification, it was necessary for Freud to relate it to more than data obtained from psychoanalysis. It was, I believe, his continuing experience with psychoanalytic patients that impressed upon Freud, in the first place, the importance of the role which aggression plays in man's mental life. It was his clinical experience that made him more and more clearly aware of the manifold presence of self-directed aggressive trends, particularly of unconscious ones, as evidenced by an unconscious need for punishment, suffering, self-injury, or self-destruction.[1] However, for Freud these purely psychoanalytic data were apparently not enough. He demanded of himself support for his new theory from some area of biology other than analysis, just as he had done 15 years earlier, when he formulated his theory of a sexual drive. This support he felt he had found in the concept of a death drive.

In any discussion of the source or origin of the aggressive drive, it is essential to note clearly the difference between it and the sexual drive with respect to the very point I have just mentioned—namely, the degree of support for it which is available from branches of biology other than psychology, specifically, other than psychoanalysis. In order to make matters as clear as possible, let us pause for a moment to review the situation with respect to the sexual drive in this regard. Here we cannot do better, I think, than to start with Freud's (1905) observations in his "Three Contributions to the Theory of Sexuality." Freud emphasized the role of certain parts of the body—the erogenous zones—in the psychological phenomena of sexual excitement, tension, and gratification. The findings of psychoanalysis have contributed very much to our understanding of man's sexuality; so much, indeed, that it would be hard to overestimate the importance of what analysis has added to our previous knowledge of this subject. Nevertheless, as far as sexuality is concerned, Freud could always point with assurance to the close and reciprocal relationship between the physical and the mental. Stimulation of an erogenous zone produces a psychological response and vice versa. In addition, we know that there are parts of the central nervous system that react to the presence of sexual metabolites in the bloodstream in ways that include regulation of the production of the metabolites themselves—again a reciprocal relationship. Since the brain is the organ of the mind,

---

[1] Arlow and I (1964) have suggested that these data were for Freud the basis of his concept of the superego as well as of aggression as an instinctual drive.

it is reasonable to assume, with Freud, that endocrine factors can influence the sexual drive, and that stimulation of an erogenous zone can do the same. To be sure, we believe at present that the relationship between psychological drive and sexual hormones is by no means as simple a one as Freud in 1905 hoped that it was. Nevertheless, we have every reason to assume that a relationship exists.

Thus we have good evidence from areas outside the psychological data of psychoanalysis proper both for the existence of a sexual drive and for at least some idea about its origin. We can put these ideas in their most general form by saying that the sexual drive in the mental life of man has its source in the complex interplay between the central nervous system and stimuli to the nervous system from two sources: (1) those body parts which we call the erogenous zones, and (2) from sexual metabolites.

We have no comparable data and we can make no comparable statement with respect to aggression. As Freud clearly recognized, the lack of such data constitutes a significant disparity in our theoretical formulation concerning the drives. If one is not willing to relate aggression to a universal death drive, as Freud (1920) did, one is at a loss to answer the question of its source or origin. To be sure, it was suggested at one time that perhaps aggression is related to the voluntary musculature in much the same way that sexuality is related to the erogenous zones. The lack of convincing evidence to confirm this suggestion seems to have resulted in its general abandonment. Indeed, it is fair to say that analysts who do not endorse Freud's concept of a death drive have been content to leave to one side the whole question of the source of aggression.

In 1955 I pointed to the existence of this problem area in the theory of aggression. At that time I suggested that aggression as a basic drive in the mental life of man may be considered to arise from the genetically determined form and function of man's central nervous system. Such an answer to the question of the source of aggression is hardly more than a restatement of the familiar thesis that the brain is the organ of the mind. However, I know of no better answer to date. Perhaps future observation and research will provide additional data which will lead to a more illuminating hypothesis.

You may wonder, as I have, why so little attention has been paid to this problem area in the theory of aggression. My own explanation is that our daily work as clinicians tends to obscure the difference between our knowledge of the source of the sexual drive and our ignorance of the source of the aggressive drive. As clinicians, that is, in our daily work with patients, we are concerned with mental phenomena in which the drives play only a part—in other words, with drive derivatives as they appear relatively late in life, rather than with more primitive, less adulterated, drive manifestations.

We are concerned in our practice chiefly with the conflicts aroused by infantile wishes, usually unconscious ones. These wishes, even in their childhood form, are not shaped by the instinctual drives alone. They have already been influenced by experience as well, that is by ego functioning. They are, generally speaking, expressed or expressible in terms of words, and they have to do with particular people, for example, with the child's own parents, as well as with particular memories and particular actions. To put it in another way, as clinicians we deal largely with manifestations of love and hate which derive from the sexual and aggressive drives as far as their motivation is concerned. We do not deal directly with what we conceive to be very primitive manifestations of sex and aggression. We assume that the drives themselves are, so to speak, pre-ego, that they are present from birth, and that they are consistent with the most primitive sort of mental functioning. As such, we believe that they play their part both in the development of the mind and in its later functioning, but we do not assume that either their existence or their activity arises from the thoughts, words, and memories that we subsume under the heading of ego functioning.

It may be noted, as a corollary to our discussion thus far, that these assumptions are better supported with respect to the sexual than to the aggressive drive, unless one relates aggression to a universal death drive. This, I believe, was Freud's reason for his insistence on more than psychological data as evidence for any

drive. Erogenous zones are present from birth and sexual metabolites circulate in the bloodstream of the most primitive verte-
brates. It seems natural and logical to assume that there is a sexual
drive in man the manifestations of which are determined by the
interaction between the erogenous zones and endocrines on the
one hand, and the developing form and function of the central
nervous system on the other. Is the same, or something similar,
equally true for aggression? In the present state of our knowledge
it seems hard to say.

The evidence for the existence and operation of the two drives
seems equally convincing insofar as it rests on psychoanalytic data,
that is upon the evidence from our clinical observations of the
importance in mental life of sexual and aggressive urges. It is,
however, only with respect to the sexual drive that we have
nonpsychological evidence concerning its origins and operation;
support, that is, for the idea that a sexual drive is present from birth.
In the case of the sexual drive we have evidence to support Freud's
statement that the drive is indeed a measure of the demand on
the mind of the functioning of the body. We have as yet no evidence of a similar sort with respect to aggression. We must await
the results of future investigation to reveal it, if it does, indeed,
exist.

The next problem area I should like to discuss has to do with
the aim of aggression. On this point Hartmann, Kris, and Loewenstein were inconsistent, a rare lapse for them. On page 18 they
stated that the aim of the aggressive drive cannot readily be formulated in clear or precise terms. On page 20 they wrote that full
gratification of aggression necessarily requires complete destruction
of the object. The latter formulation is the one that is generally
accepted, as far as one can judge from the literature, whether the
acceptance be explicit or implicit.

The propriety of such an assumption seems to me at least open
to question. It is one thing to say that very frequently a child
or adult is driven, that is strongly motivated, to destroy an object
utterly and completely. It is a considerable extension and generalization to say that destruction of the cathected object is an invari-
able and necessary condition for the complete or fully adequate

discharge of aggression. The adultomorphic nature of such a formulation seems obvious.

Here again the differences between the aggressive drive and the sexual one are apparent. With respect to the sexual drive, it is natural to assume, as Freud did, that even in the earliest, preverbal stage of life an erogenous zone can be stimulated in such a way as to produce that release of tension which we equate with discharge of the drive. In the case of the aggressive drive, we have only psychological data on which to rely. There is therefore the danger of misusing or misinterpreting psychological data in such a way as to attribute to the mental life of the infant or very small child characteristics which we are able to observe in the mental life of the older child and the adult. This is a tendency which some analysts, as we know, have carried to a degree which is implausible to most of us. A good example of this tendency is offered by the assumptions made by Melanie Klein and her associates concerning the mental life of infants in the first months of life (Brenner, 1968). It may well be that from the very beginnings of mental life, or at least, from the age of a year or a year and a half, satisfactory discharge of the aggressive drive implies complete destruction of the object cathected with aggressive energy. At present, however, the evidence on which to base such an assertion seems inconclusive.

The fact is that in our present state of knowledge it is difficult to give a satisfactory definition of the term "full discharge of aggression." In the field of sexuality we can relate the idea of the full discharge of drive energy, at least in a general way, to the phenomenon of orgasm. In the case of aggression there is no similar phenomenon which is, as Freud put it, in the borderland between the physical and the mental. We must rely on psychologic, that is on analytic data, and useful as these data are for many formulations concerning aggression, they leave something to be desired when it comes to deciding on criteria for "full discharge." The limitations of our knowledge in this regard would seem to make it desirable, at least for the present, that we be cautious with respect to any assumptions we may make concerning the aim or aims of the aggressive drive. It would seem that, until new evidence is available, we must be content with rather general and imprecise statements concerning these aims. It is particularly important to note the possibility of adultomorphization concerning the assumptions one may make with respect to the aims of aggression in very early childhood.

Among the consequences of assuming that the aim of aggression is "total destruction of the object," is one which deserves special mention in these times. A necessary conclusion from that assumption would be that aggressive wishes cannot be truly satisfied short of murder, and the only form of murder which is sanctioned in our society is the one we call war. Are we to conclude that the only choice is between war and self-destruction? We shall be hard put to it to avoid that conclusion if we define the aim of the aggressive drive as that of total destruction.

It seems to me that such an apocalyptic view of history is unwarranted by the facts. Mankind may very well destroy itself in the near future, but not, I think, because the very aim of the aggressive drive precludes any other possibility. The Swiss and the Swedes, who have not been at war for a century or more, are not more filled with conflicts over aggression than are the French, the Germans, the Russians, or ourselves. Nor, in time of war, are crippling neurotic reactions less frequent among combat troops, who do the killing, than among those in the supply units, who never engage an enemy in mortal combat. The aggressive drive can account for man's potential as a murderer or a soldier; it does not in itself explain his emergence as one.

We come now to the question of the relationship between aggression and the pleasure-unpleasure principle. It has been too little emphasized, particularly in the recent literature, that Freud's idea was that the vicissitudes of aggression as an instinctual drive bear no necessary relationship to the pleasure-unpleasure principle. It was precisely for this reason that he called his 1920 monograph "Beyond the Pleasure Principle." In this particular respect Freud felt that the aggressive drive is not on an equal footing with the sexual one. In the case of the sexual drive Freud assumed that an accumulation of libido is, generally speaking, associated with unpleasure, while its discharge is associated with pleasure. In the case of aggression his assumption was that if aggressive energies are fused with libidinal ones, their accumulation or discharge will then follow the pleasure principle, but only as a consequence of their association with libido. Freud believed that aggression as such is governed by a need to repeat which is older than the pleasure principle and not directly related to it, much less, identical with it. Thus, according to Freud, aggression as a drive is governed by the law he called the repetition compulsion whereas libido is ruled by the pleasure principle. The two laws may operate cooperatively in some cases and in opposition to one another in others. Only when aggression has been altered by being fused with libido does it, too, seem to follow the pleasure principle. It may be added that the clinical data which seemed to Freud to speak in favor of the assumption that aggression is governed by a repetition compulsion were those related to self-directed aggression and self-imposed suffering.

My reason for saying that these ideas of Freud concerning aggression have been too little emphasized in the recent literature is the following. It is precisely with respect to the question of the relationship between aggressive energy and the pleasure-unpleasure principle that modern psychoanalytic theory is at sharpest variance with Freud's original ideas. Hartmann, Kris, and Loewenstein (1949) stated as their opinion that aggressive energy bears the same relationship to pleasure and unpleasure as does libido. They noted, without discussing, the difference between their view of this matter and that of Freud. As far as I am aware, no one has questioned the propriety and validity of making this fundamental revision in the theory of aggression. One may, I believe, assume both from positive evidence as well as from the lack of opposition, that it is generally accepted among analysts today that the accumulation of aggression is, broadly speaking, associated with unpleasure, and that its discharge is, broadly speaking, associated with pleasure.

This revision has both theoretical and clinical consequences. From the theoretical side, it obviates the necessity for assuming a repetition compulsion which operates beyond the pleasure principle. Let me explain why I believe this is so. It seems to me that Freud's arguments in favor of introducing the concept of a repetition compulsion (Freud, 1920, pp. 22–23) are only understandable on the basis that he deemed the new concept necessary in order to explain instances of self-directed aggression. Freud did not consider such phenomena to be in keeping with the pleasure principle. He had to explain them in some other way, and the way he chose, the theory that seemed to him the most valid, is that of a repetition compulsion. If one differs from Freud, as we do today, and proposes to explain the flux of aggressive energies in accordance with the pleasure principle, there remains no necessary reason nor any compelling evidence in favor of assuming the existence of a repetition compulsion. It is a useful and necessary concept only if aggression is considered to be beyond the pleasure principle, as Freud thought it is. Insofar as we follow the suggestions made by Hartmann, Kris, and Loewenstein that aggression and libido are on an equal footing with respect to the pleasure principle, the idea of a repetition compulsion as a regulatory principle in mental functioning is unnecessary and should be discarded.[2]

From the clinical point of view, the relationship between aggression and pleasure seems to reflect the view, now generally accepted, that neurotic conflicts are related to derivatives of the aggressive drive no less than to those of the sexual one. It should be noted that this was not Freud's view of the matter. In his opinion it is the pleasure-seeking derivatives of the sexual drive that give rise to conflicts which result in neurotic symptom formation. He felt that the role of aggression is limited to such manifestations as self-destructiveness and guilt, that is, to self-punitive trends. Thus the currently accepted concept that aggression no less than libido is regulated by the pleasure-pain principle reflects the growing conviction on the basis of clinical experience that derivatives of the two drives play similar if not equal roles in the production of intrapsychic conflict.

One sometimes has the impression that the recognition of the role of aggression in intrapsychic conflict has led to an overestima-

[2] Kubie (1939) came to a similar conclusion on a somewhat different basis.

tion of its importance in this respect. There seems occasionally a danger that intrapsychic conflict may be related exclusively or at least predominantly to the vicissitudes of aggression and that the importance of the role of libidinal derivatives may be under-estimated. Freud (1937) himself advanced the possibility that the tendency to intrapsychic conflict may be related to the amount of unbound aggression present in the mind—to use Hartmann's terminology, to the amount of unneutralized aggression. This sug-gestion seems to have been taken as fact by some and even enlarged upon. Thus, in an article published just 20 years ago, in 1948, Melanie Klein said, first, that aggression plays a cardinal role in mental life, and, second, that it is the fundamental cause of both anxiety and conflict in the mental life of man. Subsequent state-ments by Mrs. Klein and her colleagues have been less extreme than the one just cited. Nevertheless, the view she maintained in 1948 is representative of a trend at least in the thinking of many psychoanalysts on the subject.

In summary I may say the following. First, as far as the source or origin of aggression is concerned, we have as yet no evidence to connect it with any body part or bodily process, other than to say that aggression, like all mental phenomena, must be related to the functioning of the central nervous system. Unless one sub-scribes to Freud's theory of a death instinct, the evidence for the concept that aggression is an instinctual drive, a fundamental, con-stitutionally determined motive force in the mental life of man, is, at present, wholly psychological. It comes essentially from the clinical data of psychoanalysis, not from the borderland between the physical and the mental. The formulation that a drive repre-sents the demand of the body on the mind is convincing with respect to the sexual drive, but problematic with respect to aggression.

Second, it is not possible at present to be specific about the aim of aggression as a drive. By the same token it is difficult to define what is meant by the term "full discharge" of aggression. To equate the latter with complete destruction of whatever ob-ject is cathected with aggression is unjustified and potentially misleading.

Third, if aggression is governed by the pleasure principle, the concept of an independent repetition compulsion which is "beyond the pleasure principle" is superfluous.

Fourth, to assume that aggression is indeed governed by the pleasure principle seems to permit fuller understanding of the role of aggression in intrapsychic conflict. At the same time, it is worth noting that there has been a tendency on the part of some analysts to overemphasize the importance of aggression in this respect.

I should like to close with the following remarks. The psychoanalytic theory of the drives is often thought of as far removed from the clinical data observable by the psychoanalytic method. It is often referred to as a theory of the second or third order, to use Waelder's (1960) terminology—as a kind of superordinate theory that is built on other theories rather than on observable data. In general I am sceptical of such a view of the relationship between theory and data, at least in psychoanalysis. In my opinion, however wrong Lord Bacon may have been some 300 years ago with respect to the role of creative imagination in formulating scientific theories, he was right in emphasizing the importance of a close relationship between theory and data in the field of science. Theories are, after all, generalizations which are supported by, that is related to, observed data. Nowhere is this more true than with respect to the theory of aggression. Whatever else one may say about the psychoanalytic theory of aggression, it seems to me that one has to emphasize its close relationship to the psychoanalytic method. Its validity must at present be assessed or tested primarily with respect to psychoanalytic data, since it is a generalization which is so far principally supported by those data. It is hardly an exaggeration to say that it rests or falls with them. In fact, the great virtue of the theory of aggression lies in the closeness of its fit with observable clinical data as well as its usefulness in explaining and predicting clinical phenomena. Far from being a superordinate theory, it is a profoundly clinical one, however ambiguous and problematic it may be in one or another respect. It may not suit theoretical biologists, or ethologists, or philosophers, but it is very useful indeed to most practicing psychoanalysts and suits them very well. It is, in my opinion at least, an excellent example of the importance, indeed the necessity, of recognizing clearly the close relationship that should obtain between theory and data—between the theoretical and the clinical in psychoanalysis.

## REFERENCES

Arlow, J. A. and Brenner, C. (1964), *Psychoanalytic Concepts and the Structural Theory*. New York: International Universities Press.

Brenner, C. (1955), *An Elementary Textbook of Psychoanalysis*. New York: International Universities Press.

—— (1968), Psychoanalysis and science. *J. Amer. Psychoanal. Assn.,* 16:675–696.

Freud, S. (1905), Three essays on sexuality. *Standard Edition,* 7:135–243. London: Hogarth Press, 1953.

—— (1915), Instincts and their vicissitudes. *Standard Edition,* 14:117–140. London: Hogarth Press, 1957.

—— (1920), Beyond the pleasure principle. *Standard Edition,* 18:7–66. London: Hogarth Press, 1955.

—— (1933), New introductory lectures on psychoanalysis. *Standard Edition,* 22:81–111. London: Hogarth Press, 1964.

—— (1937), Analysis terminable and interminable. *Standard Edition,* 23:216–254. London: Hogarth Press, 1964.

Hartmann, H., Kris, E., and Loewenstein, R. M. (1949), Notes on the theory of aggression. *The Psychoanalytic Study of the Child,* 3 & 4:9–36.

Klein, M. (1948), A contribution to the theory of anxiety and guilt. *Int. J. Psycho-Anal.,* 29:114–123.

Kubie, L. S. (1939), A critical analysis of the concept of a repetition compulsion. *Int. J. Psycho-Anal.,* 20:390–402.

Waelder, R. (1960), *Basic Theory of Psychoanalysis*. New York: International Universities Press.

# 16. VICISSITUDES OF INFANTILE OMNIPOTENCE

## Eugene Pumpian-Mindlin, M.D.

My interest in the problem of omnipotence dates back many years to student days in psychoanalysis when I was fascinated by Freud's discussion of "omnipotence of thought" in relation to the "Rat Man" and particularly to the discussion of the magical power of words and of religion in "Totem and Taboo" and "Future of an Illusion." However, as with so many fascinating ideas, it remained one more intriguing subject among many others in psychoanalysis, to be pursued some day. Then, about 10 years ago my attention was attracted to a phenomenon in youthful patients to which I felt insufficient attention had been paid, and my interest in omnipotence became more focused. I undertook to examine systematically, and in some detail, what appeared to be a developmental recrudescence of omnipotence (transmuted, to be sure) in adolescence, and eventually wrote a paper entitled "Omnipotentiality, Youth and Commitment" (1965). Since that time I have presented somewhat varied versions of this paper on several occasions.

To my knowledge, until recently there had been no systematic exposition or study of the vicissitudes and fate of infantile omnipotence, in spite of the fact that in psychoanalytic literature frequent reference is made to it as a continuing significant factor

231

in psychic life, principally however in a pathological sense. After presenting some of the formulations which follow at the Annual Sandor Rado Lecture in New York in April, 1968, my talk was called to the attention of Dr. Helen Tartakoff (1966), with whom I have since corresponded. In her paper, "Normal Personality in our Culture and the Nobel Prize Complex," a paper with which I was unfamiliar at the time I wrote mine, she has presented material in a section entitled "Genetic Considerations" in which quite similar observations and speculative delineations appear.

The concept of omnipotence, as it is usually discussed, very quickly becomes fused with the constructs of narcissism and self-esteem, so that it loses its separate identity. If my hypotheses have any validity, omnipotence must be separated out and re-examined, to see if it casts any new light on certain aspects of psychic development.

Infantile omnipotence is the primordial state of the psyche as it begins its long maturational and developmental journey through life. It represents the primal state at birth before there is any recognition of objects. The infant cannot distinguish between self and external world with which it feels merged. There is as yet no ego and therefore no nonego. In this state it is therefore the whole world and the universe is itself.

This first proto-fantasy and feeling of unlimited omnipotence (also often referred to as the "oceanic feeling") represents the primary narcissistic need. But this initial state of unlimited object-less infantile omnipotence rapidly passes. It exists only as long as there is no concept of external objects. It is belied by the actual realistic helplessness of the infant.

Under the stimulus of inner excitations which cannot be ignored or removed, random uncoordinated discharge movements occur. These are perceived by the environment (i.e., the mother) as signals. Her response results in a change, a relief of tension, a diminution of disturbing excitation. Ferenczi characterized this stage as one of "omnipotence of movements." Tartakoff (1966) states " . . . the inference has been drawn that the forerunners of fantasies of omnipotence and causality have a common origin in the infant's own activity" (p. 241). She quotes Spitz (1965) in this connection as follows:

> In this achievement of enlisting the mother's help . . . through screaming, the human being experiences for the first time the post hoc ergo propter hoc in connection with his own action . . . [This] principle will subsequently branch into two directions. One of them will remain in its crude form as a basic mode of functioning of the primary process. The other will be progressively refined until it becomes one of the most potent ideational tools of man in the form of the principle of determinism [p. 153f].

Due to unavoidable frustrations and inevitable delays in tension reduction which the infant experiences, he is forced into a recognition of the existence of the external world. This is the earliest beginning of ego formation. With the awareness of externality the rudiments of ego structure are developed.

Parenthetically, let me state that I am, of course, aware of the concept of autonomous ego functions, particularly those connected with the various perceptual modalities. What I am discussing here is the development of psychic reality rather than of perceptual or cognitive reality. We are concerned here with the earliest phases of the development of psychic processes, which we might call proto-thought (preverbal) processes. Much of the work of recent years in the study of infants and children by psychoanalytically trained observers relates to observations concerning sense organ perceptions and motor responses. Such work must perforce be confined to these areas since the inner (psychic) processes cannot, by their very nature, be observed, but only inferred.

Let me briefly discuss some of the bases upon which these inferences rest. The earliest stage of unlimited objectless omnipotence can be seen reflected in various mystical sensations of being at one with the universe, which have been described through the ages. Although they are extremely difficult to describe and to analyze scientifically in a satisfactory manner, these feelings undoubtedly represent genuine experiences reported by numerous people at various times. They may be dissociative abreactions of the infantile "oceanic feeling." With no apparent cause, one may experience a sense of fabulous joy and well-being, in which all the emotions that go with delightful discovery, profound insight and a sense of immortality are rolled into one.

Various drugs, including the hallucinogens or psychedelics, may produce such reactions as illumination, cosmic consciousness, or oneness with all things. Several months ago a graduate student at a large university attempted to depict for me his experience on "trips" under the influence of LSD. Although couched in highly sophisticated and partly scientific language it was a vivid description of an unlimited objectless omnipotent (and omniscient) sensation. He stated (and I paraphrase but I believe with fair accuracy) that under the influence of LSD his body lost its limited defined boundaries; it became fused with the molecules and atoms of all the world around him (all people and all things) so that there were no separate and distinct entities, but only the universe, which was himself, and himself, who was the universe and all that was in it. He stated that although he perceived all this, he did not use the word "perceive" to mean through his sense organs, but intended rather to imply a fundamentally primitive yet highly sophisticated comprehension, beyond the limits of the ordinary functions of the human mind. Characterizing the experience as that of becoming all-powerful, as if one were the "hub of the universe," he ended up by bemoaning the inadequacies of words to formulate this remarkable state of being. It is the very primal preverbal nature of the experience of infantile omnipotence which makes it so difficult to express verbally or to formulate clearly and precisely.

I might add that he informed me that one could only experience this in a mystical way and recommended that I try it, naturally with the help of LSD. After his vivid description it was indeed a tempting offer, but one to which I have not succumbed—at least not yet!

While it is true that much of what has been said is speculative and not based upon empirical observation, we have ample data from neurotic and psychotic patients which justify such theoretical assumptions.

The phenomenon of "omnipotence of movements" we see manifested on occasion in the catatonic schizophrenic patient, who later tells us how he felt that any movement he might have made would have affected, even destroyed, the whole world.

Certain aspects of compulsive rituals, in addition to the usual factors of anxiety reduction with which we are familiar in individual patients, contain elements of the "omnipotence of movements" in a primitive magical effort to control and dominate the world and thereby reduce tensions while magically fulfilling inner needs of which the patient is, of course, unaware.

In the manic patient, we see the omnipotence and omniscience of words and movements. The illusion of invulnerability, the enormous pathological self-aggrandizement and self-esteem, the supreme confidence in their ability to do anything and everything, all betray their infantile omnipotent narcissistic origins.

Returning to the infantile developmental aspect of omnipotence, we find that the resultant development of the ego forces the infant to recognize the existence of the seemingly all-powerful adults outside of himself, and his own weakness and helplessness. A "reversal into the opposite" occurs whereby the infant now attributes to the adult the omnipotence he once felt was his. It is in this stage that Freud's concept of the "purified pleasure ego" belongs. The primitive mechanisms of introjection and projection begin to develop, in which that which is pleasant (i.e., reduces tension and unpleasure) is incorporated into the ego, and that which brings unpleasure is attributed to the external world (i.e., nonego). Thus the beginning recognition and cathexis of objects is achieved.

The child now tries to participate in the omnipotence attributed to the adult by partial or total incorporation of the object, or by the reverse fantasy of being incorporated by the omnipotent adult and thereby sharing in his omnipotence. The contrast between the child's growing awareness of his own relative helplessness, and the adult's presumed omnipotence, further enhances the need of the child for objects, through which he seeks to regain his lost omnipotence.

It is during the stage at which the child attributes omnipotence to the adult that language begins to develop. Omnipotent feelings and fantasies become linked with words and verbal concepts. Since the adult exercises his omnipotent power principally through verbal productions, words come to acquire magical powers of their own. The acquisition of language, then, aside from being a powerful tool in dealing with the external world, at an unconscious level also represents an attempt to acquire the power which the child realistically sees his parents possess, as well as an attempt to regain his own earlier omnipotence, with which he has now invested them.

If the child becomes involved in too fierce a struggle for power at this time, the result may be a fixation at this level, in which the omnipotence of thought and the magic of words, which we usually associate with the obsessive-compulsive character, become dominant. The magical potency that the obsessive-compulsive patient attributes to words is well known and need not be described in detail here. Suffice it to say, on the basis of clinical experience, that the fantasies of omnipotence and the magical power of words are factors that must be dealt with as significant issues in the psychoanalysis of obsessive-compulsive neurotics if therapy is to be successful.

It is interesting to recall that Freud (1939) attributed unusual significance to the magic of words and the omnipotence of thoughts, as evidenced in the following quotation from "Moses and Monotheism":

> In our children, in adults who are neurotic, as well as in primitive peoples, we meet with the mental phenomenon which we describe as a belief in the "omnipotence of thought." In our judgment this lies in an overestimation of the influence which our mental (in this case, intellectual) acts can exercise in altering the external world. At bottom, all magic, the precursor of our technology, rests on this premise. All the magic of words, too, has its place here, and the conviction of the power which is bound up with the knowledge and pronouncing of a name. The "omnipotence of thoughts" was, we suppose, an expression of the pride of mankind in the development of speech, which resulted in such an extraordinary advancement of intellectual activities. The new realm of intellectuality was opened up, in which ideas, memories and inferences became decisive in contrast to the lower psychical activity which had direct perceptions by the sense-organs as its content. This was unquestionably one of the most important stages on the path of humanization [p. 113].

A few parenthetical remarks must be made here. Freud limits the omnipotence of thoughts to children, adult neurotics, and primitive people. While it may be true that this phenomenon appears to be of special significance in these groups, it is certainly not limited to them. The fantasy of omnipotence remains a significant factor in all individuals and societies regardless of stage of development, with only its relative dominance varying to some degree. Certainly we see the fantasy of omnipotence manifested in religion, of whatever faith. All religions, as was long ago pointed out, have in common either a pantheon of omnipotent gods, or one godly figure to whom omnipotence is attributed. The believer presents himself as helpless in order to appeal to the omnipotent figure to use his power in favor of the supplicant. In fantasy, unconsciously, the individual not only regains his omnipotence by identification with his god, but also extends it by having the god act in his favor, thus in a magical way becoming more powerful than the god himself.

This is a maneuver which one often encounters in compulsive and borderline patients who oscillate between fantasies of omnipotence and total helplessness. As a patient once stated, "If I can force you to use your all-powerful magic to help me, by making myself so helpless that you must do something, I will be more powerful than you—super-powerful."

The same fantasy in highly institutionalized form can be found in the most sophisticated religious practices, even in our current society which, while it may be savage, cannot be considered by other, more usual criteria, primitive. After all, it is not only incantations and spells which depend upon the magic of words; prayers also attest to the underlying longing for the belief in omnipotence.

In addition we see similar psychic maneuvers in social systems dominated by powerful political figures to whom followers attribute omnipotent powers in which they share by identification. It would be comforting to feel that this occurs only in societies and social orders which differ from our own, but this element is certainly not absent in our own society, although perhaps it is somewhat more disguised than in an obviously authoritarian social order.

Let me add one further parenthetical remark regarding Freud's statement quoted above. It is an interesting and curious fact that, while language and verbal concepts are among the most significant attributes of human beings, we have very little systematic psychoanalytic knowledge of their origin and development. A most interesting area of study would relate to the question of how the omnipotence of thought and the magic of words become decathected and lose their primitive potency, not only in terms of the further development of the ego, but also in relation to the inner dynamics and outer pressures which change their valences, so to speak. Certainly a systematic psychoanalytic study of the evolution of the shift from predominantly primary process activity and verbalization to predominantly secondary process functioning would represent an enrichment of our knowledge of the human psyche.

From what has been outlined above it appears then that infantile omnipotence is a major component of the most primitive core (or nucleus) of ego structure, around which primal psychic activity revolves. It is the prototype for the primary process which mediates the direct discharge of tension. It is also an analog force in the development of primary process activity with its modes of condensation, displacement, etc. and in the most primitive mechanisms of defense. It continues throughout life in many different forms as the background for magic, fantasy, dreams, myth, and legend, not to mention multitudinous aspects of our daily lives—now more submerged, now more dominant, but always present. It might even be stated that infantile omnipotence represents the primordial fantasy, the anlage, from which all fantasy formation stems, the deepest underground stream from which our rich and varied fantasy life derives.

As the infant matures and develops, the dominance of the omnipotent fantasy becomes further submerged (repressed) in the increasing awareness of external reality. With the realization of his own impotence, and the attribution of omnipotence to the adults around it, the child comes to depend upon them for his self-esteem, originally based upon his own narcissistic omnipotence. In transferring omnipotence to the adult, the child then comes to depend for love upon the all-powerful adult, who becomes thereby the regulator of his self-esteem. As Fenichel (1945) states: "Self-esteem is the awareness of how close the individual is to the original omnipotence" (p. 40).

In the oedipal situation the intense struggle for narcissistic gratification in relation to the parental figures results finally in the internalization of the conflict, and in the establishment of that uniquely human institution which we call the superego, with its supremely sapient concomitants, guilt and shame. The superego becomes the repository for omnipotent needs, fantasies, and strivings, and also becomes the storehouse for the magical modes of thought through which it manifests itself. I omit here any discussion of the ego ideal as it is frequently differentiated from the superego. However, *pari passu,* it also shares in absorbing some of the omnipotent fantasies and feelings. Tartakoff (1966), in her article on the Nobel Prize Complex, discusses significant aspects of the relation of the development of the ego ideal to omnipotent fantasies, particularly as it relates to the gifted child in whom these fantasies are reinforced by the environment.

The resolution of the oedipal situation, which uniquely stamps each individual, institutes the beginning of the struggle for dominance on the part of the secondary process psychic activity over the primary. With the establishment of the superego ego-ideal as a separate psychic system to which magical (primary process) psychic activity is relegated, the child is in a position to begin the systematic acquisition of secondary process thinking—i.e., reality oriented thought and action. I do not mean to imply in any simplistic way that secondary process function is not present long before the oedipal period. What I am speaking of is its relative dominance and significance at different periods.

From this point of view the so-called latency period assumes a somewhat different significance. It is a period of rapid ego development, primarily related to mastery of the secondary process which is necessary for the acquisition of the specifically human skills required by the particular social and historical environment in which the child is growing. But always, in the background, can be discerned partially submerged omnipotent needs, in the form of fantasy, play activity, the delight in fairy tales, (or, in more modern terms, cartoons), etc. At puberty, this relative dominance of what we might characterize as the cognitive aspects of ego development is disturbed by the emergence of the powerful sexual drives, together with the characteristic final growth spurt. The earlier psychosexual stages are recapitulated at this new level of development. Under this impetus the ontogeny of omnipotence is also recapitulated, with much greater resources at its disposal.

We are all familiar, perhaps too familiar, with the turbulence of adolescence precipitated by biological maturation. One of the most striking and disturbing aspects of adolescence is the apparent fluidity of the psychic apparatus. The boundaries of the psychic structures which had achieved some relative stability and demarcation, now seem to loosen significantly. It is this aspect of youthful development which creates so much difficulty for us in evaluating these youngsters. Primary process psychic activity breaks through unexpectedly. Conflicts from earlier levels of development are suddenly activated in order to be worked through again. It is not surprising then, that infantile omnipotence with all of its ramifications should reappear in some form at this time. I coined the term "omnipotentiality" to indicate the relationship of this seemingly new manifestation to the omnipotence of infancy which, after all, had never truly disappeared, and (as we have just seen) exercises a significant and continuous influence beneath the surface.

The fundamental thesis of my previous presentation was that there exists a particular facet of development of the ego, or perhaps more appropriately of the "self" (Hartmann, 1950), during the period which we now call late adolescence (roughly from 16 to 22) which was heretofore largely unnoted, except perhaps in a negative sense, or at most in passing. This aspect of development is sufficiently characteristic to warrant a separation of adolescence into two relatively distinct periods: (1) adolescence proper, which dates from the onset of puberty to the age of about 16, and (2) youth, from 16 until approximately 22 by which time the transition to young adulthood is usually complete. Naturally, the chronological age is only approximate in any specific case. Parenthetically, it may be noted that this dividing line is institutionalized in our society by our national "pubertal rite" of the automobile license at 16.

During this particular aspect of youthful development there emerge many of the phenomena of "omnipotentiality." It appears to be an essential and vital element in the maturation of certain aspects of ego development, particularly as these relate to the concept of the "self." It consists primarily of the feeling and conviction on the part of the youth that he can do anything in the world, solve any problem in the world if given the opportunity. If the opportunity is not given, he will create it. There is no occupation which is inaccessible, no task which is too much for him. As his perspective of the world broadens, as his horizons widen, he begins to question everything which his elders have come to accept. Nothing is impossible; nothing can be taken for granted. He can indulge in wild flights of the imagination, soaring speculations, incredible adventures. He knows no limits in fantasy, and is loathe to accept any limits in reality. Yet, at the same time, he finds it difficult to do one thing and follow it through to completion, because to do so would mean to commit himself to one thing primarily, and this he is not yet prepared to do because it would mean abandoning all the other possibilities, thus restricting his potentialities.

Limitation, reining-in, focusing, remain for the future, for the next stage: the transition to young adulthood. This characteristic coming to grips with one's real potentialities, and the willingness to apply them to a specific line of achievement, may be characterized psychologically as commitment. This represents the recognition of limitations (both external and internal), the acceptance of the fact that one must forego one's omnipotentiality for the sake of the acquisition of a particular skill or accomplishment, the realization that one cannot do anything and everything equally well, the understanding that one must establish priorities for one's self in life. The step from omnipotentiality to commitment channelizes the diffuse omnipotential energy into specific directions. If the individual finds the conflict too great to be more or less successfully resolved, he may retreat into fantasy, often regressing to the level of infantile omnipotence and magical thinking.

The resolution of omnipotentiality in the normal, healthy youth comes about from the "acting out" of omnipotential fantasies in reality, thereby submitting them to testing. Gradually, as they are tested and retested against reality, the diffuse omnipotential energies are bound to modify the omnipotential fantasies in keeping with the demands of reality. Only then can the youth establish for himself his own priorities and commit himself to some specific task; i.e., assume some specific role and place in society—in short, make the transition to adulthood.

It is exactly this continuous testing against reality which appears so bizarre, and so disquieting to the adult, who has already committed himself. It leads the youth into what the adult calls "excesses." The fantastic confidence of the youth in his ability to do things which the adult has come to accept as impossible is genetically related to the roots of omnipotentiality in infantile omnipotence.

The anxiety of the adult about the omnipotentiality of the youth stems both from its genetic relation with and its basic difference from the omnipotence of the infant. The latter is a wish-fulfilling fantasy belied by and related to the infant's actual physiological and psychological impotence. The youth, however, is both physiologically and psychologically potent—in fact, more potent than most adults. His omnipotentiality is therefore threatening and anxiety-producing to the adult, because it is closer to that of the adult and can therefore be more easily reactivated, and because it is much more real than infantile omnipotence. Infantile omnipotence lies in the realm of unrealizable fantasy; however, the youth, with his omnipotentiality, is much closer to the reality of the adult in time, and thus has the physiological and psychological potential of being a threat. The adult, having struggled to master his own youthful fantasies, is made uncomfortable and anxious in the presence of the fantasies and activities of the youth, particularly if it appears that the youth might be able to realize and fulfill them. In order to control their own anxiety, many adults vigorously suppress such tendencies in the youth. The wildness, the exuberance, the excesses, the dedication, the intensity, the devotion, the single-minded pursuit, and above all, the fantastic confidence which characterize so many youthful activities are exactly those qualities which such adults find secretly fascinating and consciously frightening. Other adults may deal with the threat in other ways, ranging from ignoring—and neglecting—the youth, to an inappropriate clinging to (or attempting to return to) what amounts to the phony youthfulness of the aging but perennially uncommitted adult.

Another common adult reaction to the expressions of omnipotentiality in the adolescent is that the young person is pursuing will-o-the-wisps, holy grails, vain illusions. From his own position of commitment he reacts with scorn or alarm to youth's ecstatic involvement, unreserved hero worship, glowing faith, idealistic devotion to the pursuit of "the impossible dream." For the adult who has committed himself to a specific course in life, often irreversible, it all appears to be an illusion. But for the youth, not yet having made his commitment, it is not illusion. It is very real, very meaningful, very important, and at this stage of development very valid for him.

Adults tend to stress the turbulence, the distress, the helplessness and the confusion engendered by the maturational psychophysiological surge during this period. At the same time they underestimate the gratifications which arise from the process of growth, maturation, and the eventual attainment of adult status. Youths do not challenge merely out of perversity, defiance, rebellion, and spite, but rather out of definite inner need to question, to "challenge an axiom," to use Einstein's wonderful phrase, because of their omnipotential striving. Only by testing his newly acquired strengths, his new mastery, can the youth temper himself to the reality of the adult world, on whose threshold he stands.

The very suddenness with which young people shift their vocational goals, immerse themselves in one field, and work assiduously therein for longer or shorter periods of time, only to discard such involvements just as suddenly and turn to something else with equal or greater intensity, is related to the feeling of omnipotentiality and to their inability as yet to accept the commitment which is necessary for the passage from youth to adulthood. The feeling of omnipotentiality, while it continues, permits the teenager to roam far and wide in many fields before responding to the social and maturational necessity of commitment.

Indeed, the free exercise of this omnipotentiality is a necessary and salutary occurrence in youth. The wider the range of exploration, the more adequately prepared is the youth to relinquish his omnipotential strivings and channelize them into specific priorities, to choose the necessary, appropriate, inevitable commitment. Unfortunately, adults, out of their own anxiety, often make this essential exploration and experimentation as difficult as possible for the youth. The youth resent this and they rebel against it—which leads to further repressive measures, both social and individual.

Herein perhaps lies a major implication of the concept of omnipotentiality: that' the omnipotentiality of youth arouses fear and hostility in many adults through reactivation of their own struggles therewith. This unrecognized resentful anxiety in the adult is rationalized both socially and individually. It manifests itself in eternal complaints against the rashness and folly of the younger generation, and more seriously in repressive measures which take the form of narrowing and restricting the opportunities for expression of these impulses by the young and demanding a commitment from them at an earlier time than they are prepared to make it, or than it is possible for them to accept.

The resultant anger of youth manifests itself in many ways, all of which have as their common denominator the expression of the omnipotential desire to be free and able to do anything— whether in earlier generations as seemingly bizarre as goldfish eating, as risqué as panty-raiding, as dangerous as hot-rodding, or any other activity which expresses the contempt for the limitations and commitments of adulthood. In our current turbulent scene, one can see elements of these feelings of omnipotentiality in the background of many of the social struggles which grip our society. It is very much to the point that these involve predominantly the youth, who do not accept the impossibility of change. In the colleges and in the ghettoes alike, it is the youth who dare to "challenge the axioms" accepted by their elders.

If the red thread of infantile omnipotence runs through all developmental periods up to the point of young adulthood, one might well ask what its further fate is in the adult life.

We know quite well the varied neurotic and even psychotic forms it may take if it has not been adequately worked through in earlier stages of development. But its persistence universally in some form or other into the years of maturity is an area that has been ignored. Even in the healthiest and most well-adjusted people, infantile omnipotence ultimately triumphs in the form of immortality through the propagation of children.

## REFERENCES

Fenichel, O. (1945), *The Psychoanalytic Theory of Neurosis.* New York: W. W. Norton & Co.

Freud, S. (1939 [1934–38]), Moses and monotheism. *Standard Edition,* 23:7–140. London: Hogarth Press, 1964.

Hartmann, H. (1950), Comments on the psychoanalytic theory of the ego. *The Psychoanalytic Study of the Child,* 5:74–96. New York: International Universities Press.

Pumpian-Mindlin, E. (1965), Omnipotentiality, youth, and commitment. *J. Amer. Acad. Child Psychiat.,* 4:1–18.

Spitz, R. A. and Cobliner, W. G. (1965), *The First Year of Life.* New York: International Universities Press.

Tartakoff, Helen H. (1966), The normal personality in our culture and the Nobel prize complex. In: *Psychoanalysis—A General Psychology,* eds. R. M. Loewenstein et al. New York: International Universities Press, pp. 222–252.

# 17. PERCEPTION, AN EGO FUNCTION, AND REALITY

Edward D. Joseph, M.D.

---

Psychoanalysis began as a conflict theory of human behavior and it was assumed that all mutual development evolved out of conflictual situations. These were of course intrapsychic conflicts between various systems of the mental apparatus. It is to Freud, and later Hartmann (1939), and others more recently, that we owe the recognition that not all human behavior stems from intrapsychic conflict. Rather much of what is seen when mental functioning is examined arises outside of conflict with some functions being innate and others serving adaptive processes as well. Even functioning which may have its origin in conflict may continue to operate after the conflict is resolved and this type of functioning may also serve adaptive purposes.

For the sake of theoretical codification it is possible to group the psychic functions of the human mental apparatus under three headings—the first is the basic inner instinctual needs of the organism; second, those functions which mediate between these needs, their gratification and the situation in the external world, and finally those special functions which determine moral and ethical behavior first provided by the environment and later as internalized within the mental apparatus. This is the tripartite concept of mod-

246

ern structural psychoanalytic theory—id, ego, and superego. Note that this is a division based on groupings of functions to which are assigned arbitrary names. It is functions we observe in operation in examining a patient or in describing mental productions. It is possible to spell out in greater detail the various functions observed—perception, memory, motility, relationship to reality, thinking in all its aspects, affects, defensive operations, relationship to objects, and to the self, etc. Some of these functions are innate qualities of the mental apparatus (perception, memory, motility) while others develop through the interaction of these innate givens, instinctual needs, environmental factors and conflict, and are built up of more complex components. Hartmann assumed that the given functions of the apparatus exist prior to conflict calling this a state of primary autonomy (i.e., functioning free of conflict). The other functions develop out of conflict, but may attain levels of autonomous functioning, a state of secondary autonomy.

An important aspect of mental functioning is that there is in practice a constant interaction and interdependence between the various functions grouped together in the concept of ego. For the purposes of this paper, the function of perception will be separated out for examination and comment recognizing that doing so does violence to the interrelationships which exist between the various ego functions.

It is important to differentiate between perception and sensation. Sensation is the neurophysiologic response to a stimulus and is mediated through neurophysiologic processes. Perception is the psychologic aspect of the response to a stimulus and involves among other things the quality of consciousness. (The work of Fisher and others in regard to registration outside of consciousness will be discussed later.) This distinction between sensation and perception was common in philosophic and psychologic writings until recent times (see for example, Binet, 1907) and is still valid from a psychoanalytic point of view. Modern psychologists, on the other hand, tend to ignore this differentiation. For example, Forgus (1966) in his recent book wrote: "Perception will be defined as the process of information extraction" (p. 1). This definition which is the one accepted by most modern psychologists and many neurophysiologists includes the whole process of the gathering of data as well as the sorting and the use of it. From this point of view perception includes both learning and cognition. Psychologists and neurophysiologists regard the process of perception as one resulting from an input into an apparatus and a response to that input. It is a process that seemingly ends at some level of brain functioning. For the psychoanalyst, however, the process ends not in the brain but continues into the mental realm bridging the mind-body gap in a manner as yet unknown. For the psychoanalyst, this latter portion of the process is perception and apperception and is of particular concern to him. It is the area in which he has a unique contribution to make for the psychoanalyst is in the position to consider the vicissitudes of the end product of this information-gathering process bringing to bear upon it all of his knowledge of the various aspects of ego functioning; that is, the psychoanalyst is concerned with what happens in the apparatus between input and response.

The following clinical example will be of value in the discussion to follow. A 40-year-old business man who had been in analysis for several years at the time of this event arrived somewhat early for his afternoon session. It was a warm spring day so he decided to wait outside the building in the fresh air rather than go into the waiting room inside. While standing in front of the building he saw a white convertible driving up the street and to his surprise recognized his analyst as the driver. He watched me pass the building and maneuver into a parking spot. Responding to my greeting as I entered, he followed me into the office within a few minutes. At the start of the session he mentioned how unusual it was for him to have come early, but because a particular piece of business had been finished more quickly than anticipated he had some extra time on his hands. He had been enjoying himself in the warmth of the spring day and was contemplating some of the benefits of his country home now that the weather was becoming good. He went on to express his surprise at seeing me since he had assumed I was inside my office. As he was saying this, he suddenly realized he could not remember the color, make, or type of my car, and in fact as he thought of it he really was not certain if he had even seen me outside. He fell to ruminating on this, knowing on the one hand that he had in fact seen me, although he could no longer remember anything about the vehicle, but on the other hand there was an element of uncertainty, or unreality about the knowledge he had just acquired. Suddenly he added, "I know it must have been you because I made particular note of the license plate number." He then gave my license plate number and he commented on the vividness of this visual percept of the license. Actually, for some months later he was able to recall the license number of my car, always with a visual image of the license plate itself.

This series of events can be examined in somewhat greater detail. According to his perception an object with mixed familiar and unfamiliar features had entered his field of vision. He had an immediate recognition of the familiar part of the object, and certainly, even the unfamiliar part (the vehicle) was not that unfamiliar to him. He also had a glimpse of a completely unfamiliar series of numbers and letters on the license plate. It is possible to separate the processes that went on and to conceptualize the process by seeing part of it as taking place outside the person of the patient, namely the movement of the object and the emission of lightwaves from the object which reached and stimulated his visual apparatus. From then on the remainder of the process took place within the person of the patient. There was presumably stimulation of the retina and transmission of impulses along nerve pathways until they reached the occipital lobe of his brain. There the object was registered after which it was mentally perceived and represented. This representation was then compared with already existing representations and with this came the cognitive process of recognition of both the person and the nature of the object.

Within the body of the patient the transmission processes along the retinal pathways belong to the realm of the neurophysiologist. The establishment of a representation of these nervous impulses within the perceptual apparatus of the patient is within the province of the psychoanalyst. Before turning to the latter portion, a brief comment on the neurophysiologist's contribution to this process is in order. Lord Russell Brain (1965) wrote: "Perception depends upon the existence of receptors which are sensitive to the particular forms of physical stimulation" (p. 8). He further stated that the nerve impulses which carry information about the different forms of sensation are basically alike. Therefore it follows that what leads to vision, hearing, smell or fear is the excitation of the relevant areas of the brain by electrical impulses which in themselves are similar. From this he concluded that the nerve impulses which are concerned with sensation are in fact a form of code. To spell out this process further the work of Hubel (1959) and Hubel and Weisel (1965) might be cited. In essence their works show that the excitation of individual receptory units in a sense organ, the retina, excites a single nerve fiber. A number of these nerve fibers converge upon and excite or inhibit a single retinal ganglionic cell at what might be called a higher level of the hierarchy. In turn a group of nerve cells at this level converge upon and excite a single nerve cell in the lateral geniculate body from which an impulse goes to the visual area in the occipital lobe. The relationship between these retinal units and their nerve fibers is in itself extremely complex, but as a result of this mode or organization the retina is equipped to respond to shapes and movements. In other words there is an organization of a stimulus proceeding at a neurophysiologic level of functioning.

The organization of the stimulus is a more complex function than had previously been recognized. There seems to be a subcortical organization of stimuli so that movement, shape, size and direction can be determined depending on the nature and quantity of retinal cells which are stimulated, the order in which they are stimulated, as well as the nature of certain neurophysiologic inhibitory processes. This organization of sensory stimuli can lead to innate modes of response that would account for such phenomena that seem to be highly organized reflex responses. Although the stimuli may be highly organized and the behavioral response also an organized one, this would be sensation in the terms defined above and would not be perception in the psychoanalytic sense as was previously defined. Lord Brain in his article stated, "the passage of the nerve impulse along the nerve pathways to the brain is not accomplished by consciousness; we become conscious of the sensation only when the nerve impulse reaches the brain." Thus he assumed that in the human the additional factor of consciousness enters into this process, in contrast, presumably, to what might occur in lower forms.

At this point the interest of a neurophysiologist such as Lord Brain and the psychoanalyst begin to coincide. Brain (1960) raised the issue about the nature of the representation established by this process and the state of the physical object which it represents. He pointed out there are physical reasons (aside from psychological reasons) as to why the representation of the external object cannot be the same as the actual object. There is, for example, the time taken for lightwaves to reach the eye of the observer and for the sensations to pass from the retina to the brain. This, at times, infinitesmal period of time means that the representation of an outside object is always of something as it was, not necessarily as it is. By and large there is the tendency to neglect this time interval as being of no consequence, but in instances where the time factor may be a very large one, as for example a light from a distant celestial object, the stimuli do not give information about the state of the star as it is but rather as it was at some point in the past. It is conceivable that in the vast amounts of time required for light to travel celestial distances the star may in fact have changed or disappeared, or something may have happened.

Brain concluded that objects are not perceived directly but rather the stimulation gives rise to a representation of the object. An objection to representationalism is that we have no way of determining that the representation reflects external objects as they actually exist. Brain discussed this question, which is of more than philosophic nature, since it touches upon the whole concept of reality and concluded that, by putting together the facts and information supplied by sensations, it is possible to infer such additional factors as speed and distance, thereby arriving at the inference that some elements in perception are "subjective." Bertrand Russell felt that the whole of the perceptual world is inside the brain and as such each individual has his own private perceptual world. Russell thought that there is one physical space but there are as many perceptual spaces as there are conscious persons. Whitehead (1932) felt that the concept of a private perceptual space is a form of misplaced concreteness. He said that this information is private and personal and it is the awareness of this information that is personal, not the spatial or perceptual relations that are determined.

It is important to keep in mind the representational nature of the perception for what is perceived psychologically is not the physical world as such but rather a representation of it. Actually for the psychoanalyst mental processes go on between mental representations within the hypothetical mental apparatus made up of the theoretical constructs of id, ego, and superego.

From a psychoanalytic point of view, stimuli and sensations stream in constantly from all the receptor organs of the body bringing information not only of events and objects outside the body but also of events and processes within the body itself. All of these sensations may give rise to perceptions and certainly may leave memory traces behind. Freud was concerned in his earliest writings onwards with the relationship between perception and consciousness as well as the relationship between perception and memory. He equated perception and consciousness, suggesting that they were, in terms of his earlier theory, coextensive and linked together as one system, the perceptual-conscious system. The relationship between memory and perception he found more difficult to deal with, but ultimately concluded by the time of papers such as "Notes on the Mystic Writing Pad" and "Negation" that perception and memory were mutually exclusive. If there were a perception with its quality of consciousness there would not at the one and same time be a memory trace at that instant of that perception. Similarly if there were a memory trace there would not simultaneously be a conscious perception of that event. A memory trace may be activated by the direction of cathectic energy to it so that it can acquire the quality of consciousness and become a percept once again. If it is a percept once again it is no longer a memory trace but may through the withdrawal of energy be returned once more to its status as a memory.

Perception as Freud considered it in his earlier writings, included not only the stimulus and the awareness of the stimulus but also the existence of "attention cathexis" so that the percept had not only the quality of consciousness but a degree of interest attached to it. Another form of phrasing of this same type of concept is that there is a "hypercathexis" so that the percept acquires the quality of consciousness. These phrases and terms can be of use as long as it is clear that they really fail to fully explain either the quality of consciousness or of attention.

The factor or quality of consciousness which is attached to perception has led some recent writers to consider the nature of the registrations of stimuli that occur in altered states of consciousness. Klein, for example, in 1959, stated: "Perception, for all its immediacy and the experience of direct contact with things-in-themselves which it gives in contrast to imaginal modes of experience, is also a cognitive event, framed by the context of meanings or concepts" (p. 19). He went on to consider the events that occur in altered states of consciousness such as dream states, hypnagogic reveries, drug-induced cloudings of consciousness, etc. In the course of these he made the point that the registration of stimuli may occur without their acquiring the quality of perception, that is the quality of conscious awareness. The work of Fisher (1954) and others repeating the pioneering experiments of Poetzl, have shown that there are areas of registration outside of consciousness. In fact perception may deal only with a central target area of stimulation with stimuli from peripheral areas of the target being registered but not being perceived. That this is a commonplace of observation in the psychoanalytic situation is known to all analysts who for example have patients who suddenly "see" an object in the consulting room which has been there for some long period of time. Or it may be that such an object may appear in a dream and only through the appearance in a dream will the patient "see" it in the consulting room.

To illustrate this phenomenon I submit the following example from a schizophrenic patient with benign auditory hallucinations that could best be understood as being derived from identifications and fantasies relating to the beloved and protecting father of her childhood. Frequently the patient would carry on conversations with the auditory hallucinated masculine voice which in turn would provide her with observations and cautions concerning her daily life. One day this patient while walking down the street, was lost in her reveries, as was often her wont, when she heard her "voice" say to her, "Wasn't that a lovely dress the bride was wearing?" She was startled and looked around to see that she had in the course of her walk just passed a church. From the door of this church a bridal couple had just emerged surrounded by a crowd of people. The bride was radiant in white, but of interest here was the fact that as she had actually passed the church she had had no conscious awareness of the stimuli or sensations until the hallucinated voice of her dead father called her attention to these and made them percepts. This is an illustration of the fact that there is registration outside of consciousness of external stimuli, which acquire the quality of perception only when some aspect of attention is attached to them. This instance shows the scanning function (often described as one of the superego functions but probably an ego activity here) and indicates the nature of the need to have attention directed to the registrations before they become perceptions.

Altered states of consciousness seem to have another effect on perceptions. Ordinarily with attention directed toward the central area of registration, the more peripheral areas of registration occur outside of consciousness and are not perceived. It seems that with altered states of consciousness, these more peripheral registrations acquire a degree of perception, but without belonging to a highly organized series of images or schemata. Thus they appear, as patients may report them from the couch, as disembodied percepts which have an unfamiliar or distorted quality. These would-be stimuli from more peripheral areas of registration (sight, sound, bodily sensations, etc.) by their lack of familiarity may be frightening or unacceptable. This may be part of the explanation of LSD experiences in which the drug affects the state of consciousness (a toxic effect?) so that some of the registrations outside of consciousness are perceived in the reverielike state following the drug intake. A similar effect may occur in hypnagogic periods, with anesthesia, etc., and finally it may occur in the state of freely wandering attention associated with the enforced suspension of concentration that occurs on the analytic couch.

These events in altered states of consciousness focus on another problem associated with perception. Many stimuli arising from both within and without the body stream into the mental apparatus. Relatively few of these are perceived so there apparently is a screening process which determines this. To say that the mature ego directs attention in accord with its interests describes the conditions which determine perception, but what can be said about the state of affairs before maturity is achieved? One answer was provided by Freud. It was felt that the young infant would in fact be inundated by stimuli with which the immature apparatus would be unable to cope. Yet aside from unusual stimuli whether in the nature of loud sounds or bright lights there seemed to be no untoward reactions present in the infant. This led Freud (1920) to the concept that the perceptual apparatus had an inborn screening and protective mechanism which he called a stimulus barrier. He conceived of the perceptual apparatus as having at least two layers: the first being an external protective shield (the stimulus barrier), within which was the second, that is the perceptual-conscious system. The concept of stimulus barrier allowed for the idea that the immature apparatus would not be overwhelmed by the quantity of stimuli impinging upon it. This concept of a mental apparatus surrounded by a protective shield has been utilized by later writers as being of value in understanding, for instance, some possible traumatization of the early infant by excessive stimulation so that the immature apparatus has more stimuli to deal with than it is capable of at its given age. This concept is found in some of the writings of Greenacre and is used by others who suggest that there may be an inborn defect in the stimulus barrier which accounts for the findings in certain autistic children where even normal stimuli are reacted to with a great deal of anxiety and withdrawal.

Analogous to the concept of a stimulus barrier serving to keep stimuli out, is the concept of stimulus need which suggests that there is a minimal amount of perception necessary for the adequate functioning of the mental apparatus. Recent work on sensory deprivation has suggested that, in individuals who are deprived of external stimuli through the nature of the experimental situation, there is an attempt via imagery and hallucinations to replace the missing perceptions. Early reports had been anecdotal experiences of individuals who were in isolated situations. The whole study of sensory deprivation and isolation has opened up since the publication of the first reports by Bexton, Heron, and Scott (1954) of the work that they performed in Hebb's laboratory at McGill. Since that time a variety of experiments have been done in which various sensory modalities have been interfered with so that the individual is deprived of stimulation via that sensory pathway. The most extreme form of sensory deprivation has been demonstrated in the experiments done by Lilly (1956) who immersed his subjects in water, enclosed in a helmet and breathing apparatus, so that the surroundings were completely neutral. The early reports contained mention of the frequent occurrence of hallucinatory experiences but later work, in which the experiments have been at times of a more acute nature, have not repeated these findings (Solomon, 1961; Ruff, 1966). Varying criticisms have been made of the experimental procedure such as the fact that there is not only a sensory deprivation but also a prevention of motor discharge through the particular form of the experimental situation. It has been therefore somewhat difficult to determine whether the lack of sensory input or the failure of motor discharge has played a part in the findings. However, there is no question that under the conditions of the experiment, as well as under the natural conditions in which individuals have been isolated, such as in prison, shipwreck, etc., that there have been psychologic changes associated with the loss of sensory input. These changes may include some alteration in intellectual functioning as well as the appearance of either projected imagery or actual hallucinatory experiences. Workers in this field very early called attention to the fact that the psychoanalytic situation is one in which there was a marked diminution in the usual sensory input. The quiet of the room, the reclining position, the lack of visual stimulation, the lack of auditory feedback from the analyst as might occur in a more normal social situation, all help in reducing sensory input and favoring regressive processes producing more primitive forms of thinking and imagery.

This fact is of importance in the treatment of certain borderline patients where the analytic situation poses too great a regressive threat. One technical device is the supply of more sensory stimuli than usual either through increased verbalization on the part of the analyst or the use of a face-to-face approach which allows for sensory stimuli which can be perceived within a more structured framework. This may assist in the operation of certain ego functions which are threatened by involvement in regressive fantasy formations leading in turn to misperceptions of the current reality. That these sensory inputs from the analyst may have other meanings is clear from the associations of many patients (e.g., "When you speak, I feel soothed as by a lullaby." "It doesn't matter what you say, as long as you speak—then I know you're not angry with me," etc.) but the reduction of the sensory isolation with its regressive pull is one factor.

This brings up the question as to whether perception is a passive or active process, a question that goes back to the Greeks who were unable to answer it. The general tendency is to regard perception as a passive process, yet in the paper on "Negation" Freud (1925) said ". . . perception is not a purely passive process. The ego periodically sends out small amounts of cathexis into the perceptual system, by means of which it samples the external stimuli, and then after every such tentative advance it draws back again" (p. 238). This repeated an earlier suggestion (1924) he had made in a brief note on the "mystic writing pad" though in the latter he had said it was the unconscious which sends out the feelers into the perceptual system. Freud (1920), however, appeared to have an additional consideration in mind for he seemed to be thinking of these cathexes going into the stream of stimuli so as to pick out relevant stimuli, relevant to ego interests of the moment. This would be along the lines of satisfying a need for stimulus nutriment. In the absence of external stimuli this searching could lead to regression to the primitive level of hallucinatory wish-fulfillment.

Miller (1962) considered the impact of sensory deprivation experiences on the phenomenon of ego autonomy concluding that sensory deprivation does not increase the freedom of the ego from the environment. He added that the ego's dependence upon stimuli from without ("stimuli nutrient" to use Piaget's term) in fact leads to regressive manifestations and impairs the freedom of operation of the ego.

Perceptions have been described up to this point as though it were possible to consider individual perceptions of and by themselves. But perceptions do not remain discrete, separate mental products and probably are never those from the earliest levels onwards. Rather there is a degree of organization of percepts which when established, aids in the recognition and classification of later perceptual experiences. Rapaport (1951) speaks of an early organization of perceptions around drive gratifications and of a later organization around reality-directed activities. This is in line with the development of the thinking processes. It might, however, be more useful to consider the organization of perceptions in terms of the development of the various ego functions and to describe each of these separately, even if somewhat artificially.

For instance, in early life, perceptions are the basis of the development of a sense of reality. This important ego function is built of representations of perceptual experiences which are joined together by the organizing function in such a way as to provide a representation of the world. Pleasure and unpleasure determine this ("what is perceived as good is taken in; what is bad is cast out" [Freud, 1925]). Either way a perception is involved and representations are built up. Memory traces of these representations are established so that in the course of time reality becomes a comparison of the new representation with an old one. Freud (1925) stated, "It is now no longer a question of whether what has been perceived (a thing) shall be taken into the ego or not, but of whether something which is in the ego as a presentation can also be rediscovered in perception (reality) as well" (p. 237). Later perceptions in other words are compared with earlier representations. One form of reality testing is based on this type of comparison, or as Klein (1959) suggests, perceptions are fit into a schema of pre-existing perceptions. This is an extremely schematic sketch, for the pre-existing perceptions used for comparison may be (and often are) made up not only of actual perceptual experiences, but also of fantasies, images, defensive maneuvers, expectations, etc. Freud gave just such an example in his late paper (1936) and Arlow (1959) used this in his explanation of *déjà-vu* phenomena. These comparisons are part of the sense of unreality associated with rapid transitions in space or time that people normally experience with foreign travel and as Gombrich (1956) pointed out in his studies on art, lead some to reject nonrepresentational art as being "alien to their expectations." That is, the perception cannot be recognized since there is no prior representation existing to fit together. Repeated exposure can make it acceptable since it will fit into a previously present frame of reference. This is a form of adaptation to reality.

To return to the patient described earlier: he had perceived a mixture of familiar and unfamiliar elements upon seeing the analyst's car. His compulsive need for order and regularity allowed acceptance of those parts of the perception which were familiar, but the unfamiliar aroused anxiety in him. This same patient had difficulty orienting himself to the office when he saw it at a different time of the day, whenever something forced a change of hour. The different shadows and shades caused by variations in the lighting were disorienting to him. In the patient's representation of the world he felt himself endangered by the strange and unfamiliar, so that like an infant he had to examine his environment to be sure it was safe. (The patient's unconscious fantasies, transference, etc., will not be introduced here.) His behavior is similar to the sensory hyperactivity of the paranoid individual who constantly scans the environment for potential danger. This hyperactivity is particularly evident in the hyperacusis such individuals show, for hearing is a sensory modality that is difficult to shut off and which brings information from both far and near in the environment (see Knapp, 1953).

Perceptions have an immediacy of experience which lends itself to testing of reality. If the current perception and the earlier representation coincide, the validity of the experience is accepted. If there is a discrepancy between the current perceptual experience and the earlier representations there is a tendency for the ego's organizing function to bring order out of this. The end result may be a distortion of the current experience in the service of maintaining the earlier, established representations (reality as it appeared to the patient described who doubted his experience) or a distortion of the sense of reality in the service of maintaining the validity of the current perception. Minor adjustments in both occur all the time and actually it seems, from the findings of sensory deprivation experiments, that the sense of reality needs constant perceptual input to maintain an optimal level of functioning.

The function of thinking is another ego function which is built up out of early perception and perceptual experiences. In fact, Freud's (1900) early definition of thinking was of an attempt to *re*-establish a perceptual identity between a memory trace and a present experience of frustration. From this early start the thinking function evolves and is interposed between perception and response. Thinking in fact often becomes the response to a perception replacing a motoric act. Thinking in the form of fantasy is often an attempt to provide order or causality in a series of perceptions, while earlier fantasies in turn may determine which stimuli are perceived and which are not. The complex interplay between fantasy and perception can be seen in a patient whose castration anxiety is great and who sees potential threats to his bodily integrity in every perception of sharp or cutting tools. Many misperceptions reported by patients can be analyzed in terms of such pre-existing, important fantasies. Recently a patient described a quarrel with his wife concerning the question of having another child. He spoke of her yelling and shouting at him until the noise simply overwhelmed him. Something in his recounting of this episode led to questioning his account of her yelling. He then reported that she had been speaking in her normal voice but that as she spoke her words appeared to become louder and louder. Further analysis of this led to scenes between the parents in which he felt mother was always yelling at father and then to fantasies of a primal scene nature having to do with a sadistic, violent attack of one person on the other. His masochistic fantasies had in this current situation led to a distortion of perception and a conviction about the distortion that only analysis could disclose and correct.

The function of thinking in all its aspects is a complicated one in which perception plays an important role. The process of symbolization upon which language and more mature thought depends can be regarded as the use of a conscious perception (of a word, image, etc.) in place of an unconscious mental representation. Imagination in terms defined by Beres (1960) is regarded as the capacity to form a mental representation of an absent object, affect, body function, or instinctual drive. This, he regarded as an advanced form of thinking characteristic only of man and one which develops as the mental capacity develops. This is a form of perception without outside stimulation and marks more mature functioning of the individual. Piaget (1930) in his description of the development of stages of perception lends experimental evidence to Beres' concept by dividing the states of perception into six levels (based partly on a study of the development of relationship to the object):

*Piaget's Stages of Perception*

1 and 2—Response to actual excitation.

3—Search for object as continuation of the action in the presence of the object.

4—Search for the vanished object where he *first* saw it.

5—Search for the object where he *last* saw it.

6—To deduce without perception ("real evocation") (16–18 months).

In regard to the development of object relations perceptions play an important role in the separation of self- and nonself-representations. The concept of body image (as one part of the self-representation) is based upon representations built up of perceptions from both within the body as well as from the body surface. The nature of object representations is a composite of perceptions of the outside object (once self and object have been differentiated), such perceptions including not only physical characteristics, but attitudes and desires of the outside objects. These may be registered, rather than perceived, and enter into the representations of the object. Fantasies, aggressive wishes, etc., may also determine the actual object representation. These can often be separated out through the misperceptions of a patient as shown in the transference reactions during the course of an analysis. The gentlest of analysts can be perceived as harsh, cruel, demanding, in accordance with transference distortions. Such transference distortions may also serve a defensive function. In the clinical example cited of the patient who saw the car, part of the patient's disbelief in the reality of his perception had to do with a need to dehumanize the analyst, so that he existed only within the analytic situation. Admitting the analyst's existence as a person put him in the position of having to admit to certain feelings, wishes, and fantasies about the analyst which he had been warding off as being anxiety-producing and dangerous. Rather than accept these, he denied the perception itself.

The ego's defensive functions often operate against perception, as in this last instance. Denial is the defense per se which by definition is concerned with the handling of external perceptions (Freud, A., 1936). The classic example of this in psychoanalytic writings is the perceptual denial of the reality of the female genital; of the various defenses against this perception the fetishist undergoes the greatest defensive distortion through the splitting of ego functions which enables him to consciously accept the reality while unconsciously denying it. Other defensive maneuvers (repression, projection, isolation, etc.) can all be utilized to ward off dangerous perceptions leading to perceptual distortions or misperceptions. Projection is often used to externalize an internal perception which can then be denied or accepted.

Of an opposite order is the defensive use of perceptual distortions as may occur when a patient "mishears" an interpretation during a session. Analysis of such an event often shows that the patient cannot accept the interpretation because of the conflict and anxiety it might produce. Misperception thus serves a denying function. At other times a patient may use perceptions (usually visual) in a defensive manner to "screen" out unwelcome perceptions (cf. Reider, 1960). Again to use the clinical example described earlier, the patient's clear image of the license plate with its series of unfamiliar numbers and letters served to replace the whole of the disturbing perception by a neutral, nonconflictual, visual percept. This is a process analogous to a screen memory as well as to symbol production in which a conscious percept stands for an unconscious representation; here the unconscious representation consists of a series of perceptions, feelings, and fantasies associated with them. For this patient the sight of the analyst's car was associated with earlier visual percepts having to do with fantasies of his wife's unfaithfulness in recent years and voyeuristic activities of his childhood associated with the parental bedroom.

## SUMMARY

This paper has attempted to consider an ego function in many of the aspects of its interplay and interdependence with all other ego functions. Although we cannot assert that some ego functions are more basic than others, it is within reason to consider many ego functions as a complex of more basic ones. Perception is one of the basic functions of the ego apparatus and as such enters into the development of more complex functions (e.g., reality testing, thinking). Still more complex functions result from the interaction of these modalities thereby making it possible to speak of the ego functions which enter into object relationships or into such a complicated, highly developed function as the sense of identity. Thus there would seem to be a hierarchical layering of ego functions from the simplest to the most complex. The constant interdependence at all levels of this hierarchy of functioning makes for the complicated behavior observed clinically. It is only for theoretical discussion that an exercise such as this paper attempts to separate out some of the basic interrelationships.

## REFERENCES

Arlow, J. (1959), The structure of the déjà vu experience. *J. Amer. Psychoanal. Assn.,* 7:611–631.

Beres, D. (1960), Imagination, perception, and reality. *Int. J. Psycho-Anal.,* 41:327–334.

Bexton, W. H., Heron, W., Scott, T. H. (1954), Effects of decreased variation in the sensory environment. *Canad. J. Psychol.,* 8:70–76.

Binet, A. (1907), *The Mind and the Brain.* London: Kegan, Paul, Trench, Trubner, & Co., Ltd.

Brain, Lord R. (1960), *The Nature of Experience.* London: Oxford University Press.

—— (1965), A trialogue. *Brain,* 88:4, November.

Fisher, C. (1954), Dreams and perception. *J. Amer. Psychoanal. Assn.*, 2:389–445.

Forgus, R. H. (1966), *Perception.* New York: McGraw Hill.

Freud, A. (1936), *The Ego and The Mechanisms of Defense.* New York: International Universities Press, 1946.

Freud, S. (1900), The interpretation of dreams. *Standard Edition,* 4 and 5. London: Hogarth Press, 1953.

—— (1917), A metapsychological supplement to the theory of dreams. *Standard Edition,* 14:217–236. London: Hogarth Press, 1957.

—— (1920), Beyond the pleasure principle. *Standard Edition,* 18:3–66. London: Hogarth Press, 1955.

—— (1924), A note on the 'mystic writing pad.' *Standard Edition,* 19:227–234. London: Hogarth Press, 1961.

—— (1925), Negation. *Standard Edition,* 19:235–242. London: Hogarth Press, 1961.

—— (1936), A disturbance of memory on the Acropolis. *Standard Edition,* 22:239–250. London: Hogarth Press, 1964.

Gombrich, E. H. (1956), The vogue of abstract art in "Meditations on A Hobby Horse." New York: Phaidon Publishers, Inc., 1963.

Hartmann, H. (1939), *Ego Psychology and the Problem of Adaptation.* New York: International Universities Press, 1958.

Heider, F. (1959), *On Perception* [*Psychological Issues,* Monogr. 3]. New York: International Universities Press.

Hubel, D. H. and Weisel, T. N. (1965), Neural organization. *J. Neurophysiol.,* 28:229.

Klein, G. (1959), Consciousness in psychoanalytic theory. *J. Amer. Psychoanal. Assn.,* 7:5–34.

Knapp, P. (1953), The ear, listening and hearing. *J. Amer. Psychoanal. Assn.,* 1:672–689.

Lilly, J. C. (1956), Mental effects of reduction of ordinary levels of psychical stimuli on intact persons. *Psychiat. Res. Rep.,* 5:1–28.

Miller, S. C. (1962), Ego autonomy in sensory deprivation, isolation and stress. *Int. J. Psycho-Anal.,* 43:1–20.

Piaget, J. (1930), *Child's Conception of Causality.* London: Kegan, Paul, Trench, Traubner, and Co.

Rapaport, D. (1951), *Organization and Pathology of Thought.* New York: Columbia University Press.

Reider, N. (1960), Percept as a screen. *J. Amer. Psychoanal. Assn.,* 8:82–99.

Ruff, G. E. (1966), Isolation and sensory deprivation. In: *American Handbook of Psychiatry,* Vol. 3, ed. S. Arieti. New York: Basic Books.

Solomon, P., et al. (1961), *Sensory Deprivation.* Cambridge, Mass.: Harvard University Press.

# 18. ISSUES IN RESEARCH IN THE PSYCHOANALYTIC PROCESS

Robert S. Wallerstein, M.D. and
Harold Sampson, Ph.D.

The purpose and focus of this essay is simply the justification of the need to formalize (that is, to go beyond) the clinical case study method as the central research instrument and research access to the therapeutic process in psychoanalysis. It is concerned with the place of formal systematic research on the psychoanalytic process and the numerous problems and issues thereby raised in devising and executing such research in a manner at once meaningful and responsive to the subtlety and complexity of the phe-

This presentation from the Mount Zion Hospital and Medical Center, San Francisco, California, is condensed from a fuller manuscript published in the *Internat. J. Psycho-Anal.* (1971). It was presented in this condensed form as the Frieda Fromm-Reichmann Memorial Lecture at the Department of Psychiatry, Stanford University School of Medicine (May, 1969), at the Los Angeles Psychoanalytic Society (April, 1970), the NIMH Research Scientist Career Development Committee conference for research awardees, Estes Park (June, 1970), the Association for Psychoanalytic Medicine, Columbia University, New York (September, 1970), and the San Francisco Psychoanalytic Society (October, 1970). It is from a study of the issues in research in the psychoanalytic process which has been in relation to the Therapeutic Process Study on the Modification of Defenses in Psychoanalysis of the San Francisco Psychoanalytic Institute and the Mount Zion Hospital Department of Psychiatry (supported by NIMH Grant MH-13915) and the Psychotherapy Research Project of the Menninger Foundation (supported by NIMH Grant MH-8308, and previously by the Ford Foundation and the Foundation's Fund for Research in Psychiatry). Their generous assistance is gratefully acknowledged.

nomena, while at the same time scientific in the best sense of that term (loyalty to the reality principle, as here embodied in appropriate canons of scientific inference).

There is no need to document the extraordinary reach of the traditional, specifically psychoanalytic, case study method innovated by Freud. The whole corpus of psychoanalysis, the closest in existence to a general psychology, comprehending the phenomena of both normal and abnormal personality development and functioning, attests brilliantly to the explanatory power of the theory derived from the data of the consulting room. It has flourished in the hands of its founding genius and of those who have come after, and has provided a truly extraordinary range of insights into the structure of the mind, the organization of mental illness, the forces at work in the treatment situation, the processes of change, and the requirements of technique. By contrast, it is the sobering appraisal of Strupp, a dedicated psychotherapy researcher, that despite the recent spectacular growth of formal research method and research inquiry in psychotherapy, these advances have to this point exerted but very slight influence on the theory and practice of psychotherapy. Strupp (1960) states the issue bluntly: ". . . If the advances of psychoanalysis as a therapeutic technique are compared with the experimental research contributions, there can be little argument as to which has more profoundly enriched the theory and practice of psychotherapy. To make the point more boldly, I believe that, up to the present, research contributions have had exceedingly little influence on the practical procedures of psychotherapy" (p. 63). And he goes on to cogently explore the schism that for the most part divides practicing therapists and investigators doing research on the therapeutic process and the issues involved in the search "to reconcile successfully scientific rigor with the richness and subtle complexity of interpersonal dynamics" (p. 70).

Valid as we recognize Strupp's argument to be, on balance we need be at least equally cognizant of the limitations of the case study method as a source of prospective continuing knowledge. These limitations have been clearly and variously summarized. Shakow (1960) spoke to the intrinsic inadequacies of psychoanalytic data that are reported by a *participant*-observer (the analyst); as observers and reporters analysts are "handicapped sensorially, memorically, and expressively. . . . Put simply, they are limited in how much they can grasp, in how much they can remember of what they do grasp, and in how much and how well they can report even the slight amount they have grasped and remembered" (p. 83). Glover (1952) focussed on the distorting biases fostered by the very conditions of analytic life. "Analysts of established prestige and seniority produce papers advancing a new theoretical or clinical viewpoint or discovery. If others corroborate it they tend to report that; but if others feel reason to reject it, this scientific 'negative' does not get reported. So ultimately it is canonized 'as so-and-so has shown'" (p. 403). For this reason, Glover sees it as almost inevitable in psychoanalysis that "a great deal of what passes as attested theory is little more than speculation, varying widely in plausibility." Such defect is not corrected within the training situation which Glover feels tends rather to perpetuate error through its hothouse atmosphere and the ready ascription of dissent or question to "resistances" that the candidate must overcome.

Gill has commented on the limitations of the treating analyst as the sole research observer and reporter, to wit, the problems of the countertransference—to which we think we pay far more attention in our actual operations, than, at least in research, we actually do. In Gill's statement (Brenman, 1947) the research problem created by the countertransference is that of properly calibrating and recording oneself (the analyst) as the observer (in researches that rest, after all, on human assessments and not on dial readings).

> The psychoanalyst's recognition of the phenomena of "countertransference" is, in a sense, a first revolutionary step in the direction of the individual observer making correction for his own selective blindnesses. Yet in a case report we hear nothing of the subtleties of the analyst's attempt to understand and evaluate his own role in the "experiments" he conducts with each patient, and thus we must take on faith that individual idiosyncracies have played a minimal role in the observations and in the conclusions drawn from them. This is not to belittle the problems which would beset a man who attempted to record in his case report his own countertransference reactions and

his method of dealing with them, but it must nevertheless be pointed out that in no other branch of science are we willing to refrain from inquiring into the possible sources of error inherent in a recording apparatus or in the experimental design itself [p. 216].

This discourse has not been one-sided however. Not only are most analysts ready to agree with Strupp's discouraged caveat that after all, heretofore more formal research has not been able to demonstrate any real improvement over what can be learned out of the psychoanalytic process. There is the additional argument advanced so vigorously by Ezriel (1951, 1952) and supported as well by Bellak and Smith (1956), Hartmann (1959), Ernst Kris (1947), and Kubie (1956; and in Bronner, 1949) that the nature of the standard psychoanalytic situation is such as to permit it to be considered from a perspective which is analogous to a research (even a quasi-experimental) method. According to this view, the psychoanalytic situation is a relatively stabilized, recurring experimental situation in which the experimenter (the analyst) introduces independent variables (interpolations and other specifiable interventions) and can then predict and ascertain their impact on all the dependent variables within the situation in which, after all, he has the fullest conditions of access to the subjective data that enter consciousness (no matter how seemingly remote or trivial) ever devised. Using this model, of the "controlled conditions of the analytic relationship" (1951) Ezriel feels that the analyst "can state the necessary and sufficient conditions to produce a predictable event during that session" (1952). Kubie (1956) attempts to spell out these controlled conditions. He speaks of the "formal constancy of the observational situation" powerfully established by the "analytic incognito" which helps insure "that the variables which are brought into each session are brought in predominantly by the analysand" (p. 125). Into this system the analyst then intrudes interpretations as deliberate and calculated variables. In this sense, "An interpretation is nothing other than a working hypothesis to be tested by certain implicit or explicit predictions" (p. 129). Therefore, "to an unexpected degree analysis, as an experimental design, is an excellent model" (p. 133). Kris (1947) states that it is through its "rules of procedure" that the psychoanalytic situation establishes itself in this way as (almost) an experimental setting.

Appealing as this thesis is, it is clear that the terms of the argument have been subtly shifted by recourse to it. Truly following it, in its implications, takes us in fact far along the road towards more organized, i.e., more formal, research with its invoking of such words (and the concomitant implementation of the principles they subsume) as "control, keeping factors constant, dependent and independent variables, hypotheses, and predictions." The issue is now that such more systematized study is necessarily predicated on data more reliable, more replicable and more public than that yielded by the traditional case study alone, and additionally, of necessity involves more operations than simply considering the analytic hour from the point of view of a quasi-experimental situation.

It should be clear from the preceding discussion why two apparently diametrically opposed, but actually also complementary, sets of questions have arisen from the two sides of this dialogue. From that of the practicing analyst, the questions have been: Why such concern with formalizing psychoanalytic research? Does that make sense? Do not all agree that it is our traditional case study method, developed by Freud, and essentially unimproved upon since, that has developed all of our really useful knowledge of the inner workings of the mind in health and in disease, of psychopathology and of its unraveling via psychotherapy? The subjectivity of our data and of our method are of its essence; why destroy its demonstrated fruitfulness in an arid quest to render it objective? From the side of the friendly nonanalyst, the sympathetic clinical researcher, the questions have been: Why such lack of concern with formalizing psychoanalytic research? Does that make sense? Do not analysts realize that despite the extraordinary insights achieved by the clinical analytic case study into the workings of the mind and the way it can change, that the method is necessarily far less effective in verifying hypotheses (subjecting them to definitive empirical "test"), and in resolving differences between the insights (hypotheses) of different equally qualified investigators studying the same material.

Among other ways, the tension in this dialectic has been expressed in Gill's aphoristic statement of the problem of formalized clinical research as that of "the dilemma between the significant and the exact." Loevinger (1963) aptly maintains that no one-sided resolution of this issue should be sought, that "the function of the researcher is to look for what is objective, behavioristic, and quantifiable without losing the sense of the problem. The function of the clinician is to preserve the depth and complexity of the problem without putting it beyond the reach of objective and quantifiable realization. As in the battle of the sexes, so in the clinical research dialogue, if either side wins, the cause is lost" (pp. 242–243). In this respect, analytic clinicians can rightly and suspiciously point to too many instances where focus on the exact (the quantifiable) has redundantly affirmed the obvious and the trivial, or has led to misleading implications, being divorced from a larger qualifying context.

The serious investigator of the psychoanalytic process cannot, then, simply accept this dilemma at face value, and accept the necessity of choosing between significance and objectivity. He must address significant problems by as exact methods as his ingenuity and persistence can develop, recognizing that if established research methods cannot cope with the significant problems in his field, then new methods must be sought (Sargent, 1961).

A further dilemma confronting us in this field of study is that of methods advance before substance advance. Those who have attempted to study the psychoanalytic process and/or the outcome and effectiveness of psychoanalytic therapy in a systematic way have *inevitably* been more preoccupied with the development of methods which can be both relevant and objective (exact), which promise to validate appropriately, that is, within the theoretical system, and yet with due safeguards against error, against circularity of reasoning, and against argument by tradition and authority while searching out the degree of precision, that is, of mathematization, more appropriate both to the nature of the data and to the investigative methods than they have been involved to this point with the definitive investigation of specific substantive issues. We say *inevitably* because there are real and formidable scientific (as well as practical) difficulties in the way of studying the therapeutic process in psychoanalysis. These difficulties must not be allowed as arguments against formal, systematic research but they do emphasize the compelling need for psychoanalysts with a research bent to address seriously these complex technical problems which require solution if our research is to be faithful to the complexities and nuances of mental life, and at the same time rigorous, empirical, and bold.

Carrying the argument even further, exclusive reliance on the "informal" case study method has hindered, and promises to more gravely hinder, the further scientific development of psychoanalysis. In its thrust to this point in history, psychoanalysis has indeed profited enormously from the natural (and the fortuitous) observations of gifted individual observers who, within a supple and comprehensive theory, have been free to evolve ideas about how the mind hangs together, and to test these ideas by further observations of their own, and in informal consensus with their colleagues, until they arrive at an inner conviction concerning the inherent degree of credibility of these ideas.

Such conviction rests upon basic shared assumptions about how one acquires knowledge within psychoanalysis, assumptions that have been rendered explicit by a number of psychoanalytic theorists. Erikson (1958) in a little noted article on "The Nature of Clinical Evidence" spells out the nature and role of what he calls "disciplined subjectivity" in the handling of evidence and inference. Waelder delineates this further in defending the role of "introspection or empathy" in this regard (1962). He argues that though introspection and empathy are not infallible ways of knowing, neither are they negligible and that this is at least one advantage our science has, qua science, over physics. Kris (1947) avers that interpretation works not by "producing" recall, but by completing an incomplete memory, thereby implying that validation consists of the judgment of the goodness of fit. It is Schmidl (1955) who has developed this concept of validation within the system by goodness of interpretive fit most fully, arguing for the fit of the specific Gestalt of what is interpreted and how it fits the Gestalt of the interpretation (a homely example being the unerring fit of the two halves of the torn laundry ticket).

But at the same time we must agree with Kubie's (1956) cautious statement about the limits of the explanatory precision achieved within this approach to the crucial problem of validation. He stated that in analytic work we arrive at circumstantial evidence of the plausibility of an interpretation (at best), not of its unique necessity. If we are to move beyond these criteria of plausibility sustained by inner conviction towards the more usual scientific criterion of replicability, then the procedures of traditional psychoanalytic case study need to be formalized, especially in their verification phases.

How then may the basic data of psychoanalysis be made available to more scientific study? The issue here is one of creating the conditions that allow for independent and concurrent observation of the phenomena of the analytic consulting room. The historical method, bequeathed to us by Freud, consists of the study of the case material as reconstructed by the analyst, perhaps after completion of the case, in more or less detail, and with indeterminate accuracy, omissions, and selective distortions (biases). Freud's (1912) advice proscribing any note taking during the analytic hour was quite categorical. He stated simply that note taking in analysis, because it meant a conscious, i.e., logical, secondary-process, selection of data, was inimical to the proper analytic stance of evenly-hovering attention, that Freud intended as the analytic-counterpart to the patient's effort at free association; such focussed selection would be clinically detrimental to the analytic unfolding, in effect partially cancelling the gains in advancing the analytic work achieved through the free association effort, and also incidentally deflecting the analyst from the fullest attention to his interpreting task. Another advantage of his data reconstruction method, not mentioned by Freud at this specific point, but an issue with which he gave ample evidence of being much concerned, is that the avoidance of note taking obviously makes for the most secure ethical, as well as necessary technical, safeguards of the patient's right to proper privacy and confidentiality.

Nevertheless the many scientific liabilities of an essentially totally private and memory-based method of data generation are obvious and have been in part already presented under Shakow's (1960) and Glover's (1952) statements on the limitations of the traditional case study method as a source of continuing knowledge in psychoanalysis. The fallibility of human memory is itself the focus of a vast body of research in general psychology.

Beyond this issue of fallibility, the reliance on the treating analyst's memory alone as the central and unsupplemented data gathering instrument in analytic research is beset by many other equally powerful limitations. These can be listed as follows: (1) The unchecked, or at least not systematically checked, subjectivity of the observer (see Gill's remarks on the inadequate attention to the countertransference as a potent distorter of the data perceived and reported). (2) The unknown systematic biases introduced by any process of selecting data for presentation according to unspecified canons of procedure for determining relevance, an issue linked to but by no means coextensive with possible countertransference distortion. (3) The lack of public character so that concurrent or independent evaluation is precluded. (4) The lack of repeatability or reproducibility of a forever vanished circumstance. Clearly systematization must begin, rather than rest, at this point.

At first glance, the use of process notes (a summary by the analyst-observer of his most salient observations), even assiduously written and in considerable detail right after or at least on the day of each analytic session, would not seem to promise any significant advance over the above described schema of memory only, supplemented by ad hoc note taking, and retrospective reconstruction after the treatment. Process notes seem indeed subject in full measure to some, and in some measure to most, of the limitations already adduced for the "memory only" method. Certainly the charges of both incompleteness and distortion seem equally applicable. For after all, process notes, however detailed, are a highly selective, i.e., biased, sampling of the universe of events actually occurring during the analytic sessions.

But despite these real and obvious limitations, process notes may have some formidable advantages for clinical research purposes, and may indeed have a critical place at this stage of research on the psychoanalytic process. Keeping and studying systematically recorded process notes as the essential research data may actually be a large step forward in the direction of formalizing and sys-tematizing the clinical research enterprise. The notes provide a permanent and "public" record of a systematic series of observa-tions by a highly trained participant observer. They constitute a record which therefore does allow for independent and concurrent observation and study (though the record itself, by its very nature, must distort the universe of events of which it is a sample). Notes may be obtained with relatively little special effort and with mini-mal disruption of the natural analytic situation. Daily process notes are fuller, more detailed, and more descriptive-observational than notes written for summary purposes to be periodically entered on a chart; at the same time they effect roughly a 30-fold reduction of the material that would be obtained per session from a typescript of a tape-recorded hour. There is the vast gain then of having a relatively brief account, even of a long analytic treatment, which the human mind can process so that large sweeps of material, dis-closing major configurations and sequences of change, can be en-compassed. Such notes are obviously unsuitable for study of verbal interactions, or for any kind of microanalysis; but they do allow, may indeed enhance, detection of recurrent configurations (not buried in such a morass of deadly detail). In that notes for virtually a year of analysis may be read in a few hours, the clinically experi-enced reader will be able to retain a gross picture of the overall course of events, and perhaps of some obvious turning points. The material may be reread repeatedly, and gone over together in a group, until each investigator has a highly differentiated cognitive map of the terrain. Patterns may be tentatively identified, and then checked and rechecked against observations; similarities and differ-ences between groups of sessions become visible.

   The implication should be clear in all of this that to the extent that process notes represent equally well the phenomena of particu-lar research interest as do the more complete verbal account of the audiotapes transcribed into the verbatim typescripts (a still open, empirical question); that is, to the extent that they are "good enough" or "equally good" for the particular research purpose at hand, process notes may indeed have research advantages over the theoretically fuller recording of the audiotape, since they can well make not only for greater manageability of data but also for greater visibility and hence extractibility of centrally relevant data. And they can have a further evident advantage in the very realm of completeness itself. The usual assumption in the use of the un-supplemented tape recording as the essential research data is "that analysis all takes place in the space between the analyst and the patient and that it is fully represented by their verbal behavior" (Schlesinger, unpubl. manuscript). But it is clear that what is here necessarily missing is the unspoken activity in the analyst's mind, the overall meanings he grasped in the patient's material, and the basis on which he made decisions for or against intervention. For in analysis, only the patient is under the injunction to try to say everything that comes to mind. It is precisely however this mental activity by the analyst that should be captured by properly written process notes. In this area, process notes can have a "completeness" denied to the tape recording.

That this process can work, and in this way, is attested to by the reliance on just this data method in our entire clinical and teaching enterprise in psychoanalytic work, supervision, the case conference, the continuous case seminar. With all the acknowl-edged limitations in the method, people do conduct psychoanalyses, and learn under supervision how to do so, with process notes as the primary media of exchange and study. That the clinical and educational enterprise "works," however imperfectly, is not a scien-tific argument but it at least makes of this an issue worthy of systematic scientific scrutiny. This issue is the particularized version of the question—how good/bad are process notes anyway?—par-ticularized to the modifying question, for what purpose? The clini-cian has the impression that he *can* supervise a case from process notes, and be reasonably comfortable that he has a fairly good grasp on what is going on. There is no real body of other empirical evidence—pro or con—in regard to this issue, which is not simply a restatement of the proposition that distortion occurs, upon which everyone agrees. We need to know rather whether for a particular purpose process notes provide a "good enough" account, or per-haps at times, even a better one.

Knapp (1966) is one of the few analysts who has actually collected side-by-side data (tape recording and independent process notes) and subjected them to comparative study in order to begin to provide empirical evidence on this question of whether patterns of change demonstrable in the process notes would also be documented in the same ways in the actual tape recorded verbal transactions between the patient and analyst, a question of such major import for clinical practice and teaching, as well as research.

Nevertheless, process notes continue to be a biased sampling of the universe of events which interest us. Many investigators in calling for recourse to verbatim recording have squarely challenged any reliance on the therapist's process notes. Shakow (1959) has urged that investigators should "Love, cherish and respect the therapist—but for heaven's sake don't trust him . . ." (p. 108). Our own position is clearly more tempered. Despite all that we know about distortion, and despite the striking demonstrations that distortions of magnitude and significance regularly occur we nonetheless dissent from the widely held view that process notes are useless for serious objective work. In fact we hold the almost contrary view that for many kinds of clinical research questions they may be as good—if indeed not significantly better, for the reasons already outlined.

However, verbatim recording has in recent years been increasingly vigorously proposed as the essential methodological advance if research into the psychoanalytic process is to progress beyond the inherent limitations of subjective memory-based data upon which all other approaches rest. It was introduced into clinical psychoanalytic research as early as 1933, when Earl Zinn was known to have made dictaphone recordings of psychoanalytic sessions with a patient at the Worcester State Hospital (Carmichael, 1956). Since then this method has been advocated and used by a widening array of analytic investigators; certainly Freud's early expressed concern that the introduction of any such outside element would not be possible has been amply laid to rest.

The most obvious advantage of the recorded session is that of the greater completeness, permanence, and public character of the data record. Gill and his co-workers (1968) contrast this with the by now oft-repeated question concerning the limitations of the analyst's memory, necessarily distorted, since he remembers and synthesizes according to his conception of the case, since he is unwittingly, albeit necessarily, influenced by the nature of his therapeutic commitment, and since any such intense human relationship is inevitably clouded by scotomata. Kubie (in Brenman, 1947) further contrasts recording as an operational technique with the difficulties that arise in any effort at similar comprehensiveness of data recording by any other method. "Months of daily observation of a process which waxes and wanes continually by just perceptible increments and decrements gradually dulls the perceptions of even the keenest observer, paralyzes the memory through the monotony of repetition, and renders the written word literally useless as an instrument of record . . ." (p. 199).

Gill and his co-workers (1968) speak additionally of what they see as an equally compelling advantage of tape recording, beyond the improvement of the data record, that is, the facilitation of the separation of the therapeutic from the research responsibility, with the possibility of thus bypassing the inevitable biases of the analyst as a contaminant of the data filter. Haggard and his co-workers (1965) in fact wonder whether valid research on the therapeutic process can be done by the treating analyst at all if, "By objective research we mean procedures for data collection, analysis and interpretation which do not rely on the perception, judgment, appraisal or memory of a single individual—especially if he is personally involved in the therapeutic situation or process" (p. 171). Bergman (1966) who has conducted a several hundred hour long completed analytic treatment with recording and sound filming of every session felt that the recording itself became an integral part of the "structure" of the treatment. Psychotherapy has many elements of structure which provide it with a background and stable context that we regard as "natural" though there is nothing natural or usual about these elements in human discourse. To Bergman, sound recording is just another arbitrary convention which if used widely enough becomes taken for granted as one more "natural" element comprising the "cultural mores" of psychotherapy. In summing up the argument for the necessity of recording, Shakow (in Bronner, 1949) has declared it to be essential to proper data gathering for the naturalistic-observational phase that psychoanalysis at times seems in a hurry to bypass though it can no more afford to do so than can any other developing science.

Which is not to claim that recording poses no problems to analysis. The most manifest is the possible inhibiting or distorting effect upon the conduct of the analytic work. Historically, therapists have always couched their reluctances to record in terms of the presumed anxieties and sensitivities of their patients, but it seems to be an exceptionless experience that where recording has been done it is the therapist who has been the more anxious and disturbed. The patients have seemed less manifestly distressed, and have accommodated more easily and quickly. Haggard et al. (1965) have noted the possible contagious impact of the therapist's doubts and anxieties; they state too that therapists who are made anxious tend to exaggerate the extent to which their patients are anxious.

These anxieties generated in the analyst have several identified sources. Concern over professional exposure is of course uppermost. Gill and his co-workers (1968) address themselves to a deeper, less overt source of anxiety in the analyst. They point to the gratifications in the analytic situation which lead analysts to resist intrusion. "Autonomy is always relative, and the power and pervasiveness of infantile drives is such that they must find an expression. . . . The analyst would have to yield some of these gratifications if he opened his work for inspection" (pp. 241–242).

No wonder that Carmichael (1956) talked about how the majority of analysts whom he approached to participate as therapists in such a project expressed great interest in it but evaded a personal commitment; they didn't have time or didn't have a suitable patient. Carmichael said that they "preferred to remain at a distance from it, expressing doubts about the validity with which the therapeutic process could be represented under such conditions," (pp. 56–57) a viewpoint which he characterized as both a legitimate issue and a rationalization.

Whatever the case that can be made out for the presumed necessity of recording in at least some kinds of psychoanalytic research, a salient question concerns the impact of the fact of recording upon the analysis (again, no matter how well analyst and patient appear to be able to accommodate to the intrusion). Stated simply the question is: Does the analysis become vitiated in any serious way, as an analysis? This is not the same as asking whether the recording will have an effect as a major parameter—which no one can deny. Rather, as put by Haggard et al. (1965), "The question is not, Would the therapy have been exactly the same if there had been no recording? but is rather, Did this particular therapy, even though recorded, possess those components—free association, transference, interpretation, and so on—which characterize and must occur in psychoanalytic therapy?" (p. 173).

Gill and his co-workers (1968) have addressed themselves most extensively to this problem. They see the recorded research analysis as sharing at least two major attributes with another kind of different-from-usual analysis, the training analysis; these are (1) the absence of full confidentiality, and (2) the existence of goals in addition to the therapeutic. These they acknowledge to constitute special problems for the analysis; "difficulties are introduced which may on occasion be enough to tip the scales against success. By analogy, however, we argue that a recorded research analysis is not in principle impossible" (p. 237) (any more—or less—than a training analysis). Obviously, any aspect of the research context or any technical parameter of an analysis may be used defensively. Similarly, for the usual taken-for-granted safeguard of utmost confidentiality, "Whatever the desirable and rational reasons for maintaining it, it can carry hidden irrational and transference meanings as well" (p. 238). The proposed handling of all of these issues, is of course, thorough analysis, which they feel is "not in principle impossible." And this cuts both ways. Any analysis has a reality context so that "It is not merely *deviations* from the *usual* analytic situation which must be analyzed but so must the *usual* situation" (p. 238).

Haggard et al. (1965) take this whole issue further onto empirical ground. They bring a content analytic approach to a comparative study of material from recorded and nonrecorded "control" cases. They found no overall difference in the amount of concern expressed, for instance, by patients over revealing intimate thoughts and feelings and having them scrutinized by another person; but with recorded subjects these concerns were mobilized earlier in the treatment course (that is, the impingement of the reality forced the pace of the material). They summarize that there is no conclusive empirical evidence as yet, one way or the other, in regard to the existence of an undue (significant) distorting effect.

Overall, even the most vigorous proponents of recording agree that there is an indeterminate impact on the analysis, more overt in the stress aroused in the analyst than in the patient, leading to undetermined distortions in the unfolding analysis, and susceptible to analytic resolution to an unknown (to be determined) degree. To aid in the handling of analytic stress under such circumstances, almost all have come explicitly to feel the need for ongoing supervisory and/or consultative help, regardless of the analyst's sophistication and experience in both clinical and research techniques. An additional and related consideration has to do with the inevitable judgmental and evaluative aspects of any study, if those other than the treating analyst are party to the analytic proceedings, which is the case by definition in such research study based on recordings. In that sense the research is psychologically akin to supervision, and needs to be frankly faced on that basis. What follows as corollary to this, is that the therapist must be part of the research just as the supervisee is part of the supervision. This must be so not only for the analyst who tape records a case but for every analyst whose analytic material is offered for research study in whatever form. The analyst outside the research-study group will lack adequate motivation to do his part of the data-producing work, money and promised participation in authorship being unsatisfactory rewards in such situations. The treating analyst who is initially outside the research group will want to be inside it, and if he is in it at all, he should be in it all the way. Whether in or out of the group, the analyst will be concerned with the scrutiny of his work by professional colleagues, and we feel that these anxieties are most likely to be mitigated by being part of a freely communicating group of friendly colleagues. The group's inhibitions about criticizing a colleague, or temptations to do so, are part of the psychological reality of this type of study, whether or not the analyst is part of the group. His participation in the group is more likely to permit mastery of these inhibitions and temptations, and achievements of relative objectivity, than the more uneasy situation of discussing the case, as it would seem, behind his back.

It is clear from the foregoing discussion that other more arguable advantages and disadvantages aside, the recording on film of the analytic hour has the very real advantage of providing an indubitably more "complete" data record which successive and independent researchers may hear and see, again and again, and in slow motion, so to speak, to establish the objectivity, the replicability, and the validity of observations. But this completeness too needs examination, in its reality, and also in its putative advantages. For the search for ideal completeness of data is ultimately unrealizable and—a point we wish to make—also not the issue. Even the most faithful sound movie, most minutely studied, cannot reveal whole dimensions of highly relevant data. The obvious example, already stated, is that of the feelings and thoughts of the analyst, for the most part unuttered, which comprise his various reactions to the patient's material and the processes by which he selects how and what he will respond to. This consideration has led to the need stated by Shakow (1960) to supplement the verbatim recording of the analytic hour by the additional recording of the analyst's immediate post-session elucidation of his understanding of the session including all the associations that he could give to his unexpressed thought processes. In the interest of the continuing quest for ever greater "completeness" and even greater access than this, this proposal was pyramided in a round-table discussion by Shakow, Brosin and Kubie (in Bronner, 1949) to multiply the hierarchically layered observers of the therapeutic process and to tap, at both conscious and unconscious levels, the undivulged reactions of the therapist and all the observers through simultaneous concomitant access to their psyches. Such a top-heavy method would of course not only be unfeasible in any practically conceivable sense but in terms of the position we are stating, beside the point. Our thesis is rather that any manner of studying a phenomenon or a process will reveal only certain orders of data, hopefully those that are most centrally relevant to the hypotheses and the theoretical framework of the investigation, and will never be complete in the abstract sense.

Beyond this, the practical problems of the greater completeness, i.e., comprehensiveness, of the verbatim data record are simply stated. The material is voluminous, miles of tape, with roughly 30-page typescripts of each transcribed hour, and soon becomes overwhelming. Listening to the tapes and/or reading the material, especially when it is of someone else's therapeutic work is enormously time consuming and rapidly becomes inordinately tedious. We become the hapless victims of a major dilemma for research method in our field, that, like another field, electroencephalography, we mainly suffer from too much, rather than too little, data.

Which is all to say that tape recording (or for that matter any other of the data gathering methods here proposed) can be neither categorically dismissed nor categorically defended. The major issue of the detrimental effect upon the analysis is an empirical one to be answered in the specifics of the investigation, and the major issue of the value to the research is a theoretical one to be determined by the relevance of the data-gathering method selected to the phenomena being elicited.

In summary then, of what we trust to be by now a sufficiently focussed exposition of the development of a research posture, we believe that a permanent and public record is an extremely useful (actually indispensable) measure in moving from the traditional informal to the systematic and formalized in research on the psychoanalytic process—and that further delays in instituting steps in this direction are to the detriment of continuing psychoanalytic advance. The kinds of appropriate steps in this direction, of making the basic data of psychoanalysis more systematically available to scientific study may be several. We do defend the value of process notes, especially for studies of relatively molar processes taking place over broad sweeps of time, while recognizing all their fallibility, their biased selectivity, and their potential for uncontrolled distortion. We think though that steps can be taken to improve the quality of the notes used in research studies, as well as to test empirically the suitability of such notes for the intended research purpose. Important in this, is a side-by-side systematic study of how well such process notes (when compared to typescripts of tape recordings of the same hours) pick up observations crucial to the particular investigation. If such demonstration be successful for those particular purposes, there accrues the enormous research advantage of a 30 to 50-fold reduction in data volume, into truly manageable proportions without significant loss or alteration of relevant information.

Similarly, we also defend the recording of analyses for certain research purposes, as the evident impossibility of studying micro-processes effectively without recordings, but here too, it is equally incumbent that those purposes be clear in mind beforehand and that the purposes be relevant to the kind of minute interactional data being generated, because it will not really advance knowledge very far or very fast to simply have miles of tape without ideas and methods for converting that raw material into useable knowledge. At the same time, we need to urge the continuing careful study of the impact of the research procedures, not only recordings, on the processes being studied. We say this not as unfriendly critics convinced that research will "ruin" (i.e., irretrievably alter in ways that make useless for scientific research and/or render less effective as therapy) the processes under study, but rather as psychoanalytically knowledgeable investigators who recognize the powerful impact of methods of investigation on the human subjects of investigation. At the same time we recognize that the empirical evidence does not suggest that this impact renders analysis inherently impossible, or too difficult, or that the study of the impact is impossible.

Once made available, in whatever form and in whatever quantity, another whole order of problems in psychoanalytic research revolves around the question of handling the data in manageable ways, that nonetheless remain loyal to the subtlety, the complexity, and the richness of the clinical phenomena, again the dilemma between the significant and the exact. Here too there are thorny unresolved conceptual and methodological issues which will be delineated under the following headings: Of what order are the data? How do the data relate to the concepts? Are clinical judgments or inferences to be used as data? and The consensus problem or, what to do when experts disagree?

First, of what order are the data? At their most patent, the data of analysis are manifest behaviors. But, as Hartmann (1959) has put it; "While analysis aims at an explanation of human behaviors, those data, however, are interpreted in analysis in terms of mental process, of motivation, of 'meaning'; there is, then, a clear-cut difference between this approach and the one usually called 'behavioristic' " (p. 21). That is, the data of analysis are manifest behaviors, as interpreted by (to be specified) canons, according to which such interpretations can be consistently and reliably made.

The successful solution of the problems inherent in arriving at such consistent and reliable interpretation rests initially on two necessary conditions: (1) the maintenance of meaning without significant loss or distortion, as the data are compressed and are isolated from their qualifying context; and (2) adequate definitional clarity, of the nature of the events and phenomena, and the concepts according to which their meanings are understood. On the first of these, Lustman (1963) has said of the problems of categorizing and indexing psychoanalytic material for intracase and intercase analysis, in the Hampstead Child-Therapy Clinic, "The success of this approach with large masses of psychoanalytic material coming from large numbers of patients remains to be demonstrated. By that I refer to problems of compressability, fragmentation, and the loss of meaning when taken out of context . . ." (p. 70).

The second of these necessary conditions, that of adequate definitional clarification likewise represents a still major unsolved issue for psychoanalysis. Though psychoanalysis has a well established theoretical structure of explanatory constructs, on at least six levels of conceptualization and generalization varying systematically in remoteness from the observational base, and in centrality and importance for the theoretical structure (Waelder, 1962), it has not been able to achieve precise definitional clarification of even its most fundamental and most pivotal concepts.

Simple, working "definitions" can of course be formulated for ordinary clinical and heuristic purposes, as in the recently published official *Glossary of Psychoanalytic Terms and Concepts* (Moore and Fine, 1967). But there are indeed scientific complexities in the definitional process (and a major scientific labor involved in their elucidation for research purposes) that are beyond the usual capacity of conventional, pragmatic working definitions. Considerations of time preclude the discussion of examples of this problem at this point but I am sure that it is one that is painfully familiar to all who have thought and worked in this area. The need for clarification and the absence of agreement in this area of definition is presently so widespread that it almost becomes incumbent on each research group engaged in psychoanalytic research of serious scope to write its own glossary of terms, with its own idiosyncratic specifications of usage within the overall framework of psychoanalytic thinking.

Secondly, how do the data relate to the concepts? This problem is multifaceted and one of peculiar difficulty for psychoanalysis because of specific problems inherent in its structure as a science. Rapaport (1960) states the general issue and its specific difficulty in application to psychoanalysis thusly: "All sciences must subject observations to interpretation in order to establish their evidential significance for the theory. This is particularly conspicuous in psychoanalysis, where the concepts are by and large at a considerable distance from the observations" (p. 16). This issue of the remoteness of the concepts from their observational base makes for special difficulties in the task of empirical hypothesis testing in psychoanalysis because of the additional complexities automatically introduced by the psychoanalytically necessary principles of multiple determination and of overdetermination.

Rapaport (1960) has elaborated specifically on the need for, and the consequences of this principle of overdetermination. He said, "Psychoanalysis' need for this principle seems to be due partly to the multiplicity of the determiners of human behavior, and partly to the theory's characteristic lack of criteria for the independence and sufficiency of causes. The determiners of behavior in this theory are so defined that they apply to all behavior and thus their empirical referents must be present in any and all behavior. Since there is usually no single determiner which constantly assumes the dominant role in a given behavior, other determiners can hardly be neglected while a dominant determiner is explored. When favorable conditions make one determiner dominant, the investigator is tempted to conclude that he has confirmed a predicted functional relationship—as he indeed has. Regrettably, the attempt to repeat the observation or experiment in question often fails, because in the replication either the same behavior appears even though a different determiner has become dominant, or a different behavior appears even though the same determiner has remained dominant" (p. 67).

Though the problems here specified—of remoteness of concepts from observations, of multiple determination and of overdetermination and their consequences for the issues of prediction and of hypothesis testing, and of the lack of established correspondences between concepts and observations with the absence of accepted canons for clinical interpretation—are indeed formidable, they are added to, from the other side, by avoidable (and perhaps also, to some extent, unavoidable) confusions between data and inferences, and between levels of inference. For a systematic discussion of the latter difficulty (confusions between levels of inference or of theory), see the clear and rigorous exposition by Waelder (1962). In relation to the former, seemingly more surprising, confusions even between data and inference (or data and concepts) Hartmann (1958) has carefully traced some of the sources. He said:

What one calls "clinical" and "theoretical" presentations in analysis are divergent styles of abbreviation . . . due to specific features of the psychoanalytic approach the demarcation line of clinical and theoretical work is often not easily traceable. . . . Every reading of psychoanalytic literature asks of the reader a labor of reconstruction if he wants to view it in its aspect as a scientific contribution. What was the background in terms of observables? What are the hypotheses, either presupposed by the author, or deducible from his work? . . . [These hypotheses] interpenetrate with fact-finding in such a way that their hypothetical character is not always clearly recognized. Highly abstract hypothetical constructs (as libidinal cathexis, etc.) are then reported in a descriptive sense as data of observation [with consequent major confusions then in both clinical practice and theory! (pp. 133–134)].

The implications of these considerations on the difficulties in identifying the pattern of relationship of observations to concepts—difficulties then both of proper separation and of properly establishing linkages (the inferential process) in the face of the layered remoteness of the one from the other, and the multiply varying, multiply determined, and moreover, multiply overdetermined connecting links—the implications of these difficulties are that among the central tasks of psychoanalytic clinical research are those of making both descriptions and inferences as explicit, as "public," and as objective as possible, and of tracing and specifying as much as possible the relationships between observations and concepts, all as essential prerequisites to the establishment of reliability of intersubjective judgments. The pitfalls in the way are many. Space considerations allow mention of only one at this point. In proper pursuit of the task of relating the surface to the depths, the strategic emphasis may well need be the reverse of the more obvious direction. Since the theory specifically denies an isomorphic relationship between discrete behaviors (thoughts, actions) and intrapsychic states, and since the rules for inferring underlying processes from the data of observation can only be specified in the least complex and often in the least informative of instances, it may not be possible to proceed very far in the discovery or the reconstruction of complex underlying states from the configurations of elementary observational building blocks. We should expect rather, to work more the other way; i.e., to start with the more overarching concept, to differentiate its components and their various possible pathways of representation, and to discover thereby their array of possible empirical referents in the data of observation.

Thirdly, what is meant by the use of clinical judgments or inferences as "data"? In the whole process here described of according explanatory importance to both observation and inference and the fullest explication of the inferred pathway as well, the underlying state, or inferred intrapsychic organization, takes on an at least co-equal position as a relevant and manipulable base of knowledge. Sargent (1961) in an article establishing the methodological under-girding of the Psychotherapy Research Project of The Menninger Foundation in fact persuasively argued the viewpoint that the essential data of the whole clinical research enterprise are not behaviors or verbalizations, important as these are, but rather the patient's intrapsychic organization as "seen" clinically through these; i.e., the essential data are the clinical judgments.

The reader is referred to Sargent's (1961) own paper for the fuller exposition of this position, the anchoring of an entire research enterprise in clinical judgments as its essential data, and the manifold implications of this position for the methodological issues of psychologic science in its own right and in its place among the array of sciences. This position has not been argued uniquely by Sargent or from the area of therapy research alone. Schafer (1967) in discussing the uses of projective test data for clinical research purposes developed the same point, "the research unit should be interpretations and not scores or theme counts. Only then may we continue to work in context, which is to say, work with clinical data clinically. Scores, content, sequences, attitudes, behavior, and style of verbalization must all feed into the interpretations. Any one of these by itself is not a reliable, specific, and hierarchically localized indicator" (p. 81).

Fourthly, we have the consensus problem, or what to do when experts disagree? What Seitz (1966) has called the consensus problem in psychoanalytic research poses the curious paradox of being inherently probably the most difficult issue to contend with in clinical research, both conceptually and technically, and at the same time one that is studiedly underemphasized in the empirical and theoretical clinical research literature. This issue becomes crucial to any situation involving complex interpretive judgments based on inference; it does not operate importantly in the instance of simple reliability tasks performed upon sensory observational data. It is such a special problem for psychoanalysis precisely because psychoanalysis is so centrally dependent upon interpretation, and at the same time, as Rapaport (1960) has stated "there is as yet no established canon [in psychoanalysis], for the interpretation of clinical observations" (p. 113). Seitz (1966) reported one of the few clinical research projects, called the Consensus Research Project, which was directed squarely to the effort to surmount just this dilemma. The project was disbanded after the three years of work by Seitz and his seven senior analytic colleagues from the Chicago Institute for Psychoanalysis. The write-up referred to the work as a report of the failure of a research because of the "inability [over that time] to make progress in developing a reliable interpretive method, i.e., a method that would yield greater consensus among a group of analysts in making independent formulations of the same case materials" (p. 210).

The reasons for this persisting major consensus dilemma in psychoanalytic research are many. It is far more than an issue of inadequate research sophistication stemming just from an insufficient tradition of attention in clinical research to problems of method and design. Rather, in the nature of psychological (psychoanalytic) science itself there are at least three central features that characterize the field which, in principle, render consensus difficult to come by. These can be stated as (1) the principle of multiple causation or determination, (2) the principle of overdetermination and multiple function, and (3) the probabilistic nature of psychic states. The essence of each can be stated briefly:

(1) The principle of multiple causation leads clearly to the problem of the blind men and the elephant, the only partially correct views of observers with limited observational or theoretical vantage points. Strupp and his colleagues (1966) addressed themselves to this as an important contributing factor in the consensus difficulty in clinical research.

> Because many events with which the therapist deals are highly complex and far from being directly observable, and because a high level of clinical inference is often required in describing the nature of the events, it is likely that an independent observer will not traverse the same roads of clinical inference traveled by the therapist. The result is that their respective descriptions may fail to agree, or because the two observers may focus on different levels of abstraction or different facets of the matrix of events, it is difficult to determine from their respective descriptions whether they agree or disagree, or to assess the extent of their agreement [p. 371].

(2) The principle of overdetermination is related to but distinct from the above, though often confused with it. Here the consensus difficulty becomes further compounded, since beyond the array of necessary and sufficient causes to psychic events called for in the concept of multiple causation, there can be an additional superfluity of oversufficient causes. Once the elephant is fully and adequately described by bringing together the variety of partial perspectives into an integrated whole, there can still be additional descriptions, each of which, e.g., each of the metapsychological points of view, can be sufficient description to account for the entire elephant (the phenomenon under description). With regard to this concept, we have already quoted in part from Rapaport's (1960) statement of the need for it in the theory of psychoanalysis.

(3) A much less noted problem for the consensus search has to do with the probabilistic nature of patient-states. Chassan (1957) has especially elaborated the implications of this perspective. He said, "it is easy to argue from this point of view that the inability of coefficients of stability to become and to remain high is more a reflection of the underlying probabilistic aspects of patient-states than of any particular deficiencies in the testing procedures" (p. 167). He illustrates this issue from an area of "harder" data with reference to the now classical studies on the major internal inconsistencies revealed when the same panel of outstanding radiologists each reread the same chest X rays for the presence of minimal tuberculous lesions. With regard to the startling extent of the failure to agree with oneself demonstrated by this study, Chassman (1957) could of course state that "the phenomenon of a tuberculous minimal lesion . . . is a state or a process which can be said to be entirely uninfluenced by the mere act of observing it on an X ray plate, and the goal of complete agreement between all investigators is entirely unambiguous" (p. 170); in contrast, psychoanalysis is a study of interpersonal relationships, participant observation is a basic phenomenon of the therapy, countertransferences operate, etc.—all reasons for increased uncertainty and variability of interpretation.

In the face of these formidable difficulties in the way of reducing, ordering, and making summarizing judgments about the data of psychoanalysis, are there roads which nonetheless point in the direction of solving or at least mitigating the restrictions imposed thereby on empirical research yield? The problem, as we have developed it, is that we cannot reasonably work from the two platforms chiefly advanced in the research literature. The first is based on the attempt to get rid of the clinician so to speak, that is, to be free of the vagaries of clinical judgment, by the research focus on observables and measurables, on the raw observational data of manifest behaviors alone, applying then the usual statistical analytic techniques to determine their reliability. The limitation here, so clearly stated by clinician to researcher, is that these observables and measurables do not take on meanings, neither singly nor in combinations that can be inductively built up, except by interpretation in the light of concepts of varying degrees of remoteness from and varying kinds of relationships to the data, all beyond the scope of the statistical manipulations. The alternate approach is based on maintaining the skilled clinician and attempting to work from his ordinary (which can mean highly experienced), clinical interpretive judgments. The limitation here, stated equally clearly by researcher to clinician, is the consensus problem that renders these judgments not reliable enough, or rather not even sufficiently about the same things, and with a largely undetermined, and to a certain extent indeterminate, degree of difference in the things being judged. This is the problem started so cogently by Seitz (1966); the work of his project, involving highly skilled and experienced analytic collaborators, investing large quantities of time, zeal, and research sophistication in dedicated pursuit of this goal of consensus in clinical interpretive judgment is eloquent testament of the incapability of such a quest set in these terms. To seek more from that process is to ask more of the clinician judge and the concepts he essays to judge than they are in effect "calibrated" to bear.

Two other strategies less tried within psychoanalysis, derivatives and extensions beyond these, seem to us more concordant with the complexities of the issue at hand. The first is that of the Psychotherapy Research Project of The Menninger Foundation. The basic stance here has consisted of the effort to "refine" ordinary clinical judgment through a variety of operations, in part already alluded to in this essay. To the extent then that judgments about variables, successively refined, can give rise to judgments (of heightened agreement, consensus, or of known degree of disagreement, dissensus) from which empirically testable predictions can be generated, a method of successive approximations has been evolved for pushing clinical judgments of complex psychological events in the direction of more reliable, hence more measurable, statements. Put another way, such a research approach rests not on the precise measurement of behavioral observables of varying degrees of relatedness to the underlying organizing constructs, but on complex assessments (clinical judgments about the configural meaning of behaviors) that are, however, successively refined and then made to bear the burden of empirical testing via predicted consequences. It is the circling back from the observed consequences that strengthens or weakens the credibility of the inferential process built into the clinical judgments; and it is the attention to the refining process that renders these inferences more visible, hence asymptotically correctable.

An alternative approach to these same issues is exemplified in an ongoing therapeutic process study within the San Francisco Psychoanalytic Institute, in which rather than attempt to refine the clinical judgments relating to the organizing constructs, the effort is systematically made to more tightly link the constructs to their observable consequences. The strategy is to use careful clinical judgment to hypothesize relationships and then to seek out the behavioral consequents that should be evident if the relationships are as postulated, that is, to find the behavioral events that would correspond to the dimensions of the relationship. The final testing point is then in behavior observation that can be subjected to the usual specifications for reliability and validity. Both these strategic approaches exemplified in the two psychoanalytic therapy research projects then take into account the problem of the remoteness of concepts from observations, as well as of the potential for confounding the two; both too are anchored at crucial points in mensurable behavioral data. The varying but very partial degrees of success achieved to date by efforts in these directions lie in the difficulty of execution.

Closely linked to all the problems of arriving at consensus on clinical judgments is the problem of circularity contaminating the judgments so arrived at. The starting point for discussion of this problem can be taken from a statement by Rapaport (1960): "Clinical predictions are always fraught with the fact that all motivations have multiple, equivalent, alternative means and goals. Thus, such predictions usually cannot specify which of these equivalent alternatives are to be expected, and therefore, the results of experimental tests of these predictions must *first be interpreted* before their bearing on the theory can be established" (italics ours) (p. 120). The rub rests in the italicized phrase. This Rapaport (1960) discusses directly at another point:

> In the lack of a canon for clinical reesrach, it is difficult to accept as positive evidence observations which must first be interpreted before it becomes clear whether or not they confirm the predictions of the theory. We must be wary lest we smuggle in the confirmation through the interpretation. Axiomatization and/or a canon of investigation protect other sciences from such circularity. . . . [In psychoanalysis] as things stand, there is no canon whereby valid interpretation can be distinguished from speculation, though ex post facto the experimental clinician can distinguish them rather well [p. 112].

This tendency to circularity becomes inevitably built into any science relying predominantly upon the clinical retrospective method for the gathering of its data and the confirming of its hypotheses. For if we have no uncontaminated way of assessing the relative strength, the balance of forces, short of the criterion behaviors that are predicted to; that is, if we are only able to judge the antecedent state of affairs after the fact, by observing the outcome, then indeed we are in a circular bind. Waelder (1963) like Freud (1920) before him advanced just this viewpoint on the difficulty, in principle, of making clinical predictions; "i.e., a tendency is proved to have been the stronger one by virtue of the fact that it has actually prevailed" which completes the circle to "We cannot predict the outcome through measurement of the strength of the forces involved if we need that very result to make the measurement" (p. 39). The dilemma, so stated, would be insoluble in these terms if clinical research in psychoanalysis had to be strictly confined to observance of the clinical retrospective method, which was indeed the classical method of investigation used by Freud in his studies of symptoms, dreams, etc. This very powerful model which worked so successfully for Freud in unraveling the mystery of the dream, as well as his own psychic structure, became then the cornerstone of the clinical method for the study of both the abnormal and the normal phenomena of mental life. Its limitations have only subsequently become evident as psychoanalytic science has begun to move from the generating of hypotheses to the more rigorous testing of these formulations, when just such issues of hidden circularity arise. It is at precisely this point that the classical experimental model, in which antecedent conditions are specified and controlled in advance, and the subsequent consequences are then independently observed, has its locus of most potent application.

In keeping with this, the psychoanalytic discourse on prediction and on the use of prediction to cope with the problem of circularity has not been one-sidedly pessimistic. One of us has elsewhere (Wallerstein, 1964) and with collaborators (Sargent et al., 1968) reviewed the psychonanalytic literature on the place of both the principle and the tool of prediction in psychoanalytic investigation, developing a rationale and structure for the formal use of predictions to more systematically and precisely link the data of psychoanalysis to the theory of psychoanalysis, and thereby creating a wedge by which to test and extend the theory. A manual has been elaborated for such usage, together with a fully written out case illustration, including the explicit formalized predictions made in that case and the process by which these predictions were empirically tested. As stated elsewhere (Sargent, et al., 1968), despite the difficulty in making them, clinical diagnostic and therapeutic work rests on predictions that are inherent in the clinical undertaking. To quote:

> Every responsible action in diagnosis and treatment involves one or more predictions derived from clinical experience or from theoretical hypotheses. When the clinical team in a case conference assigns a patient to treatment, a prediction is implied; the course recommended is expected to benefit the patient in certain ways, some of which are

more, some less, spelled out in case discussion. In such deliberations, many other predictions are made, implicitly or explicitly, relating to possible contraindications, vicissitudes of the treatment course, and/or specific outcomes to be hoped for. Furthermore, clinical predictions, followed by observations of the course and outcome of therapy, provide myriad potential experiments which could test the hypotheses by which the predictions and treatment recommendations were guided [p. 3].

Thus, prediction is actually a pervasive, even universal, clinical phenomenon, usually implicit, and as such unremarked. The research task is to make explicit, so as to set up the conditions for formal testing, a range of predictions in a sample of patients entering psychoanalytic therapy, predictions relating, in the project discussed, to "the anticipated course and outcome of the recommended therapy, the nature of the problems to arise in the therapy in terms of expected transference paradigms, major resistances, and foreseeable external events that might (favorably or unfavorably) be expected to bear on the treatment course, and prognostic estimates in regard to expected or hoped-for changes in symptoms, in impulse-defense configurations, in manifest behavior patterns, and in level and nature of achieved insights" (Wallerstein, 1964, p. 684). It is at this point that critical control for circularity enters by setting down in advance the entire predictive complex of conditions, predictions proper, and assumptive clauses together with the predetermined evidence, in fact or in judgment, that will subsequently be necessary in order to sustain or refute the predicted outcome. It is by thus forcing the whole sequence of statements and of supporting reasons in advance, that observation is controlled and *post hoc* reconstruction, according to which almost any outcome can be plausibly rationalized in terms of a retrospective weighing of contending forces, avoided.

In this way, despite the many conceptual and practical difficulties in implementation, the systematic use of the predictive method can overcome the problems of circularity, and permit us to conduct "experiments in nature" (i.e., where we do not control the antecedent conditions, but designate their presence and hypothesize about their consequences) within the clinical research context.

This is not to say that prediction is the only way to avoid circularity or the only way to guard against confounding and error. For example, much of child analytic research is based on the direct observational method applied to the study of child development. Data from such observational and longitudinal study not only supplement but also check the retrospective and reconstructive data derived from the therapeutic process, whether of adults or of children. The congruence of the formulations derived from the data of the two independent, observational sources can be assessed. Additionally, and from within the psychoanalytic method proper, the fate of Freud's original traumatic (seduction) theory of the psychoneuroses is a demonstration not only of the major fallibility of the retrospective method, but also of the capacity of the superior mind to discern the increasing deviations from reality that such a false formulation progressively imposes, and within the method, turn it to a successful reformulation more loyal to reality; that what was once considered fact, an experiential vicissitude, is now to be considered fantasy, a maturational unfolding of an internal drive representation. This whole process of error and of rectification took place purely within the classical psychoanalytic method, without benefit either of "outside confirmation" or of predictive safeguard.

Finally, as a last major issue to be discussed we turn to the question: To what extent can one generalize from an N of 1 or of very few? Probably no one would cavil with Strupp's (1960) admiring remark, from the perspective of an empirical psychotherapy researcher, that it is a tribute to Freud's genius "that he succeeded in making valid generalizations on the basis of exceedingly small samples" (p. 63). Yet it is a fundament of modern empirical science that generalization across cases requires a sampling of many. As Janis (1958) put it:

An obvious weakness of a single case study . . . is that it can provide no indication as to whether the relationship applies to all other, many other, a few other, or no other human beings. Thus, even when a causal sequence is repeatedly found in a given person, the investigator cannot be sure that his findings can be generalized to any broad class of persons because the relationship may occur only in an unspecifiable, restricted class of persons sharing a unique constellation of complex predispositional attributes. [Or] to put the matter in more technical language . . . a major limitation of the findings is that there are zero degrees of freedom with respect to individual differences, even though each finding may be based on hundreds of degrees of freedom with respect to the samples of the subject's behavior that enter into the correlation between the independent and dependent variables [pp. 23–24].

In the face of such seemingly elementary considerations, how can one account for the success of so many N = 1, or N = very few, studies in psychological science? Support can be found both among statisticians and clinicians for the position that for many clinical research purposes more can perhaps be learned from a smaller than from a larger number of cases. From the statistical point of view, Edwards and Cronbach (1952) have stated: "Information gained from an experiment mounts more or less in proportion to factorial n where n is the number of uncorrelated response variables. By this estimate five tests can report 120 times as much knowledge as a single test in the same investigation! . . . Effort to refine measurement has the same beneficial effect on the power of an investigation as adding to the number of cases . . ." (pp. 55–56). From the clinical point of view, Gill and Brenman (1947) have stated:

> The clinical researcher must compare situations in which a number of variables are varying at once, thus differing from the experimentalist who can attempt to hold all the variables but one constant. The clinical worker must find patterns and principles of relationships which must be true to account for the observed variations. The more simultaneously varying variables he must deal with, the more uniquely determined is the hypothesis he must deduce to fit the observations. . . . Instead of saying that many variables force a multiplication of cases, we would say that they make necessary only a relatively few cases [pp. 220, 226].

The literature of experimental psychology has in fact, also reviewed the variety of circumstances under which the even more limiting condition of N = 1 can still mark an appropriate and useful, sometimes the only possible, research strategy. Dukes

(1965) in a paper entitled "N = 1," discusses the conditions that warrant employing an N of 1 under four headings:

> (1) If uniqueness is involved, a sample of one exhausts the population. At the other extreme, an N of 1 is also appropriate if complete population generality exists (or can reasonably be assumed to exist). That is, when between-individual variability for the function under scrutiny is known to be negligible . . . [(2) The dissonant nature of the findings]: In contrast to its limited usefulness in establishing generalizations from "positive" evidence, an N of 1 when the evidence is "negative" is as useful as an N of 1,000 in rejecting an asserted or assumed universal relationship . . . [(3) When there is a limited opportunity to observe: When] individuals in the population under study may be so sparsely distributed spatially or temporally that the psychologist can observe only one case, a report of which may be useful as a part of a cumulative record [and] (situational complexity as well as subject sparsity may limit the opportunity to observe). . . . (4) Problem-centered research on only one subject may, by clarifying questions, defining variables, and indicating approaches, make substantial contributions to the study of behavior [pp. 77–78].

In this connection Ebbinghaus' classic and still fundamental work on memory, done in 1885, on only one subject, himself, was quoted.

Granting then the critical importance and even the established value of the intensive study of one or a few cases in order to discover relationships or under special circumstances, is there some point at which psychoanalytic research on the therapeutic process must become large scale in order to "prove" the hypotheses developed on the few cases? If certain mechanisms can be demonstrated as components of change in the course of a completed psychoanalysis under study, just what is really involved in being able to prove that this is generally true in successful psychoanalyses? In part the answer to this is linked to the distinction delineated by Bakan (1955) between general-type propositions and aggregate-type propositions. General-type propositions assert something which is presumably true of each and every member of a designable class. They are given increased support with each successive positive instance, though never "proved" in a formal sense. With the first negative instance they are either overthrown *in toto,* or more likely, the class boundaries must be further circumscribed, to effect a new, more limiting definition that excludes the negative event and maintains the new, more narrowed, and hence more precise, proposition. In this sense, the "truth" is progressively approached via a succession of single cases. The situation is of course very different with aggregate-type propositions which assert things presumably true only of the class considered as an aggregate, and where increasing exactitude and significance accrue with the increasing size and representativeness of the sample.

Nonetheless we can and do justify our efforts on single or few cases, and the literature cited indicates that there is cogent scientific justification for this position depending on purpose and on circumstance of the study. Intensive case-by-case study may ultimately not be required for the testing of psychoanalytic propositions, and at such time appropriate canons must be devised for the transition from hypothesis-formulating studies of single or few cases, intensively scrutinized, to hypothesis-testing studies on the appropriately larger samples. But in clinical research we do start with an approximation of $N = 1$ for at least two good reasons. The first is that we want to make reasonably sure that we are not *oversimplifying* the world in abstracting certain processes, but are rather appropriately simplifying the world by identifying salient, invariant relationships. We prefer to seek these relationships within individual, intensively studied cases because this provides a needed anchorage in the complexity of clinical reality, and therefore some protection against naïve conceptions of how things hang together. Secondly, psychoanalytic researchers are historically just now in the process of developing research methods which formalize, systematize, and render explicit the dimensions of clinical practice and clinical inference that up to now have remained informal, implicit, and intuitive (the "art" of psychotherapy). In order to make sure that these methods do not distort the processes they are intended to investigate, the methods have to be devised and studied in relation to well understood individual cases. As we become more secure about our research technology in this area, we may imagine being able to deal with more extensive designs for cross-case studies.

In conclusion we would like to summarize the purposes of a discursive journey through the dilemmas posed by the many issues in research into the psychoanalytic process here discussed. We have attempted to confront side-by-side, with reference to both theory and practice, two questions relevant to our central thesis: Is it necessary to conduct more formalized and systematized studies of the therapeutic process in psychoanalysis? And, is such an endeavor possible? We maintain on grounds that we hope are cogent and persuasive, that the answer to both questions today is an emphatic yes! And yet we also hope that we have not sought, however unwittingly, to minimize the manifold conceptual and technical difficulties encountered by the investigator who seeks to combine clinical relevance with scientific rigor.

Our central conviction is that the informal clinical case study, in spite of its compelling power, has certain real and obvious—indeed formidable—scientific limitations. The major task for research in the clinical field and the clinical process is the formalization of this highly artistic method into a disciplined research instrument which transcends our clinically satisfactory operating criteria of inner coherence and clinical conviction bred of experience, while approaching the scientific criteria of systematic replicability. Psychoanalysis has historically underrated these complex problems of hypothesis-testing and verification. In part this has been because it has not wished a sterile scientism to obstruct genuine exploratory and investigative zeal; but in part this has grown out of an historical tradition—and a particular constellation of scientific problems which were conducive to that tradition—which has placed exclusive reliance on a single method of naturalistic observation by trained participant-observers. It is our belief that it is appropriate, feasible, and very necessary to supplement that tradition now in order to make further progress towards the solutions of the problems which we have here so urgently raised.

## REFERENCES

Bakan, D. (1955), The general and the aggregate: a methodological distinction. *Percept. and Mot. Skills,* 5:211–212.
Bellak, L. and Smith, M. B. (1956), An experimental exploration of the

psychoanalytic process: exemplification of a method. *Psychoanal. Quart.*, 25:385–414.

Bergman, P. (1966), An experiment in filmed psychotherapy. In: *Methods of Research in Psychotherapy*, eds., L. A. Gottschalk and A. H. Auerbach. New York: Appleton-Century-Crofts, pp. 35–49.

Brenman, M. (1947), Problems in clinical research (Round table, 1946). *Amer. J. Orthopsychiat.*, 17:196–230.

Bronner, A. F. (1949), The objective evaluation of psychotherapy (Round table, 1948). *Amer. J. Orthopsychiat.*, 19:463–491.

Carmichael, H. T. (1956). Sound film recording of psychoanalytic therapy: a therapist's experience and reactions. *J. Iowa State Med. Soc.*, 46:590–595.

Chassan, J. B. (1957), On the unreliability of reliability and some other consequences of the assumption of probilistic patient-states. *Psychiat.*, 20:163–171.

Dukes, W. F. (1965), N = 1. *Psychol. Bull.* 64:74–79.

Edwards, A. L. and Cronbach, L. J. (1952), Experimental design for research in psychotherapy. *J. Clin. Psychol.*, 8:51–59.

Erikson, E. (1958), The nature of clinical evidence. *Daedalus*, 87:65–87.

Ezriel, H. (1951), The scientific testing of psychoanalytic findings and theory. *Brit. J. Med. Psychol.*, 24:30–34.

—— (1952), Notes on psycho-analytic group therapy: interpretation and research. *Psychiat.*, 15:119–126.

Freud, S. (1912), Recommendations to physicians practising psychoanalysis. *Standard Edition*, 12:109–120. London: Hogarth Press, 1958.

—— (1920), The psychogenesis of a case of homosexuality in a woman. *Standard Edition*, 18:145–172. London: Hogarth Press, 1955.

Gill, M. M., Simon, J., Fink, G., Endicott, N. A. and Paul, I. (1968), Studies in audio-recorded psychoanalysis. I. general considerations. *J. Amer. Psychoanal. Assn.*, 16:230–244.

Glover, E. (1952), Research methods in psychoanalysis. *Internat. J. Psycho-Anal.*, 33:403–409.

Haggard, E. A., Hiken, J. R. and Isaacs, K. S. (1965), Some effects of recording and filming on the psychotherapeutic process. *Psychiat.*, 28:169–191.

Hartmann, H. (1958), Comments on the scientific aspects of psychoanalysis. *The Psychoanalytic Study of the Child*, 13:127–146. New York: International Universities Press.

—— (1959), Psychoanalysis as a scientific theory. In: *Psychoanalysis, Scientific Method and Philosophy*, ed. S. Hook. New York: New York University Press, pp. 3–37.

Janis, I. L. (1958), *Psychological Stress*. New York: John Wiley and Sons.

Knapp, P. H., Mushatt, C. and Nemetz, S. J. (1966), Collection and utilization of data in a psychoanalytic psychosomatic study. In: *Methods of Research in Psychotherapy*, eds. L. A. Gottschalk and A. H. Auerbach. New York: Appleton-Century-Crofts, pp. 401–422.

Kris, E. (1947), The nature of psychoanalytic propositions and their validation. In: *Freedom and Experience: Essays Presented to Horace M.*

*Kallen,* eds., S. Hook and M. R. Konvitz. New York: Cornell University Press, pp. 239–259.

Kubie, L. S. (1956), The use of psychoanalysis as a research tool. *Psychiat. Res. Rep.,* 6:112–136.

Loevinger, J. (1963), Conflict of commitment in clinical research. *Amer. Psychologist,* 18:241–251.

Lustman, S. L. (1963), Some issues in contemporary psychoanalytic research. *The Psychoanalytic Study of the Child,* 18:51–74. New York: International Universities Press.

Moore, B. E. and Fine, B. D. (1967), *A Glossary of Psychoanalytic Terms and Concepts.* New York: Amer. Psychoanal. Assn.

Rapaport, D. (1960), *The Structure of Psychoanalytic Theory: A Systematizing Attempt* [*Psychological Issues,* Monogr. 6]. New York: International Universities Press.

Sargent, H. D. (1961), Intrapsychic change: methodological problems in psychotherapy research. *Psychiat.,* 24:93–108.

——, Horwitz, L., Wallerstein, R. S. and Appelbaum, A. (1968). *Prediction in Psychotherapy Research:* a method for the transformation of clinical judgments into testable hypotheses [*Psychological Issues,* Monogr. 21]. New York: International Universities Press.

Schafer, R. (1967), *Projective Testing and Psychoanalysis.* New York: International Universities Press.

Schlesinger, H. J. (unpubl. ms.), Discussion of studies in audiorecorded psychoanalysis I. General considerations by Merton M. Gill et al. *Meeting of Amer. Psychoanal. Assn.* New York, Dec. 1967.

Schmidl, F. (1955), The problem of scientific validation in psychoanalytic interpretation. *Int. J. Psycho-Anal.,* 36:105–113.

Seitz, P. F. D. (1966), The consensus problem in psychoanalytic research. In: *Methods of Research in Psychotherapy,* eds. L. Gottschalk and A. H. Auerbach. New York: Appleton-Century-Crofts, pp. 209–225.

Shakow, D. (1959), Discussion. In: *Research in Psychotherapy.,* eds. E. A. Rubinstein and M. B. Parloff. Washington, D. C.: Amer. Psychol. Assn., pp. 108–115.

—— (1960), The recorded pychoanalytic interview as an objective approach to research in psychoanalysis. *Psychoanal. Quart.,* 29:82–97.

Strupp, H. H. (1960), Some comments on the future of research in psychotherapy. *Behavior. Sci.,* 5:60–71.

——, Chassan, J. B. and Ewing, J. A. (1966). Toward the longitudinal study of the psychotherapeutic process. In: *Methods of Research in Psychotherapy,* eds. L. A. Gottschalk and A. H. Auerbach. New York: Appleton-Century-Crofts, pp. 361–400.

Waelder, R. (1962), Psychoanalysis, scientific method and philosophy. *J. Amer. Psychoanal. Assn.,* 10:617–637.

—— (1963), Psychic determinism and the possibility of predictions. *Psychoanal. Quart.,* 32:15–42.

Wallerstein, R. S. (1964), The role of prediction in theory building in psychoanalysis. *J. Amer. Psychoanal. Assn.,* 12:675–691.

# Part V
# Clinical Practice

# 19. THE ROLE OF METAPSYCHOLOGY IN THERAPEUTIC INTERPRETATION

Victor H. Rosen, M.D.

The relevance of the metapsychological formulations of psycho-analytic theory to clinical practice has always been moot. In the case of Freud's theory of the "death instinct" the overwhelming verdict has been conspicuously against its applicability to the ex-igencies of everyday practice. There seems to be an increasing tendency in some quarters to emphasize Freud's clinical contribu-tions and to treat his metapsychological constructs as if they had greater historical than practical importance.

Two recent contributions (Klein, 1969; Needles, 1969) by emi-nent psychoanalytic theoreticians are illustrative. One (Needles, 1969) emphasizes the irrelevance of some of the economic aspects of drive theory to the understanding of the phenomenology of pleasure, while the other (Klein, 1969) asserts that drive discharge theory reduces the cognitive phenomena of pleasure and unpleasure to a quasi-physiological model. Both papers are representative of the objections raised in other contexts in less organized and closely reasoned form.

Having had the opportunity to discuss both of these stimulating

305

contributions at their initial presentation, I have been encouraged to elaborate those comments for whatever heuristic value they may contain.[1] My disagreement with the views of these two authors, stated briefly, is that metapsychology is not only an abstraction of clinical theory, but explicitly or implicitly determines many of the interventions that occur in the course of psychoanalytic treatment.

I will comment separately on these two papers which have different approaches to the problem before discussing the features that they share in common.

Klein's (1969) presentation is entitled "Discussion of Freud's Two Theories of Sexuality." His major premise is that the psychoanalytic conception of sexuality exists in two versions. The first he calls the "clinical theory" because it is the one that tacitly guides actual clinical work. Of this theory he says, "It centers upon the distinctive properties of human sexuality, upon the values and meanings associated with sensual experiences in the motivational history of the person from birth to adulthood, upon how nonsexual motives and activities are altered when they acquire a 'sensual' aspect and vice versa" (p. 137). The "second theory," Klein says, "translates these causal connections into quasi-physiological terms of a model of an energic force that seeks discharge. This drive discharge model is the basis of the rest of Freud's metapsychological theory which stands in a parallel relationship to the first theory without any necessary interconnection between the two" (p. 137).

My main disagreement with this statement, which is derived from clinical experience rather than theory, is concerned with Klein's (1969) implicit equation of "sensual" and "sexual" (an equation that is very common in clinical and theoretical literature). By making these terms interchangeable I think that he commits the converse of the error that he calls our attention to in examples that he gives of the misuse of the drive discharge model. It is true that Freud's early work with hysterical patients emphasized the ubiquitous character of the repression of erotic sensual experi-

---

[1] A careful reading of these papers (see Klein, 1969 and Needles, 1969) will make the ensuing remarks more intelligible and will also be of interest to the reader in their own right.

ences in both the genetic and dynamic aspects of symptom formation. In "Instincts and Their Vicissitudes" (Freud, 1915) however, where he was more explicit about his concept of "drive" than in any of his previous writings, he speaks of drives as having a "source," an "aim," and an "object." He thought that the drives had psychic representations and could be represented in psychological terms. It was only the question of "source" which seemed to cause him some confusion and for which he sought physiological explanations. Thus, a full description of the libidinal drive at a particular stage in its development, let us say the oedipal period in the male, consists, according to drive theory, of not only an unknown "force" but also of a particular aim, phallic penetration, of a particular object, the maternal one. Furthermore, the broad spectrum of clinical phenomena that have been investigated since the days of "The Studies" has given rise to revisions of such concepts as "defense," "narcissism," and "conflict." The terms "libidinization," "sexualization," "instinctualization," or Hartmann's (1964) concept of "deneutralization" as applied to activities or functions, is purely deductive and does not imply that a conscious erotic sensual experience has ever been associated by the patient with the disturbed activity or function. In such instances it is possible that it is drive discharge theory (whatever its ultimate validity) that more accurately suggests the clinical connections of diverse observations than so-called "clinical theory." (This is not meant to contradict Klein's assertion that a naïve use of metapsychological concepts can be misleading.)

Let me present a clinical example of an instance where drive theory may be more illuminating than a theory derived solely from the phenomenology of sensual experience. A 17-year-old male is being treated for a learning problem in school. In spite of a very high intellectual capacity he finds it difficult to study and does poorly in certain subjects. He is a product of "progressive schools" and parents who are "psychologically sophisticated." There has been great freedom in discussing sex in the family and an emphasis on avoiding any inculcation of shame or guilt about sexual matters in the patient. From the beginning of his therapy the patient speaks freely about his frequent but not compulsive masturbation and about his masturbatory fantasies and the sensual experiences that accompany them. His fantasies are active, heterosexual, and not unusual. Although his casualness is impressive, it does not appear to be peculiar or pathological. Sometime later in his treatment, with great difficulty the patient admits to the habit of nail biting which is accompanied by considerable guilt in the doing and shame in the telling. Why would most analysts agree that this activity should be explored as a masturbatory equivalent—that it is most likely a sexualized activity, in spite of the absence of sensual pleasure associated with it and the lack of full erotic sensual experience obtained in the seemingly unrelated masturbatory activity? In my opinion this clinical deduction (which incidentally could be validated in this patient) follows from "drive theory." I think that the general direction of inference on the part of most psychoanalytically trained clinicians would go as follows: The patient's environment has redirected his conflict. Guilt and shame have been largely removed from the conscious, erotic sensual experience but not from the drive as a whole. The patient is not conscious of the oedipal aim and object of his apparent sexual activity so that this part of the drive has been displaced to another activity where, despite the fact that it is unaccompanied by any conscious sensual pleasure, it becomes involved in the same conflicts as one that has such accompaniments. In this instance "sexualization" is not synonymous with "sensualization." Thus what Klein (1966) has described as "clinical theory" would not be sufficient to lead us to a therapeutically useful hypothesis, as in this case. There is therefore in my opinion, a use for both "clinical" phenomenological theory and an economic (metapsychological) one in the development of the interpretations that are the day-to-day stuff of clinical practice.

Leaving these objections aside, I think that Klein has raised some fascinating questions and has made some astute observations and suggestions. On the basis of one of these suggestions I can see the possibility of a revision of drive theory that would make it more consistent and perhaps increase its range of application to clinical phenomena. I think that Klein is quite right in pointing to the great clinical importance of the varieties of sensual cognitive schemata. He is also correct, in my opinion, in his statement that psychoanalysts have not been as interested as they should be in exploring the conditions, the development, and the meanings of sensual experience, and he is correct in his criticism of a tendency to confuse phenomenology in this area with theory. The neglect in the exploration of the varieties of erotic sensual experience extends to other forms of sensuality as well. I think that Klein also points out correctly that we have not even consistently assigned the cognitive aspects of sensuality, i.e., pleasure, to a special class of mental events as we have in the case of other mental phenomena. Klein's most interesting suggestion in this paper is that the consummatory aspect of the experience of pleasure may become its own "drive." Rather than replacing drive theory as he suggests, Klein offers an ingenious opportunity for making the "drive-discharge" model a completely psychological theory unencumbered by any appeal to physiology for its explanatory power.

Some of Freud's uncertainties about his own drive theory are recounted in Klein's paper. The most outspoken statement of his difficulties in relating the concept of drive "source" with the qualitative aspects of experience appears in "Instincts and Their Vicissitudes" (1915). After describing drives as having a source, an aim, and an object, Freud says:

> By the source of an instinct is meant the somatic process which occurs in an organ or part of the body and whose stimulus is represented in mental life by an instinct. We do not know whether this process is invariably of a chemical nature or whether it may also correspond to the release of other, e.g., mechanical forces. The study of the sources of instincts lies outside the scope of psychology. Although the instincts are wholly determined by their origin in a somatic source, in mental life we know them only by their aims. An exact knowledge of the sources of an instinct is not invariably necessary for purposes of psychological investigation; sometimes its source may be inferred from its aim [p. 123].

Freud then goes on to make the following statement (which seems to justify at least part of Klein's complaint that economic theory is ambiguous or equivocal):

> Are we to suppose that the different instincts which originate in the body and operate on the mind are also distinguished by different *qualities,* and that that is why they behave in qualitatively different

ways in mental life? This supposition does not seem to be justified; we are much more likely to find the simpler assumption sufficient— that the instincts are all qualitatively alike and owe the effect they make only to the amount of excitation they carry, or perhaps, in addition, to certain functions of that quantity. What distinguishes from one another the mental effects produced by the various instincts may be traced to the difference in their sources. In any event it is only in a later connection that we shall be able to make plain what the problem of the quality of instincts signifies [p. 123].

The editor of the Standard Edition says in a footnote at this point that it is not clear what "later connection" Freud had in mind. It seems doubtful that he ever returned to the issue. But since Freud was also uncertain as to whether the source and the aim of a drive can really be distinguished, Klein may offer a way out of the dilemma. He implies, if I understand him correctly, that once the cognitive schema for the sensual pleasure involved has been stimulated and experienced, the internalization of the circular process becomes the "source" of the drive much like the electrically wired rat who presses the lever to stimulate his own hypothalamic centers for sensual experience. Consummatory reinforcement of such a circular process may account for many features of "drives" such as their "peremptoriness" (Klein's term), rhythmicity, and invariance. If we also assume that the internalization of this circular process can become unconscious and secondarily autonomous, we have returned to a drive concept without invoking any mysterious "forces" that operate outside of the mind. It is important in this connection to recall that we have body image representations (i.e., psychic representations) of the organs connected with the leading erogenous zones, which are probably part of what Klein calls the "cognitive schemata for sensual pleasure." This would also clarify Freud's observation that sometimes the source of the drive may be inferred from its aim.

There is another dilemma posed by Freud's drive theory which may find a more consistent solution if these hypotheses are correct. In regard to the object of an instinct, Freud (1915) says that it ". . . is the thing in regard to which or through which the instinct is able to achieve its aim" (p. 122). "It is," he says, "what is most variable about an instinct and is not originally connected with it, but becomes assigned to it only in consequence of being peculiarly fitted to make satisfaction possible" (p. 122). This somewhat ambiguous statement, which asserts that the object is both a facultative and an obligatory part of the instinctual organization, is also implicitly clarified by the theory of internalization of a process of consummatory reinforcement of sensual gratification. The maternal object, it can be conjectured, would in this case be both the source and the object of the drive, in its inception at any rate, since in most instances it is she who sets the consummatory process of sensual experience and reinforcement into being in the first place. In *Three Essays on the Theory of Sexuality* Freud (1905) had already alluded to a similar possibility albeit somewhat tangentially. He says, "A mother would probably be horrified if she were made aware that all her marks of affection were rousing her child's sexual instinct and preparing for its later intensity . . . moreover if the mother understood more of the high importance of the part played by instincts in mental life as a whole . . . she would spare herself any self reproaches . . . she is only fulfilling her task in teaching the child to love (p. 223). In Klein's formulation there is thus another possible revision of classical notions about psychic structural development. According to such a revised view it would be the species-specific sensual cognitive schemata, ready for stimulation and consummatory reinforcement by the mother's nuturing care, which are the inborn mechanisms, rather than "drive forces." In this sense the child could be said to come into the world as an ego anlage. The id and later superego organization could be said to be determined in their inception by the degree and manner in which maternal stimulation of built-in ego schemata takes place. Far from making drive theory "parallel" to "clinical theory" such a view of the origin of the drives places them at the center of interpretable genetic phenomena. This hypothesis, incidentally, also seems to be more fruitful as an explanation of the syndrome of maternal deprivation in the first year of life than the one based upon depression due to object loss; i.e., what looks like depression is really drive deficiency. I think that it may also offer some interesting addenda to an understanding of the sensual aspects of the perversions.

Needles (1969) in his presentation, "The Pleasure Principle, the Constancy Principle and the Primary Autonomous Ego" suggests that neither the pursuit of pleasure nor the avoidance of pain is dependent upon drive-discharge phenomena. Unlike Klein, he does not suggest that all economic considerations be abandoned, but he does feel that the "constancy principle" (a corollary of the drive-discharge theory) is inaccurate and unsatisfactory for the explanation of the empirical data of the experiences of pleasure and pain. A major argument for this conclusion is that pleasurable stimuli are still perceived as such after satiation. Needles thereby infers that excitation followed by the discharge of energy is not the only avenue to pleasure.

Before confronting the main issue raised by Needles, I would like to comment on the terms "stimulation" and "excitation" which Needles uses interchangeably in his paper. He says for example, ". . . the ego plays a significant role in the experience [of pleasure] as well through its perceptual apparatus; visual, auditory, tactile, olfactory stimuli impinge upon it with great intensity and this excitation provides a preponderant pleasurable component of no mean proportion" (p. 813). In common speech the terms "stimulation" and "excitation" have overlapping meanings. It should be recalled however that Freud had an electrical model in mind when he proposed his theory of drive discharge to explain the "pleasure principle." According to the Oxford English Dictionary the electrical meaning of excitation refers to the induction of a charge in any instrument capable of discharging electrical energy, as for example, a Leyden Jar. In the same context, a "stimulus" is that which imparts the "excitation" to the apparatus which may store or discharge the energy thus induced. Hence the reaction of chemicals in food upon the taste buds is a stimulus, while the pleasure of the perceived flavors is the excitation.

The psychic model differs from the electrical in that psychic stimuli may arise within as well as outside the apparatus. If we define the concepts as I have outlined, then the processes of stimulation and excitation, although often interdependent, may at times be relatively independent of each other. For example, there may be stimulation without excitation if the apparatus is for some reason in a refractory state. Or there may be excitation and discharge of energy without prior stimulation if, for example, the capacity of the apparatus to store its charge is lowered. The possibility for this relative independence of stimulation and excitation are not included in the examples given by Needles (1969), examples which presumably refute the constancy principle. Thus he says,

> It seems to me that the acceptance of a functioning ego at birth renders more admissible the concept of a psychic apparatus that seeks excitation because it is pleasurable; and that this in turn necessitates the modification of the constancy principle which does not include seeking for excitation. Basic to this conclusion is the view that from the Id there can only be satisfaction from discharge but in the ego there can be pleasure from excitation of a certain type [p. 817].

If "stimulation" and "excitation" are different processes, this objection does not necessarily hold true. It is still possible to conjecture that the ego seeks "stimulation" rather than "excitation" (although I would prefer the passive verb "receives" rather than the active connotation of "seeks") and that the excitation produced as the consequence of this stimulation must be discharged in the interest of a homeostatic equilibrium that is necessary for optimal ego functioning. It is also conceivable under these conditions to postulate that the cognitive experience of pleasure derives from the discharge of excitation rather than from the sensory stimulation. The same reservation holds for Needle's objection to Schur's (1966) formulation. Needles says,

> It is rather puzzling that Schur retains the terms "pleasure" and "unpleasure" to designate principles that he claims have nothing to do with pleasure and unpleasure but only with energy levels. But does Schur really succeed in dispensing with feelings of pleasure and unpleasure in his formulation? Does the organism, for example, in avoiding the blistering heat of the sun react to the quantity of excitation or to the discomfort [p. 820]?

In my opinion this is a pseudo question. If the processes of stimulation and excitation are clearly differentiated there is no contradiction in Schur's formulation. One must specify whether the discomfort experienced in this hypothetical case arises primarily from psychological or physiological causes. One can imagine certain conditions under which the individual does not perceive discomfort, in spite of a powerful noxious stimulus, and others where there is intolerable discomfort from stimuli which are minimal in physiological terms.

As I have just indicated, these questions of definition are related to what I consider to be the main issue. I think that we often forget that drive-discharge theory applies to the pleasure principle as a psychological phenomenon. It was not intended to elucidate the neurophysiology of sensual pleasure. Thus to test the validity of the constancy principle it is necessary to be sure that we are dealing with psychic and not with physiological data. As Needles alluded to in his paper, it is possible that there is a tendency to equate the two which results in confusion. The problem, as in the case of Klein (1966), may arise from an indiscriminate use of the term "cognitive." To talk of the "cognitive" experience of pleasure may imply to some that only the phenomena of the peripheral organs belong to physiology and that anything which occurs in the central nervous system belongs to the realm of psychology. I think that we must consider brain physiology and mental events as different phenomena. To my way of thinking, psychology deals with mental representations. I do not think that the mental representations of pleasure and/or pain are the same thing as the ability to perceive pleasurable or painful stimuli, as for example, in a neurological examination. Freud was always quite explicit in defining the id as a psychic structure although he noted its physiological roots. If we are to be consistent, we must test Freud's formulations in terms of psychic pleasure. Nowhere is this distinction more clear and yet more likely to be confused, as Needles suggests, than in the phenomena of orgasm. How else, for example, can we account for the intensity of orgasm in dreams where there is little or no peripheral stimulation, or the orgastic phenomena of perversions where aberrant stimulation is utilized. Would it not be safer to assume that it is the meaning of the stimuli rather than the stimuli themselves that produces the difference in the cognitive experiences of orgastic pleasure.

Keeping the distinction between physiological and psychological events in the forefront, it seems to me that the same examples employed by Needles (1969) and others who have offered similar arguments, can be used to support the constancy principle. Needles cites, for example, the pleasure that an individual may derive from a liqueur following a meal which has amply satisfied his hunger. Why is this phenomenon different from that of the infant whose need for sucking pleasure continues after he has been adequately fed? Freud, it may be recalled, insisted that hunger and the oral drive for pleasure were anaclitically related and not identical; i.e., hunger is a physiological need while the oral pleasure is a psychological one. It may be argued that the pleasure of the liqueur after a full meal can be used as evidence for a residual undischarged oral excitation which can only manifest itself in undisguised form when it is no longer in the service of predominantly nutritional needs. Indeed the character trait of greed would have no referent making it discernible if it were not for the implicit concept of the constancy principle. We do not interpret behavioral phenomena as "greedy" unless the acquisitive need continues past the point of satisfaction of all the reasonable requirements of the individual.

It is generally agreed that the investigation of the phenomena of sensory physiology requires a research design that excludes psychological events as concurrent variables. Conversely we must also exclude the physiological effects of sensory phenomena before we can study their psychological effects. The same rules should apply to the "normal" psychology of what we call "cognitive" experience. I am not sure that Needles' interesting data or some of the findings of experimental psychologists deal consistently with the *psychology* of pleasure rather than its physiology. Since the economic theories of drive discharge have been derived from psychic phenomena, their validity should be tested only in terms of their ability to predict and to explain the phenomenology of the psychological aspects of pleasure and pain. On the basis of the evidence so far presented, I do not think that we are ready to discard either the constancy principle or the drive-discharge theory.

The question of the relevance of metapsychological theory to clinical interpretation cannot be separated from our view of the overall purpose of interpretation. In my opinion, both authors referred to above neglect the relationship between metapsychology and the central task of interpretation, which is to infer the *unconscious meaning* of the clinical phenomena observed and to transmit this inference to the patient in a linguistic message (Rosen, 1969). Thus in the example of the adolescent nail biter previously mentioned, we would not infer that this activity could have the meaning of a masturbatory substitute without the concept of a displaceable libidinal drive seeking alternate avenues of discharge when its usual mode of expression is blocked. Likewise, if we accepted Needles' argument that the continued seeking for pleasure-producing stimuli following satiation was a refutation of the constancy principle and Klein's concept of the irrelevance of metapsychology to clinical theory, we would probably fail to recognize the *meaning* of a variety of clinical phenomena that fall into this paradoxical category of behavioral events, including symptoms which represent "sexualization" without sensual pleasure.

## REFERENCES

Freud, S. (1905), Three essays on the theory of sexuality. *Standard Edition,* 7:223. London: Hogarth Press, 1953.
—— (1915), Instincts and their vicissitudes. *Standard Edition,* 14:111–140. London: Hogarth Press, 1957.
Hartmann, H. (1964), Comments on the psychoanalytic theory of the ego. In: *Essays on Ego Psychology.* New York: International Universities Press.
Klein, G. (1966), *Freud's Two Theories of Sexuality in Clinical-Cognitive Psychology, Modes and Integration,* ed. L. Breger. New Jersey: Prentice Hall, pp. 136–181.
Needles, W. (1969), The pleasure principle, the constancy principle and the primary autonomous ego. *J. Amer. Psychoanal. Assn.,* 17:808–825.
Rosen, V. (1969), Sign phenomena and their relationship to unconscious meaning. *Int. J. Psycho-Anal.,* 50:197–207.
Schur, M. (1966), *The Id and the Regulatory Principles of Mental Functioning.* New York: International Universities Press.

# 20. CHARACTER PERVERSION

## JACOB A. ARLOW, M.D.

In this paper I intend to describe some unusual character traits I have observed in certain male patients. What is striking about these traits is the fact that they are genetically related to sexual perversions and that structurally they are reproductions, in exquisite detail, of the defensive mechanisms which characterize the specific perversions. In the history of the development of these character traits one can observe how they substituted for or were the equivalent of perverse sexual practices. On the basis of these observations, a number of general conclusions will be offered concerning the relationship between certain character traits and perversions. I would also like to introduce the concept of character perversion. The relationship between these character traits and the antecedent perversions which they replaced may be expressed in the concept of "character perversion." Here I draw an analogy to the genesis of character neurosis. In this condition what had once been a symptomatic neurosis is, in the course of development, replaced by neurotic character traits, i.e., character neurosis. In the patients whom I am about to describe, an original perversion or tendency toward perversion was replaced in later life by an abnormal character trait, a perverse character trait. I propose to call such phenomena "character perversion."

Of the three character traits to be described the first two have a very similar organization and, in fact, are seen in close association. These traits may be observed in individuals who have difficulties in relationship to reality. Such persons are often strikingly unrealistic in their daily activities. Some of them have an additional, associated trait; they have a compulsion to tell petty lies. The third type of perverse character trait to be described demonstrates a wide range of behavior, some of which is often humorous in nature. I refer to the so-called "practical joker."

### The Unrealistic Character

In psychoanalytic experience, the unrealistic character type is by no means uncommon. It escapes notice because the disturbance is usually relatively mild and the patient does not complain of it. Furthermore, it may or may not upset the observer. Some degree of this disturbance may be seen in most male patients who suffer from intense castration anxiety.

The essential feature of this type of character trait is the refusal of the individual to face reality squarely. This may extend to many areas of his life. When presented with problems he will seize upon an insignificant detail, peripheral to the main point of the argument. Such a person may be dilatory but not out of malice or hostility. He does not derive the gratification from delay which is so typical of the anal character. Although perceiving the true nature of the problem he has a need to "beat around the bush." As much as possible, he tries to ignore the demands of reality which are measured in time intervals. In fact, in one of my patients, those two inexorable accompaniments of reality, death and taxes, were characteristically ignored. When obligations accumulate and are forcibly brought to the attention of this type of person, he often responds with panic.

This type of behavior must be distinguished from the counterphobic attitude Fenichel (1939) described. Counterphobic patients seek out dangerous situations in order to master them. The unrealistic characters *ignore* situations which they know to be dangerous. Figuratively they close their eyes to real life situations. On the couch during treatment, they literally keep their eyes closed most of the time. As one patient expressed it, he prefers to treat reality as if it were a bad dream.

In the setting of treatment, as in their daily lives, it is often hard to follow the conversation of such patients. Their speech tends to become vague and the description they give of events or people is imprecise and lacking in detail. They avoid reporting day-to-day events. When pressed for greater definition they become unsure of what they had experienced and the listener becomes confused trying to understand.

During psychoanalytic treatment the unrealistic character presents many technical problems. All the trends outlined above are aggravated and are used as resistance. The patient seems unwilling or unable to draw obvious conclusions. Sometimes the therapist feels that he is dealing with a case of pseudoimbecility. When an interpretation is offered, the patient "looks away," that is, he acts as if he had not heard what had been said or he focuses his attention on some insignificant detail, or he turns to a new subject without acknowledging the transition.

Sexually, these patients usually have some disturbance of potency, most frequently, ejaculatio praecox. One patient experienced complete anesthesia during sexual relations. He felt as though he were not participating in the act at all. The same patient suffered from a mild but chronic depersonalization and derealization. (In my experience, most of these patients have a form of detachment in the analytic situation which approaches depersonalization and derealization.) Experiences which other patients would feel as real, intense and dramatic, he treated lightly or with a feeling of estrangement. An operation, a funeral, or an accident were referred to casually and dismissed in a sentence or two. Such behavior is typical for this group of patients. It is hard for unrealistic characters to take a good look at a problem; at best, they take only a sidelong glance. They are glancers, not lookers.

In a male patient the inability to look at reality was true both in a figurative and in a literal sense. Actually, of course, he repudiated what he perceived. The data of analysis demonstrated that on one level of consciousness he was always perceiving and properly interpreting the information furnished him by his senses. In addition to the typical modes of behavior just described, this patient would make a point of "not seeing" what was in the consultation room. He could let weeks go by before noticing a new item of furniture. On several occasions he passed directly by me on the street without seeing me. He rationalized these perceptual difficulties by ascribing them to the fact that he had not been wearing his glasses. Typically, however, he would not wear glasses to the analytic sessions to insure, apparently, that he could perceive neither the analyst nor what the analyst was saying.

After this problem had been discussed for some time, the patient decided to put the interpretations to test by wearing his glasses to the sessions. He began by mentioning several of the decorative features of the office which he now actually perceived; previously he had a vague surmise that they existed. His thoughts next turned to several difficulties in his business life which he had avoided confronting directly. He had delegated responsibility for these matters to some of his subordinates and when they presented him with summaries and interpretations of their findings, he glanced through the reports very briefly. Some he put aside without reading at all, although a number of important problems pressed for solution. He lived in dread of losing certain important accounts but preferred not to think of it.

His thoughts next turned to the behavior of his three-year-old son who had been having nightmares. The boy, very articulate, had begun to ask vague questions about natural phenomena. He had been refusing to go to the park to play with certain friends whose company he had hitherto enjoyed. At night he got into bed, pulled the blanket over his head and said, "Can't see anything." The patient reported that his wife claimed that these difficulties in the little boy began after the following incident took place in the park playground: The child was playing when she suddenly noticed that "his eyes froze." He was staring at a little girl whose diaper was being changed. It took him a while before he could communicate with his mother again and when he did, he began asking all sorts of questions about playgrounds, structure of benches, etc.—nothing at all about the little girl.

The patient's mother had been staying at his home. She behaved in the household as she had when the patient was a child; she was careless of her dress. When the patient reproached her for the effect this could have on his son, his mother had answered him, "It's good for him, he has to learn the truth sometimes." Further associations continued the theme of shock connected with seeing the female genital, with recollections from many periods of his life. He reported a dream in which he saw the genital area of a woman; all details had been obliterated by a firm white girdle. The dreamer could see "nothing" and his attention focused on the very edge of the girdle where a long white garter belt dangled.

In a short essay on the nature of reality, Lewin (1948) comments on the fact that the idea "reality" as it appears in free association often stands for the female genital. The patient whose character disturbance has just been described lived out this unconscious equating of the female genital with reality. Such patients behave as if they were repetitively abreacting the traumatic confrontation with the female genital. The defense which they use represents a combination of denial in phantasy to which is added a compulsive need to focus attention on some distracting, peripheral, reassuring substitute item.

One of my patients came to understand how this reality denying part of his character was connected with his choice of professional career. He was the son of a carpenter. His training went in progressive stages from the study of electronics, to physics, and then finally to mathematics. He felt that mathematics was the "queen of sciences." It was superior to all other studies because there was no need ever to have any references to real events. "If you began with a hypothesis or an assumption, you can continue to elaborate or refine the system without ever having to turn to real facts or to deal with nature. It is an invulnerable and foolproof system." When he was a little boy he spent hours phantasying about how he could erect an invulnerable castle, one that would be invulnerable against any kind of assault. His appreciation of the defensive function of his character structure and choice of profession was revealed in the following short story which he made up about a person like himself. This material came up in the context of his fear of penetrating the female genital.

A carpenter once came home to discover that the television set was not working. He tried his hardest to find out what was wrong.

After many hours of labor, he gave up because he did not know enough about electronics. Consequently, he decided to study electronics and in time became an outstanding expert. He then realized that electronics is only a form of applied physics, so he bent his mind to the study of this field and soon became an eminent physicist. After a number of years he realized that physics is based upon mathematics and, as might be expected, he went back to study. Before many years he was acclaimed one of the world's great mathematicians. Years later, after many successes and honors, he sat with his wife musing on how his professional interests had developed. "Just imagine," he said to his wife, "how it all began. From not being able to fix that television set I went from one academic study to another until I reached the pinnacle of success in mathematics." "Just imagine," his wife answered, "if I had told you that day that you had forgotten to insert the plug into the wall socket."

In the clinical examples mentioned above, one may have noted indirect references to the typical male perversions of voyeurism and fetishism. These perversions, together with the others to be mentioned below, have a common origin in the need of the male child of the Oedipus phase to ward off intense castration anxiety. The perversion represents in part an attempt in the presence of overwhelming castration anxiety to make sexual gratification possible through certain behaviors which serve to reassure the individual against the danger of castration. The most common reassurance consists of some form of denial of the perception in reality of the penis-less female genital.

In my experience the voyeur and the fetishist are part of a complementary series. The voyeur is compelled to look but not to see. When he is unavoidably confronted by the truth (in the form of the penis-less female genital) he will have nothing to do with it. The patient whose amusing phantasy of professions was just reported was intensely scopophilic throughout childhood and adolescence. Like most voyeurs, his scopophilic activities were pursued under conditions which guaranteed that he would never really see, at close range, a completely nude woman's body. He avoided sexual relations and marriage for a long time and although unusually intelligent, he managed to keep himself ignorant of sexual information. After marriage he had sexual relations infrequently and sustained his potency either by perverse phantasies or by some distracting preoccupation with abstract concepts connected with his work. On the day following sexual relations with his wife or after being confronted with evidence that she was menstruating, his reality-denying activity would become most pronounced. It was under such circumstances that he would be driven to some perverse voyeuristic adventure or to some inappropriate, unrealistic act. When reporting these activities he seemed pseudo imbecilic. During sessions when the events were being interpreted to him, he would blink his eyes, close them, shield them with his palm or move his head as if he were shaking off some unbearable sight. Thereafter he would either change the subject (look elsewhere) or fasten onto some peripheral detail of what had been said.

In general, patients with this kind of problem have in common a wide repertory of eye-shielding mannerisms during sessions. One patient had long-standing voyeuristic and fetishistic impulses which he had only begun to control to some extent in recent years. For the first few years of his active sexual life it was a necessary condition for potency that his partner come into bed and get under the covers wearing a full girdle or underpants. Only under the covers would he permit her to be completely nude. He was also fascinated by garter belts, particularly by long dangling garters. He had an interest in photographs, which never completely revealed a woman fully nude, and was intrigued by "see through" clothes.

Another patient of this unrealistic character type passed through a very difficult latency and adolescence in which multiple perverse activities were prominent. Outstanding among these were voyeurism, exhibitionism, and fetishistic interest in shoes and bras. This latter type of defense serves as the transition to the role of fetishism in the genesis of this character trait. The fetishist in his defensive needs goes a step further than the voyeur. Not only does he look away in order to deny the unbearable reality of the female genital, he has a compulsive need to fasten his attention onto some reassuring, peripheral object. As is well known, the item upon which he fixes his attention and which becomes the obligatory condition for sexual fulfillment, unconsciously represents an actualization of the reality-denying phantasy of the female phallus. Perceiving the external, realistic representation of a female phallus negates the earlier unnerving perception of the real truth regarding female anatomy.

What determines which item the fetishist selects to represent the female phallus? According to several authors (Freud, 1927; Lewin, 1950; Fenichel, 1945) the fetish is selected on the basis of some contiguous visual impression which preceded or followed immediately upon the traumatizing view of the female genital. The garter, girdle, or some other item of woman's underclothes, close to or actually covering the genital, lend themselves as distracting perceptions. Upon these the frightened viewer may concentrate in order to look away from the heart of the matter. Displacing his gaze upward, the future fetishist may come upon the breast (Lewin, 1950) or the bra. Looking downward he finds the heel or the shoe. The perception of the fetishistic object thus becomes a screen obscuring the truth or concealing it completely.

Thus, in these patients, the character trait of being unrealistic derives from the need to fend off the danger of castration. In my material, the danger of castration was connected with the typical conflicts of the oedipal phase and was conditioned by traumatizing exposure to the female genital. Two mechanisms are fundamental in this particular form of defending against castration anxiety. First is the mechanism of denial, i.e. the perception is acknowledged consciously but is denied unconsciously. To this is added a second factor, a factor which is common to fetishism as well. When confronted with reality the individual can feel secure only if he can turn his attention to some realistic external perception which is distracting and reassuring because it corresponds to his unconscious phantasy of a female genital with a phallus. The character trait of being unrealistic is the equivalent of a constant, repetitive abreaction to the traumatic confrontation with reality in the form of the female genital.

## THE PETTY LIAR

For some patients the fetish must have a certain gauzy, filmy quality. Such patients require an item which is neither totally opaque nor fully transparent. They would love to look, in fact they have to look, but they do not want to see what is really there. In a patient who had such a requirement, a defensive shift from passive (looking) to active (showing) helped us to understand one of his pathological character traits. He was a petty liar. He was also a "Peeping-Tom" who kept complaining of the frustrations connected with voyeurism. At the last moment some item of clothing, for example, a nightgown, would obscure his view of the object he was observing at a distance; or the window shade would come down, etc. He managed never to quite see what he thought he was looking for. Actually, to be free from anxiety he required that something be interposed between himself and the truth of the world of anatomy. The object which excited him during masturbation had to be something insubstantial and filmy. As a youngster at camp he used to peek at staff members' wives when they were getting undressed. Several times he stole some items of lingerie, kept them near his tent, and concentrated on them while masturbating.

In his daily dealings he was always telling petty lies. As a rule these were not the kind of lies from which he obtained any material benefit. He told lies even when there was no need to conceal the truth. His productions during the session were usually unclear. He himself commented on the nebulous, *veil-like* quality of what he had to say, observing once that he never liked to tell "the naked truth." When he was able to deceive people into accepting his fabrications he felt a sense of mastery. Even if he did not tell a petty lie it was important for him to adorn or embellish what he was describing. Sometimes when he succeeded in having people accept his petty lies as real, he almost began to believe them himself. His character disturbance thus resembled the structure of certain types of imposters as well as the type of pseudologia phantastica described by Fenichel (1939b). The statement which conveys the unconscious import of this kind of behavior may be expressed in the following words: "If I am successful in preventing others from seeing the truth then I need not fear that I myself will be confronted by the shocking truth." This is an example of denial by proxy (Wangh, 1962).

A sublimation of this fetishist-like defense against castration anxiety may be seen in the choice of such occupations as hairdressing, fashion design, interior decoration, etc. There are many references, especially humorous ones, to the "deceptive" quality of female adornment and embellishment.

To recapitulate: The petty lie is the equivalent of the fetish—it is something which is interposed between the individual and reality in order to ward off the perception of the true reality and to substitute instead perceptions which facilitate ambiguity and illusion, both of which can temper for the patient the harsh reality of female anatomy. The fetish is, in a sense, a "screen" percept.

### THE PRACTICAL JOKER AND HOAXER

It is a short step from grasping the fetish and having phantasies about women possessing penises to dressing up in a fetish-like outfit or in women's clothes and then acting out the phantasy of being a woman with a penis. These fundamental features of the transvestite may be transformed and may become the basis of the pathological character trait of the practical joker.

The following features characterize the type of joker or hoaxer to whom I refer:

1.  The need to inspire panic or anxiety in others.
2.  The gratification of aggression and the sense of power which comes from perpetrating the hoax.
3.  The pleasure of exposing the hoax.

The joker or hoaxer acts out the defenses used by the exhibitionist and the transvestite. Certain exhibitionist perversions have in common the mechanism of identification with the aggressor. As the unprepared little boy was frightened by the shocking sight of the woman's genitals, so he turns and shocks girls by causing them to see his genital, a sight for which they are unprepared. There is a difference however. Whereas originally he *saw nothing,* in his perversion he *shows something.* Transvestism constitutes a reassuring denial. In essence, the transvestite says, "You have nothing to fear. There is no such thing as a body without a male organ. On the surface it seems female, but get a good look underneath and you will discover that the opposite is true. You thought something was missing but it was there all the time." Correspondingly, the hoax has the meaning of, "It was foolish of you to be frightened. Once you know the underlying truth you can see that from the very beginning nothing really was amiss."

The following case illustrates the genesis and elaboration of such defensive measures in a joker and how this part of his character was shaped. This material is from the analysis of a young adult who suffered from very intense anxiety. Whenever a situation developed which represented the danger of castration to him, he would resort to playing practical jokes or perpetrating some hoax. His hoaxes had the quality of arousing fear in his victims. When their suffering reached a certain degree of intensity, he would bring the hoax to an end.

There were many ways in which he played this game. He took advantage of his massive bulk and muscular development to act tough and threatening. Sometimes he played the imposter. Acting as if he were a detective or an FBI agent, without actually saying so, he would inspire anxiety by asking questions of individuals who were potentially vulnerable to investigation. Sometimes he would use the telephone and pose as an FBI agent, without saying explicitly that he was one. At other times he would call up a teacher or a relative and tease him while concealing his identity.

One aspect of the psychology of this patient's hoaxing combines identification of the aggressor with the mechanism of mastering anxiety through a proxy. In this case, the patient used his sister as well as his classmates as proxies. The pattern for this kind of hoaxing could be traced back to early childhood. In school he used to upset his classmates by spreading false rumors. For example, he told his class that a comprehensive examination was scheduled for the next day and that this test would determine the semester's grades. With his younger sister he would act out scenarios of the latest monster pictures so effectively that she was terrified. Sometimes he dropped the play quality. When they were home alone he once awakened his sister to tell her that there was a burglar in the house and that she should be very still. He went to the door of the bedroom and behaved as if he were watching a thief, returning from time to time to report what was happening. Another time he insisted that he heard a knock at the door. He proceeded to answer the knock and had a frightening conversation with an imaginary policeman, making sure all the time that his sister heard his side of the conversation.

In the treatment, he would exaggerate his symptoms, trying to create the impression that he was going insane. He complained of feelings which could be interpreted as the beginnings of psychotic depersonalization, delusions, or hallucinations. His description of anxiety feelings was most florid.

The meaning of this hoaxing activity could ultimately be understood in terms of his childhood relationship to his mother and sister. They lived in close quarters and he frequently saw them unclothed. He was very angry with his mother for exposing herself but could not tell her how he felt. Certain childhood games which he played had the purpose of reassuring him that the dangers he imagined were not real. In one such game he would play being blind, walking along the street for a predetermined distance, and then opening his eyes and experiencing great pleasure at being able to see again. In the same way he played being a cripple. These activities are part of a typical form of children's play which I have described elsewhere (1969c). Sometimes he would come home from school limping badly, complaining of some physical symptom, or reporting some academic catastrophe. After his mother was sufficiently wrought up, he would calm her down by revealing the truth.

When this behavior was being discussed in the context of castration anxiety and a phantasy of the vagina dentata, the patient recalled an incident which had been very important to him. One day at school he found some black paper which he could wrap over his three front teeth to create the illusion that the teeth were missing. So outfitted, he came home and went about his business as if nothing were amiss. Suddenly his mother caught a glimpse of his mouth. She panicked and wanted to know what happened. At this point, with great glee, he took the paper off, revealing that the teeth were intact. He recollected that at the age of five or six he would regularly play with himself before the mirror. He would press his penis back between his thighs so that his genital area corresponded to what he had seen on his little sister. With great delight he would relax the pressure on his thighs permitting the reassuring reappearance of his penis. On several occasions in latency and adolescence he dressed up in various items of his mother's clothes, used her cosmetics, and masturbated.

The same mechanisms became clear in another patient who was a practical joker. He was a 30-year-old-man, a Don Juan, who suffered from intense castration anxiety. He had the phantasy of the dentata vagina and could be potent only when he was certain that the relationship with the woman would not last and that he was free to extricate himself at will.

The patient had the following dream the night before a date with a sexually aggressive woman. He had been avoiding her because he was afraid that he would be impotent. The last time he had seen her he aggressively said many things to shock her.

This is the dream: "I saw a cat which had been run over. It was badly mutilated and bloody. It was lying on the street under a piece of clothing. I raised the piece of clothing and exposed the cat to a woman."

The patient made the following associations: His girl friend had inadvertently crushed a mouse. Its intestines protruded but it was still alive. She was disgusted with sight. The patient, although disgusted himself, removed the mouse.

His friend is afraid of mice. He often plays practical jokes on her by pretending he hears mice in the room. Once, as a birthday joke, he presented her with a gift package containing a live mouse. On another occasion he wanted to call her attention to a crushed animal on the street, knowing she had a horror of such sights. In bed with another girl friend he once made believe that he had died.

When he was an adolescent, his parents gave a dinner party to which they had invited some new friends. The patient made his appearance without greeting anyone. He sat down and for a long time did not say a word. Suddenly he began to distort his features and to make grimaces "like an idiot." The guests were shocked and his parents were embarrassed. Then just as suddenly, he smiled charmingly and began to talk in his normal fashion. "Everyone was relieved."

His girl friend wears no underclothes. When he drives with her he will suddenly throw up her dress and expose her.

At the party, the night before the dream, he shocked his hostess and several of the women guests by making crude comments about their clothes or appearance.

He is not afraid of menstruating women, he says. On the contrary, he often goes out of his way to have relations with them. However, when he sees blood on women's legs he is disgusted. His next association was, "The animal in the dream was bloody, all cut up. I am disgusted by the idea of the dead animal."

The character trait of practical joking was interpreted in terms of an identification with the aggressor plus the reassuring element of denial—i.e., what looks so terrible is not real; it is just a joke.

The patient responded with the memory of another practical joke. At the age of 15 he had been the guest of a family friendly with his own. Sometime after he left them he wrote a thank you note, in which he bemoaned his unhappy fate, hinting that he had either been locked up in jail or confined in an insane asylum. Shortly thereafter, his mother received a letter from these friends expressing regret at what had happened to the patient. When his mother confronted him he laughed and said that it was all a joke.

His next association was, "My mother exposed herself so much I am sure I must have seen her bleeding. She was very open and must have left her pads around." (There is considerable evidence to indicate that this was true and that the patient may have witnessed some obstetrical accident.)

The patient does not recall wearing any of his mother's clothing. However, he admitted to using her facial cream and eyelash curlers as well as some of her ski clothes and snow boots. To this information, the patient added, "those things are about the same for a man as for a woman."

At camp at the age of 15 he used to play the game of putting his penis between his thighs to simulate the vulva. He would then separate his legs and would be amused at the sight of the penis popping out.

Confirmation of the interpretation of his hoaxing came in the form of a striking bit of acting out. At the following session, after a long holiday weekend, the patient stated that he did not have relations with the aggressive, seductive woman. The morning after the date with that woman, in the company of several friends and his girl friend, he went away for the week end. He watched his friend putting pink curlers in her hair. As a joke he put them in his own hair and dressed in her nightgown. Thus attired, he entered a room occupied by some of his friends, sideling in backwards, whereupon he suddenly turned around and faced them fully, all the while speaking in a deep, base voice. His friends were shocked and then they all laughed. The patient then told the analyst, "I often imitate women for short periods of time."

## DISCUSSION

In the development of these patients the element of traumatic exposure to the female genital was prominent in the data. There was intimate, repeated contact with the female genitals and early exposure to female sexual hygiene in the form of menstrual pads, douche bags, and similar items. For these patients, as young boys, the confrontation with the female genital had proved to be profoundly traumatic. The intensity of the impact was determined in large measure by the degree to which the young boy was prepared for what he saw. The fact that the child was repeatedly exposed to the female genital by an aggressive mother seemed to be of greater significance than the element of the suddenness of the exposure, although in the patient's formal organization of memory, the latter element seemed to be stressed. Vulnerability to castration anxiety, of course, must be related to the concomitant events and conflicts operative during the oedipal phase, as well as to the manner in which experiences during the prephallic phases served to shape the structure of the ego's system of defenses and its propensity to anxiety.

During the latency period and extending further into the early phases of adolescence, a trend in the direction of developing perversions could be noted. These trends were not very serious nor did they necessarily eventuate in a solidly structured perversion, that is, they did not come to dominate all sexual activity nor did they constitute a regular, unfailing concomitant of masturbation. On the contrary, there was something playful, something tentative and mobile about the perverse behavior. In some cases, relatively stable perversions did develop. In both perverse tendencies and in the organized perversions, analytic study showed the various ways in which the ego had tried to master castration anxiety. The most important methods used consisted of a combination of un-doing, denial, and isolation. Through these mechanisms of defense the ego attempted to secure freedom from anxiety. Essentially the young patient tried to convince himself that the testimony of his senses had been faulty. The compelling need to deny is striking in all of these cases.

No matter how intricate the system of defenses employed, it was never completely successful in accomplishing its purpose. The inner pressure of instinctual drive and the force of external stimula-tion made repetition of the perverse practices imperative. The per-verse practice was based upon a reassuring daydream, essentially a form of denial in phantasy (Anna Freud, 1946). This phantasy was unconscious. It was, in fact, in connection with fetishism that Freud (1927) had demonstrated that the reassuring phantasy of the fetishist is characteristically unconscious. In general, the spe-cific form which a perversion takes depends upon the defense mech-anism employed by the ego in the organization of the reassuring phantasy. Essentially the perversion is the phantasy acted out. This accounts for the fact that so frequently perverse activity is con-nected with masturbation. The methods employed by the ego to attain reassurance against anxiety are varied and are not mutually exclusive. It is not uncommon, therefore, to find several different perverse trends existing side by side in the same person. I would suspect that this is the rule rather than the exception.

Some mention must be made of the role of the superego in the organization of the perversion. Fear of retaliation and guilt seem to play only a minor deterrent force regarding the practicing of the perversion itself. It would seem that in individuals who ex-hibit the character traits described above, one observes a superego corrupted not by bribery as Alexander (1930) described, but rather a superego subverted by anxiety. Frequently the model for perverse solutions to internal conflict had been suggested by significant individuals in the patient's environment, with whom the patient had identified. It is not only the possible traumatic seduction into perversion which is significant but also the insinuation by way of identification of a specific type of defense. The deterrent influence of the superego is also mitigated in these cases by the playful quality which seems to attend the practice of these perverse acts. Up to a certain point they may seem like a game and in slightly disguised form, it is easy enough for the seemingly innocent little boy to beguile an audience of adults with his pantomime of perversion. In so doing he enlists their aid in overcoming superego reproaches by casting the unsuspecting adults in the role of a permissive auxiliary superego (Arlow, 1969c).

In previous communications (1953, 1969a, 1969b) I have described the value of analyzing the details of unconscious phantasy activity in order to understand symptoms and altered ego states. The same approach may be applied to understanding the relationship between symptom, character trait, and perversion. The conflicts which grow out of the oedipal period usually find concrete expression in the form of an unconscious phantasy. Depending on how the ego defends itself against the anxiety associated with the phantasy, different forms of psychological resultants may be observed. Accordingly, out of the same conflict it is possible for the individual to develop a symptom, a character trait, or a perversion. Furthermore, it is possible for these three different kinds of solutions to exist side by side in the same person. In the patients whom I have discussed above, a number of defensive maneuvers on the part of the ego united in the form of a perverse tendency. After the passage of time, usually toward the latter period of adolescence, in some of these patients a second attempt was made to control the castration anxiety which was being fended off through the perversion. In some instances the perverse activity was given up entirely and only a miniscule token act persisted. It is my impression that this was the rule rather than the exception. Some disguised residue of both perverse activity and phantasy can usually be found if searched for carefully enough. The perverse activity may be so symbolic and so distant from any recognizable sexual expression as to give the impression that the problem, from all external indications, has been resolved. This may account for the great number of patients who report that they have daydreams of a perverse nature but no actual perversions. For some patients entertaining a perverse phantasy during intercourse becomes the obligatory condition guaranteeing potency. In other instances the perverse activity forms part of the manifest content of the dream which is dreamt after sexual relations. In any event, in many of these patients careful investigation shows that at some time during adolescence perverse activity had been practiced and then had been overcome more or less as the adult sexual identity took its final form. What appeared in consciousness was a distortion of character or the emergence of certain unusual character traits. In this paper I have described the origin of certain such traits. The genesis of these unusual characteristics is analogous to the genesis of the character neurosis. In the latter, a distortion of behavior or character takes the place of what had once been a psychoneurosis. In the patients discussed above the distortion of behavior or character takes the place of what had once been a perversion or a perverse trend. Accordingly, I suggest that such distortions of character may properly be designated as character perversion.

### CONCLUSION

In this communication I have attempted to trace the origin of certain unusual character traits through the study of the vicissitudes of defense directed against the emergence of unconscious phantasy. What was stressed particularly was the combination of defense mechanisms employed by the ego to ward off the anxiety associated with the danger situation. During latency and adolescence these unconscious phantasies were part of perverse trends or of an organized perversion which had been practiced. All of these patients for various reasons suffered from intense castration anxiety. Particularly traumatic was the exposure to the female genital. The traumatic impact of this event depended in large measure upon antecedent experiences and conflicts. The young patients responded with intense castration anxiety which they tried to master primarily through using the mechanism of denial in phantasy. Acting out of these phantasies led at some point to perverse sexual practices. These practices constituted a concretization of the phantasy which attempted to deny the reality of the female genital. The phantasies together with the perversion formed the major portion of the masturbation complex during adolescence. During the latter part of adolescence a second attempt was made to control the anxiety bound by the perverse activity. This attempt was partially successful; for the most part the perverse activity stopped and in some instances the concomitant phantasy disappeared from conscious mental life. Either alongside a severely attenuated set of perverse activities or in place of such activities, there appeared some unusual character trait which unconsciously served the same reassuring function which previously had been vested in the perversion. Typical for these character traits was the fact that the defensive mechanisms utilized corresponded precisely to the ones typical for the perversion. Accordingly, the unusual character traits had an origin and function in common with the perverse sexual activity; both tended to fend off castration anxiety. The same could be said of symptom formation. It is possible for symptom, character trait, and perverse activity to exist side by side in the same patient representing different methods by which the ego attempts to master a danger situation. In the setting of psychoanalytic treatment, through the analysis of resistance and transference, it becomes possible to observe the defensive import of the perverse character trait and to demonstrate how both the incipient perversion and the subsequent character trait had a common structure, a common origin, and a common function.

## REFERENCES

Alexander, F. (1930), *The Psychoanalysis of the Total Personality.* New York and Washington: Nervous & Mental Disease Publishing Co.

Arlow, J. A. (1953), Masturbation and symptom formation. *J. Amer. Psychoanal. Assn.,* 1:45–58.

—— (1969a), Unconscious phantasy and disturbances of conscious experience. *Psychoanal. Quart.,* 38:1–27.

—— (1969b), Phantasy, memory, and reality testing. *Psychoanal. Quart.,* 38:28–51.

—— (1969c), A type of play in latency boys. In: *Essays in Honor of Margaret Mahler.* In press.

Fenichel, O. (1939a), The counterphobic attitude. *Int. J. Psychoanal.,* 20:263–274.

—— (1939b), The economics of pseudologia phantastica. *Int. Ztschr. f. Psychoanal.,* 24:21–32.

—— (1945), *The Psychoanalytic Theory of Neurosis.* New York: W. W. Norton & Co.

Freud, A. (1946), *The Ego and the Mechanisms of Defense.* New York: International Universities Press, Inc.

Freud, S. (1927), Fetishism. *Standard Edition,* 21:152–159. London: Hogarth Press, 1961.

Lewin, B. (1948), The nature of reality, the meaning of nothing, with an addendum on concentration. *Psychoanal. Quart.,* 17:524–526.

—— (1950), *The Psychoanalysis of Elation.* New York: W. W. Norton & Co.

Wangh, M. (1962), The evocation of a proxy. *The Psychoanalytic Study of the Child,* 17:451–469. New York: International Universities Press.

# 21. DEVELOPMENTAL ASPECTS
# OF THE
# TRANSFERENCE NEUROSIS

## Carl P. Adatto, M.D.

In this presentation I will reexamine the phenomenon of what is subsumed under the concepts of transference and the transference neurosis from the viewpoint of their importance as findings resulting from the application of the psychoanalytic method, and then comment on some theoretical propositions regarding the developmental aspects of the transference neurosis. The ubiquitous presence of transference phenomena in both human relationships and the analytic situation has been well established.[1] The existence of the transference neurosis is also well accepted by analysts; however, its definition, meaning, and existence in every analysis is subject to debate as evidenced by a recent panel on the subject at the American Psychoanalytic Association (1968). If the transference neurosis is seen as closely tied in with the phenomenon of resistances, then it is necessary to view its development within a given analysis over a course of many months. From there it is not a far reaching step to consider the whole phenomenon of the

---

[1] Rapaport (Gill, 1967) differentiates between transference phenomena in everyday life and in analysis, and transference as . . . "a theoretical explanatory construct issuing from the method of interpersonal relationship, adopted and employed by psychoanalytic theory" (p. 205).

transference neurosis, and what it represents, as something which undergoes development along with the development of the individual who has maturational forces available to him. By examining this important and central finding of the analytic situation, fertile areas for further investigation of mental processes are likely to open up. The transference neurosis is a major source of data and the crucible of investigation in which there is an interplay of clinical findings, technique, and theory; it is subject to examination at the lowest theoretical levels. Freud (1912) conceptualized the transference neurosis on the one hand as rigid, regressive, rooted in the infantile neurosis, and on the other as a developing, progressive phenomenon. I intend to focus only on the latter aspects, and will not attempt to discuss Freud's conceptualization except as it applies to this topic, nor will I attempt to formulate a tightly knit theory.

One might best understand Freud's theories of transference by assuming his stance of being a physician who, having chosen a method of treatment for his patient, then proceeded to apply the method with the rigor of a scientist. In this way one can trace his theoretical development of transference from its origins as an incidental finding, which he viewed as the "worst obstacle" in treatment, to his last theoretical considerations of the subject. In "Studies on Hysteria" (1893–1895), following his discussion which points to the fact that there is an obstacle to treatment "when the patient's relation to the physician is disturbed" (p. 301), he outlines his principal reason for failure to elicit a reminiscence as follows:

> If the patient is frightened at finding that she is transferring on to the figure of the physician the distressing ideas which arise from the content of the analysis. This is a frequent, and indeed in some analyses a regular, occurrence. Transference on to the physician takes place through a *false connection* [p. 302].

Later he comments: "To begin with I was greatly annoyed at this increase in my psychological work, till I came to see that the whole process followed a law" (p. 304).

Rather than pursue in detail Freud's investigation of this "law," I shall proceed to the case of Dora where he describes transferences as a "special class of mental structure," and says that "They are new editions of facsimilies of impulses or fantasies which are aroused and made conscious during the progress of the analysis—they replace some earlier person by the person of the physician" (p. 116). He goes on to theorize that some transferences which do not differ in content from their model are "merely new impressions or reprints," whereas others are sublimated and are revised editions. The latter are constructed by the patient "cleverly taking advantage of some real peculiarity in the physician's person or circumstances and attaching themselves to that" (p. 116). It is noteworthy that he describes this phenomenon as occurring without the physician's direct participation. He goes on to state that "Psychoanalytic treatment does not *create* transferences, it merely brings them to light, like so many other hidden psychical factors" (p. 117).

In "Dynamics of the Transference" Freud (1912) states: "The part transference plays in the treatment can only be explained if we enter into its relation with resistance" (p. 154). He explains why transference appears on the scene and dominates the analysis as a resistance. It is at that point where there is a resistance to the analysis of the unconscious roots of the pathogenic complex that transference enters the scene. "We infer from this experience that the transference-idea has penetrated into consciousness in front of any other possible associations *because* it satisfies the resistance" (p. 103). This is repeated over and over again in the course of an analysis, and the longer the treatment lasts the more resistance is expressed through the transference. "These circumstances tend towards a situation in which finally every conflict has to be fought out in the sphere of transference" (p. 104). It is the "strongest weapon of the resistance" (p. 104) and its intensity and persistence are "an effect and an expression of resistance" (p. 104).

In "Remembering, Repeating and Working Through," Freud (1914) describes transference as a repetition of the forgotten past; the aim of the analyst is to have the patient remember rather than repeat his past.

It is here that he describes the transference neurosis:

> The main instrument, however, for curbing the patient compulsion to repeat and for turning it into a motive for remembering lies in the handling of the transference. We render the compulsion harmless, and indeed useful, by giving it the right to assert itself in a definite field. We admit it into the transference as a playground in which it is allowed to expand in almost complete freedom and in which it is expected to display to us everything in the way of pathogenic instincts that is hidden in the patient's mind. Provided only that the patient shows compliance enough to respect the necessary conditions of the analysis, we regularly succeed in giving all the symptoms of the illness a new transference meaning and in replacing his ordinary neurosis by a "transference-neurosis" of which he can be cured by the therapeutic work. The transference thus creates an intermediate region between illness and real life through which the transition from the one to the other is made. The new condition has taken over all the features of the illness; but it represents an artificial illness which is at every point accessible to our intervention. It is a piece of real experience, but one which has been made possible by especially favorable conditions, and it is of a provisional nature. From the repetitive reactions which are exhibited in the transference we are led along the familiar paths to the awakening of the memories, which appear without difficulty, as it were, after the resistance has been overcome [pp. 154–155].

Freud (1914) notes that one must become acquainted with resistance "to *work through* it, overcome it, by continuing, in defiance of it, the analytic work according to the fundamental rule of analysis" (p. 155). If one can accept this as current day analytic practice, regardless of the theoretical orientations involved, it is hard to view the transference neurosis—not transference—as anything but the outcome of the analysis of resistances to analysis over a period of time, to the point where it becomes the main resistance. This in turn requires the full scale working through of resistance and defense. Hence, I feel that transference neurosis is a phenomenon brought about through the application of the psychoanalytic method and is not seen in any other condition. Stated another way, one achieves a transference neurosis by analyzing the transference resistance over a period of time; and this is accomplished only by the psychoanalytic method. Thus, transference is distinguished from transference neurosis by the former being a ubiquitous phenomenon seen in and out of psychoanalytic treatment, whereas the latter technically can be viewed as a by-product or artifact—artificial illness—of the analytic method. Freud is clear in his position that the working through of resistance distinguishes analytic treatment from any kind of treatment by suggestion. "It only deserves the latter name [psychoanalysis] if the intensity of the transference has been utilized for the overcoming of resistances" (Freud, 1913, p. 143).

In his chapter on Transference in the "Introductory Lectures" (1916–1917 [1915–1917]), he establishes a developmental viewpoint both in regard to neurosis proper and the transference neurosis. It is essentially this statement which I address myself to in the present paper:

> We must not forget that the patient's illness, which we have undertaken to analyze, is not something which has been rounded off and becomes rigid, but that it is still growing and developing like a living organism. The beginning of the treatment does not put an end to this development; when, however, the treatment has obtained mastery over the patient, what happens is that the whole of his illness's new production is concentrated upon a single point—his relation to the doctor. Thus the transference may be compared to the cambium layer in a tree between the wood and the bark, from which the new formation of tissue and the increase in the girth of the trunk derive. When the transference has risen to this significance, work upon the patient's memories retreats far into the background. Thereafter it is not incorrect to say that we are no longer concerned with the patient's earlier illness but with a newly created and transformed neurosis which has taken the former's place. We have followed this new edition of the old disorder from its start; we have observed its origin and growth; and we are especially well able to find our way about in it since, as its object, we are situated at its very center. All the patient's symptoms have abandoned their original meaning and have taken on a new sense which lies in a relation to the transference; or only such symptoms have persisted as are capable of undergoing such a transformation. But the mastering of this new, artificial neurosis coincides with getting rid of the illness which was originally brought to the treatment—with the accomplishment of our therapeutic task [p. 444].

While expressing more optimism with regard to the outcome of the analysis at this juncture than he did later, Freud nonetheless has clearly taken the position that growth processes influence both the illness and the transference neurosis. I think it is consistent to maintain that a portion of the transference is simply a repetition of the infantile neurosis because it apparently has not been modified by a maturational process to any degree. It is also consistent that transference neurosis as a growing phenomenon is influenced by the growth processes which are already available to the patient as well as those which are liberated by the analytic treatment. This is in keeping with observations and histories of nontreated individuals.

In his chapter on Analytic Therapy, he explains the mechanism of cure "by clothing it in the formulas of the libido theory" (p. 453). He describes how analysis divests the symptoms of libido and then attaches it to the relation with the doctor. "Thus the transference becomes the battlefield on which all the mutually struggling forces should meet one another" (p. 454).

In "Beyond the Pleasure Principle" Freud (1920) again speaks about the patient's repeating instead of remembering the unconscious repressed material, and states that these reproductions "are invariably acted out in the sphere of the transference, of the patient's relation to the physician. When things have reached this stage, it may be said that the earlier neurosis has now been replaced by a fresh 'transference neurosis'" (p. 18). He describes many of the unwanted situations and painful emotions that are repeated in the transference and the effect they have on interrupting the analysis. At this point Freud addresses himself to the rigid, nonprogressive aspects of transference. He enlarges on this point in "Analysis Terminable and Interminable" (1937), where he discusses negative transference and the question of prophylactically stirring up conflicts by artificially producing new conflicts in the transference. In discussing the limitations of such a procedure he states: "The patients cannot themselves bring all their conflicts into the transference; nor is the analyst able to call out all their possible instinctual conflicts from the transference situation" (p. 233). Thus Freud is saying that in its use as an instrument in the treatment situation, transference has its limitations.

To recapitulate, I will review the insights at which Freud

arrived. Transference, discovered as an incidental finding—an obstacle—follows a "law," and is not created by analysis. Freud's interest focused on the relationship of transference to resistance and the opportunity it gave the analyst to view the repeated infantile neurosis. The development of transference neurosis is the result first, of the transference becoming a resistance, then of working through of resistances over and over until transference neurosis becomes the central resistance.

Freud's contributions to developmental concepts include the following. In the case of Dora he distinguishes between reprints of old editions and newly formed editions. Transference neurosis is a newly formed neurosis caused by the shift in libido from symptom to mental representation of analyst. Finally he describes illness as growing like a living organism, and likens transference to the cambium layer of a tree.

Resistances as repetition compulsion, negative transference, and negative therapeutic reactions; the relationship between positive and negative transference; technical management of transference, etc., are areas not covered.

The concept of neurosis and neurosis as recapitulated in the transference neurosis follows a developmental course. Hence, neurosis and its recapitulation in the transference neurosis follows a developmental course influenced by maturational factors. Perhaps Freud concerned himself with the rigid, regressive aspects of the transference neurosis because it delineated areas of obstacles to his work. It seems to me that a better understanding of the developmental aspects may lead to routes whereby these obstructions to analytic work may be removed; that is, we must determine how to ally with developmental forces which in the final accounting are responsible for the changes in the favorable outcome.

## THESIS AND PROPOSITIONS

Propositions regarding transference neurosis in this thesis are as follows: *The transference neurosis reflects a developmental continuum—the highest point being the transference neurosis as seen fully developed in an adult, the lowest being a totally autistic, nonobject related individual incapable of manifesting any semblance of it.*

The transference neurosis:

A.   Results *only* from the application of the psychoanalytic method over an extended period of time by working through of resistance to repressed conflicts, and in this sense is an artifact (artificial illness).

B.   Reflects not only the nature of object relationships, but other psychic activity as well.

C.   Is observed *fully*—analyst is persistently central—only in adult neurotic patients (presuming normal individuals are not analyzable) because of their developmental achievement of object relationships, psychic functions, etc.

D.   Is observed *incompletely, episodically, or not at all* in preadults, psychotics, and others because they have immature development.

E.   Reflects the developmental changes occurring prior to analysis and also changes induced by the analysis.

F.   Reflects the impact of maturation on the infantile neurosis, which, though retaining its core in the repressed, changes in structure and is a basis for the phenomenon being suitable for resistance—hope for gratification and defense against it.

G.   Can be an instrument not only for achieving therapeutic aims, but also for measuring the level of the development of the psychic apparatus.

Hence transference neurosis is a complex phenomenon reflecting not only the capacity to form object relationships and to transfer cathexis from one mental object representation to another, but also is inseparable from aspects of psychic functioning not related to object relationships *per se.* It reflects the developmental achievement of the individual attained prior to analysis, as well as developmental changes occurring as the result of analytic treatment. The infantile neurosis undergoes constant modification under the impact of developmental changes, even though the core of the infantile neurosis is retained in the structure of the transference neurosis and is the basis for the phenomenon of transference being suitable for resistance.

While the phenomenon of transference neurosis as described by Freud is rather distinct in adult neurotics, one can see it as the highest level of developmental achievement of a continuum observed in analyzed patients. Hence it is possible to see it not only as an all-pervasive attachment to the analyst and symptoms related to him, but also occurring sporadically and partially as the capacities of the individual and the vicissitude of the analysis permit. By adhering to the analytic method the analyst can not only achieve his therapeutic aims, but also have at his disposal in the transference neurosis an instrument for measuring the level of development of the psychic apparatus and for measuring subsequent developmental changes occurring as the result of analysis.

## CLINICAL BASIS

This thesis grew out of clinical experience in which I analyzed five late adolescents, and following an interruption of several years, reanalyzed them as adults (1958, 1966). In 1957 I reported the results of the analyses of the first patients. Following an intensive working through of their conflictual material, there was a period of psychic equilibrium and absence of analytic motivation. This usually coincided with the formation of a heterosexual attachment, a marked diminution in anxiety, and by and large a disappearance or ignoring of the symptoms which brought them to analysis. I postulated that this phenomenon is a manifestation of the terminal phase of normal adolescent development, reflecting an ego activity aimed at restoration and reintegration of the psyche. In 1964 I reported the outcome of the analysis of three of these patients who returned to me for analysis following marriage and the birth of children. This arrangement offered an excellent opportunity to correlate their developmental progress into adulthood with analytic data. I discovered that the transference and emotional investment these patients made in me, which had been sketchy or incomplete in the first analysis, were more analyzable in the second. The transference manifestations which were accessible to analytic interpretation were meager during the first analysis and stopped entirely once a heterosexual love attachment was established. During the second period of analysis a transference neurosis became manifest, making the transferences accessible to interpretation. I discovered that during the first analysis there were indeed transference reactions of which I had no confirmation. Insofar as these reactions were never accessible to me as hard data, they could not be subject to interpretation. A sample of the data will illustrate (1966). Several sessions after resuming the second analysis one patient reported a dream:

> I had to leave your office early. I left you and walked down the street and saw Jill (wife) who told me that you wanted to see me in a half hour. I said "no," saw several old friends, and then I was in Chicago and tried to phone you. I couldn't because I couldn't use a new dial system which had no letters or numbers, and no one could tell me how to use it. You were angry at me in the dream and had a round head, round thin-framed glasses, and thin metal ear pieces.

The patient reported some masturbatory activity in association to the dialing of the phone, and then indicated his surprise at the difference both in the analysis and myself as compared to his past impressions. Apparently I was more real to him and did not look like he expected me to. His thoughts of Chicago were that his mother had been born there, and he commented how I looked somewhat like a woman in the dream. He noted that leaving the session early would give him a chance to eat breakfast earlier. The day previously he had arrived at this early morning session, as he had this day, without breakfast, and had planned to eat after the session. He preferred to eat breakfast in a downtown restaurant (equivalent to my office) rather than have his wife prepare it for him. In commenting about the round head his first association was to a football, whereupon he laughed, saying, "you're a prick-head," and wondered why he had me wearing glasses when I didn't have any. That the earrings were feminine led to his thought about wedding rings and then another outburst of anger toward his wife and how she was "eating away" at him. He was able to associate to these distortions of me more easily than before, and talked about me as though we had been in contact during the time elapsing since the previous analysis. For instance, he said, "You remember how nervous I was when the baby was born?" I had no knowledge that he had become a father.

It is my feeling that while transference and cathexis to me was present during both periods, these patients seemed unable to lend their psychic energy to the purpose of introspection, hence to the development of resistances, transferences, and transference neuroses.

The literature is replete with cases of children and adolescents who have transference reactions and specific episodes or areas of transference neurosis; however, there seems to be a consensus that children and adolescents do not present the phenomenon of transference neurosis in full measure as described in the adult patient.

The mere openness of transference manifestations and their intensity does not qualify as classification of transference neurosis as defined by Freud because the analyst does not become the central person in the patient's life, and the neurosis is enacted in other relationships with equal if not greater depth. For instance in analyzing a 15-year-old boy with epileptic seizures, I was able to observe strong transference reactions which gave me considerable information about the structure of his neurosis as well as the anxiety-producing thoughts and fantasies. When the homosexual transference in one instance reached considerable intensity, the patient had a seizure apparently as a way of warding me off. During this period of analysis he had seizures only during his analytic sessions and was symptom-free at all other times. This kind of data frequently emerged during the analysis, but there was an elusive quality to the patient in that he would move over to other relationships which, according to his report, involved transference reactions. These reactions however did not appear to be displacements from me, but more directly from the parental figures who were still actively on the scene, or displacements onto the parental objects directly. I feel at times that it is tempting to attribute such responses to the analyst and the transference neurosis, even though the data for such a conclusion is lacking.

There have been cases of child analyses reported that attest to the fact that transference neurosis episodes exist in children; however, none claim that the mainstream of the analysis was carried out in the transference neurosis. Harley (1967) reports a case of a five-year-old girl in which a transient transference neurosis—a fear of the analyst's toilet flush—and a more persistent transference neurosis phenomenon, in the form of a dog phobia, appeared in the analysis. She states:

> Transference neurosis, as defined in the sense that a neurotic symptom formation, arising from regressed conflicts activated by the analytic situation, is centered on the analyst or his surroundings, is sometimes observable, albeit in limited or circumscribed form, in certain phases of treatment even with young children [p. 116].

Fraiberg (1966) reports an analysis of a latency-aged child in which a part of the child's neurosis, repressed memory of primal scene and repressed libidinal aims, were manifested in a transference neurosis symptom of a dog phobia that manifested itself in relationship to the analyst and her house. Fraiberg constructs this to revival of memories reexperienced with the original objects. Numerous other cases have been reported in both children and adolescents in which transference neurosis phenomena or episodes were reported as a part of the analytic findings and analyzed in a manner analogous to the adult model. This evidence indicates that the transference neurosis is capable of forming at an early age, as a result of the analysis of the resistances to the repressed.

Melanie Klein's (1948) views on the transference neurosis as related to her work with children indicate that she observed the transference neurosis more extensively than some other child analysts:

> In my experience a full transference-neurosis does occur in children, in a manner analogous to that in which it arises with adults. When analyzing children I observe that their symptoms change, are accentuated or lessened in accordance with the analytic situation. . . . Parents who watch their children carefully have often told me that they have been surprised to see habits, etc., which had long disappeared, come back again [p. 166].

She states that these reactions are "for the most part" kept within the confines of the analytic hour. How central a part they play in the entire analysis is not stated.

Perhaps the most outstanding and classical example of this problem is demonstrated in Freud's (1905 [1901]) case of 18-year-old

Dora. This was an analysis of three months' duration which terminated abruptly and prompted Freud to comment that he did not succeed in mastering the transference in good time. In his review of the case Freud comments: "But when the first dream came, in which she gave herself the warning that she had better leave my treatment just as she had formerly left Herr K.'s house, I ought to have listened to the warning myself" (p. 118). He goes on to postulate various confrontations he would have made to clear up the transference, adding: "But I was deaf to this first note of warning, thinking I had ample time before me, since no further stages of transference developed and the material for the analysis had not yet run dry" (p. 119). One could describe this case as having been interrupted before the transference neurosis developed. It is conceivable that it was not necessarily Freud's faulty technique in not interpreting the transference that caused this phenomenon, but perhaps Dora's lack of developmental capacity and readiness to respond to the analytic method with a transference neurosis.

## DISCUSSION

The clinical facts are that transference neurosis may occur in episodes or during parts of an analysis with children or adolescents but never to the degree of central importance observable in the analysis of some adult neurotics. I do not feel that this phenomenon is necessarily clear-cut and distinct because neurotic symptoms are not always well delineated and sometimes shift into what seems to be unsatisfying, compulsive ego-alien character traits, habits, or mere attitudes toward the analyst. The patient cited who had a transference dream in which I became the object of his oral desires, originally directed toward his mother, manifested no clear-cut symptom although his breakfast habits had changed in concurrence with the transference. His fear of exhibitionism, however, seemed directly related to the transference and was a clear-cut symptom.

There is a problem of delineating which phenomena can be subsumed under the concept of transference neurosis, even if one adheres to the concept of symptoms occurring in the transference, in relation to the analyst. Clinically one sees the phenomena of the patient converging on the analyst who represents the central and persistent libidinal object, endowed with the characteristics of infantile objects, as well as parts of the patient's own psychic apparatus. The neurotic symptoms may not always be clear-cut and characterological attitudes are part of the picture. Perhaps this phenomenon can be called *transference-resistance primacy* if one wishes to limit the concept of transference neurosis to neurotic symptomatic manifestations in relationship to the transference. Freud stopped using the term transference neurosis in his later writings and referred only to transference when discussing the above set of phenomena. It is not clear why this is so. At any rate, whether we speak of transference neurosis, transference-resistance primacy, etc., what we are referring to is endowment, in a central and persistent manner, of the psychic representation of the analyst with certain characteristics and aims. These are part of the patient's psyche, together with its representations, and reflect the structure of the conflictual state. What is of conceptual importance is that when analysis is at least partially successful in effecting derepression, the instinctual impulse finds a substitute in spite of repression.

Some adult patients present only partially developed transference neurosis phenomena, in which the patient seems to come to the edge of plunging into it, but does not do so, apparently because the derepression is only threatened but not materialized. I will defend the position that the data emanating from the application of the psychoanalytic method demonstrates full transference neurosis only in adult neurotic patients and that we cannot expect this phenomenon to occur, except partially, in preadult patients. Hence the psychoanalytic method yields data which reflects the developmental achievements of an individual as reflected by the intensity, character, and presence (or absence) of the transference neurosis.

*Relationship of Transference Neurosis to Psychic Structure*

If we assume the transference neurosis to be a reflection of the psychic functioning of an individual, especially his neurotic conflicts, we can follow developments in the psychic apparatus as reflected in the transference neurosis.

*Id.* The residue of drive organization in the infantile neurosis apparently undergoes modification along with transformation and developments in the instinctual development through life. With the physical transformations of puberty come psychical transformations which modify and perhaps reshape the repressed conflicts. This would imply that the "stereotype plates" Freud describes also are altered in some way, that their conflictual character is retained, but put into a new constellation. With the resolution of adolescent conflicts and the attainment of adult sexuality the transformation of the stereotype plates (or psychic structures) undergo still further modifications. For one thing we might assume that the infantile needs are revised in such a way that they achieve more discharge through the medium of the newly transformed sexual patterns. The act of genital adult sexual gratification may in itself not only offer discharge, but also may reduce the feeling of danger surrounding sexual activity by virtue of its experiential impact. By being less dangerous to experience it may thereby be more easily transferable and experienced. The danger is lessened but nevertheless retained in its basic repressed configuration.

This reasoning would imply that in turn we would have to assume that such theoretical functional units as psychic structures are not as immutable as is implied on occasion, and that considerable transformation takes place even in the neurotic individual who is plagued by the persistence of repressed infantile conflicts.

*Ego.* From the viewpoint of ego functioning, transference neurosis becomes a major resistance to the analysis, a resistance which we can view as a defense mechanism generated during the course of an analysis. It can come about in full force only when the ego develops to the point where it is used as a refined defense. It was the resistance aspect of the transference that interested Freud the most and that he felt was worthy of great attention. But in order to use transference neurosis in this way the patient must have undergone transformation in his psyche which lessens the danger in the conflict and correspondingly increases his abilities to throw up this barrier to tampering with his repressed conflicts. This is consistent with the development of ego functioning—the capacity to regress in the service of the ego and analyze at the same time. An adolescent, who is lacking in such stability in ego function, is much more threatened by regression than the adult neurotic whose reality testing, synthetic functioning, etc. have been reexperienced many times over. Hence the less developed and stable the ego functions, the less the capacity to engage in the regression required to develop a transference neurosis. The ability to use transference neurosis as a central resistance and defense is an indication of sophisticated ego functioning in which gratification and defense are combined at a level closer to consciousness than previously, thereby indicating a higher level of ego functioning.

*Superego.* One of the achievements of adulthood is the modification of the superego, permitting the admission and expression of the instinctual urges in fuller range with correspondingly less aggressive expression. Adolescents, on the other hand, frequently reel back from their pubertal developments and adolescent genital drives because of the guilt generated by conflict with the superego as well as the aggressive or destructive drives connected with it. Patients who are unable to endure these prohibitions have difficulty in forming object-directed cathexis. The immature superego and the process of the reorganization of the superego functioning make adolescents vulnerable to castration and other basic anxieties, along with the upsurge of pubertal drives and an ego incapable of completely mastering these anxieties. The ego-ideal is also fluid and hence not a stabilizing force in the psyche of the adolescent as compared with the adult. The prepubertal superego is even more rigid and stabilized around the infantile objects. Hence, immature individuals cannot risk the expression of transference wishes because they are so threatened from within the psychic apparatus.

*Object Relationships.* The ability to manifest a transference neurosis implies a sufficient freedom from infantile objects to form new object relationships, to transfer from one mental representation to another (implying a lack of adhesiveness of the libido), to overcome the danger involved in such a relationship enough to establish it, and an orientation in favor of objects as opposed to narcissism. All these points represent different ways of expressing developmental achievements. The shift from infantile to new object relationships incorporating adult sexuality in the adolescent is a requisite for becoming an adult. Intermediate objects of a non-threatening nature are frequently chosen in the process of such a shift, the analyst frequently representing such a person under certain circumstances. The patient, however, fears the regression involved in such a transference because it means reversion to a parental figure and all the dangers implied in an incestuous relationship. On the other hand, such a patient will often avoid transference in order to achieve an intermediary object relationship relatively free from the intensity of such transference. Evidence from my patients indicated that the process of transference was an ongoing thing and would remain out of the sphere of consciousness, as discovered by the later analysis of the same individuals. One must then distinguish not only between the capacity to form object relationships in the transference, but also the ability of the patient to derepress such cathexes for the purpose of analysis. It would imply that often the transference relationship is established, but quickly repressed because it is associated with the pathogenic complexes.

*Narcissism.* A corollary to object relationships is the degree of narcissism or libidinal investment in the self. Under the threat of the danger of object relationships the preadult patient will retreat to a narcissistic position in his libidinal economy. This is a topic which deserves considerable attention in its own right because it involves the reassessment of transference neurosis as a phenomenon which apparently springs out of object need or hunger, but which conceivably can use this object relatedness as a defense to preserve a narcissistic position. Frequently I have been impressed in adult patients by the patent transference manifestations being screens for more narcissistic involvement. What appear to be deep regres-

sive object ties and oral dependency often turn out to be detachment from the analyst and narcissistic cathexis. The patient seduces
the analyst by transference gratifications in order to keep his
narcissism protected and undisturbed. Another point is the distinction Freud made between the transference patients and the
psychotics. The latter could not be analyzed because they were
unable to involve themselves in the analytic situation via the transference. This is an area of investigation for those who work with
psychotic patients or with patients who are narcissistically oriented
and have little apparent desire for object relationships. The transference psychosis must be distinguished from the transference
neurosis although both may appear to be similar in the intense
attachment to the analyst, as well as in the symptoms emanating
from the analytic situation. The difference in part rests on the
evidence of defective ego functioning and narcissistic predominance
in the transference psychosis as compared to the transference
neurosis. In turn, the latter implies a capacity for object relationships involving evidence of distinguishing objects from self. The
interrelation between the development of narcissism and object
relationships in normal development, and the degree to which both
modes of libidinal cathexes exist, indicates that the adult is able
to carry on object relationships rather safely and still not threaten
his narcissistic needs. In normal adults the object relationships
serve to satisfy the narcissistic needs.

## What Is Transferred in the Transference Neurosis?

The patient, according to Freud, transfers the libido from symptom to the mental representative of the analyst which resides  in
his ego, thereby causing the symptoms to be manifest in the transference itself; hence the transference neurosis. Both the neurotic
gratification and the defense against remembering the repressed
conflict emerge in this phenomenon, a central feature of which
is the almost total engrossment the patient has in the analysis and
the analyst. Other people in the patient's life become secondary
in importance to the analyst who is seen both as powerful and
desirable as well as threatening and oppressive. Individuals with
little or no capacity to cathect new objects or those who are

threatened by such a transfer from an old object representative to a new one do not demonstrate the transference neurosis. Nor does this occur in what Freud called the narcissistic neuroses in which the libido is narcissistically committed and cannot be reinvested in other objects, as is true of psychotic patients.

More is transferred to the analyst than simply libidinal and aggressive drives. Freud (1940 [1938]) noted: "If the patient puts the analyst in place of his father (or mother) he is also giving him the power which his superego experiences over his ego, since his parents were as we know, the origin of his superego" (p. 175). Hence part of the transference neurosis includes externalization onto the analyst of other aspects of the patient's psychic structure. This is an important consideration because it offers a wide range of externalized psychic activity which presents the analyst with the workings of the mind. Such projections of the id, ego, and superego, as well as libidinal and aggressive cathexes are described by A. Freud, although she distinguishes these from transference proper. The projection of the superego onto the analyst is a fundamental proposition of the technique of Melanie Klein.

It not only encompasses the projections and displacement onto the analyst, but also the introjection and internalization of the analyst. For this reason the problem of seeking out new object relationships has its impact in the formation of the transference neurosis. The new editions Freud speaks of are contingent upon the analyst's becoming an internalized mental representation in the patient's psyche. This phenomenon is easier to observe in the analysis of adolescents where transference phenomena are colored by internalization of the analyst. For instance the changes occurring in the superego make it possible for adult sexual activity to commence out of identification with the superego and ego-ideal of the analyst. This takes place despite or perhaps *because of* overt efforts of the analyst to remain neutral, that is to assume and maintain his stance as an analyst using his method. The present discussion would be led astray by further pursuit of this topic; however, the developmental aspects of this interplay phenomenon which goes on in the midst of application of the analytic method is worthy of note. Adult patients engaging in the same processes seem to be less threatened by possible identification, and are more likely to form a full transference neurosis which serves both as a resistance to uncovering the repressed conflicts, and at the same time, a development of new psychic structure using the internalized analyst as scaffolding for the process. Thus it would appear that throughout development, even into adult life, object relationships serve as a catalyst for the genesis of psychic changes. From a teleological view one could say that such use of objects is mandatory for survival during the infantile period, but also necessary, although less obvious, for continued development during adult life as well.

CRITIQUE AND LIMITATIONS

It is clear that this thesis is open to criticism on several major grounds, thereby limiting its usefulness. I will try to present some of the criticisms and limitations as I see them:

A.   *Limitations Involving Method.*

1. *Free Association.* Emergence of transference neurosis is dependent upon the ability, willingness, and desirability of the patient to free associate. Hence, any interferences with free association will of necessity alter or inhibit manifestations of the transference neurosis. By definition free association is a verbal process. So as not to minimize the complications in this area, it is well to note Freud's observation that transference resistance was often manifested by the patient's abandoning the basic rule of free association. At this point he felt it necessary to make a transference interpretation in order to proceed with the flow of associations, only to find again and again transference resistance made itself known by this abandonment of the fundamental rule. The capacity to free associate, however, is a basic premise of use of the analytic method, for through it one reaches the repressed instinctual conflicts. Hence, a patient must have sufficient psychic development as well as motivation to be able to free associate sufficiently to even enter a transference neurosis. For this reason A. Freud (1965) notes, "Without the use of free association not all the evidence for the child's trans-

ference appears in the material" (p. 56). Children and adolescents lack the ability to engage in sustained free association to the extent that adults do. This fact in itself alters the scientific investigation and leads us to candidly state that the analytic method is limited by such a restriction. Thus the entire investigation of transference neurosis is hampered by the limits of the method which brings it into view. It might be noted parenthetically that the equation of play activity with free association is not acceptable to many child analysts; hence this route, too, is open to question as a source of data.

2. *Theories on Role of the Ego.* There exist major differences among analysts regarding the degree of ego autonomy and its freedom from the underlying unconscious conflicts. Hence analysts who are partial to the view that the therapeutic alliance is an expression of mature and relatively autonomous ego functioning, approach the analysis of transference differently from those who see in transference, from the beginning, unconscious conflicts and primitive psychic functioning (Zetzel, 1956). Freud's position was that the positive transference enabled the analyst to carry out his method and sustain the analysis during periods of transference resistance to the analysis in general. However, it appears to me that he plunged into the analysis once he considered that this agreement was in force, essentially maintaining his alliance with the patient by analyzing the resistance and by uncovering the repressed conflicts. These differences will of necessity produce different data and make the comparison of data complicated.

3. *Conceptualization of Resistance.* This is a specialized version of the above. If on the one hand resistance to the analysis is seen in terms of the transference neurosis embodying all levels of ego activity and primitive defense, it will be handled promptly as it presents itself as resistance. On the other hand resistances are also seen as emanating from sources of psychic activity other than the transference and occupy a large part of the analytic work especially prior to the formation of a transference neurosis. Since transference neurosis is a complex phenomenon, it is possible to

consider it as a defense itself (among other functions), along with such defenses as repression, denial, displacement, etc. In fact since it becomes the major resistance to analysis, its analysis as a defense proper is consistent with ego analysis. The theoretical achievements of ego psychology have perhaps obscured the fact that mental functioning at the level of transference neurosis is a conglomeration of different phenomena just as are dreams. Hence until this theoretical impasse is clarified, one must place restrictions on the value of the thesis I am presenting.

### B.    *Patients Who Do Not Manifest Transference Neurosis.*

There are individuals who approach the analyst with hopes of achieving something far beyond the boundaries of reality. The strength of the repressed wish combined with an underdeveloped ego functioning might combine to create a state of psychic functioning which renders a person unanalyzable. Individuals who overtly wish for direct control of their lives or dependency gratification beyond the call of professional capabilities, immediately alert the analyst to the danger of attempting to use the analytic method. Some other therapist or another therapeutic technique is often recommended to such patients.

There are also some adults who are not psychotic and who appear to have relatively sufficient mature psychic functioning such that a skilled analyst considers them candidates for analysis, but who fail to develop a transference neurosis. With such patients, the beginning of the analysis appears to go along smoothly. There are analyzable transference resistances which, after a period of many months of analysis, suggest that the patient is on the verge of breaking into a transference neurosis, but this never occurs. The transference is analyzed in bits and pieces and seems to be separated from the main core of the neurotic conflict. There are many possible reasons for such a phenomenon among which are:

1.    Failure to understand the defenses and transference because much of the neurotic conflict remains ensconsed in an all-pervasive, well-concealed defensive stance.

2.    The occurrence of neurotic gratification outside the analysis, with such happenings as split transferences.

3.   Inherent lack of psychic capacity or flexibility.

4.   No consistent outcome in applying the analytic method, hence the analyst must be content to use other routes to the analysis of repressed conflicts.

5.   Insufficient knowledge about the phenomenon of transference.

6.   Failure of agreement on defining transference neurosis.

My thesis rests on the assumption that transference neurosis is an inevitable outcome of an analysis with a relatively mature individual, who is motivated and in whom the resistances are detected and analyzed. The above considerations may prevail and limit this thesis.

## SUMMARY

This paper considers Freud's fundamental theories of transference and transference neurosis as phenomena occurring as a result of application of the psychoanalytic method, and enlarges on his developmental concepts of the transference neurosis. A thesis is presented: The transference neurosis reflects a developmental continuum, the highest point being the transference neurosis as seen fully developed in an adult, the lowest being a totally autistic, nonobject-related individual incapable of manifesting any semblance of it. It is discussed from the viewpoint of the psychic apparatus, object relationships, and narcissism, as well as to theories regarding what is transferred. Finally, it is subjected to a critique regarding its limitations.

## REFERENCES

Adatto, C. P. (1958), Ego reintegration observed in analysis of late adolescents. *Int. J. Psycho-Anal.*, 39:172–177.
—— (1966), On the metamorphosis from adolescence into adulthood. *J. Amer. Psychoanal. Assn.*, 14:485–509.
Calef, V. (1968), Chairman Panel on Transference Neurosis, Meeting of the American Psychoanalytic Association, May.
Fraiberg, S. (1966), Further considerations of the role of transference in latency. *The Psychoanalytic Study of the Child*, 21:213–236. New York: International Universities Press.
Freud, A. (1965), *Normality and Pathology in Childhood*. New York: International Universities Press.

Freud, S. (1893–1895), Studies on hysteria. *Standard Edition*, 2:1–305. London: Hogarth Press, 1955.

—— (1905 [1901]), Fragment of an analysis of a case of hysteria. *Standard Edition*, 7:7–122. London: Hogarth Press, 1955.

—— (1912), The dynamics of transference. *Standard Edition*, 12:97–108. London: Hogarth Press, 1958.

—— (1913), On beginning the treatment. *Standard Edition*, 12:121–144. London: Hogarth Press, 1958.

—— (1914), Remembering, repeating and working through. *Standard Edition*, 12:145–156. London: Hogarth Press, 1958.

—— (1916–1917 [1915–1917]), Introductory lectures on psychoanalysis. *Standard Edition*, 16. London: Hogarth Press, 1963.

—— (1920), Beyond the pleasure principle. *Standard Edition*, 18:7–64. London: Hogarth Press, 1955.

—— (1937), Analysis terminable and interminable. *Standard Edition*, 23:216–253. London: Hogarth Press, 1964.

—— (1940 [1938]), An outline of psychoanalysis. *Standard Edition*, 23:144–205. London: Hogarth Press, 1964.

Gill, M. M. (1967), The scientific methodology in psychoanalysis. In: *The Collected Papers of David Rapaport*. New York: Basic Books, 1967.

Harley, M. (1967), Transference developments in a five-year-old child. *The Child Analyst at Work*, ed. E. Geleerd. New York: International Universities Press, 1967.

Hoffer, W. (1956), Transference and transference neurosis. *Int. J. Psycho-Anal.*, 37:377–379.

Kepecs, J. G. (1966), Theories of transference neurosis. *Psychoanal. Quart.*, 35:497–521.

Klein, M. (1948), *Contributions to Psychoanalysis, 1921–1945*. London: Hogarth Press, 1948, p. 34.

Orr, Douglas W. (1954), Transference and countertransference: a historical survey. *J. Amer. Psychoanal. Assn.*, 2:621–670.

Waelder, R. (1956), Introduction to the discussion on problems of transference. *Int. J. Psycho-Anal.*, 37:367–368.

Zetzel, E. R. (1956), Current concepts of transference. *Int. J. Psycho-Anal.*, 37:369–376.

# 22. THE MARRIAGE-SEPARATION PENDULUM: A CHARACTER DISORDER ASSOCIATED WITH EARLY OBJECT LOSS

Irwin M. Marcus, M.D.

There are certain character disorders that may be distinguished by the individual's tendency to persist in clinging to seemingly hopeless relationships, which are full of conflicts and frustrations and fundamentally represent object relations on the oral level. The entire spectrum of the person's infantile neurosis unfolds in these relationships and in the eventually emerging transferences to the analyst. This description is not to isolate and simplify a syndrome as such, for man's uniqueness and the plurality of determinants is one of the basic principles in psychoanalysis. However, the multitude of factors which contribute to the understanding of an individual does not preclude efforts to single out certain determinants which appear to occupy a central position in the formation of character symptomatology.

In this paper, I have singled out for discussion patients who experienced cumulative trauma through separation from the mother in early childhood because of a variety of reasons such as her death, withdrawal due to personality problems, or the birth of a sibling. These patients reacted with excessive internalization

361

of the idealized maternal object rather than with a sense of loss and mourning. They later establish a façade of sociability associated with impulsive qualities, often including a variety of sexual partners and experiences which occur in a compulsive, acting out manner, having the features of autoerotic activity. A secondary projective identification with the father's penis, perceived as the magic power that can control and possess the mother, provides a phallic coloring to the personality. The mother-breast equation, as the lost object, and the primary narcissistic self are fused into an undifferentiated unit with a resultant withdrawn state of chronic anguish. Mother surrogates such as a nursemaid, a grandmother, or a foster or adoptive mother are not sufficiently cathected to alter this internalized affective state and to disrupt the fixed psychic relationship between the internalized object and self. The same appears to be true for their later social relationship. The loneliness, depressiveness, and sense of isolation make reality tenuous and frightening at times, hence the counterphobic efforts to grasp at relationships. These patients function well in society and are successful in their work. They are bright and often endowed with considerable talent and sensitivity. They are respected and liked by friends, and, although others may recognize that they may have some problems in living, they are not looked upon as having an illness. Freud once referred to the simultaneous existence of regressive and normal thinking as "double thinking."

The patients under discussion discovered their penis during this childhood period of abrupt weaning from the mother-breast, and the penis became their consoling substitute. Thus the equation becomes mother-breast-penis which is protected and loved, with a resultant intense fear of castration. Through projective identification, the oral sadism felt toward the frustrating mother and directed at her breast produces additional problems when the female genital is perceived. The vagina is reminiscent of the child's biting mouth (vagina dentata), and the genital region becomes the focus of the perceived danger. It is not unexpected that homosexual conflicts either entirely unconscious or partially conscious, with or without acting out, would be present. Competitiveness and anger at males provoke fantasies of biting off the penis. Friendliness arouses wishes to suck the penis or to be sucked. The ambivalence in these fantasies and the secret passive wishes accompanying them stir anxiety, guilt, depression, hypochondria and other symptoms.

In addition to confusion of mother-breast-penis and vagina-mouth, there are other combinations such as penis-feces and vagina-anus. Anal symptoms with itching and rubbing as disguised masturbation, wishes to finger and rub the woman's or man's anus, avoiding loss of feces (penis-breast) as in constipation, anal fissures, hemorrhoids, and pleasure in explosive defecation associated with fantasies of destroying the breast-mother may occur. The narcissistic overevaluation of the feces intensifies the toilet training conflicts, continues the disturbance in object relations, and generates obsessional mechanisms in the character structure. The buttocks are equated with the breasts. The more traumatic the oral experiences and the feeling of loss and abandonment, the greater will be the likelihood of fears and primitive rages influencing the reaction to toilet training and closely linking the oral and anal patterns which in turn will infiltrate the phallic and oedipal conflicts. One male followed both males and females who wore underpants that were well outlined through the clothes. The outlines were associated with brassieres. Breast envy as a consequence of early object loss in another male was so intense that his exclusive overt homosexual pattern was a sucking activity in which both his penis and his partner's unconsciously represented the breast.[1] More frequently, these patients manifest a dread of becoming homosexual. Breast envy also occurs in women who remain fixated on the trauma of the original deprivation of the mother-breast and do not accept their own later breast development to complete their maturation as an adult. They continue to search for the caretaking-feeding, mother-breast in their relationships with both men and women.

The preoedipal crystallization of character in these patients fosters a pseudo maturity and pseudo independence. Their

---

[1] These two cases are not included in the case presentations.

strengths reflect the fact that they have received adequate care by the mother or mother figure, but that the mothers were unable to deal with the child's rage or anxious reactions. The mother's inability to help the child recover from these episodes of conflict motivates a premature withdrawal from her and a search for more supportive adults. The child's effort to avoid the violent rage and dependency needs, combined with high intellect, encourages verbal qualities, aloofness from other children, a preference for acceptance and praise by adults for their apparent maturity, as well as an attraction to the helping professions. However, when the frustrations are too great to bear, there is an eruption of tantrums, suicidal fantasies or acts, either conscious or unconscious, or direct attacks upon their mates or companions. In early childhood and even later, the mothers of these patients would complain to their husbands whenever the child's rage would burst forth. The father usually sided with the woman against the child, thereby reinforcing the submissive-passive defenses in the child. The impression given by the father is: "You and mother can have each other with my blessings, and, dammit, you better behave yourself because I can't stand her complaining and nagging." Thus, the child's real experience with the father undermines any incentive to relinquish the preoedipal attachment (Marcus, 1956). We now know that a father must actively participate in his child's development (boy and girl) and cannot delegate his role to the mother without having the child pay the price through disturbances in psychosexual development and overall character structure. Healthy fathering should promote the separation of the child from the original mother-child unit, a process which should begin before the oedipal period. A father who genuinely wants his son to mature into a man who can master his own destiny will help his son to structure the inner chaos the child feels as he struggles through the preoedipal conflicts with his mother. This fatherly help ushers in the stage of masculine identification with the father. A father who absents himself or who beats his son into submission abandons his son to identify with the destructive qualities in the mother and enhances the child's frightening image of the father. Thus, the child's superego is fed with elements that will increase his need for punishment. An example of this may be seen in Freud's (1909) Rat Man case.

The pseudo maturity defense against the mother-breast fixation, its associated rage and guilt, and the wish to avoid and deny the oedipal conflicts, because peaceful relations with the father are the child's only hope for acknowledgement as a man, often lead to a premature flight into marriage. The pseudo mature patient's wife usually represents a mother-breast figure to him. When the patient is a woman, her husband is the mother-breast who is to give constant loving care and make no demands or criticisms. These patients are unusually sensitive to criticisms or any indication that they may not be the sole focus of attention at all times. Therefore, they tend to compete with their own children for attention and may develop almost paranoid jealousy about any other adult their mates may notice or admire. Hypochondria or actual poor health from psychosomatic disorders, fatigue from overwork, depression or irritability, general discontent and/or addiction to drugs, alcohol or smoking are techniques which elicit constant nursing care and concern from their spouses. If the spouse does not or cannot provide this concern, or lets down at times, or becomes exasperated, depressed, and withdrawn, then the patient will transfer his nurturing needs to his own children and extract the mother-breast from them. Such patients are also prone to forming symbiotic regressive unions with other men or women for the same reason. Thus, where the preoedipal narcissistic attachments persist, the patient is actually limited in his ability to give mature love and instead seeks narcissistic gratification in being loved, meaning being mothered. Sexuality serves as a means of captivating, controlling, punishing, or feeding the mother when in the latter instance there is a role reversal. Since all their relationships are heavily colored by the sexual and phallic aspects, the anxiety and conflicts aroused in their daughters and sons frequently drive their children toward premature sexual experience, intense clinging relationships with their peers, flights from home to "hippy-land," addictions to smoking, alcohol, or drugs, severe depressions, psychotic breaks, or suicide. In order to offer children desexualized affection during the significant phases in their development, parents must have made sufficient progress in solving their own preoedipal and oedipal conflicts.

Although I consider crucial the fixation on the introjected preoedipal mother-breast object, and the repetition compulsion to revive and relive it through the mechanism of projection and in transference, I do not feel that the oedipal phase is less significant or bypassed in the development of these patients. However, they do continue to seek the preoedipal maternal-breast qualities in their mates and a major segment of the ego appears to be captivated at the oral-sadistic level. The original maternal introject reigns as a queen in the infantile ego nucleus. When the defense against the oral-sadistic impulses is reversed, the child becomes passive and helpless, offering himself as an object to be devoured by the preoedipal mother figure. The masturbatory activity in these patients also reveals the persistent intimacy between the preoedipal object and the infantile self. Such unconscious wishes for fusion with an absorption by parental introjects is felt as a serious peril to survival; consequently, anxiety and withdrawal reactions are generated.

The varied defenses include the denial of oral-sadistic and passive wishes; instead, we see the impulse to conquer, possess, and sexually assault the maternal object. The pseudo maturity also denies the self-image of a weak, dependent child. Compulsive eating binges, smoking, alcoholic bouts, and masturbation dramatically proclaim their independence, ability to satisfy their own needs, and the illusion of their magic omnipotent and invulnerable powers. As a word of advice to those who might suggest or imply to the patient any disapproval of these patterns, caution is of the utmost importance. If it is a wife, she may end up with a black eye or worse. If a friend, well, that might be the end of the friendship; and if an analyst, a strong reaction of resistive acting out can be predicted. The withdrawal and primitive rage deny the wish for symbiosis. The compulsive acting out of the drives is usually self-destructive and the capacity to delay and redirect or sublimate the needs appears to be impaired. Thus, in terms of the structural theory, the dynamics involved may be interpreted as a victory for the id over the ego. Some may question my view of the apparent weakness in sublimation, given my initial statement that these patients are bright and typically successful in their work. In fact some sublimation of the aggressive aspect of the oral drive does take place. This pattern seems to be related to the desire for power and control, especially as a means of having contact with people, winning the admiration of the parents and others, and successfully winning in competition with the father and other men. In slightly different terms, the sublimation is in the service of possessing the mother-breast-penis. At times the oral-sadism and associated guilt entering the intellectual sphere may produce severe stammering or inhibitions in communication. There are other consequences for the oral-sadism, among which is the severity of the superego. As Arlow and Brenner (1964) have noted, the regressive transformation of superego derivatives can make the function of the superego as impulsive and intractable as the derivatives of the id. Freud (1930), Hartmann and Loewenstein (1962), Jacobson (1964), Nunberg (1926), and others have indicated that a link exists between the preoedipal precursors of the superego and the child's own aggressiveness. The tendency of these patients to overwork is not entirely a greedy attitude towards money, possessions, or power, but also a self-flagellating, self-defeating pattern which deprives them of pleasurable relaxation and of creative productivity due to lack of time and fatigue. The reasons for this behavior appear to lie in the severity of the superego, the partial identification with an industrious, stoic father, and secret competitiveness with him as well as other men. In certain instances the money needs were denied, and, in combination with guilt over these impulses, the patients handled money poorly, were in constant debt, and acted out this aspect in the transference with problems in paying the fee.

The compelling, repetitive urges of these patients may tempt us into thinking of this phenomenon as an obsessive-compulsive character disturbance. I am inclined to view these as pre-ego mechanisms which are born of the repetition compulsion and are driven by the id impulses; they are not basically ego mechanisms of a defensive nature. This view is not to say that the ensuing

anal-sadistic drives do not exert a powerful influence on the evolving character structure. These drives do color the symptomatology
with an obsessional overlay. Where excessive amounts of aggression
must be turned inwardly early in childhood due to the environmental conditions herein described, the normal ambivalences, such
as between love and hate, passivity and activity, or feminity and
masculinity are greatly increased. The intrasystemic conflicts are
then accelerated by the developing ego structure and its inevitable
intersystemic conflicts. The cyclic feed-back under these circumstances is such that constant discontent and environmental conflict
are inevitable.

The patient's need to disrupt and subsequently reestablish relationships, and to engage in this process repetitively for years, all
the while suffering from unhappiness and frustration, both with
and without the object, reflect the clinging tendency I described
at the onset of this paper. In many instances, the mates were
selected prematurely and on the basis of the patient's oral needs.
These mates fulfilled their caretaking role for their spouse only
partially, but the other essential qualities and needs were just not
available to them. Whether or not their spouses would or could
provide a greater satisfaction is beyond the scope of this paper.
But by the time my patients came into analysis, the feeling of
love as felt by both partners for each other was a dead issue. I
postulate that these patients are playing the "peek-a-boo game"
with their mother-breast objects. Under the influence of the repetition compulsion they are attempting to assimilate the intense emotions associated with the original traumatic separation and chronic
frustration as experienced in early childhood. They play the same
game with their smoking objects and with the liquor bottles.
Kestenberg (1965, 1966) in her discussion of motility suggests
that the repetitious sequence of pain and reassurance is modeled
not only on the anal rhythm but also on holding and releasing
play activities as seen in six to 12 month old infants. Spitz (1937)
observed that the reptitious pregenital games of the infant become
boring to him later, and Kris (1940) stated that these early
rhythms in the service of drive discharge are superseded by ego
controlled rhythms for purposes of expressing affect. In any event,

we can see that each of these early phases is characterized by a changing relationship toward the mother, of wishes to be close to her and experimentation with distance.

As a first clinical example, I shall present fragments from the analysis of "A," a young man in his late twenties who worked in a successful medical group practice in a rural area. Part of his symptomatology centered on his anguish, despair, suicidal fantasies and fears; chronic struggles with his wife; dissatisfaction with the several women with whom he maintained sexual relations; fears of and rage at controlling authorities in his work situations; poor physical health occasioned by overweight and eating, smoking, and drinking binges; vague hypochondriacal fears of a cancer developing somewhere in his body; and chronic severe headaches.

Certain relevant biographical data to be noted are his mother's death when he was three years of age and his being cared for by a nursemaid who was overconcerned with his bowel habits. He was negativistic and defied her by withholding patterns. His father kept himself constantly busy with business activities and apparently did little to establish a close relationship with his son. His two sisters, one of whom developed asthma, were only a few years older than the patient. He felt that his father preferred them. For the most part he appeared to be a quiet child who remained uninvolved with his sisters. In later childhood his father remarried but the patient did not feel any attachment to his stepmother. His schooling proceeded favorably for a few years with a gradual increase in learning difficulties. Compulsive masturbation continued through his teens and into early adulthood. In his middle adolescence he enjoyed reckless high speed driving and proceeded to wreck a car. Thereafter, he wandered around the country on his own for several months. He and his wife met in their late teens and married a few years later. The relationship continued to be a sadomasochistic struggle throughout the years without the feeling of security developing in either party. Divorce talk and separation fantasies and acts were frequent. They had three sons.

"A" began to express his hatred for the analyst early in treatment and was puzzled by not being able to find grounds for it. He acknowledged strong competitive feelings with regard to both his peers and authorities, but was inhibited in asserting himself with them when issues arose. "A" spoke of not letting himself get close to anyone but recalled a period in his life when he was "in love" with a male peer and later with a second one. He eventually wondered why he was always engaged in a struggling situation and realized how anxious he feels when he finally "gets his head above water" and is temporarily free of a conflictual relationship. He said that he sought out analysis to see if there were a possibility to change this way of living but warned the therapist that he did not think he had ever felt a sincere, enduring alliance with anyone. When he severed relationships he liked to leave things unfinished and the door open so that he could always go back. This included leaving books partially read and experiencing an intense fear of considering any issue really ended. "A" would come to his sessions with a hangover at times, revealing the satisfaction in attempting to give up drinking, smoking, and overeating and then resuming them. "When I get fat," he explained, "I can always go back to getting a new slim body." He enjoyed getting intensely involved with people and then going back to his loneliness.

When "A" was confronted with the acting out of certain inter-personal conflicts during the analysis, he revealed his intention to maintain his messed up life style so as to prevent the therapist from deriving any pleasure from his improvement and to avoid allowing closeness and affection to develop. One of his early dreams follows: He and a woman were surf-board riding. There were sharks in the water, and he was frightened about being bitten. His associations included his life-long fascination with water and dangerous situations, such as the three separate occasions on which he almost drowned. There were also happy experiences with mother figures who would take him to the beach. He is afraid that the therapist will find out about his distrust and fears that he might stop hating the therapist and become a little boy again. There was also a strange feeling of smelling the odor of his father and fearing that he might disintegrate and start crying. A later fantasy depicted his father's watching with admiration as "A" had inter-course with his stepmother. The following phase was marked by a revival of suicidal impulses, insomnia, restless street-walking, hypochondriacal fears of cancer, and painful sensations when urinating. During one of these sessions, he had the urge to see if the burning cinders of his cigarette had set fire to the waiting room. His wishes to kill the therapist and his father led to his first overt crying bout and verbalization of feeling unloved by everyone. "A" was not able to admit that his loneliness was associated with a sad feeling. However, the grandiosity in his defensive self-sufficiency came to the surface. He became aware of lonely feelings and lack of relationship even during intercourse with various women whom he thought he liked. Although Markovitz (1968) reported that his patients felt a sense of well being and clearer body image with smoking, "A" had a vague body image when smoking. "A" associated smoking and drinking with being filled up, being close to mother, and losing his manly image. When he stopped smoking, began to diet, and radically cut down his drinking habits, he became "more aware of his muscles" and sensed that "his body was more sharply defined." In short, he felt like a man. During what he experienced as his withdrawal stage, he felt as if his mother were "leaving him through every pore." His improved figure elicited both the wish and the fear of being envied and admired by the therapist and other men. He felt that as a result he could stand more erect and the associations were in line with Lewin's (1933) contribution on the body as a phallus. However, it soon developed that the boys and men he had admired over the years, and with whom he had made transient identifications, were those whom he thought were worshipped by their own mothers. He maintained that he was a much better mother than his wife and therefore was concerned about leaving his children in the event of a separation. A childhood fantasy was recovered: His father had killed his mother, but his mother did not really want him either, yet if "A" could become "a beautiful man, his mother might return to him from heaven." The bitterness toward his father kept the war alive and caused him to reject his father's efforts to show approval. "Whatever father would do for me, I'd turn it into shit" is "A's" interpretation of his own behavior. He began to experience oral panics—fears that he would lose his friends, money, clinic, and status in the community. He and the world were empty. His girl friends and wife were sucking too much from him, but he had to keep feeding them and others to protect himself from being devoured. "A" portrayed them as "dinosaurs" with huge gaping mouths. His suicidal fantasies and irritability intensified, and his fantasy evolved into the theme of his going crazy. If he reached a state of complete helplessness and misery, then his mother would return. "A" indicated that the empty feelings had always been there but were concealed from me because were they to be exposed I would think he was really crazy. He expressed the wish that he and I could share a huge baby bottle together and wondered what a man really feels when with a woman. The fear of allowing himself to take in feelings from others was paramount, but he said he was beginning to feel a relationship with me. Two of his fantasies concerned our sitting together at a table inside his head and of him sitting with me beneath a cherry tree beside a pool, a favorite area in his childhood. Although in the past he had had to force himself to take in new information, he now began to read books for pleasure. "A" felt that the therapist had been "gentle" and appreciated that I did not force him to "shape up and face the cold world the way it is." He found himself becoming more kindly toward others. Memories of closeness to mother during her illness were interwoven with more data about his masturbation, incestuous fantasies, and having a magic sword. At a later phase he revealed the wishes and fears of becoming his father's wife and of being engulfed by his father's anus. A renewal of hatred for his father and all men followed with the wish that his father had died instead of his mother. A memory of passionate excitement in viewing the corpse of a woman at a funeral came to the surface at this time as well as the thrill in fighting with his wife and fantasies of killing her or being killed during these rageful episodes. "A" and his wife decided to experiment with another separation, and she initiated therapy in a nearby community. It became increasingly clear to the patient that his work was equated with mother's feeding him; therefore, he could not give up long hours and thereby separate from her. If he gave up having mother in his mind and allowed others in, he would have to accept her death. His many fantasies and dreams of being in an empty room were equivalents of the dead mother symbol—the empty breast. He was in his mother, and she, in him. "A" began to experience an inner calm about seeing himself as a separate person not involved in intensive struggles with others and felt this separation period from his wife was necessary for his own growth and hers. His self-awareness was that he did not feel like a little boy anymore. He noticed the old urge to bite a woman's breast was diminishing and verbalized an increased confidence in psychoanalysis. At this point he was in his fifth year of analysis.

The second observation concerns "G," a young successful man in his thirties who suffered from chronic gastrointestinal disturbances. His psychosomatically oriented physician recommended that "G" consider psychoanalysis. The patient had married in his late teens, divorced his first wife after a few years and promptly re-married. This second marriage produced a son and a daughter. Gradually increasing dissatisfaction, frustration, and conflicts had led to a series of separations and reconciliations, "G" having embarked upon a series of affairs with single women and fantasies of similar involvement with married women. "G" said his problem was an inability to express his anger while he had "to take a lot of shit" from everyone.

"G's" background included knowledge that his mother had had two miscarriages before his birth and two subsequently. His sister was born when he was six years of age. His mother seemed withdrawn from him early in his childhood—"she was sick all the time." He turned to his grandmother and spent a good deal of time away from home. His father did not get along with his mother and spent most of his time with business activities. "G" described his mother as "hot-headed" and complaining about his badness. She was overconcerned about his becoming dirty or hurt in play. He felt a preference for his father. There was a memory, placed at three years of age, of seeing a doctor treat his mother and there being blood and a dead baby. Further associated memories were of his mother wringing chicken necks. At six years of age, an older man told him about masturbation and parental intercourse. Years of conflicts and struggles over masturbation followed.

An early dream involved a tame animal, the mascot of a football team. While the patient watched the game, the animal suddenly tried to bite him. In another dream, a large fish approached a smaller fish he had just caught and swallowed it. Other dreams included being bitten or almost bitten by snakes. The patients "G" and "A" had similar struggles with overweight, dieting, and efforts to control smoking and drinking. "G" had been irritable and depressed while dieting and angry that his wife would not prepare foods he could eat. He was angry with himself for being preoccupied with his hostility to his mother and puzzled about not having overcome it after all these years. He was also disgusted with his inability to find happiness with any woman. There was a growing awareness of marked jealousy of his sister, whom he felt was much closer to his parents. "G" had fantasies of cutting his mother's belly, like draining a bag of water, of whipping women, and other punitive actions. He continued to have severe depressions, vacillating with rages during the analysis. His desires, regrets, and fears regarding closeness to father and other men, and fears of his own destructive fantasies were prominent. A common fantasy was biting off the penis of those he feared or with whom he competed. He finally acknowledged that he could neither trust nor feel an attachment to anyone. However, he was highly regarded and liked by his friends and business associates and socialized quite well. He feared that the analysis would lead him toward better relations with his wife and would constitute a repetition of his father's making him submit to mother. "G" also made a point of not wanting me to think that I meant anything to him and was ashamed to expose how much he needed a woman. He usually initiated the reconciliations after separations. The patient's denial of wanting his mother or needing a woman was further reflected in his lack of interest in money, clothes, and other possessions. He felt that if he acted as if he had a penis, no one would be interested in taking care of him. The increased recognition of his dependency needs opened a phase of expressing warmth for me and of working with passive strivings toward his father. However, a new phase of gastrointestinal upset and rage followed. Competitive oedipal conflicts and castration anxiety were experienced with me and other men, and an upsurge of more intense longing for his mother was expressed by increased smoking and drinking. Professing disdain for me, he described me as a methodical, conservative man, much like his father. He dreamed of large stores with gourmet food, of giving large parties, and of huge lakes, restaurants, and bars. During the third year of analysis, "G" acknowledged that the many times he had belittled me or tried to diminish my interpretations were expressions of fears of accepting anything from me. The exploration of this admission led to the evolution of childhood fears of and wishes for pregnancy and to the recovery of many early childhood memories, fantasies, and feelings. The hypochondriacal fears, anti-Semitic, anti-Negro, and anti-woman feelings were further clarified. "G" felt as though his viscera were a big empty hole which only felt warm and full when filled with alcohol. He considered whiskey a "vital force" like milk, something which was alive, and referred to alcohol as "his life-line." He wanted his father to fill him with milk, because he could not get it from his mother. The bottle was the mother-breast-penis. "G" and "A" both played the game of separation and reappearance in episodes of being "off and on the wagon"—the peek-a-boo game. He found that alcohol only dulled the pain of emptiness and loneliness and that the compulsive sexuality and masturbation were a pretense and fantasied union rather than attempts at real relationships and love experiences. There followed much more working through of the various themes mentioned. It was his feeling that the need for involvement in conflicting relationships and his inability to understand issues, were related to his desire to be like his mother. He was pleased with recognizing progress in his analysis, but angry at me and the analytic process because it was extracting something from his personality. The behavioral change had unconscious maternal significance for him and produced panicky feelings of dying. He dramatized the experience as a gradual realization that he had spent his life trying to survive and had yet to learn the process of living.

## DISCUSSION

The breast-penis linkage as a contributing factor to severe castration anxiety was described over 30 years ago by Bergler and Eidelberg (1933); Eidelberg (1952, 1961); S. Freud (1926, 1930); F. Alexander (1923); Stärcke (1921); and others. It has been the undertaking of this paper to reflect upon the specific defensive organization that may be set in motion by early object loss and partial recovery. Patients manifesting these character disorders can maintain a selective type of acting out, wherein they are apparently mature, stable, and effective in their work and peripheral social life yet isolate an unyielding, repetitive, self-destructive struggle to restore the original unity and become the mother's only child in their intimate object world. In the attempt to reestablish fusion with the mother, they may appear as the "borderline" patients described by R. Knight (1954) or the depressive and psychotic patients of Bychowski (1960). Assessing the complexity of character phenomena can be aided by including the views from genetic, dynamic, structural, and adaptive references. Compartmentalization or splitting of the ego, with maintenance of early object relationships and the self-image of an infant on the one hand and a contrasting, realistic image on the other was observed by Freud (1927), Fairbairn (1952), Kernberg (1966), and others. In any event, a considerable cathexis seems to be committed in the service of maintaining a section of the ego for the intact original introjects. The primitive wish to bite and incorporate the mother-breast-penis thereby reestablishing a fusion with mother and the fears and wishes to be passively eaten, which are associated with the dread of losing masculinity and identity, were noted in Lewin's (1950) contribution on the oral triad. In other words, the preoedipal origins of castration anxiety combined with oral sadism and regressive altered ego function appear to have greater disruptive influence on character than essentially oedipal castration anxiety. In this regard, the Wolf Man's fears of being devoured can be contrasted with those of Little Hans, who feared his finger would be bitten off.

Cases "A" and "G" enjoyed their ability to exercise magic

omnipotence by filling themselves with mother-breast symbols of food, smoke, and alcohol, and by flirtations with suicide fantasies and death. According to the psychoanalytic theory of symptom formation, the orally shaped wish for nirvana and absorption by the mother also incorporates the defense against the impulse. The patient rationalizes his actions as proof of self-sufficiency and masculine identity and then suffers the punishment of poor health and self-condemnation. The secondary gain of concern and care from others completes a cycle. These patients also enjoyed the omnipotence of changing their body from the round, flabby, pregnant mother to the muscular, strong young man who appears to be ready for a new venture into an independent life without the mother. The decathexis of frustrating love objects is never complete even though inanimate objects take over and become important symbols. The complexities of this style of living are better appreciated when we accept the fact that the impulses and needs are not only generating defenses but are also achieving conscious and unconscious fulfillments. The decathexis of objects and instinctual regression and aggression is not as widespread and is under better ego control than in psychotic patterns.

Both "A" and "G" suffered cumulative narcissistic trauma. "A" lost his mother early and was cared for by a series of surrogates with only limited contacts with his father. "G's" mother withdrew from him during repeated miscarriages, probable depressive reactions, and then with his sister's birth. Greenacre's (1941) contribution on early childhood experiences in the predisposition to anxiety would agree with the foregoing. The degree of ambivalence—the love-hate, libido-aggression—toward the mother and the child's capacity for identification are significant factors in the ability to form satisfying relationships in adult life. Although ambivalence is a characteristic of all relationships, the predominance of the preoedipal hostile mother identification is a serious interference in ego maturation and integration. "G's" mother image was split between her caretaking role and her ability to reproduce, to kill babies, and to wring chicken necks. His wife's pregnancies always increased his anxiety and hostility, sent him searching for other relationships, and intensified his oral needs. Intellectual overcompensation, reaction-formations, and regressive identifications with the mother combine as defenses against the masculine destructive impulses, sexual oedipal competitive feelings, and castration anxiety. The patient's rejection of interpretations were reluctantly and sheepishly acknowledged later as meaningful. The fear of substituting the analyst for the maternal introject and as an object for identification is part of the issue. The wish to destroy the therapist's mind and the envy were equated with the oral-sadistic feelings toward the breast-penis. "A" and "G" were both exposed to compulsive mothering in their toilet training and to an environment that was generally hostile to their instinctual impulses; that demanded submission, passivity, and cleanliness; and that aroused stubborn defiance and withholding. They were also forced into excessive dependency upon aggressive phallic women and felt that their sisters were the preferred siblings. Having maternal introjects and later identification as a reaction to separation is not unusual, but its nuclear position along with the oral and anal-sadistic components of development is the problem. The patient's ability to come to terms with the rage against a mother who turned away from him; with the father and siblings who are associated with the crime; with the rivalry for and envy of each parent for having the other; and with the synthesis of the split-off self image of a helpless child are all necessary prerequisites toward an appropriate, integrated adult personality. In working with these patients I felt free to allow my emotions and compassion to color the interpretations, rather than appear impersonal. Such an attitude helps the patient maintain an image of separateness and ego integration.

Of further importance in these considerations is the relationship between prolonged periods of frustration of the aggressive and sexual drives and the establishment of sadomasochistic patterns. The inhibited aggression will vacillate between the ego and the object and will increase the fantasies surrounding the psychic trauma; the inhibited sexual drive enhances the self-love and self-pity. Patients with the "breast complex" have a very active fantasy life as their early substitute for the gratification they were denied. Thus, the production of associations in the analysis is plentiful. The transference components in their object-choice must be detected, although the discovery is difficult because of the ease with which they stimulate reactions in others which justify their suffering position. It is easier to detect the transference to the analyst, but the amount of acting out and the hectic life experiences interfere with a concentration of the affect in the analysis. The contempt from the preoedipal period, the passive striving, and later rivalry and identification from the oedipal and latency periods, and revivals in adolescence can all be identified in the transference. Fenichel (1945) compared acting out and transference by stating that they have

> . . . in common an insufficient differentiation between the present and past, an unwillingness to learn, a readiness to substitute certain rigid reactive patterns for adequate responses to actual stimuli. . . . The patterns may be mere emotional attitudes—it is transference when directed toward specific people and acting out if it has to be done regardless toward whom [p. 297].

Freud (1914) initially considered acting out a replacement of memory, but later recognized the role of unconscious wishes. Anna Freud (1936) expanded the concept to include the instinctual impulses or wishes and the defenses against them. She cautions that interpretation of the acting "affords us some valuable insight" but "the therapeutic gain is generally small."

In the analysis of the character problems in this constellation, the self-esteem is dependent upon being loved, on receiving or taking in, because of the predominance of oral mechanisms. The conflict is between the urge to react with rage when frustrated and to repress or supress the aggressiveness because of guilt and fear of loss of love and self-esteem. The techniques for avoiding the depression started early and must be analyzed consistently to bring the depression to the surface and into the treatment situation. Acting out is more dangerous than transference struggles with the analyst, because the former has more real consequences. The patient's conscience does react strongly after the act, but, at the time, the behavior is ego-syntonic. The patient learns, through repetitive doses of experiencing depression in analysis, that it will not destroy him. His tolerance for stress will gradually increase, and the acting out will eventually diminish. The analysis helps the patient see his own responsibility in producing the "neurosis of fate" by actions that repeat the same attitudes in each relationship. The trauma of a premature separation from the mother and projection of the child's rage onto her makes separations from the analyst on weekends or trips especially threatening. In both clinical examples, drinking bouts were more of a problem on weekends, and I was punished by the patient's not attending the session on Monday. The intensity of rage, the convictions of my possibly retaliating, the depreciation of me or my work, the temptations to engage in physical struggles or to destroy my office, as in the cigarette incident, all reflected transient regressions to a fusion of mother-breast-self-analyst transference psychosis. Such reactions would be provoked by my withholding an answer or a demand for reassurance or by a memory or fantasy of an encounter with me. Interpretation of a projection or an introject would be rejected as my defending myself. However, the reliability of the analyst, together with the patient's ability to deal with reality and view the split ego area, brings about a gradual shift from narcissistic to object relations as well as a more consistent transference neurosis and therapeutic alliance. The tendency to severe regression revives vacillation between the narcissism and object relatedness and necessitates a prolonged period of working through the patterns. The analyst's attention must be directed toward knowing at each phase who is who in the oscillating transference relationship. Analyzing the superego not only in terms of oedipal identifications but also in terms of the preoedipal persecuting introjects is part of the task. The patient is his critical, rejecting parent in punishing the analyst-child for leaving him, for being independent, and not obeying his demands. When this process is interpreted, the patient feels he is being attacked by the hostile parent who rejects his hostility. Then the patient counterattacks with the child's ego against the analyst as a parent. As Freud (1940) indicated, the hostile objects in both the ego and superego must be slowly demolished. Both the analyst and the patient may feel these power struggles as a strain (Money-Kyrle, 1956; Woodmansey, 1966) but, where the analyst's superego is sufficiently mature, he can interpret without guilt and without blaming the patient or himself.

The oedipal components of the superego, with guilt and conflicts over phallic sexuality and lack of parental endorsement of masculine aggressiveness, reinforce the child's fixation at oral and anal levels in a sadomasochistic pattern. The counterphobic element of repeating separations with objects and transitional objects confirms the continued presence of a high anxiety level and the efforts at denial and digestion of the trauma. This reaction reminds me of the repetitious play of children in therapy. The hunger for a better, more fulfilling relationship must not be overlooked in understanding the patient's search for new experiences or his hopes of finding it in the old attachments. Attempts to interfere with the acting out by premature interpretations are due to anxiety aroused in the analyst and will comply with the patient's wish to involve the analyst in the struggle with his controlling parent-images. Also, premature interpretation is not likely to promote as complete an understanding of the pattern. Although the preoedipal conflicts penetrate into oedipal and genital phases, the ego functions have sufficient strength to present the picture of a neurosis in work and peripheral social function. These patients were not without protective, affectionate mothering and an adequate home life, but the combination of certain environmental responses and their own specific techniques for handling the early separation produced a circumscribed area of personal and social maladjustment. Superego development is completed through the oedipal experiences but is overly harsh from preoedipal primitive rage. The oedipal fantasies seem closer to the surface, are less repressed, and more readily recognized by the patient because of clinging to the preoedipal sexualized relationships.

In conclusion, the death of a mother, her withdrawal due to pregnancies, personality problems, work obligations, or early separations due to physical illness in the child or parent can all disturb the child's ability to master reality. Primitive aggression toward the original object and introjection to avoid abandonment can cause the mother-breast-child unit to remain entombed in a split-off section of early ego development. The intellectual and fantasy powers allow the child to turn away from the parents, to deny the mourning reaction, and to move toward pseudo maturation. He recathects himself and the internalized parental image with sexuality, which increases the image of their power and significance in his life, as well as his own magical omnipotence. The ego externalizes the original situation, and it is reenacted through the repetition compulsion and transference making the individual vulnerable to symbiotic dependency relationships and an acting out style of living. The acting out has oral components in its nucleus and is a repetition of the impulses, fantasies, and defenses. To the analyst it also serves as a valuable communication, a form of resistance to analysis and to change, and an effort to seek fulfillment in life. Transitional objects as noted by Winnicott (1953, 1956) and symbols of food, smoke, and alcohol may be treated to the same ambivalent struggle as interpersonal relationships. These patients appear to lead a sadomasochistic existence, but it is confined to their intimate life and does not impair occupational and peripheral social success.

Relationships are sexualized as a means to an end, to achieve fulfillment on the oral-narcissistic level of a mother-breast-child unity. The syndrome as herein described is analyzable and may be a more common phenomena in character disorders than has been generally considered.

## REFERENCES

Alexander, F. (1923), The castration complex in the formation of character. *Int. J. Psycho-Anal.,* 4:11–42.

Arlow, J. and Brenner, C. (1964), *Psychoanalytic Concepts and the Structural Theory.* New York: International Universities Press.

Bergler, E. and Eidelberg (1933), Der mammakomplex des nannes. *Int. Zeitschrift für Psychoa.,* 19:547–583.

Bychowski, G. (1960), The structure of chronic and latent depression. *Int. J. Psycho-Anal.,* 41:504–508.

Eidelberg, L. (1952), *Studies in Psychoanalysis.* New York: International Universities Press.

—— (1961), *The Dark Urge.* New York: Pyramid Books, Almat Pub. Co.

Fairbairn, W. D. (1952), *An Object-Relations Theory of the Personality.* New York: Basic Books.

Fenichel, O. (1945), Neurotic acting out. In: *The Collected Papers of Otto Fenichel,* Vol. 2. New York: W. W. Norton & Co., pp. 296–304.

Freud, A. (1936), *The Ego and the Mechanisms of Defense.* New York: International Universities Press.

Freud, S. (1896), Further remarks on the neuropsychosis of defense. *Standard Edition,* 3:159–188. London: Hogarth Press, 1953.

—— (1908), Character and anal erotism. *Standard Edition,* 9:167–176.

—— (1909), Notes on a case of obsessional neurosis. *Standard Edition,* 10:153–318.

—— (1914), Remembering, repeating, and working through. *Standard Edition,* 12:145–156.

—— (1926), Inhibitions, symptoms, and anxiety. *Standard Edition,* 20: 77–178.

—— (1927), Fetishism. *Standard Edition,* 21:149–158.

—— (1930), Civilization and its discontents. *Standard Edition,* 21:59–65.

—— (1940), An outline of psychoanalysis. *Standard Edition,* 23:141–208.

Greenacre, P. (1941), The predisposition to anxiety. In: *Trauma, Growth and Personality.* New York: W. W. Norton & Co., 1952.

Hartmann, H. and Loewenstein, R. M. (1962), Notes on the superego. *The Psychoanalytic Study of the Child,* 17:42–81. New York: International Universities Press.

Jacobson, E. (1964), *The Self and the Object World.* New York: International Universities Press.

Kernberg, O. (1966), Structural derivatives of object relationships. *Int. J. Psycho-Anal.,* 47:236–253.

Kestenberg, J. S. (1965), The role of movement patterns in development. *Psychoanal. Quart.,* 34:1–36.

—— (1966), Rhythm and organization in obsessive-compulsive development. *Int. J. Psycho-Anal.,* 47:151–159.

Knight, R. P. (1954), Borderline states. In: *Psychoanalytic Psychiatry and Psychology,* ed. R. Knight and C. Friedman. New York: International Universities Press, pp. 97–109.

Lewin, B. D. (1933), The body as phallus. *The Psychoanal. Quart.,* 2:24–47.

—— (1950), *The Psychoanalysis of Elation.* New York: W. W. Norton & Co.

Marcus, I. M. (1956), Psychoanalytic group therapy with fathers of emotionally disturbed preschool children. *Int. J. Group Psychother.,* 6:61–76.

Markovitz, E. (1968), On the nature of the addiction of cigarettes. Unpublished paper.

Money-Kryle, R. E. (1956), Normal countertransference and some of its deviations. *Int. J. Psycho-Anal.,* 37:360–366.

Nunberg, H. (1926), The sense of guilt and the need for punishment. In: *Practice and Theory of Psychoanalysis,* Vol. 1. New York: International Universities Press, 1948, pp. 89–101.

Starcke, A. (1921), The castration complex. *Int. J. Psycho-Anal.,* 2:179–201.

Winnicott, D. W. (1953), Transitional objects and transitional phenomena. In: *Collected Papers.* London: Tavistock, 1956, pp. 229–242.

—— (1956), The antisocial tendency. In: *Collected Papers.* London: Tavistock, 1956, pp. 306–315.

Woodmansey, A. C. (1966), The internalization of external conflict. *Internat. J. Psycho-Anal.,* 47:349–355.

# NAME INDEX

Abraham, K., 52, 54
Adatto, C. P., 337–359
Aichhorn, A., 67
Alexander, F., 333, 376
Allen, F. L., 51
Altman, L., 184
Altshuler, K. Z., 141, 148
Anthony, E. J., 89
Arlow, J. A., 52, 153, 168, 182, 259, 317–335, 367
Armstrong, R. H., 161
Aserinsky, E., 138, 139, 151

Baekeland, F., 160
Bakan, D., 298
Baldridge, B. J., 157
Balint, M., 17, 19, 20, 21, 22, 23
Bellak, L., 268
Benedek, T. F., 21, 27, 37, 38, 43, 45
Beres, D., 261
Berger, R. J., 156
Bergler, E., 376
Bergman, P., 277
Bernfeld, S. C., 18, 33, 113
Bexton, W. H., 256
Bibring, G. L., 19
Binet, A., 247
Bizzi, E., 157
Blitzsten, N. L., 44
Blos, P., 66–88, 106, 114, 116, 129
Bornstein, B., 192
Brain, R., 249, 250, 251
Brenman, M., 267, 277, 279
Brenner, C., 52, 153, 168, 182, 216–230, 367

Bronner, A. F., 268, 277, 281
Broughton, R. J., 147, 148, 201, 206
Bunney, W., 162
Buxbaum, E., 18, 26, 27
Bychowski, G., 376

Carmichael, H. T., 276, 278
Chassan, J. B., 290
Coles, R., 64
Cronbach, L. J., 297

Dement, W. C., 138, 144, 145, 147, 151, 156, 158, 188, 189, 206
Deutsch, H., 100, 105
Dewan, E. M., 141–142
Dubos, R., 99

Ebbinghaus, H., 298
Edwards, A. L., 297
Eidelberg, L., 376
Eissler, K., 18, 24
Eitingon, M., 3, 19, 22, 44
Erikson, E. H., 13, 53, 271
Evans, C. R., 141, 142
Evarts, E. V., 141
Ezriel, H., 268

Fairbairn, W. D., 376
Farrow, E. P., 40
Fenichel, O., 52, 129, 168, 173, 175, 192, 197, 238, 318, 324, 325, 379
Ferenczi, S., 14, 16, 20, 21, 22, 23, 37, 52, 232
Fine, B. D., 285
Fisher, C., 136, 141, 151, 152, 153, 154, 156, 157, 158, 159, 160, 188, 189, 190, 203, 205, 206, 247, 253

384

# SUBJECT INDEX

387

Authoritative institutions, affecting adolescents, 70, 72, 73, 76

Bed-wetting, and dreaming, 136, 195–196
Biological trends, in adolescent development, 99, 103, 108, 112
Bisexuality, theories of, 32, 34, 35
Body image, in adolescence, 111–131
  case studies of, 119–128
Body management, development in, 60

Car thieves, adolescent, 70, 77
Castration anxiety, 322, 324, 328, 329, 331–332, 334–335
  and early object loss, 362, 375, 376
Catatonia, and omnipotence of movements, 234–235
Changing reality, and adolescence, 98–110
Character perversions, 317–335
  and castration anxiety, 331–332, 334–335
  petty liars as, 324–326
  practical jokers and hoaxers as, 326–331
  superego role in, 332–333
  unconscious phantasies in, 332, 333
  unrealistic character types as, 318–324
Childhood, 51–132
  accommodation to new experiences in, 91, 93
  concrete operations in, 91, 94
  defense mechanisms in, 61
  developmental lines in, 59–62, 90
  and diagnostic profile of Anna Freud, 57–64
  dreams and sleep in, 187–206
  formal operations in, 91, 94–95
  moral development in, 95–96
  object concepts in, 92–93
  omnipotence, infantile, 231–245
  pathology in, concepts of, 58, 61
  and Piaget's developmental psychology, 89–97
  preoperational thought in, 91, 92–93
  regression in, 60–61
  REM sleep in, 145–146
  transference neurosis in, 347–348, 349
  traumatic neurosis in, 189, 203

Clinical practice, 305–382
Cognitive development studies, by Piaget, 90–97
Communication
  and action, 68–72
  impact of, in adolescence, 101–103
  see also Language
Compulsions
  and early object loss, 366, 367–368, 381
  and magical power of words, 236, 237
  repetition, 226–227
  and rituals, 235
Concretization, in adolescence, 66–88
  see also Adolescence
Conflict
  absence of, in delinquency, 70–71
  and aggression, 227–228, 229
  and behavior, 246
  resolution of, in dreams, 159
Consciousness, and perception, 253–254
Counterphobias, 318, 362, 381
Countertransference, 17, 18, 41
  from Fliess to Freud, 31, 32, 36, 38–39
Critical periods, concept of, 54
Cultural factors, in adolescent development, 99–100, 112

Daydreams, in adolescence, 69
Death drive, 218, 221, 222, 228, 305
Defense mechanisms
  in childhood, 61
  and perception, 262
  in perversions, 332, 334–335
Delinquency, 66–88
Denial of reality, 318–324
  in adolescence, 72, 77
  and perception, 262
Depression, sleep patterns in, 162
Destructiveness
  adolescent attitudes toward, 103, 104, 106–107
  as aim of aggression, 223–225, 228
Development in adolescence, 98–110
  and concretization, 71–74, 76, 79
Developmental lines, concept of, 59–62, 90
Developmental psychology, of Piaget, 89–97
Diagnostic profile, of Anna Freud, 57–64